CHAPTER

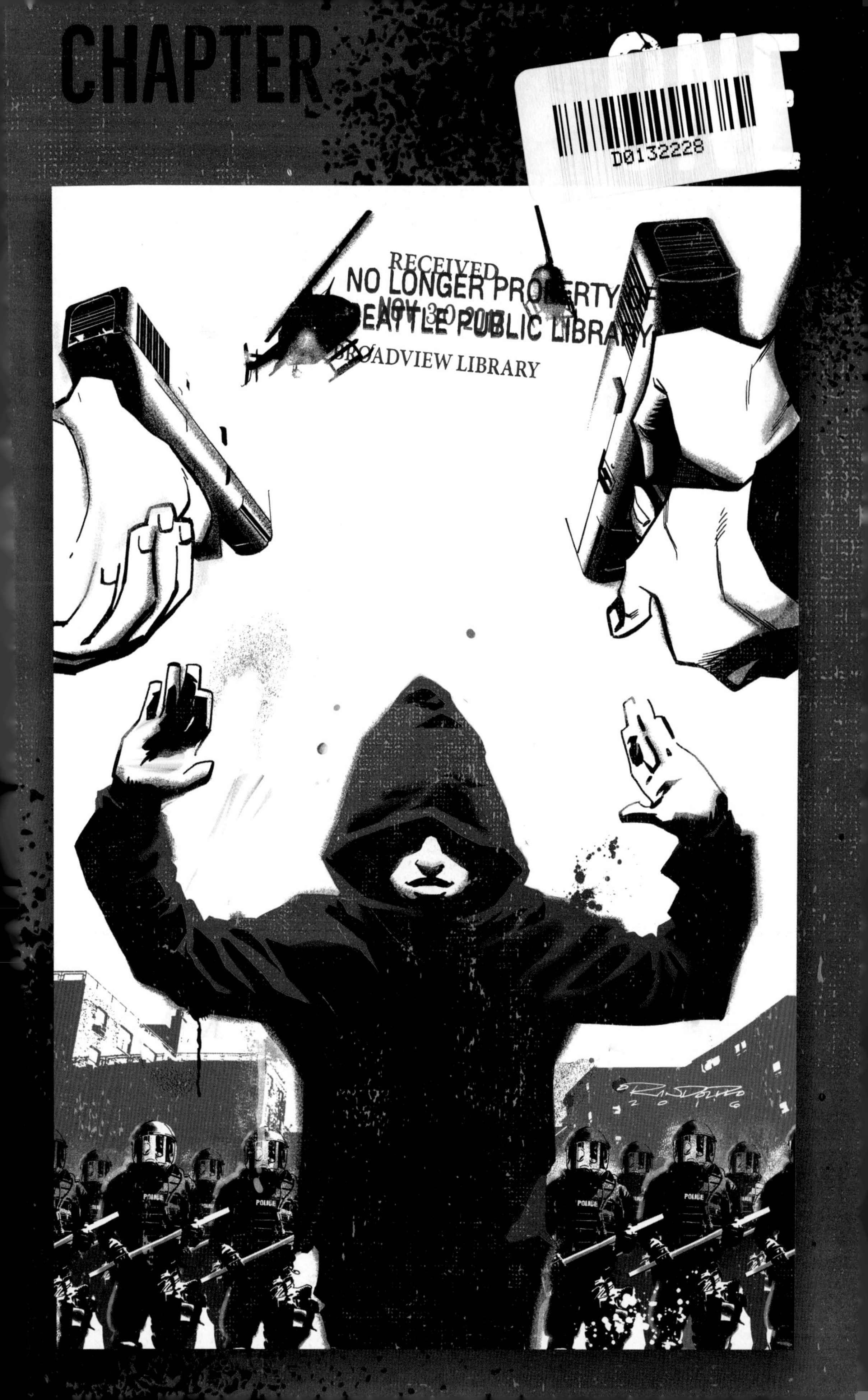

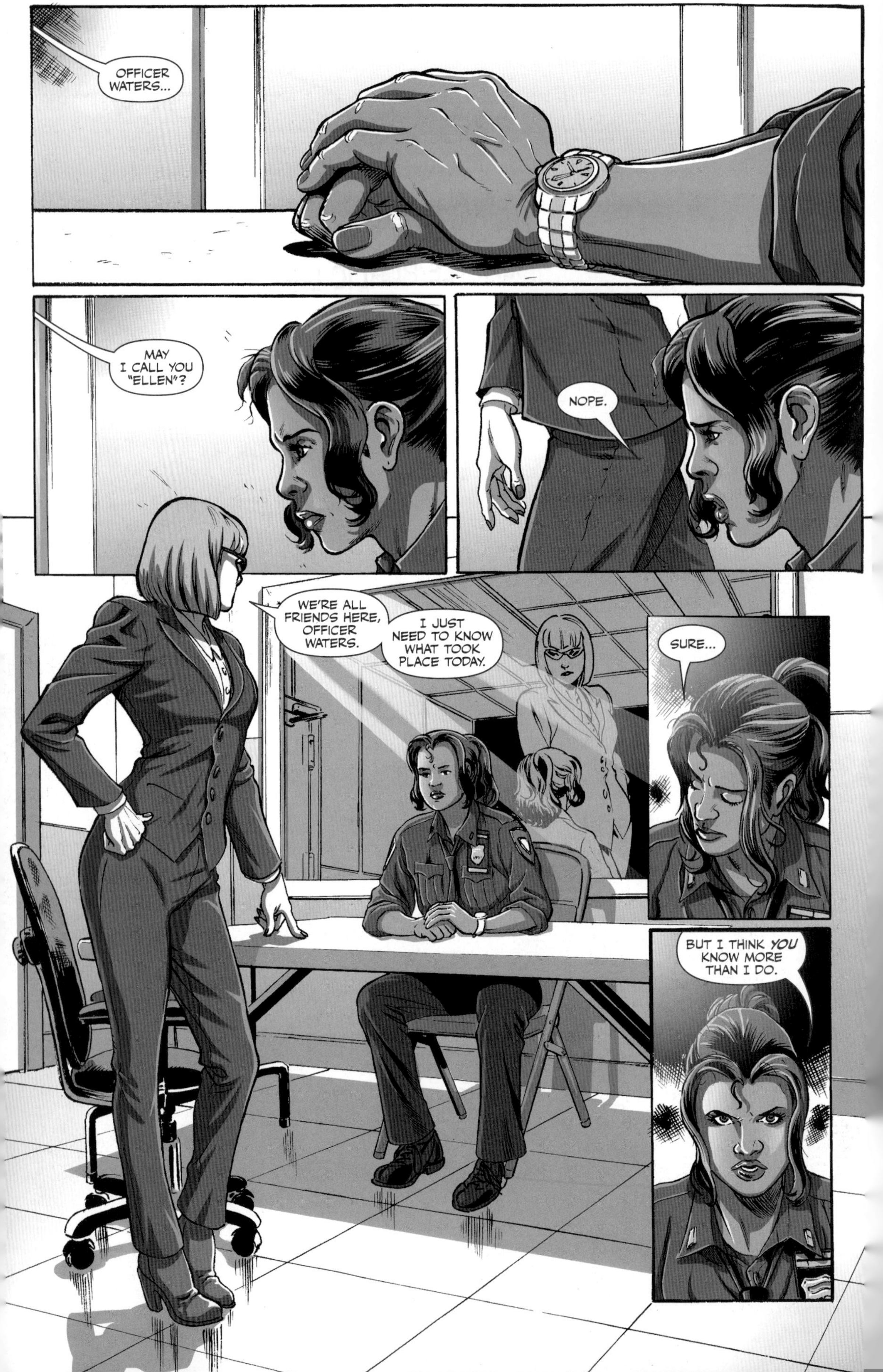
OFFICER WATERS...
MAY I CALL YOU "ELLEN"?
NOPE.
WE'RE ALL FRIENDS HERE, OFFICER WATERS.
I JUST NEED TO KNOW WHAT TOOK PLACE TODAY.
SURE...
BUT I THINK YOU KNOW MORE THAN I DO.

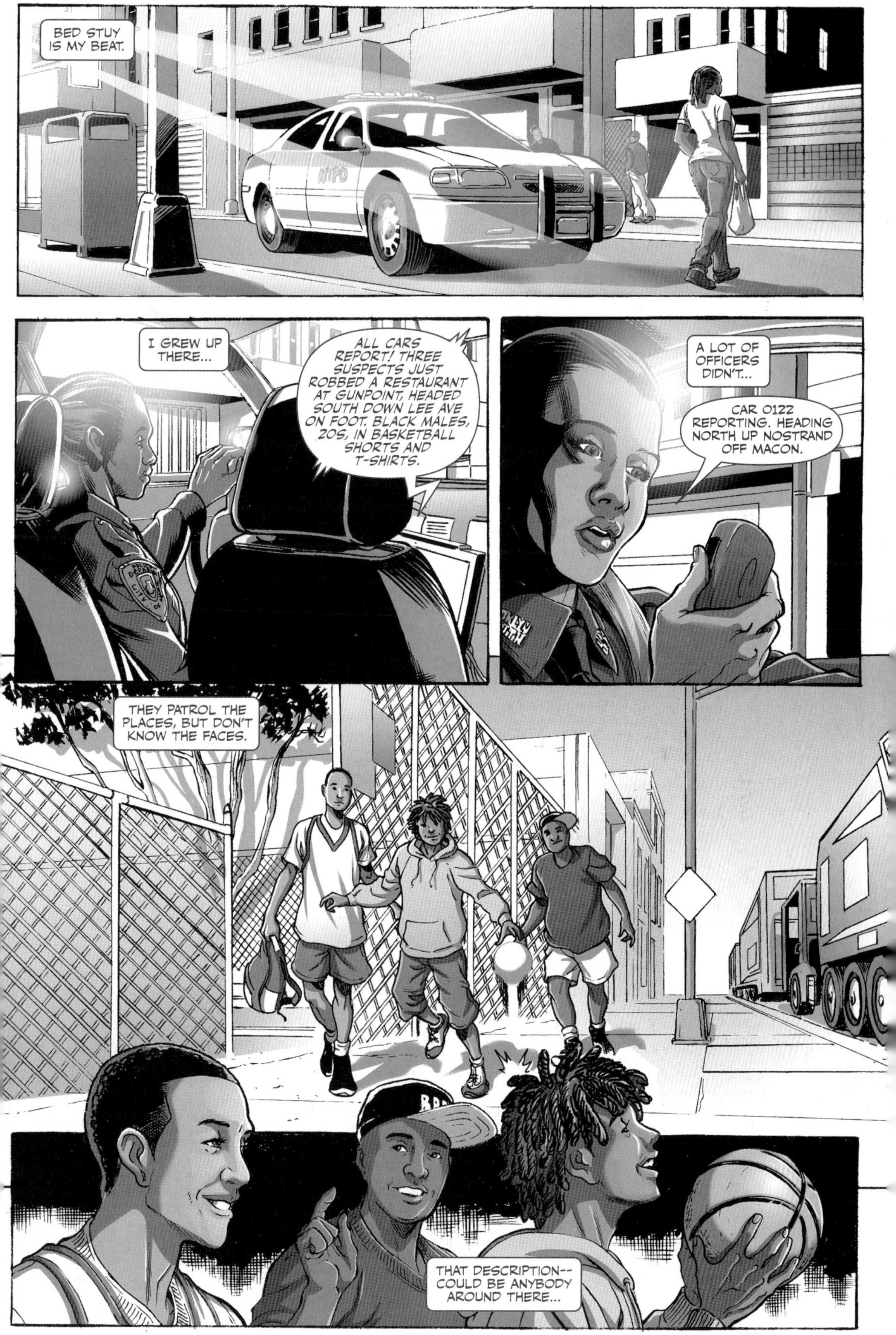
BED STUY IS MY BEAT.
I GREW UP THERE...
ALL CARS REPORT! THREE SUSPECTS JUST ROBBED A RESTAURANT AT GUNPOINT, HEADED SOUTH DOWN LEE AVE ON FOOT. BLACK MALES, 20S, IN BASKETBALL SHORTS AND T-SHIRTS.
A LOT OF OFFICERS DIDN'T...
CAR 0122 REPORTING. HEADING NORTH UP NOSTRAND OFF MACON.
THEY PATROL THE PLACES, BUT DON'T KNOW THE FACES.
THAT DESCRIPTION-- COULD BE ANYBODY AROUND THERE...

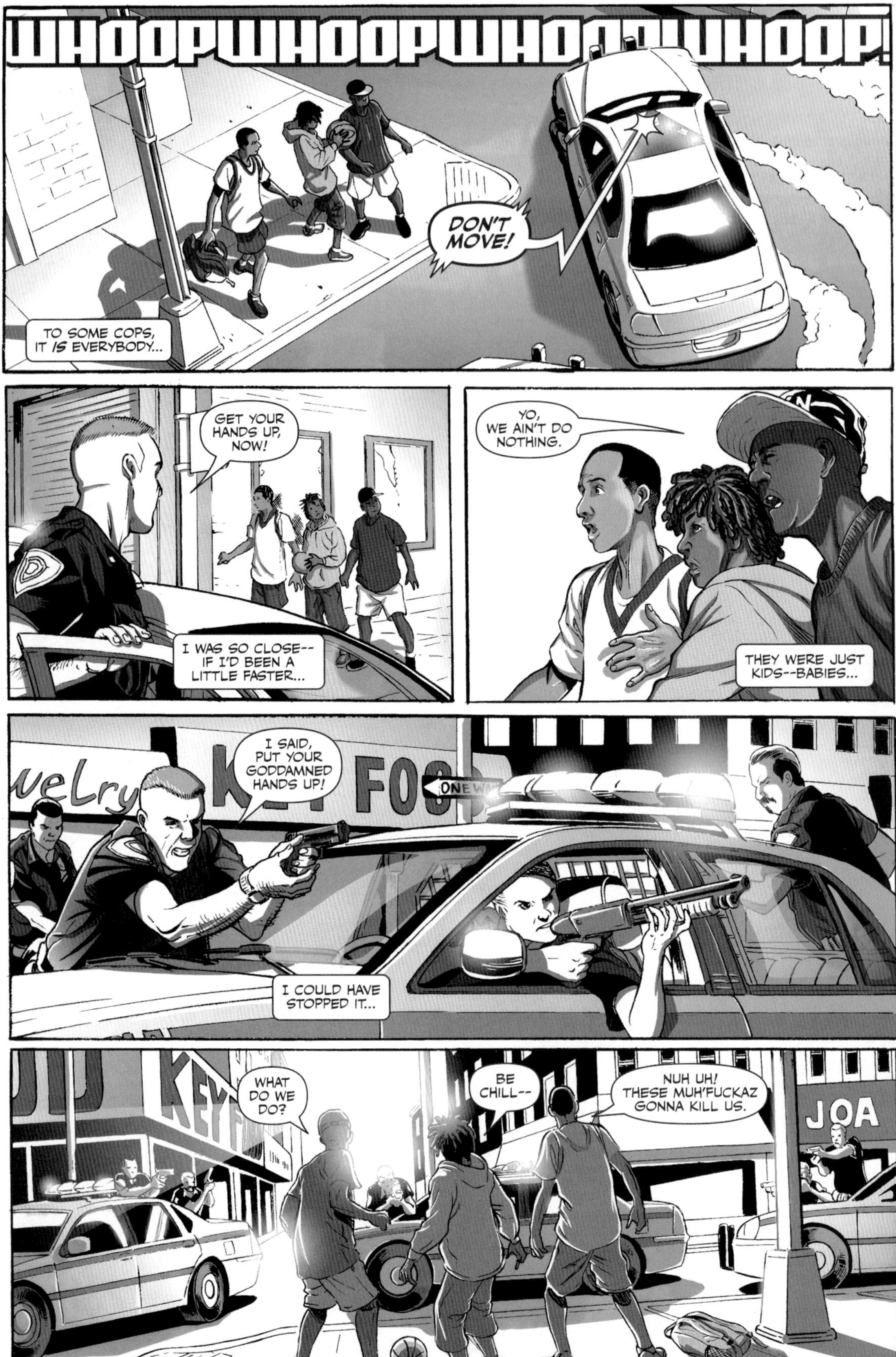
WHOOPWHOOPWHOOPWHOOP!
DON'T MOVE!
TO SOME COPS, IT IS EVERYBODY...
GET YOUR HANDS UP, NOW!
I WAS SO CLOSE--IF I'D BEEN A LITTLE FASTER...
YO, WE AIN'T DO NOTHING.
THEY WERE JUST KIDS--BABIES...
I SAID, PUT YOUR GODDAMNED HANDS UP!
I COULD HAVE STOPPED IT...
WHAT DO WE DO?
BE CHILL--
NUH UH! THESE MUH'FUCKAZ GONNA KILL US.

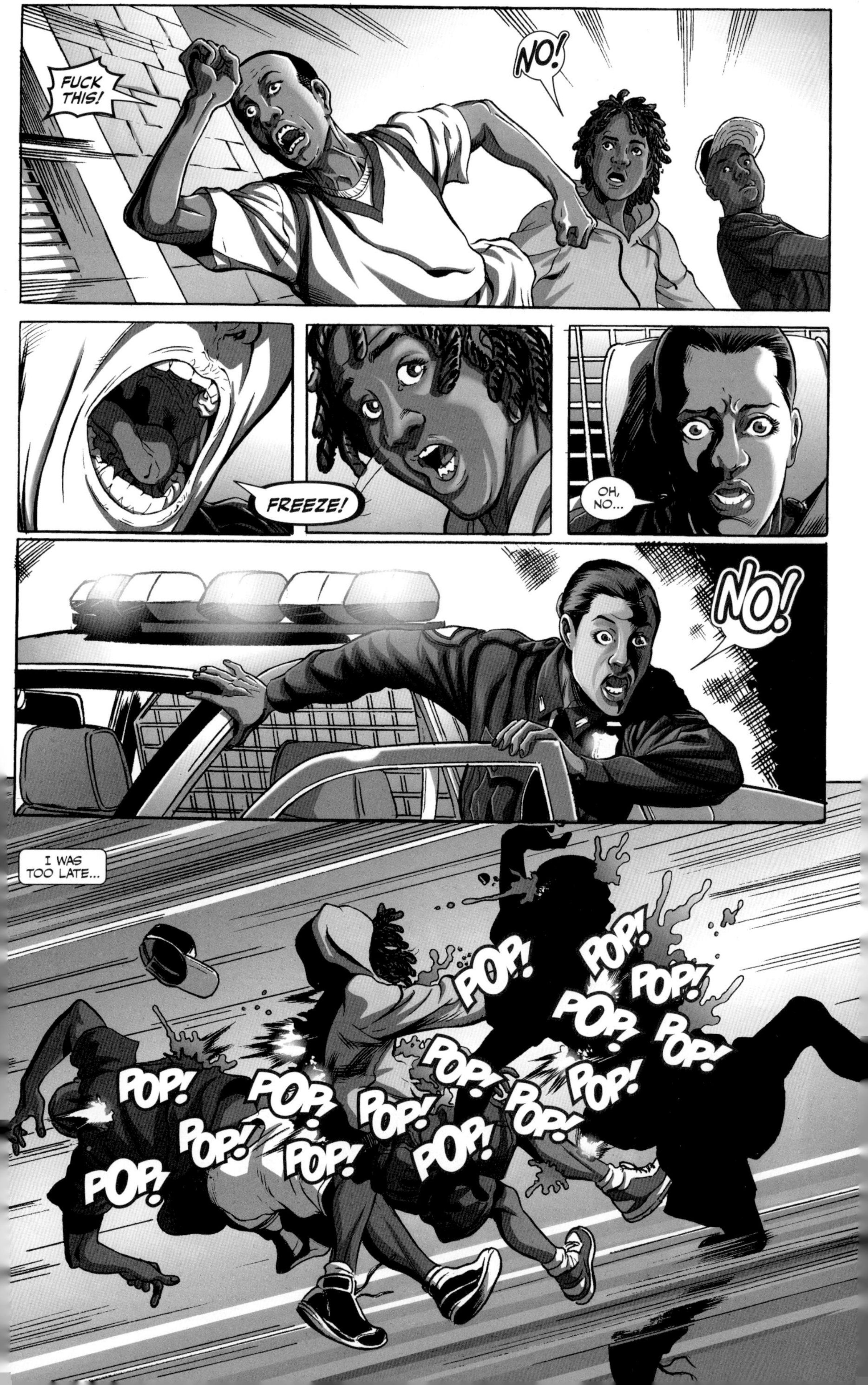
FUCK THIS!
NO!
FREEZE!
OH, NO...
NO!
I WAS TOO LATE...
POP!
POP!
POP!
POP!
POP!
POP!
POP!
POP!
POP!
POP!
POP!
POP!
POP!
POP!
POP!
POP!

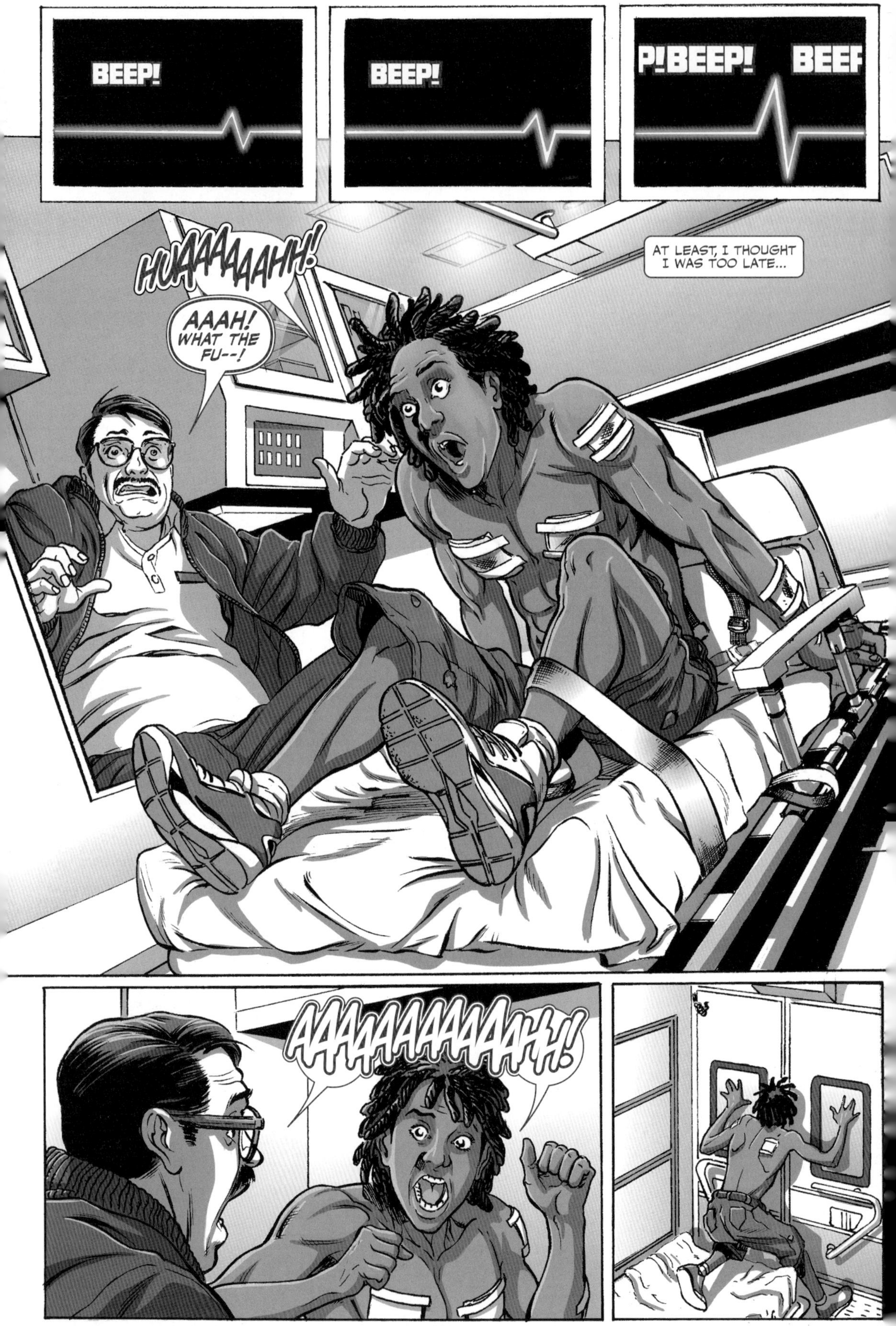
BEEP!
BEEP!
P!BEEP! BEEF
HUAAAAAAAHH!
AAAH! WHAT THE FU--!
AT LEAST, I THOUGHT I WAS TOO LATE...
AAAAAAAAAAAHH!

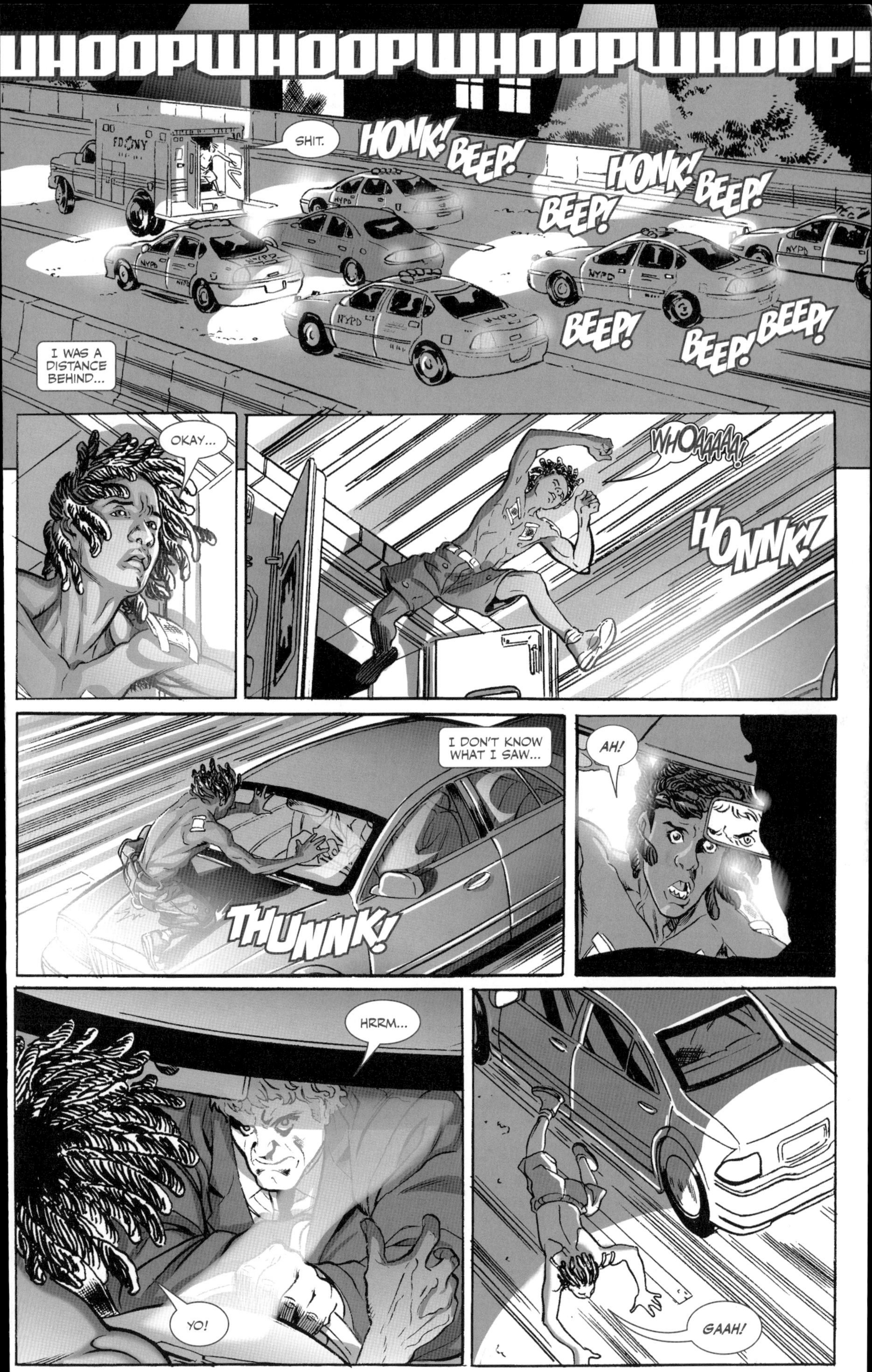
WHOOPWHOOPWHOOPWHOOP!
SHIT.
HONK!
BEEP!
HONK!
BEEP!
BEEP!
I WAS A DISTANCE BEHIND...
BEEP!
BEEP!
BEEP!
OKAY...
WHOAAAAA!
HONNK!
I DON'T KNOW WHAT I SAW...
THUNNK!
AH!
HRRM...
YO!
GAAH!

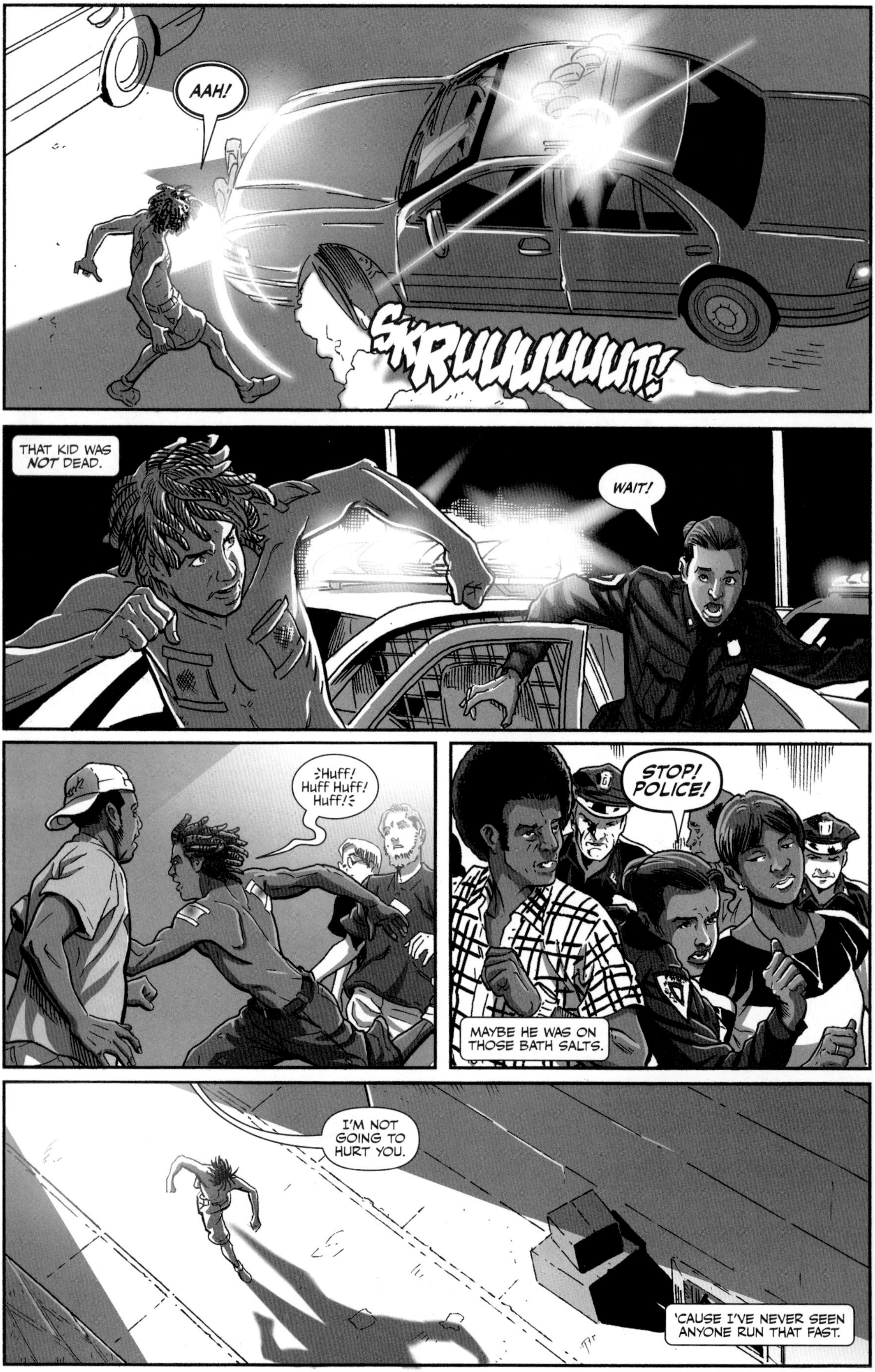
AAH!
SKRUUUUUUT!
THAT KID WAS NOT DEAD.
WAIT!
Huff! Huff Huff! Huff!
STOP! POLICE!
MAYBE HE WAS ON THOSE BATH SALTS.
I'M NOT GOING TO HURT YOU.
'CAUSE I'VE NEVER SEEN ANYONE RUN THAT FAST.

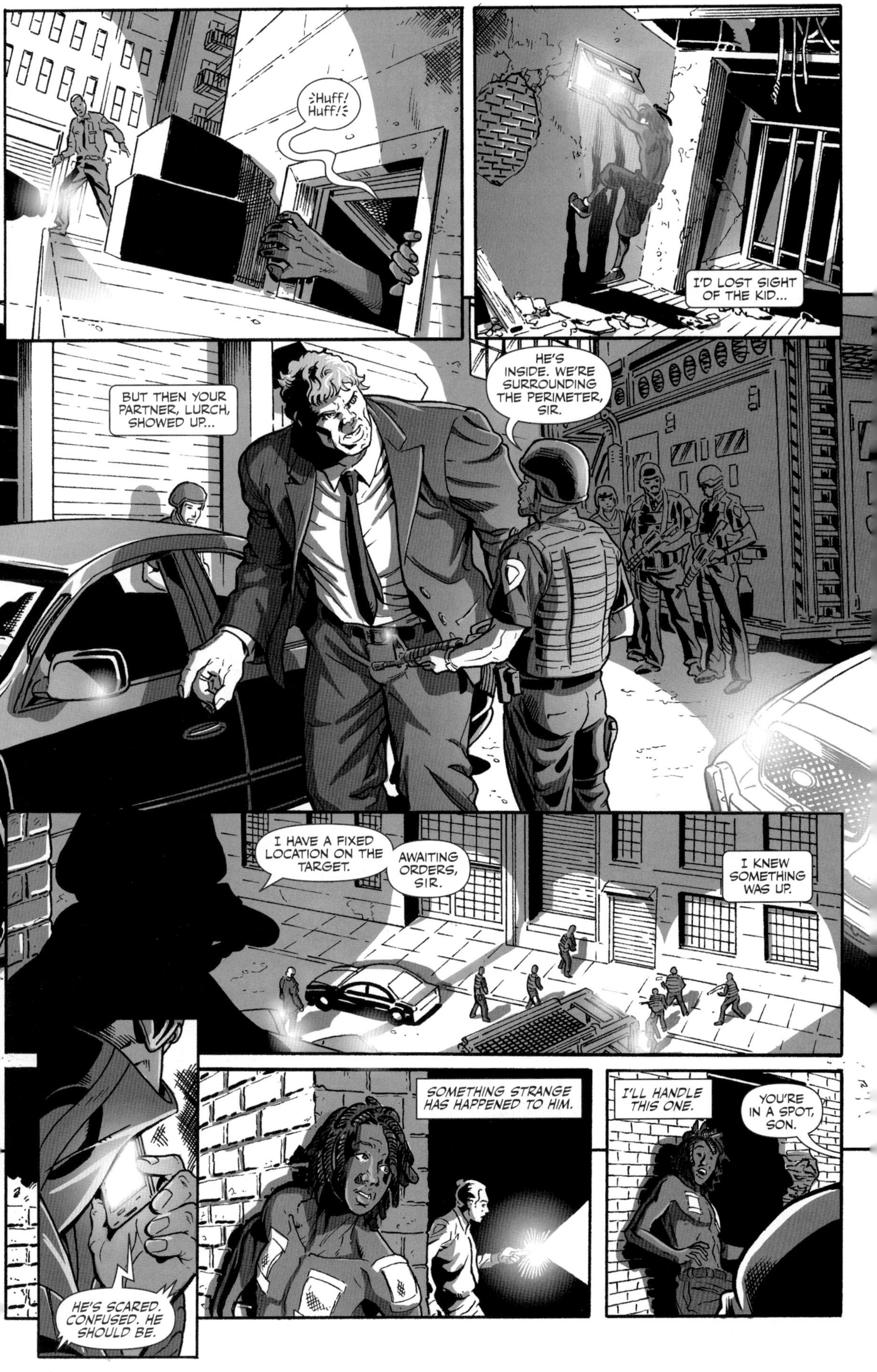

Huff! Huff!
I'D LOST SIGHT OF THE KID...
BUT THEN YOUR PARTNER, LURCH, SHOWED UP...
HE'S INSIDE. WE'RE SURROUNDING THE PERIMETER, SIR.
I HAVE A FIXED LOCATION ON THE TARGET.
AWAITING ORDERS, SIR.
I KNEW SOMETHING WAS UP.
HE'S SCARED. CONFUSED. HE SHOULD BE.
SOMETHING STRANGE HAS HAPPENED TO HIM.
I'LL HANDLE THIS ONE.
YOU'RE IN A SPOT, SON.

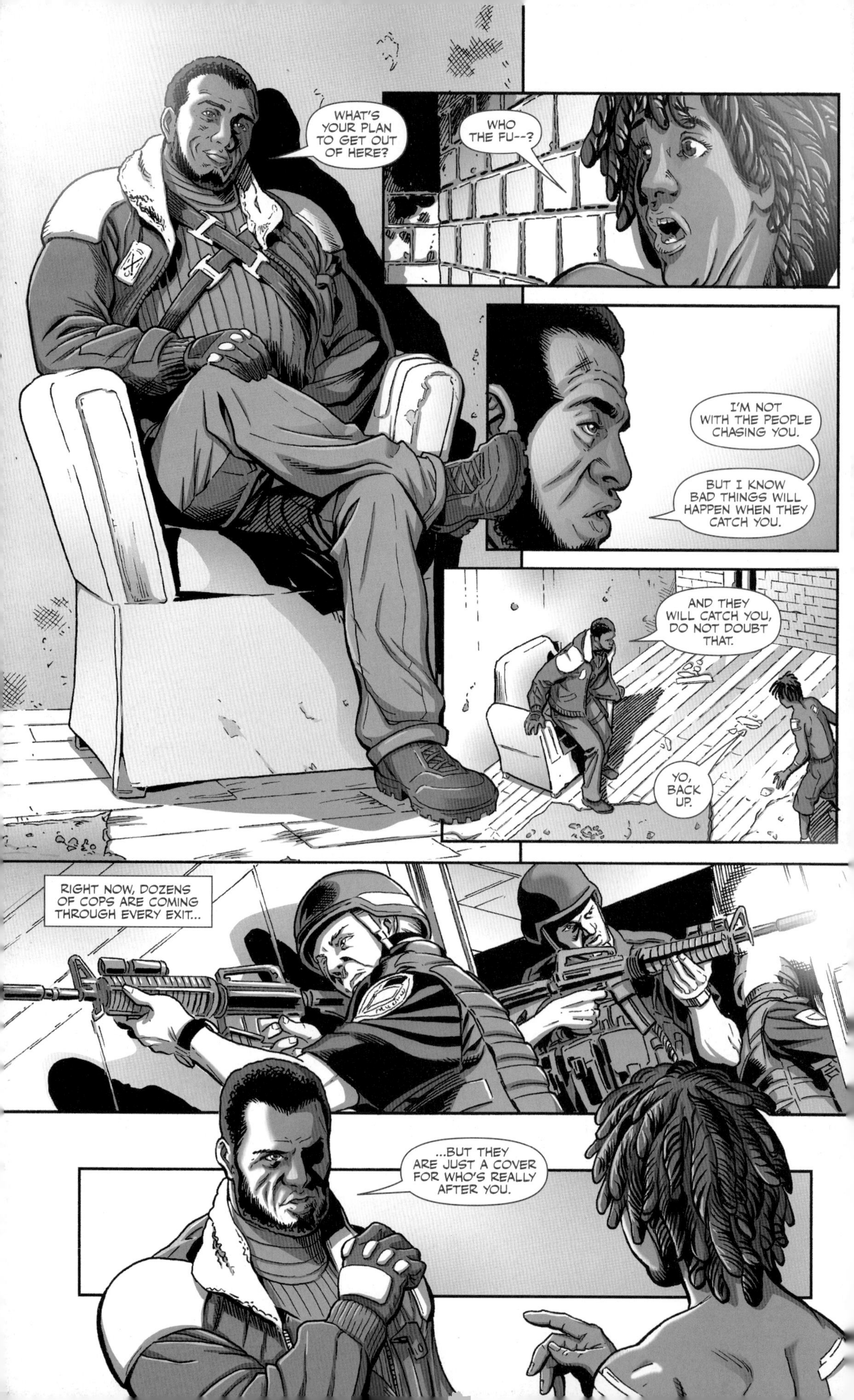
WHAT'S YOUR PLAN TO GET OUT OF HERE?
WHO THE FU--?
I'M NOT WITH THE PEOPLE CHASING YOU.
BUT I KNOW BAD THINGS WILL HAPPEN WHEN THEY CATCH YOU.
AND THEY WILL CATCH YOU, DO NOT DOUBT THAT.
YO, BACK UP.
RIGHT NOW, DOZENS OF COPS ARE COMING THROUGH EVERY EXIT...
...BUT THEY ARE JUST A COVER FOR WHO'S REALLY AFTER YOU.

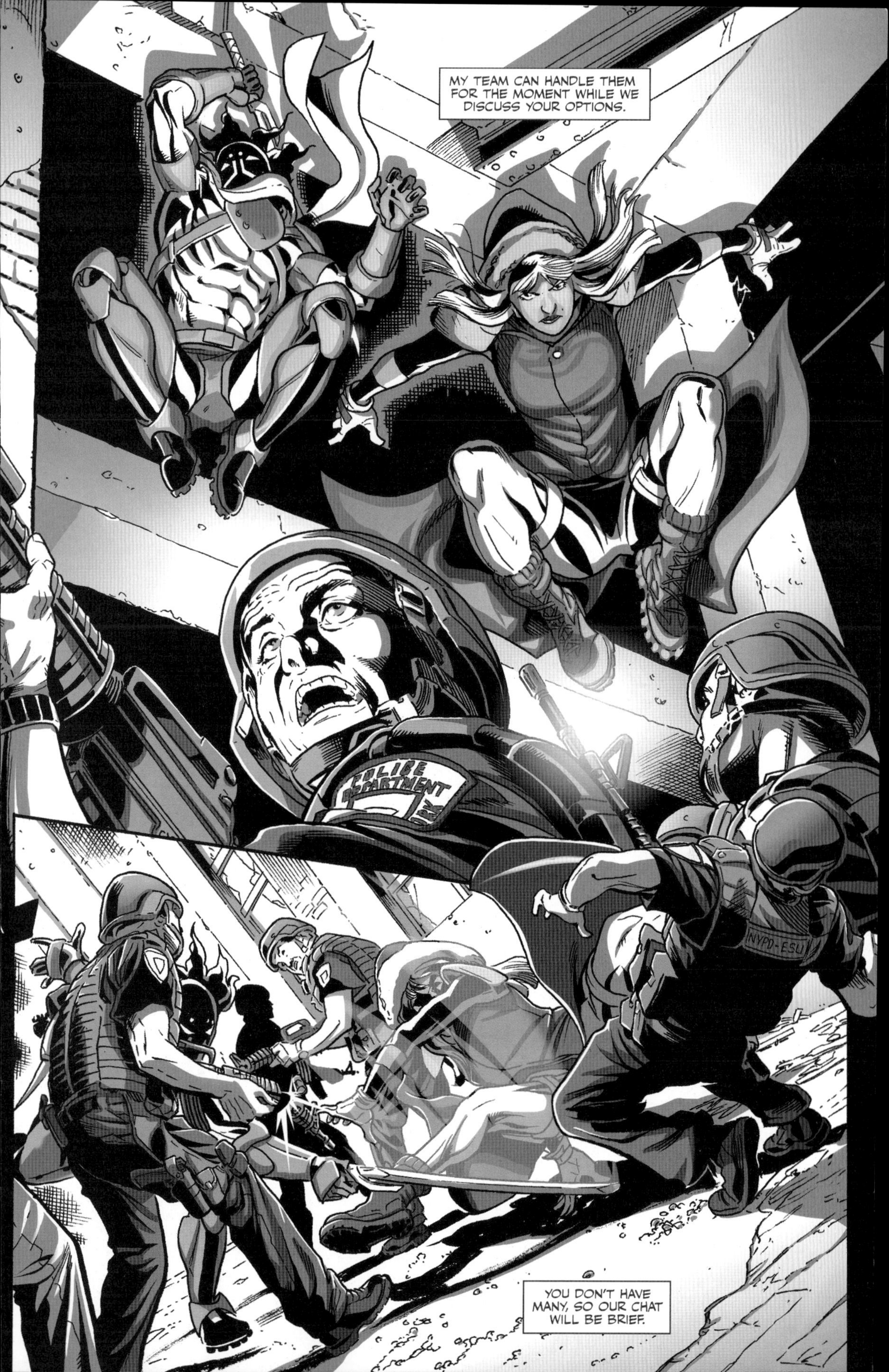
MY TEAM CAN HANDLE THEM FOR THE MOMENT WHILE WE DISCUSS YOUR OPTIONS.
NYPD-ESU
YOU DON'T HAVE MANY, SO OUR CHAT WILL BE BRIEF.

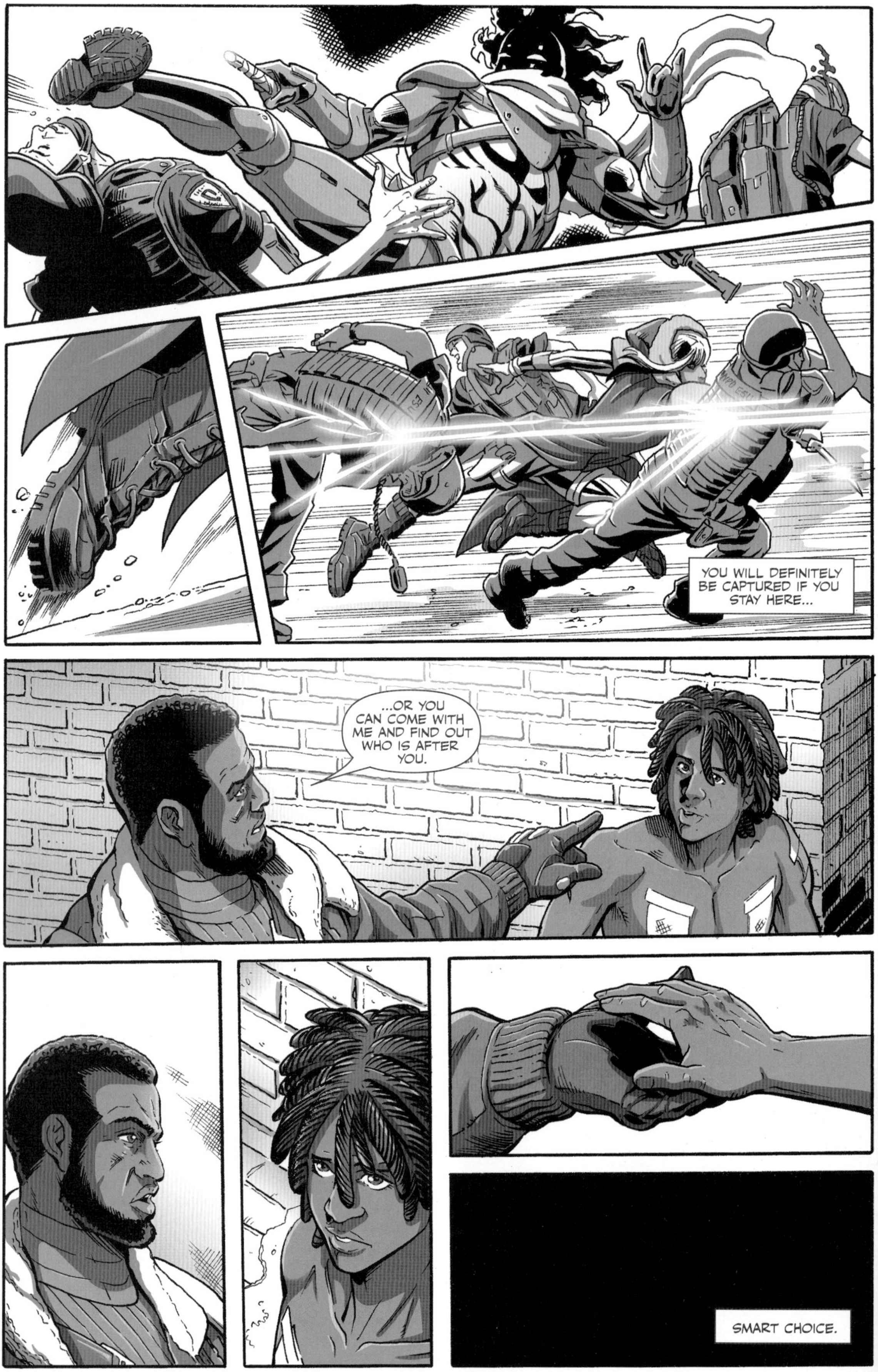
YOU WILL DEFINITELY BE CAPTURED IF YOU STAY HERE...
...OR YOU CAN COME WITH ME AND FIND OUT WHO IS AFTER YOU.
SMART CHOICE.

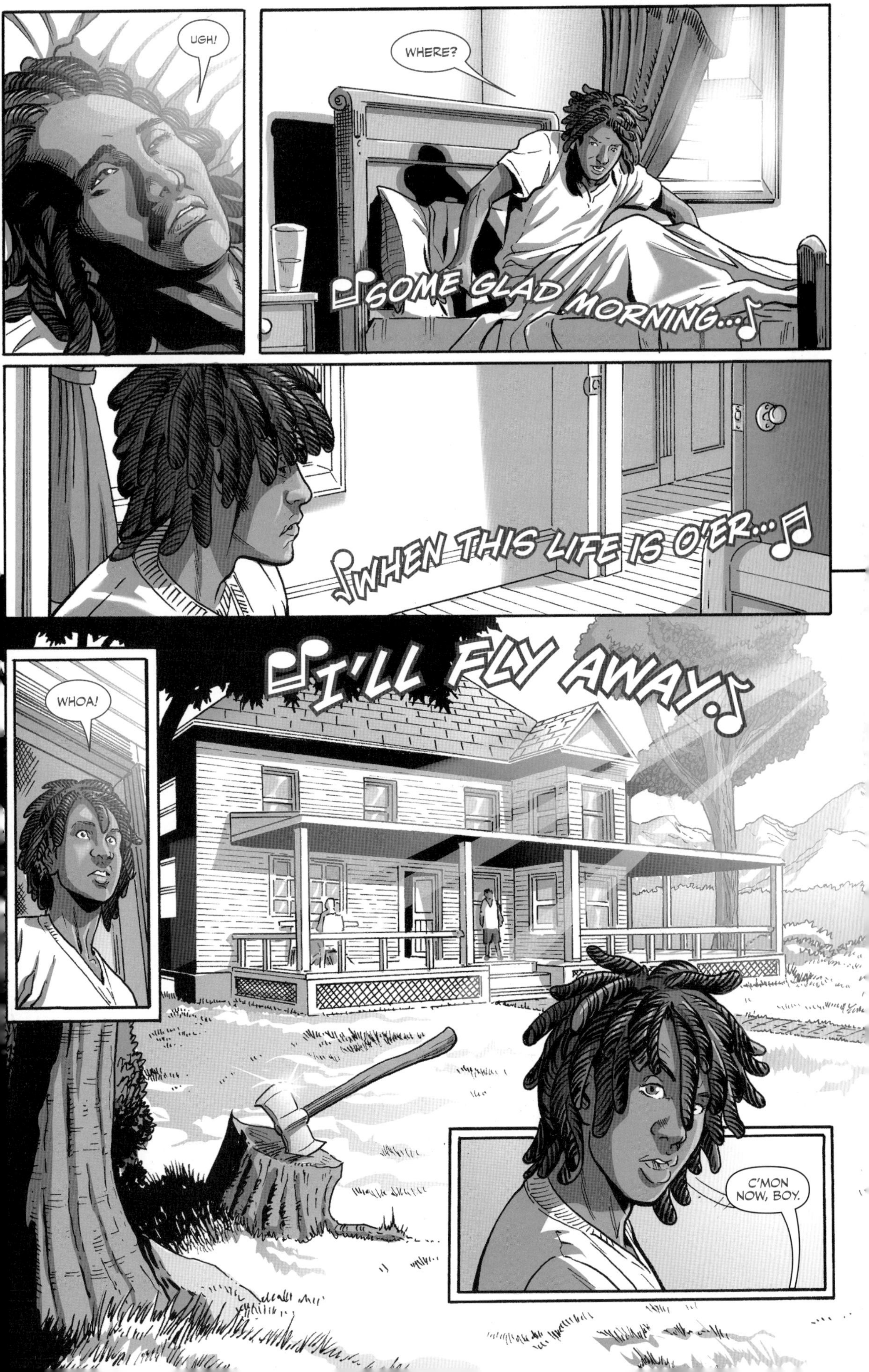
UGH!
WHERE?
SOME GLAD MORNING...
WHEN THIS LIFE IS O'ER...
I'LL FLY AWAY.
WHOA!
C'MON NOW, BOY.

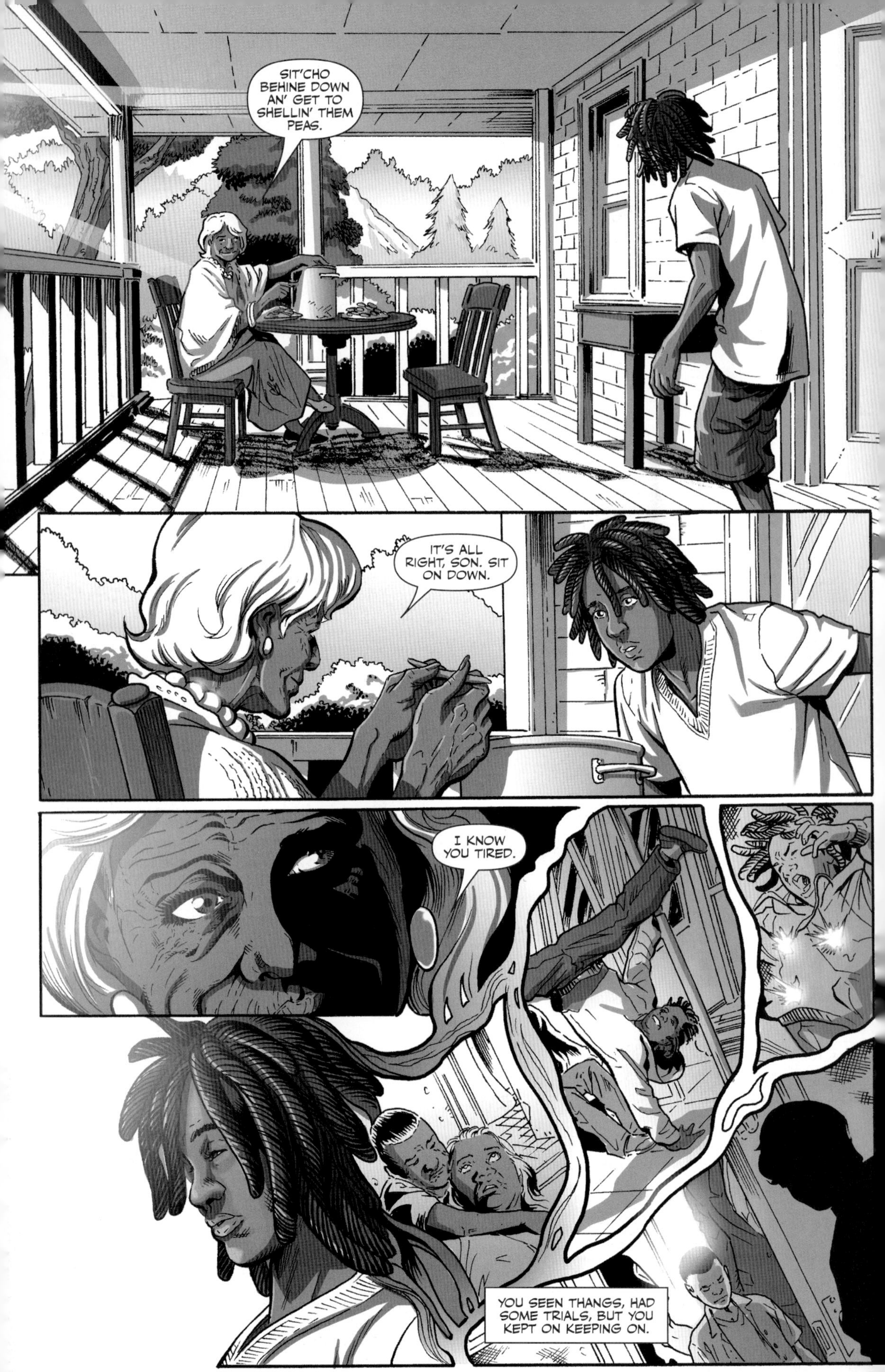
SIT'CHO BEHINE DOWN AN' GET TO SHELLIN' THEM PEAS.
IT'S ALL RIGHT, SON. SIT ON DOWN.
I KNOW YOU TIRED.
YOU SEEN THANGS, HAD SOME TRIALS, BUT YOU KEPT ON KEEPING ON.

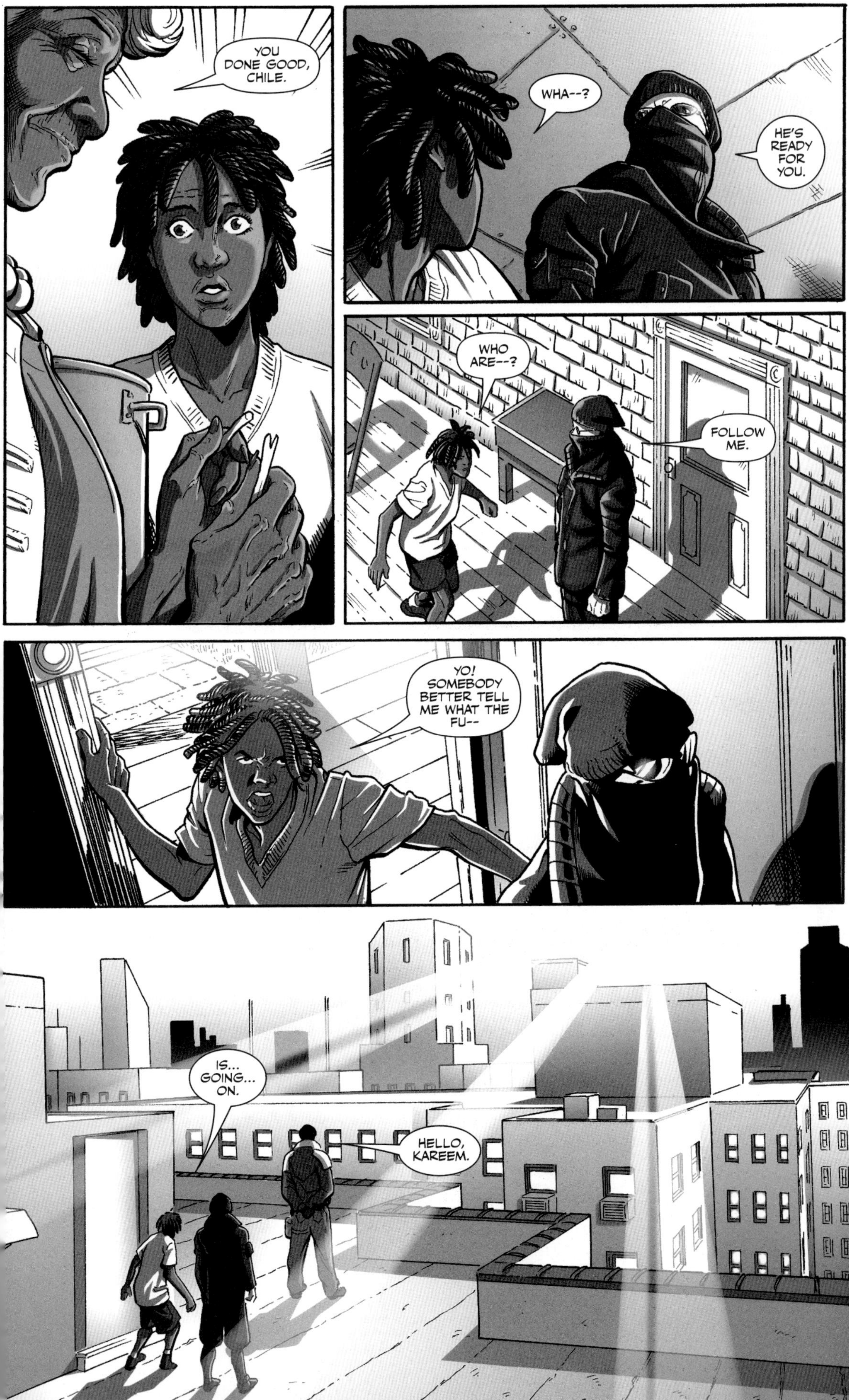
YOU DONE GOOD, CHILE.
WHA--?
HE'S READY FOR YOU.
WHO ARE--?
FOLLOW ME.
YO! SOMEBODY BETTER TELL ME WHAT THE FU--
IS... GOING... ON.
HELLO, KAREEM.

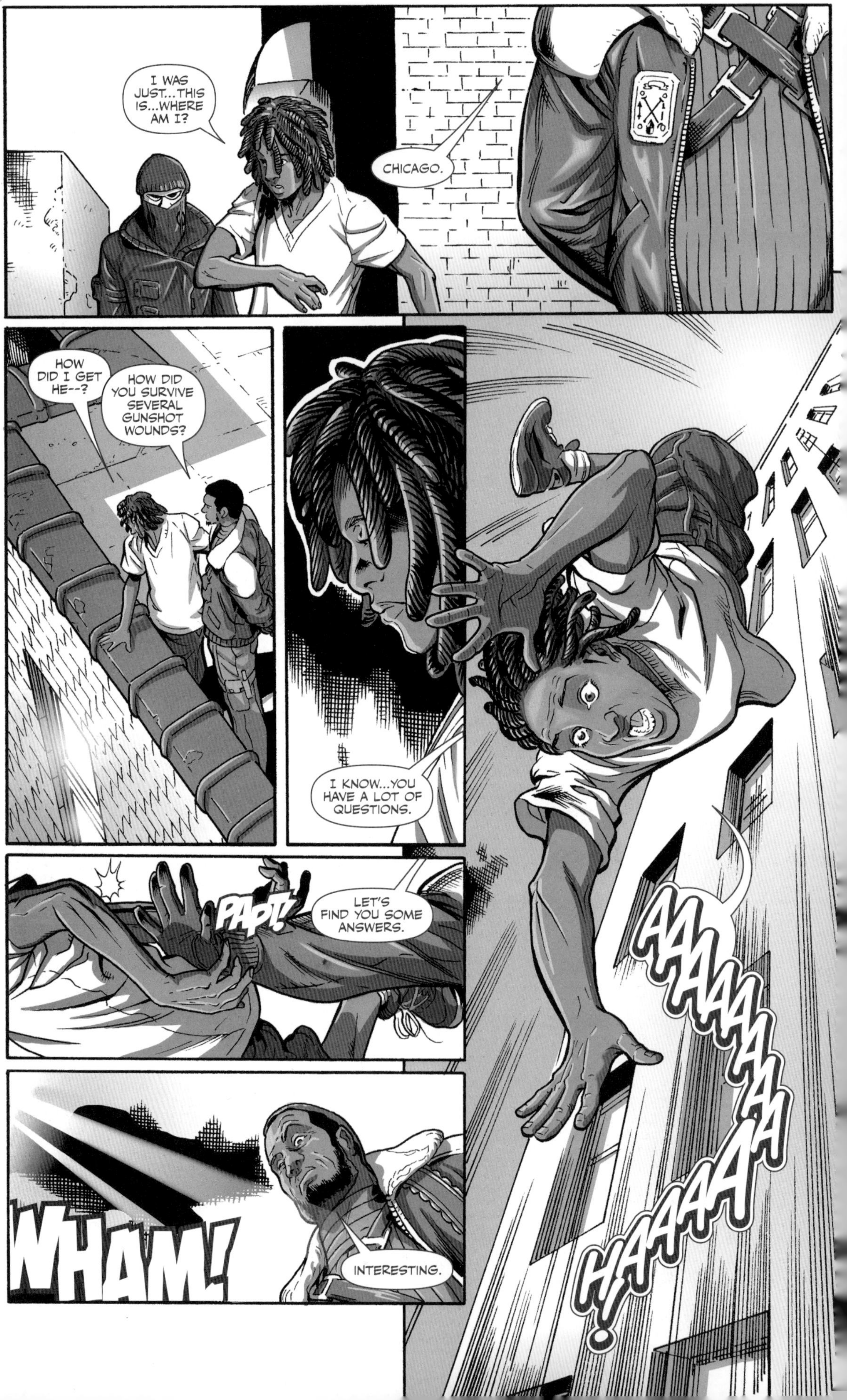
I WAS JUST...THIS IS...WHERE AM I?
CHICAGO.
HOW DID I GET HE--?
HOW DID YOU SURVIVE SEVERAL GUNSHOT WOUNDS?
I KNOW...YOU HAVE A LOT OF QUESTIONS.
PAPT!
LET'S FIND YOU SOME ANSWERS.
WHAM!
INTERESTING.
AAAAAAAAAAHAAAAA!

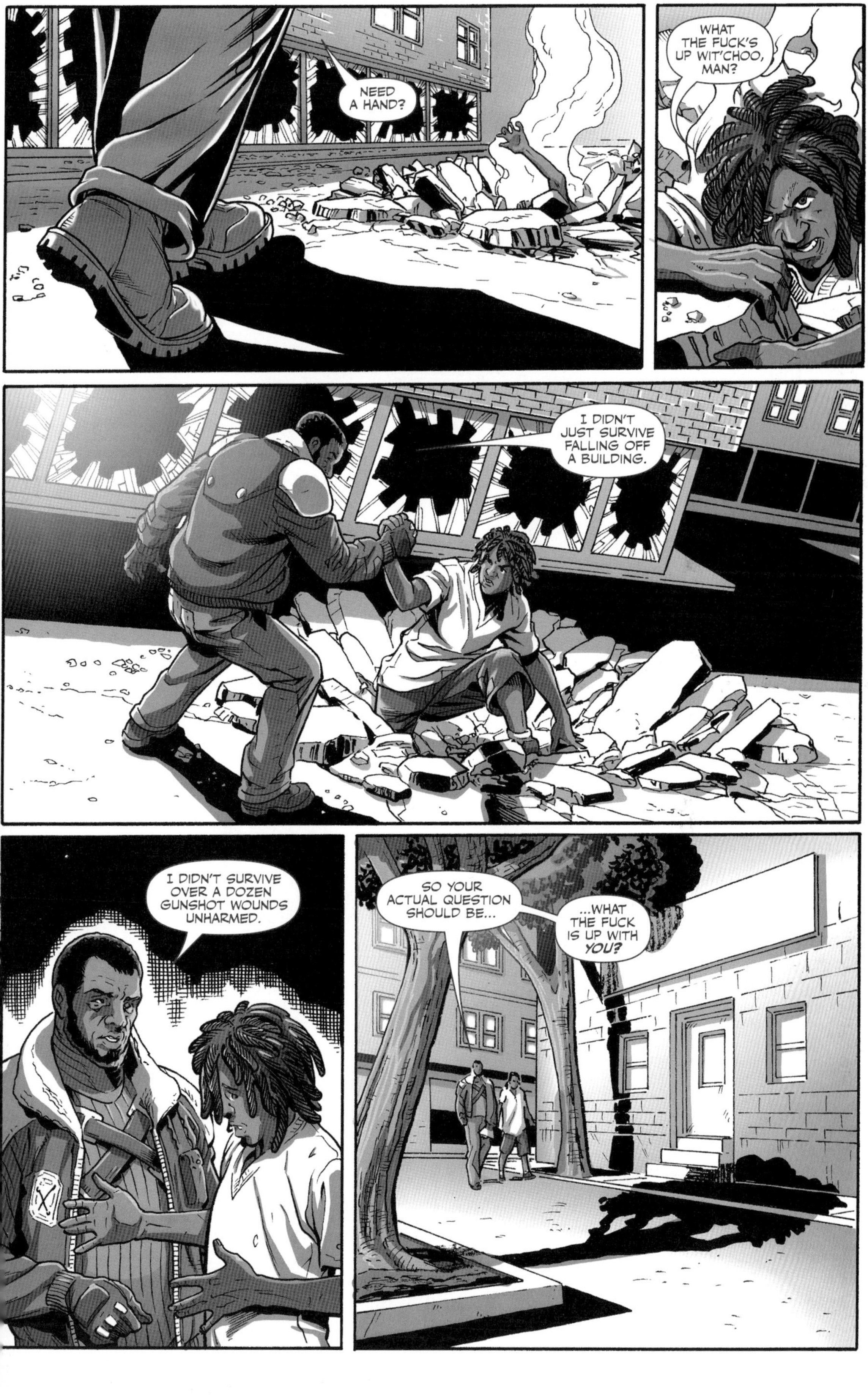
NEED A HAND?
WHAT THE FUCK'S UP WIT'CHOO, MAN?
I DIDN'T JUST SURVIVE FALLING OFF A BUILDING.
I DIDN'T SURVIVE OVER A DOZEN GUNSHOT WOUNDS UNHARMED.
SO YOUR ACTUAL QUESTION SHOULD BE...
...WHAT THE FUCK IS UP WITH *YOU?*

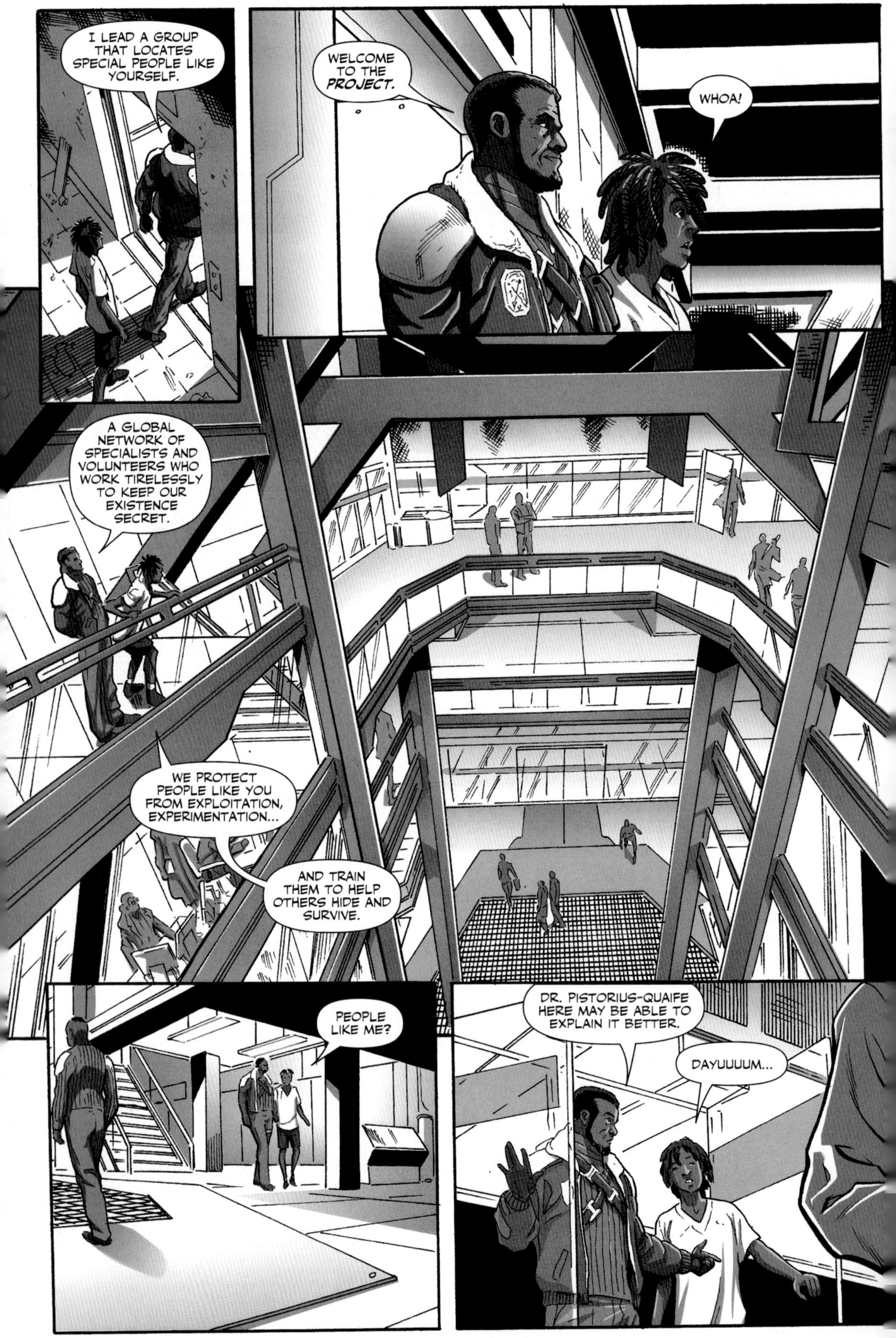
I LEAD A GROUP THAT LOCATES SPECIAL PEOPLE LIKE YOURSELF.
WELCOME TO THE *PROJECT*.
WHOA!
A GLOBAL NETWORK OF SPECIALISTS AND VOLUNTEERS WHO WORK TIRELESSLY TO KEEP OUR EXISTENCE SECRET.
WE PROTECT PEOPLE LIKE YOU FROM EXPLOITATION, EXPERIMENTATION...
AND TRAIN THEM TO HELP OTHERS HIDE AND SURVIVE.
PEOPLE LIKE ME?
DR. PISTORIUS-QUAIFE HERE MAY BE ABLE TO EXPLAIN IT BETTER.
DAYUUUUM...

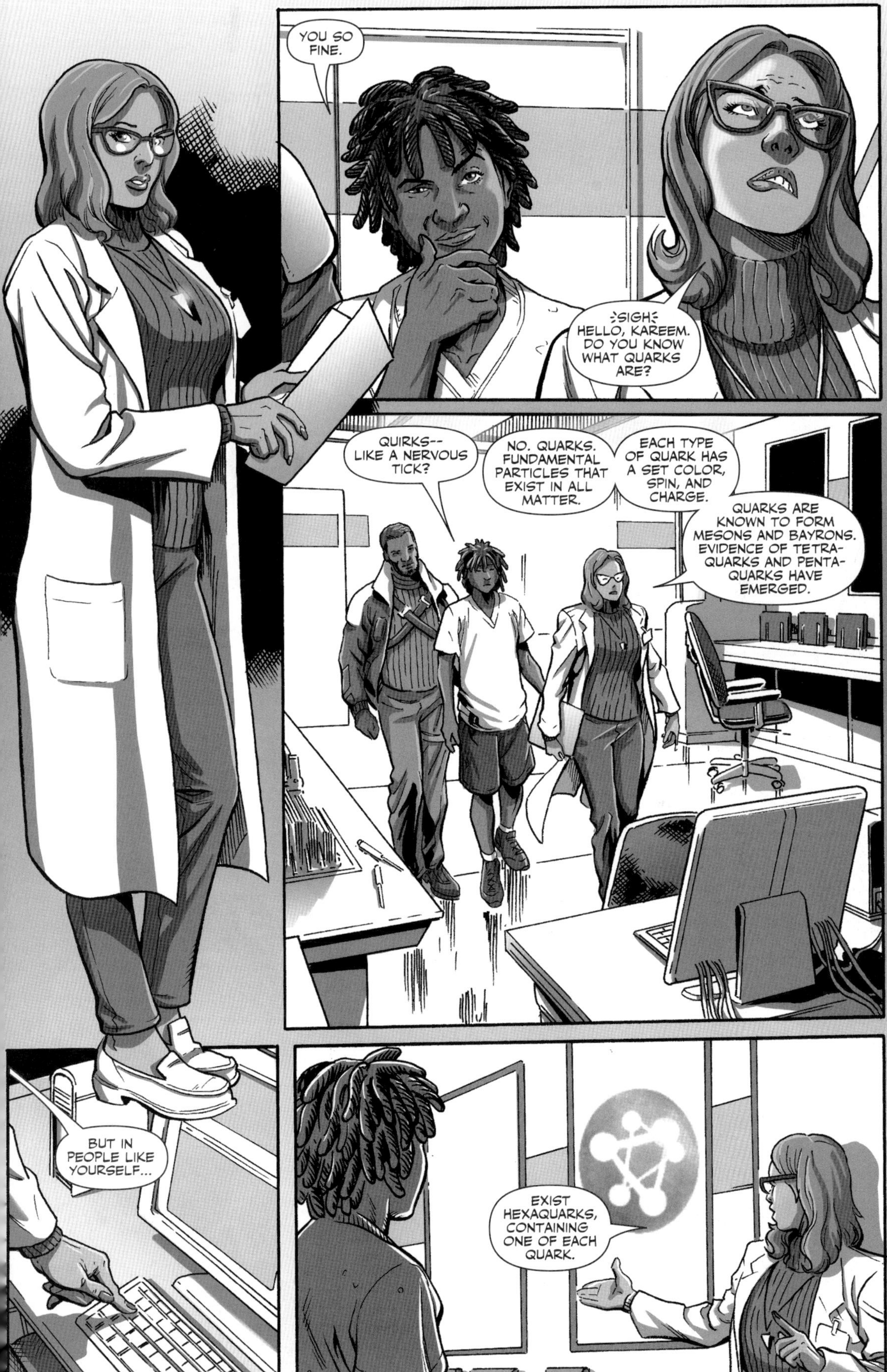
YOU SO FINE.
⁒SIGH⁒ HELLO, KAREEM. DO YOU KNOW WHAT QUARKS ARE?
QUIRKS-- LIKE A NERVOUS TICK?
NO. QUARKS. FUNDAMENTAL PARTICLES THAT EXIST IN ALL MATTER.
EACH TYPE OF QUARK HAS A SET COLOR, SPIN, AND CHARGE.
QUARKS ARE KNOWN TO FORM MESONS AND BAYRONS. EVIDENCE OF TETRA-QUARKS AND PENTA-QUARKS HAVE EMERGED.
BUT IN PEOPLE LIKE YOURSELF...
EXIST HEXAQUARKS, CONTAINING ONE OF EACH QUARK.

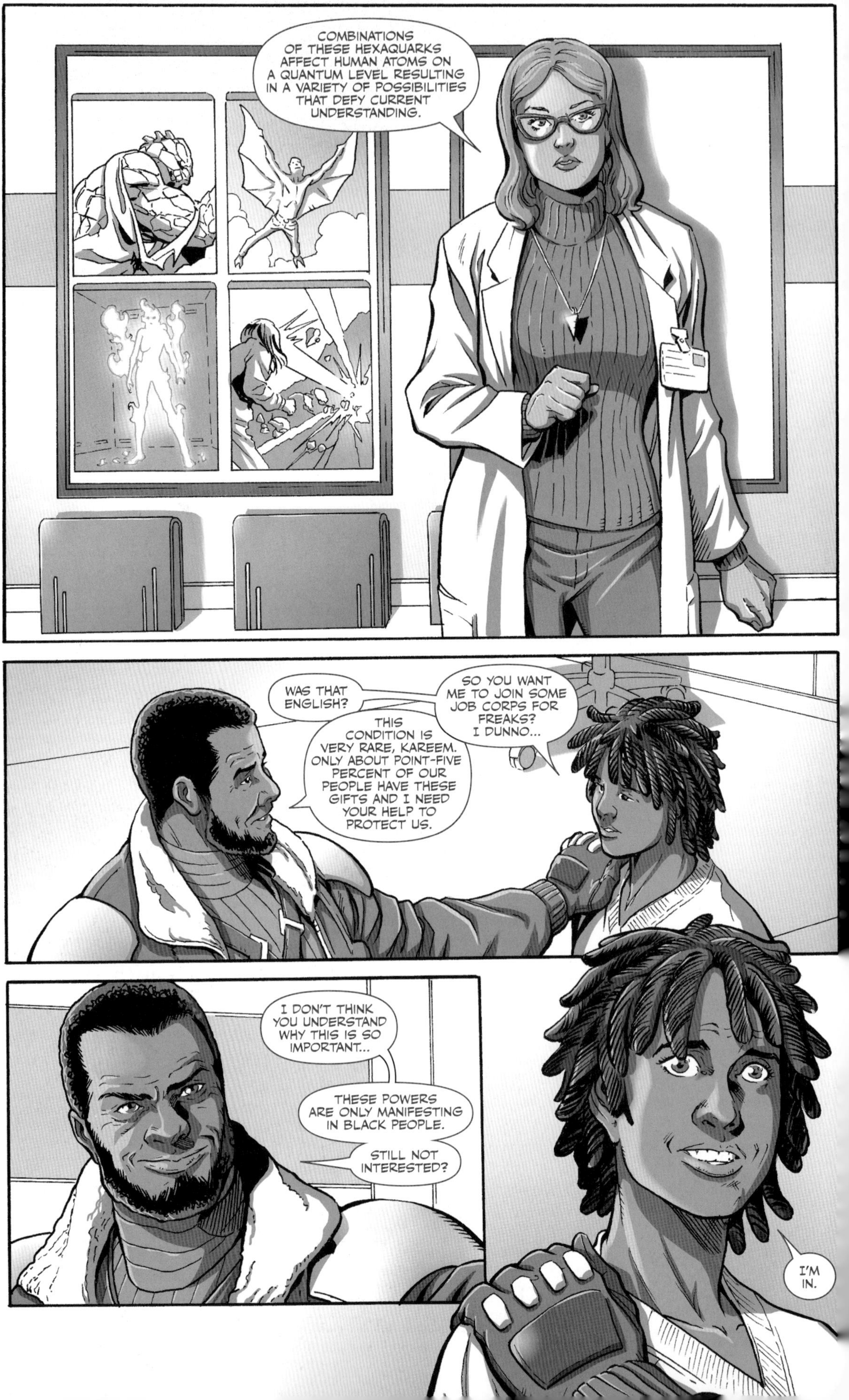
COMBINATIONS OF THESE HEXAQUARKS AFFECT HUMAN ATOMS ON A QUANTUM LEVEL RESULTING IN A VARIETY OF POSSIBILITIES THAT DEFY CURRENT UNDERSTANDING.
WAS THAT ENGLISH?
SO YOU WANT ME TO JOIN SOME JOB CORPS FOR FREAKS? I DUNNO...
THIS CONDITION IS VERY RARE, KAREEM. ONLY ABOUT POINT-FIVE PERCENT OF OUR PEOPLE HAVE THESE GIFTS AND I NEED YOUR HELP TO PROTECT US.
I DON'T THINK YOU UNDERSTAND WHY THIS IS SO IMPORTANT...
THESE POWERS ARE ONLY MANIFESTING IN BLACK PEOPLE.
STILL NOT INTERESTED?
I'M IN.

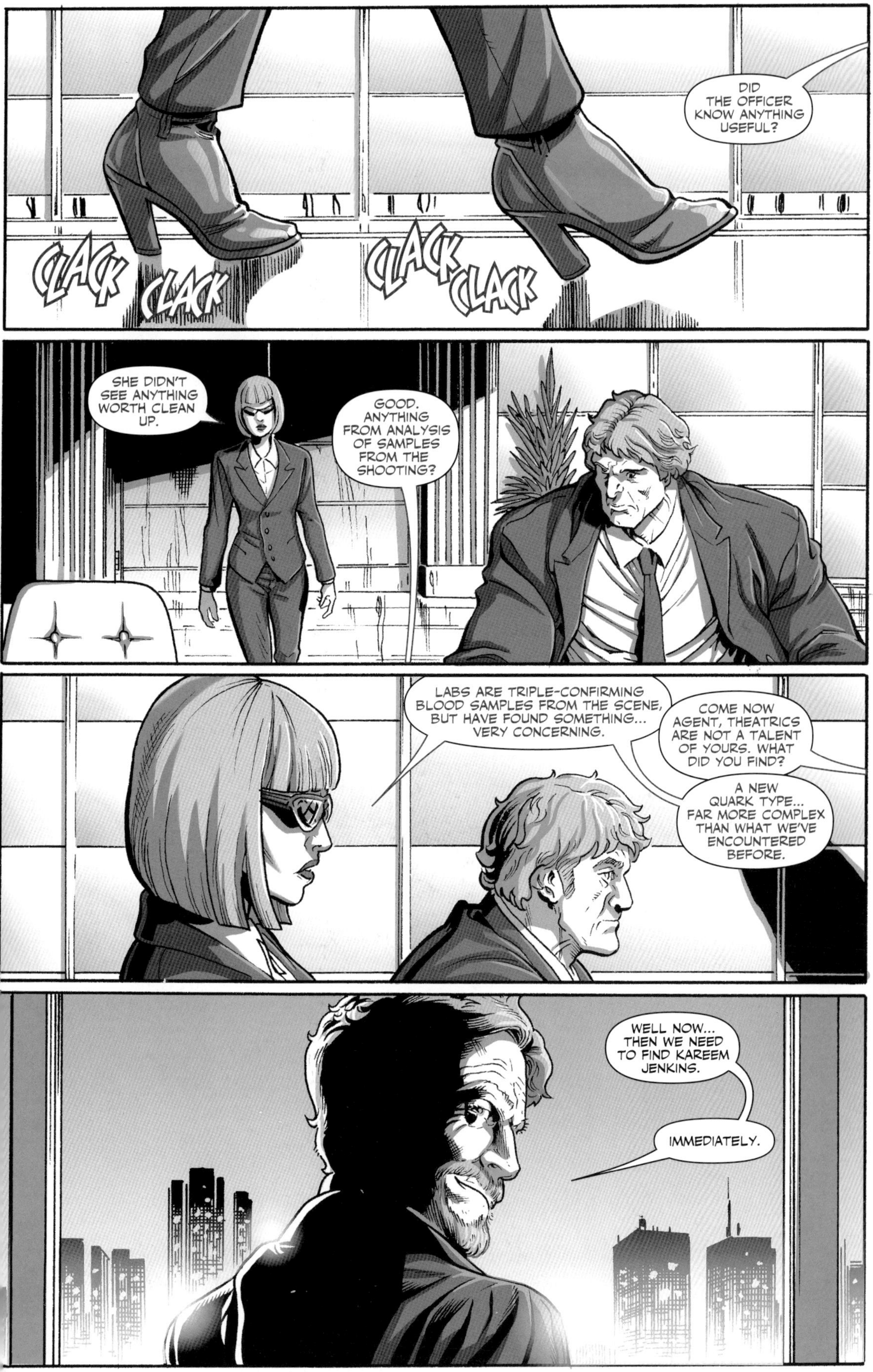
DID THE OFFICER KNOW ANYTHING USEFUL?
CLACK CLACK
CLACK CLACK
SHE DIDN'T SEE ANYTHING WORTH CLEAN UP.
GOOD. ANYTHING FROM ANALYSIS OF SAMPLES FROM THE SHOOTING?
LABS ARE TRIPLE-CONFIRMING BLOOD SAMPLES FROM THE SCENE, BUT HAVE FOUND SOMETHING... VERY CONCERNING.
COME NOW AGENT, THEATRICS ARE NOT A TALENT OF YOURS. WHAT DID YOU FIND?
A NEW QUARK TYPE... FAR MORE COMPLEX THAN WHAT WE'VE ENCOUNTERED BEFORE.
WELL NOW... THEN WE NEED TO FIND KAREEM JENKINS.
IMMEDIATELY.

CHAPTER TWO

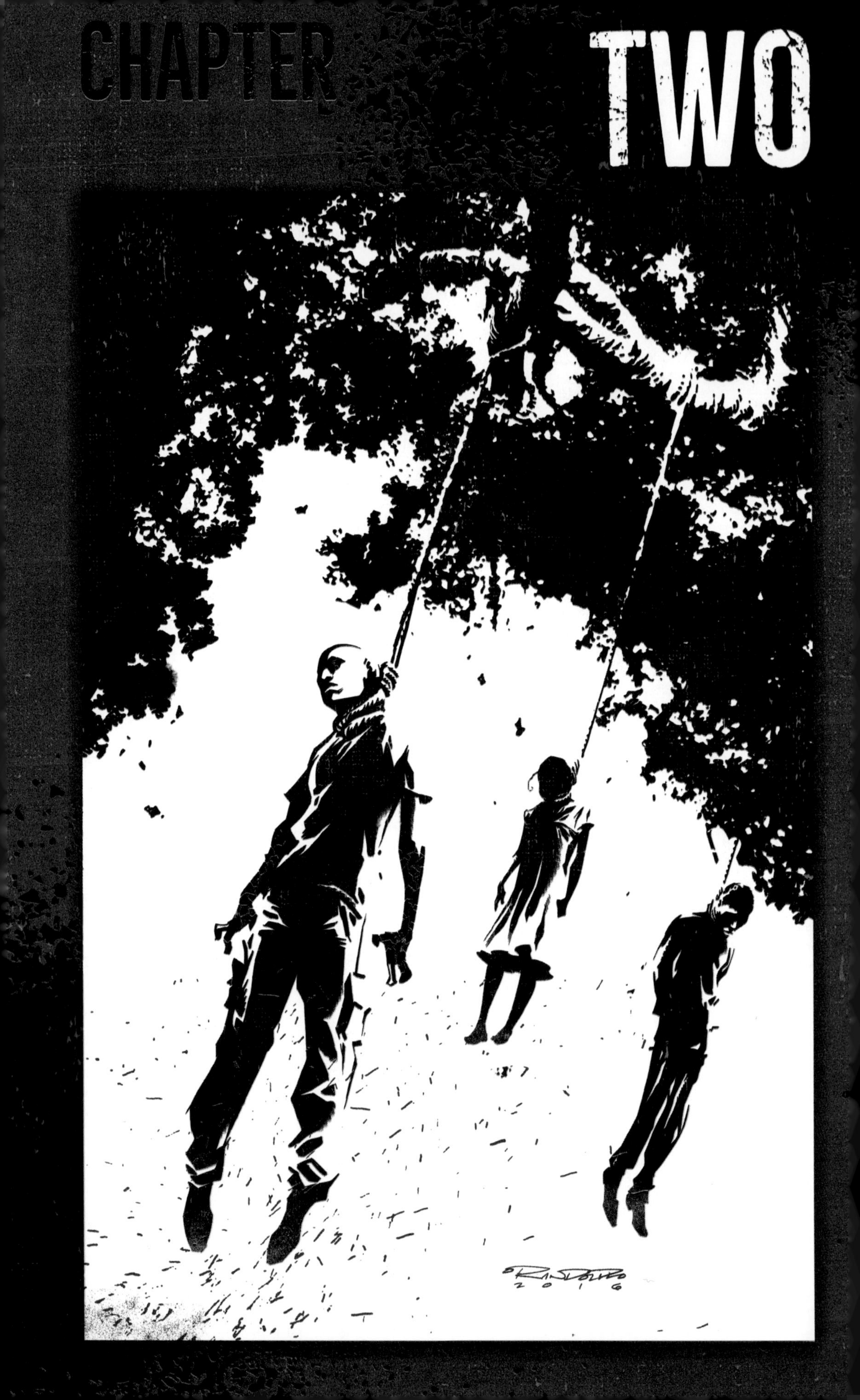

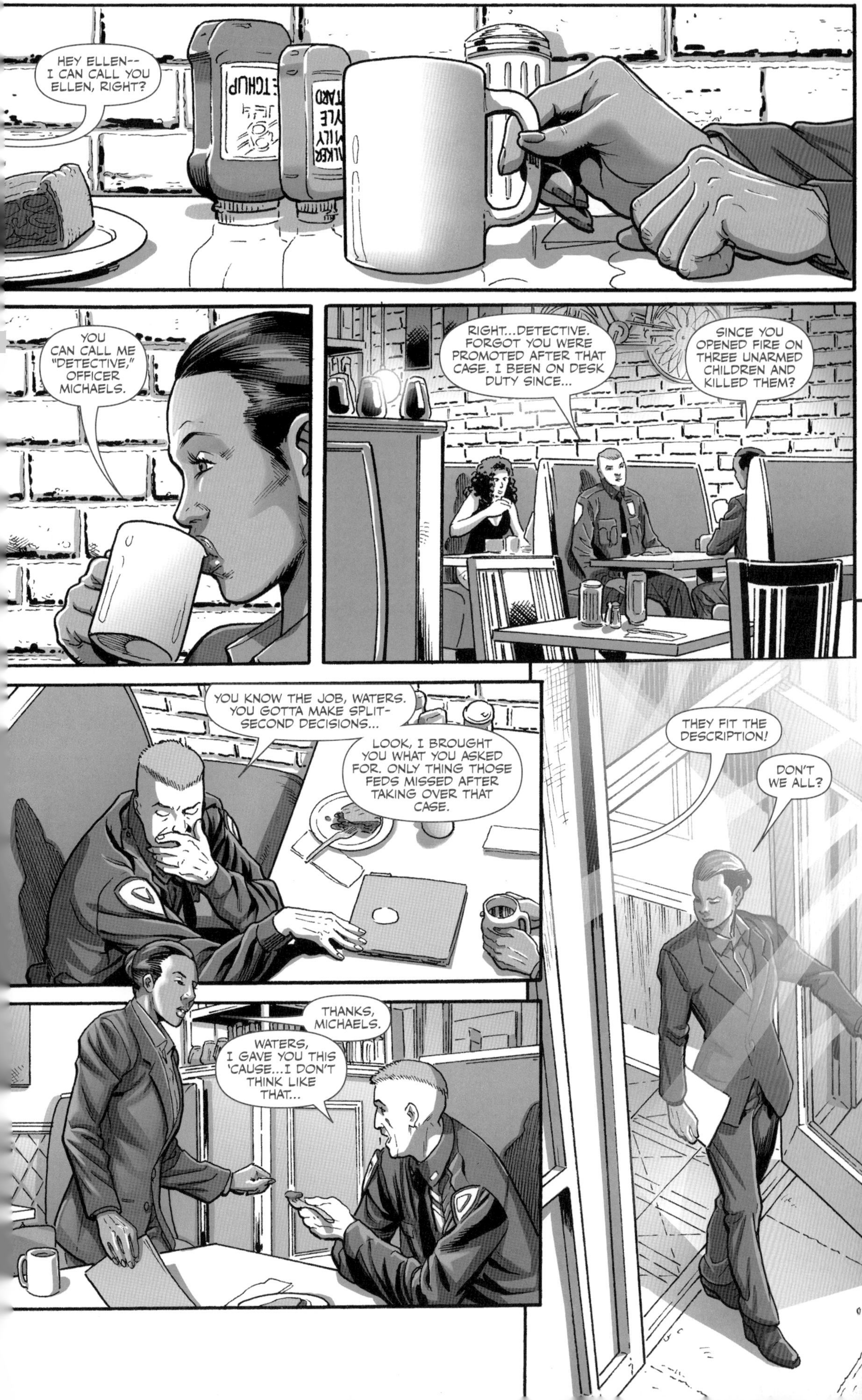
HEY ELLEN-- I CAN CALL YOU ELLEN, RIGHT?
YOU CAN CALL ME "DETECTIVE," OFFICER MICHAELS.
RIGHT...DETECTIVE. FORGOT YOU WERE PROMOTED AFTER THAT CASE. I BEEN ON DESK DUTY SINCE...
SINCE YOU OPENED FIRE ON THREE UNARMED CHILDREN AND KILLED THEM?
YOU KNOW THE JOB, WATERS. YOU GOTTA MAKE SPLIT-SECOND DECISIONS...
LOOK, I BROUGHT YOU WHAT YOU ASKED FOR. ONLY THING THOSE FEDS MISSED AFTER TAKING OVER THAT CASE.
THANKS, MICHAELS.
WATERS, I GAVE YOU THIS 'CAUSE...I DON'T THINK LIKE THAT...
THEY FIT THE DESCRIPTION!
DON'T WE ALL?

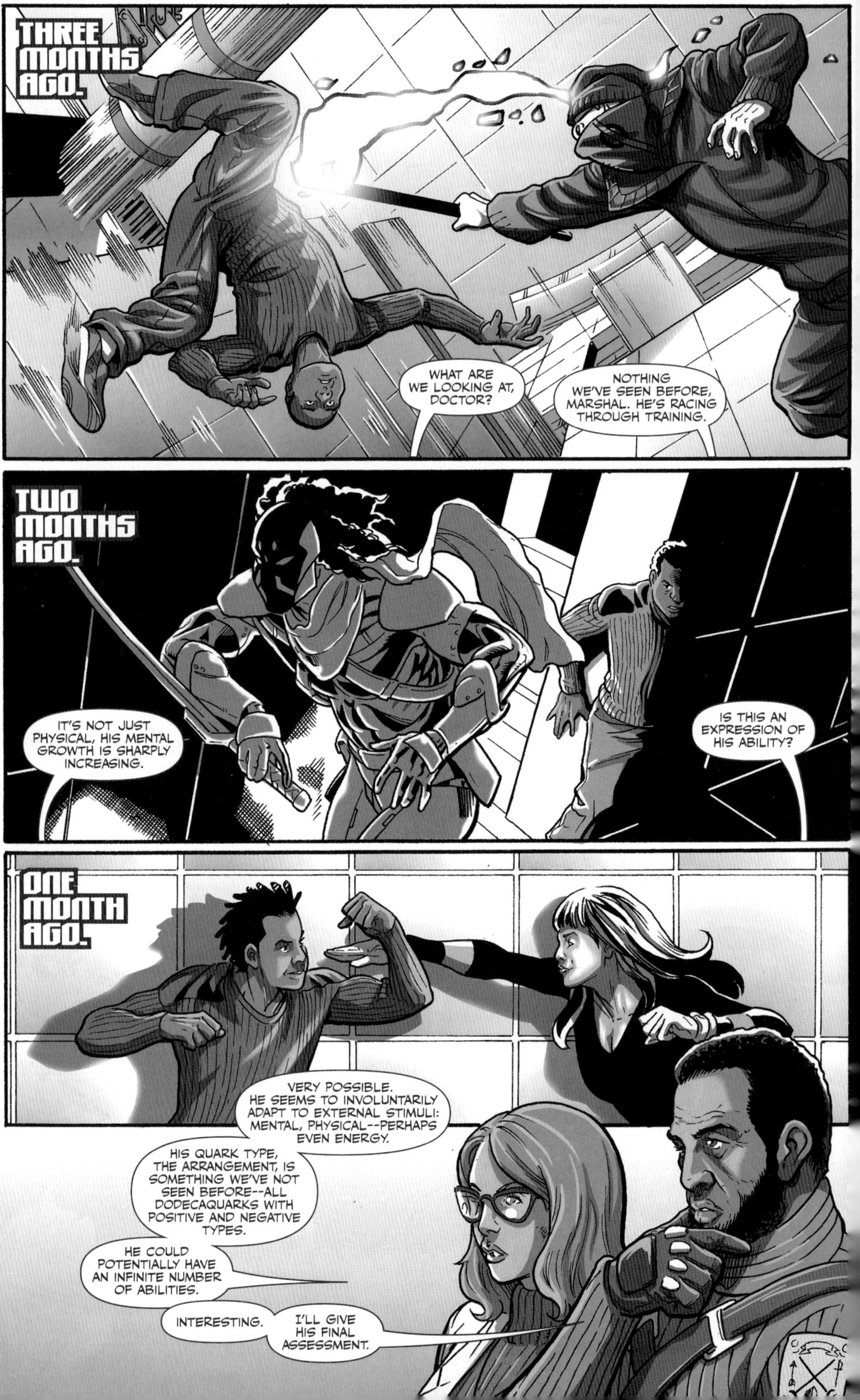
THREE MONTHS AGO.
WHAT ARE WE LOOKING AT, DOCTOR?
NOTHING WE'VE SEEN BEFORE, MARSHAL. HE'S RACING THROUGH TRAINING.
TWO MONTHS AGO.
IT'S NOT JUST PHYSICAL, HIS MENTAL GROWTH IS SHARPLY INCREASING.
IS THIS AN EXPRESSION OF HIS ABILITY?
ONE MONTH AGO.
VERY POSSIBLE. HE SEEMS TO INVOLUNTARILY ADAPT TO EXTERNAL STIMULI: MENTAL, PHYSICAL--PERHAPS EVEN ENERGY.
HIS QUARK TYPE, THE ARRANGEMENT, IS SOMETHING WE'VE NOT SEEN BEFORE--ALL DODECAQUARKS WITH POSITIVE AND NEGATIVE TYPES.
HE COULD POTENTIALLY HAVE AN INFINITE NUMBER OF ABILITIES.
INTERESTING.
I'LL GIVE HIS FINAL ASSESSMENT.

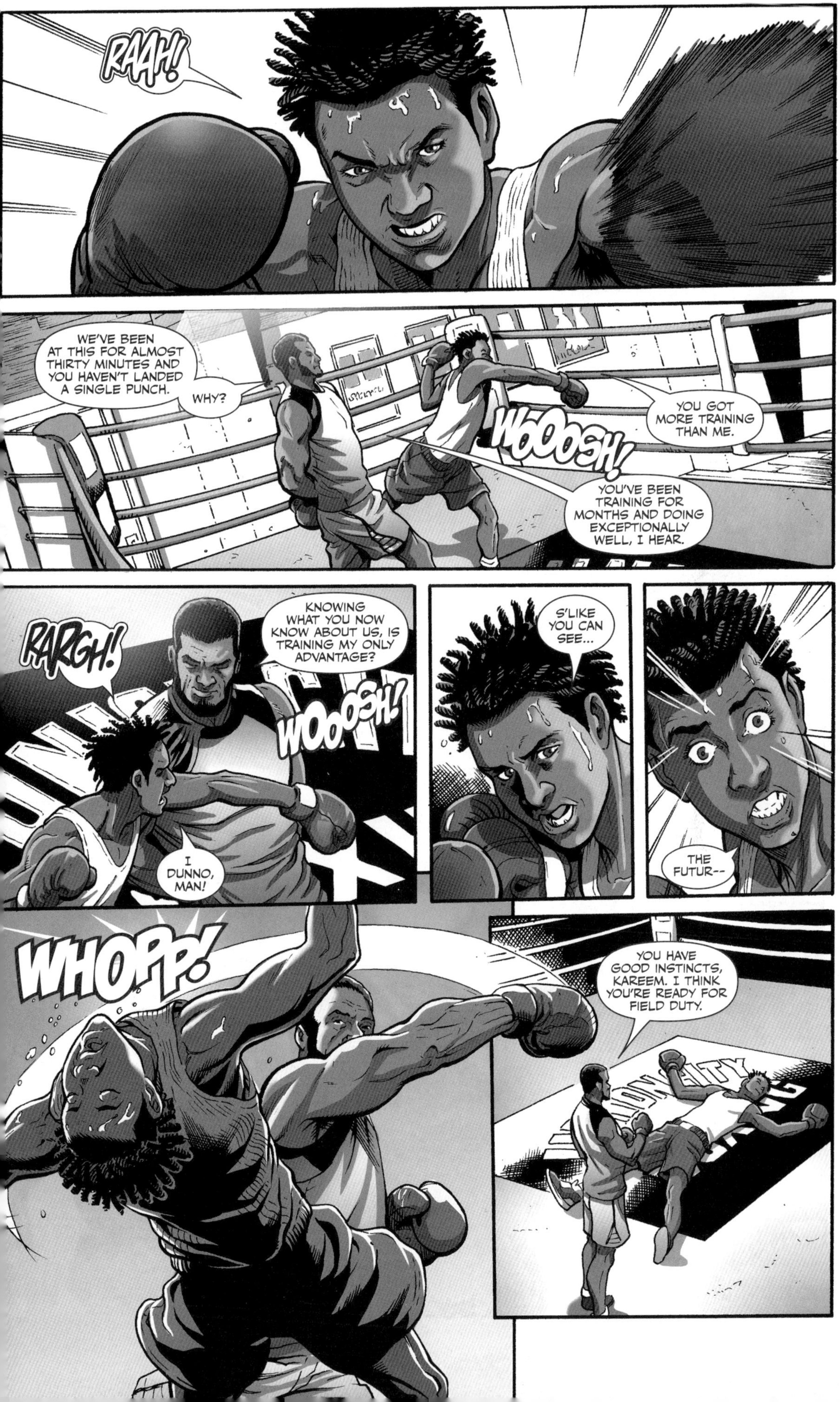
RAAH!
WE'VE BEEN AT THIS FOR ALMOST THIRTY MINUTES AND YOU HAVEN'T LANDED A SINGLE PUNCH.
WHY?
YOU GOT MORE TRAINING THAN ME.
WOOOSH!
YOU'VE BEEN TRAINING FOR MONTHS AND DOING EXCEPTIONALLY WELL, I HEAR.
RARGH!
KNOWING WHAT YOU NOW KNOW ABOUT US, IS TRAINING MY ONLY ADVANTAGE?
WOOOSH!
I DUNNO, MAN!
S'LIKE YOU CAN SEE...
THE FUTUR--
WHOPP!
YOU HAVE GOOD INSTINCTS, KAREEM. I THINK YOU'RE READY FOR FIELD DUTY.

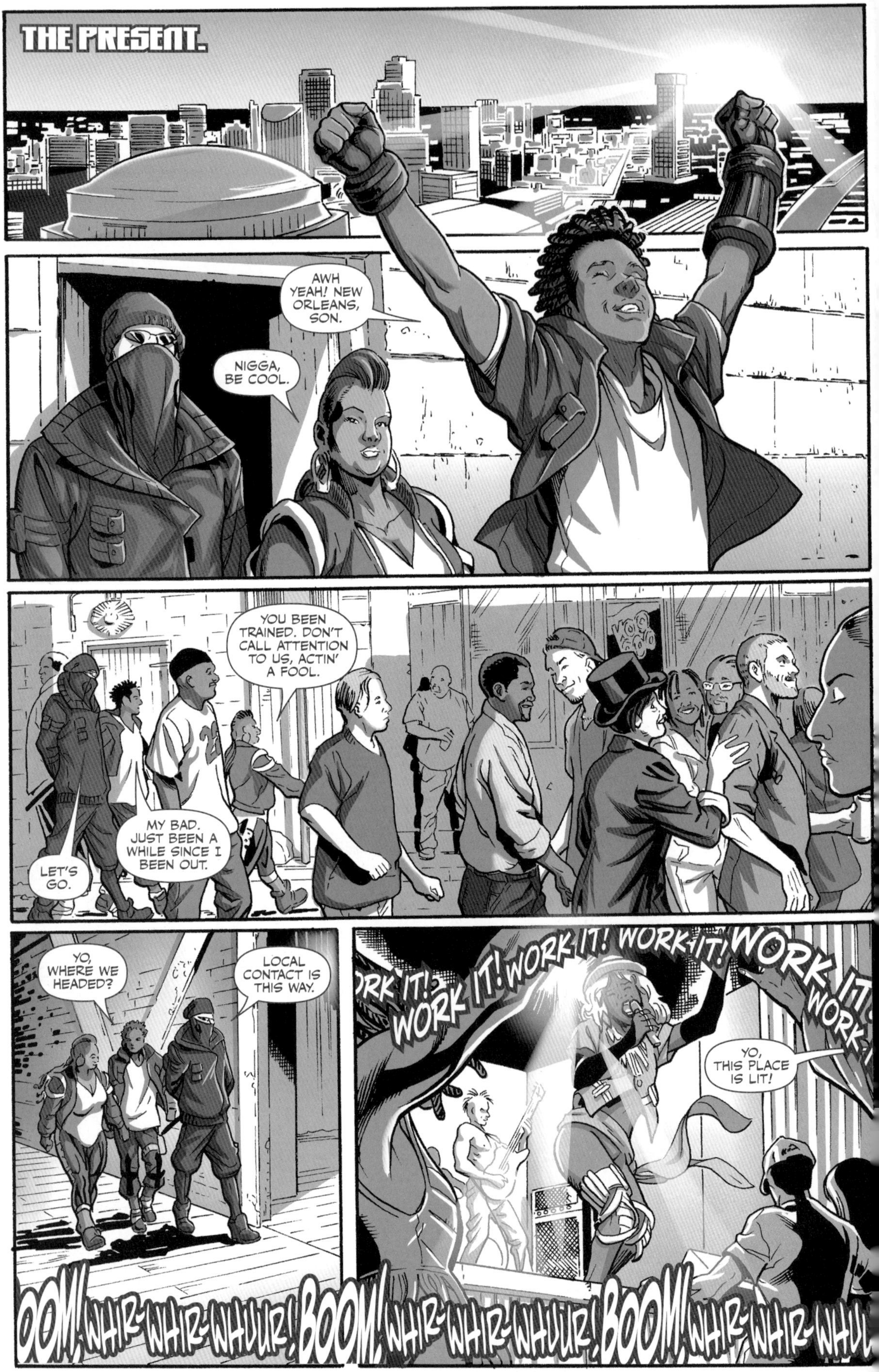
THE PRESENT.
AWH YEAH! NEW ORLEANS, SON.
NIGGA, BE COOL.
YOU BEEN TRAINED. DON'T CALL ATTENTION TO US, ACTIN' A FOOL.
MY BAD. JUST BEEN A WHILE SINCE I BEEN OUT.
LET'S GO.
YO, WHERE WE HEADED?
LOCAL CONTACT IS THIS WAY.
RK IT! WORK IT! WORK IT! WORK IT! WORK IT! WORK IT! WORK
YO, THIS PLACE IS LIT!
OOM! WHR-WHR-WHUUR! BOOM! WHR-WHR-WHUUR! BOOM! WHR-WHR-WHU

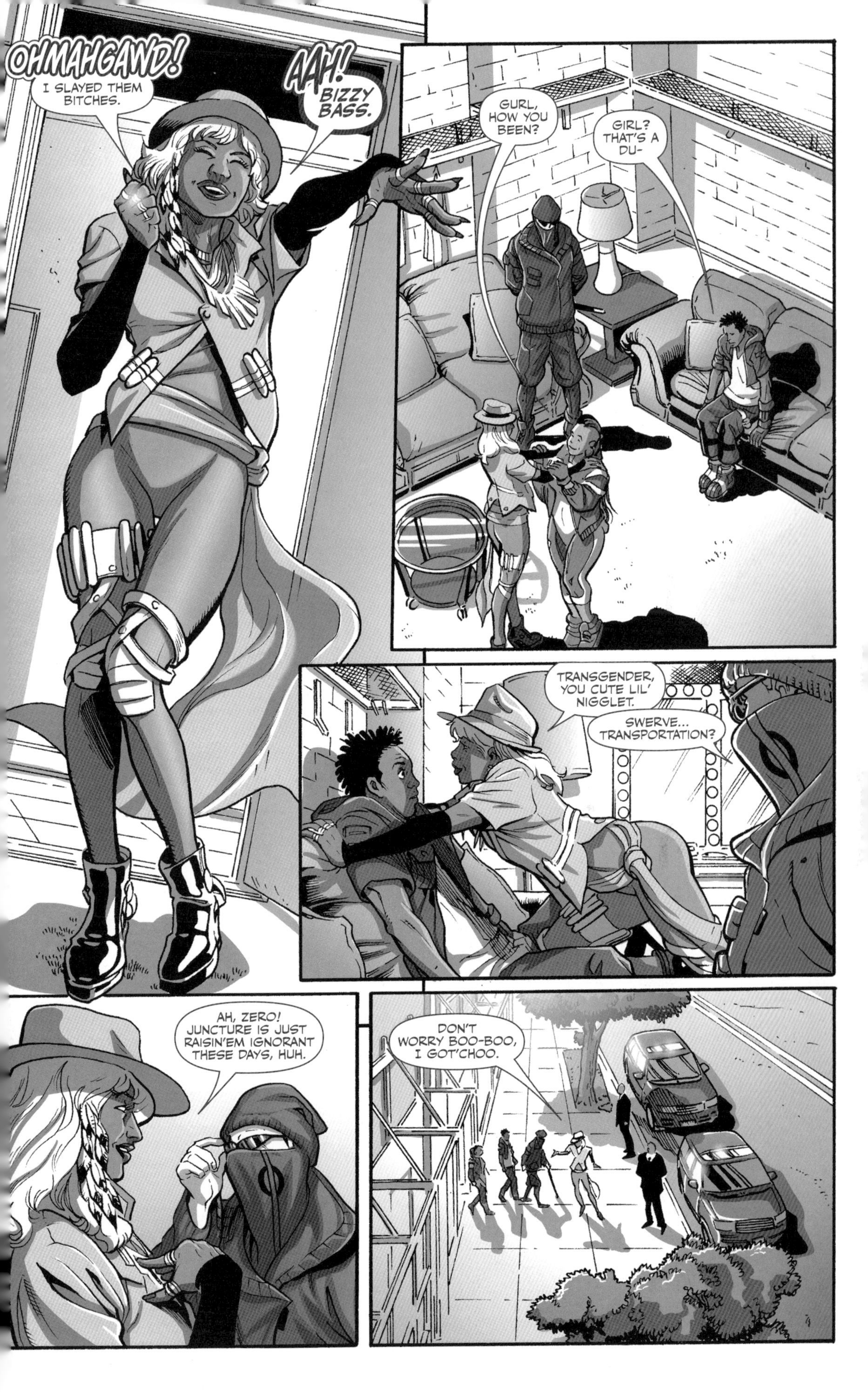
OHMAHGAWD!
I SLAYED THEM BITCHES.
AAH!
BIZZY BASS.
GURL, HOW YOU BEEN?
GIRL? THAT'S A DU-
TRANSGENDER, YOU CUTE LIL' NIGGLET.
SWERVE... TRANSPORTATION?
AH, ZERO! JUNCTURE IS JUST RAISIN'EM IGNORANT THESE DAYS, HUH.
DON'T WORRY BOO-BOO, I GOT'CHOO.

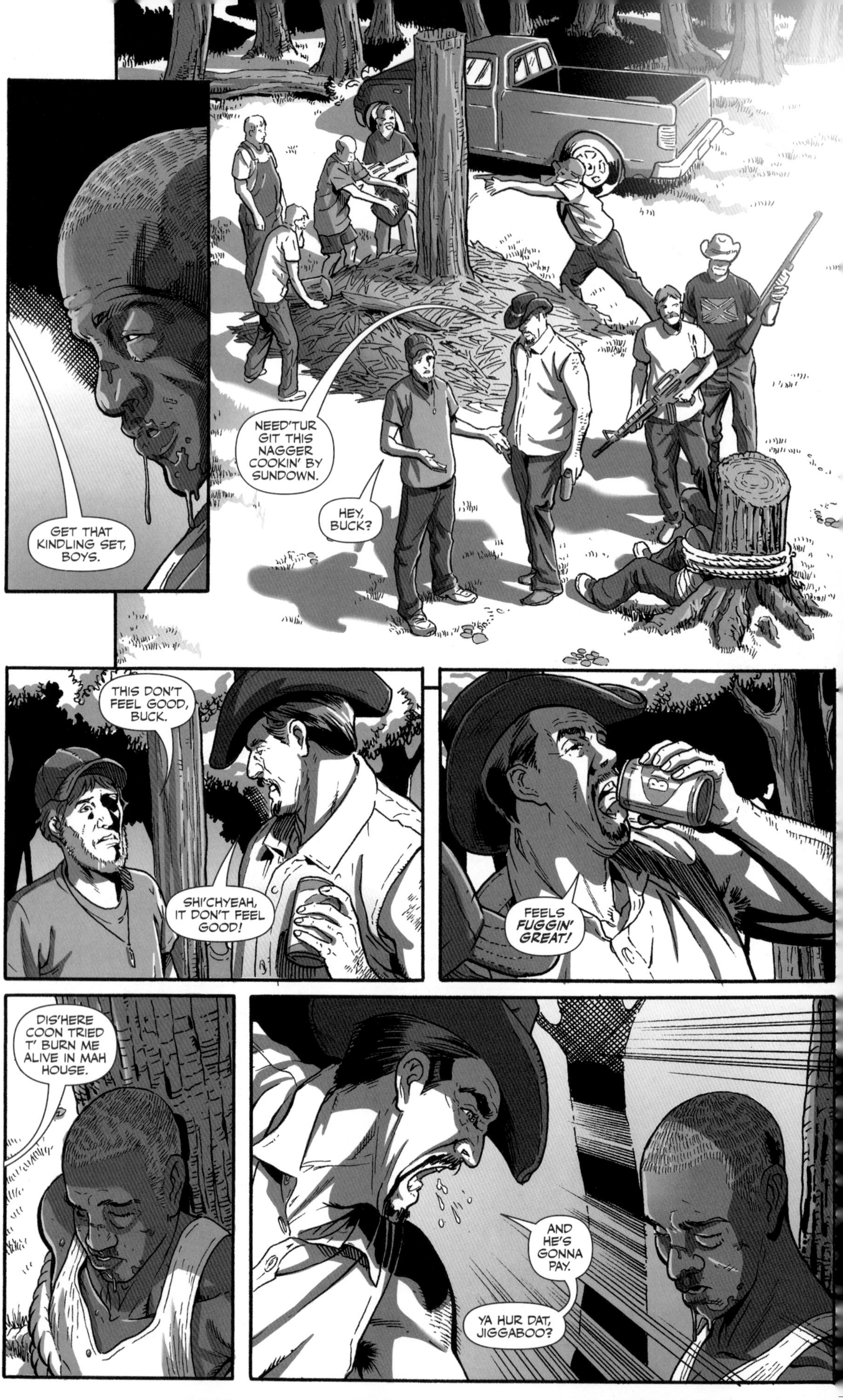
GET THAT KINDLING SET, BOYS.
NEED'TUR GIT THIS NAGGER COOKIN' BY SUNDOWN.
HEY, BUCK?
THIS DON'T FEEL GOOD, BUCK.
SHI'CHYEAH, IT DON'T FEEL GOOD!
FEELS *FUGGIN' GREAT!*
DIS'HERE COON TRIED T' BURN ME ALIVE IN MAH HOUSE.
AND HE'S GONNA PAY.
YA HUR DAT, JIGGABOO?

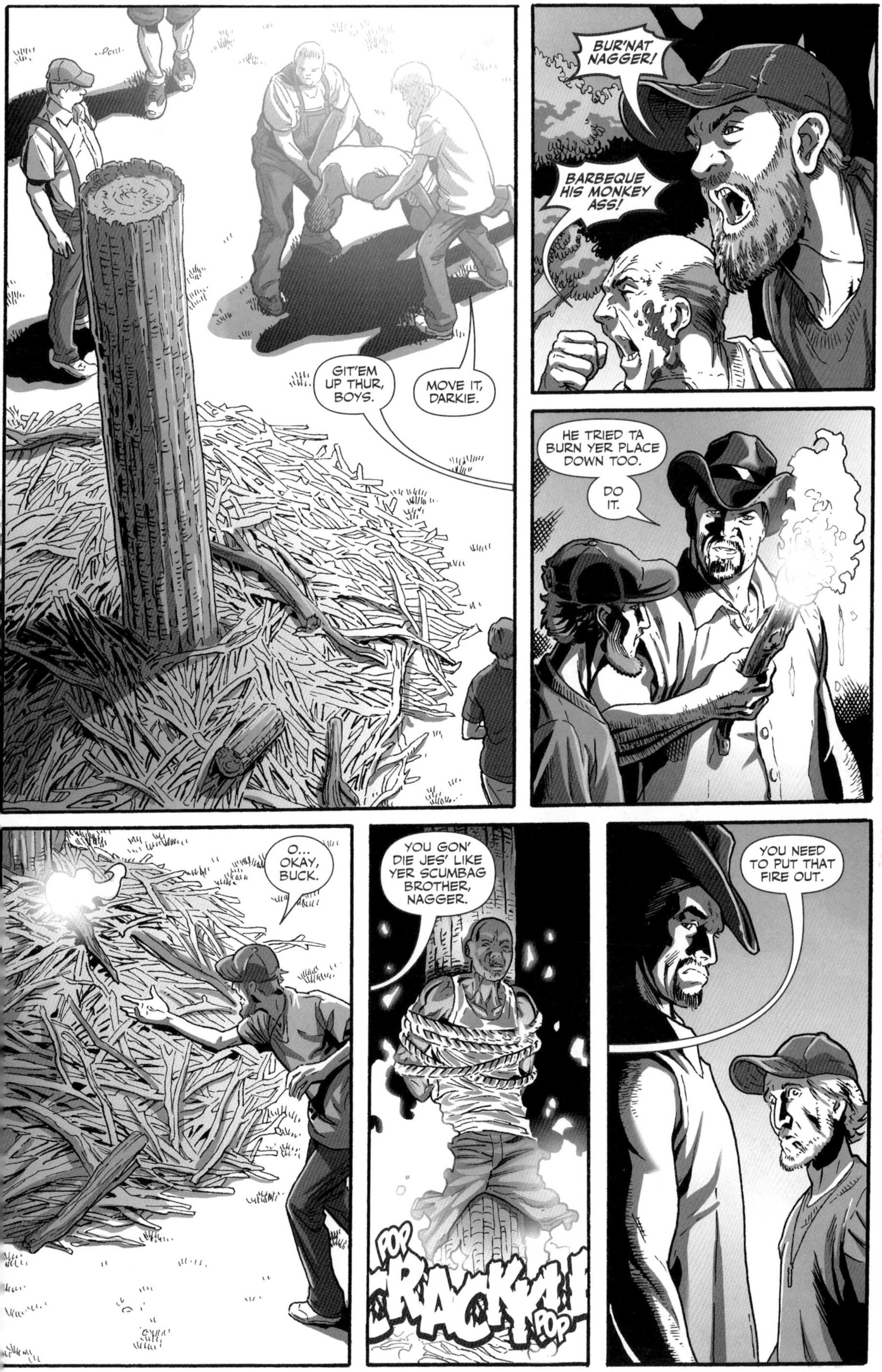
GIT'EM UP THUR, BOYS.
MOVE IT, DARKIE.
BUR'NAT NAGGER!
BARBEQUE HIS MONKEY ASS!
HE TRIED TA BURN YER PLACE DOWN TOO.
DO IT.
O... OKAY, BUCK.
YOU GON' DIE JES' LIKE YER SCUMBAG BROTHER, NAGGER.
POP
CRACK
POP
YOU NEED TO PUT THAT FIRE OUT.

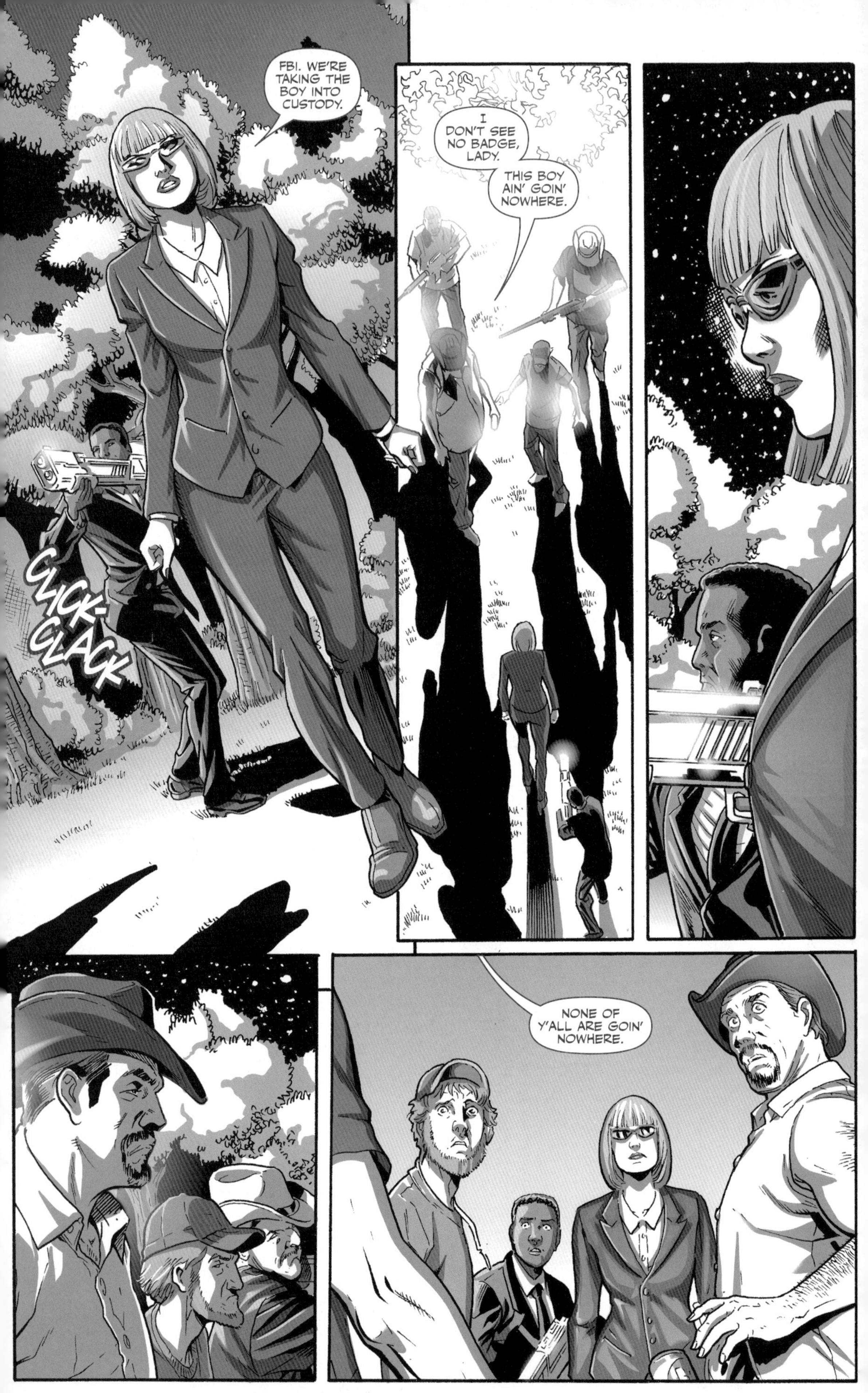
FBI. WE'RE TAKING THE BOY INTO CUSTODY.
CLICK-CLACK
I DON'T SEE NO BADGE, LADY.
THIS BOY AIN' GOIN' NOWHERE.
NONE OF Y'ALL ARE GOIN' NOWHERE.

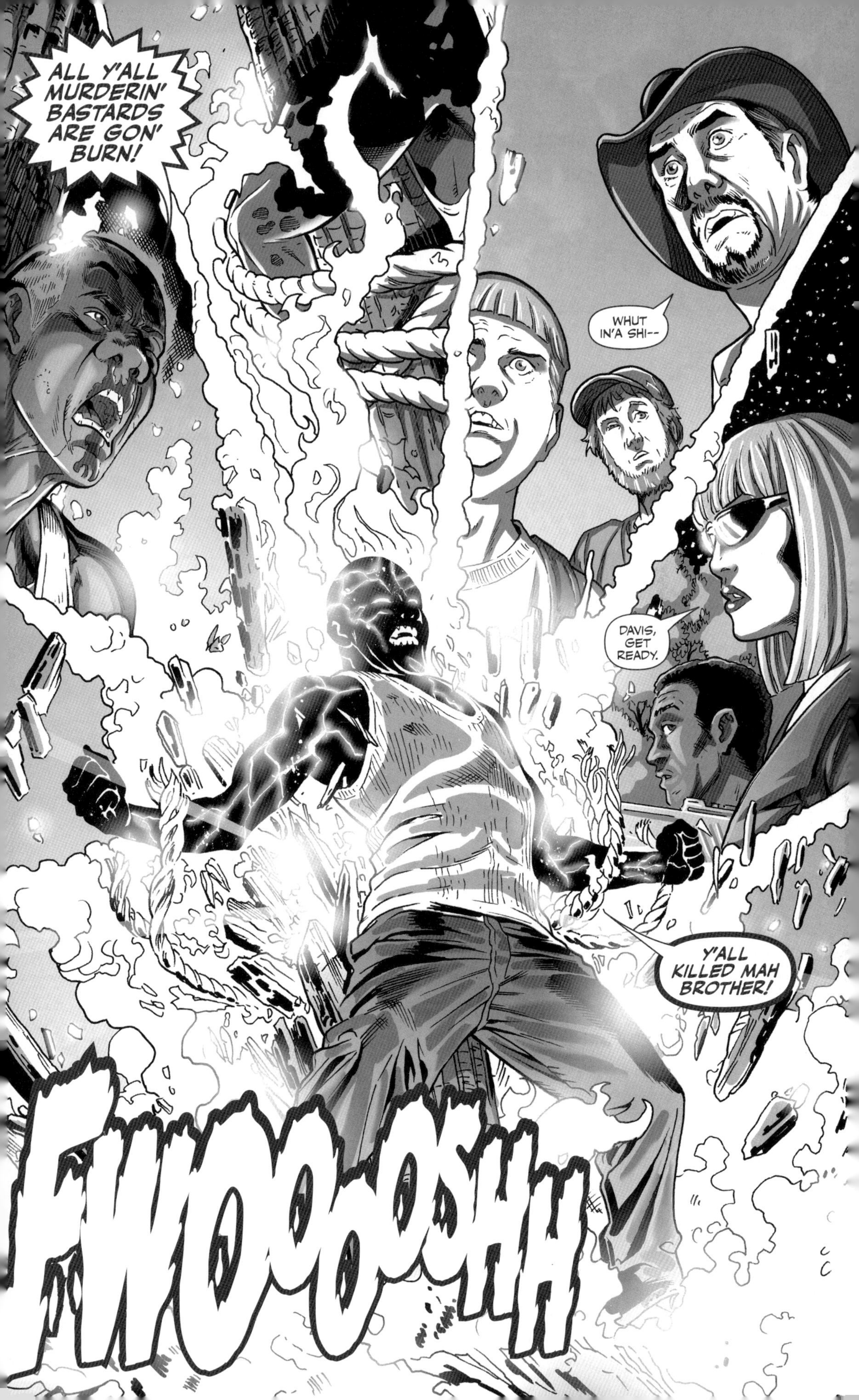
ALL Y'ALL MURDERIN' BASTARDS ARE GON' BURN!
WHUT IN'A SHI--
DAVIS, GET READY.
Y'ALL KILLED MAH BROTHER!
FWOOOSHH

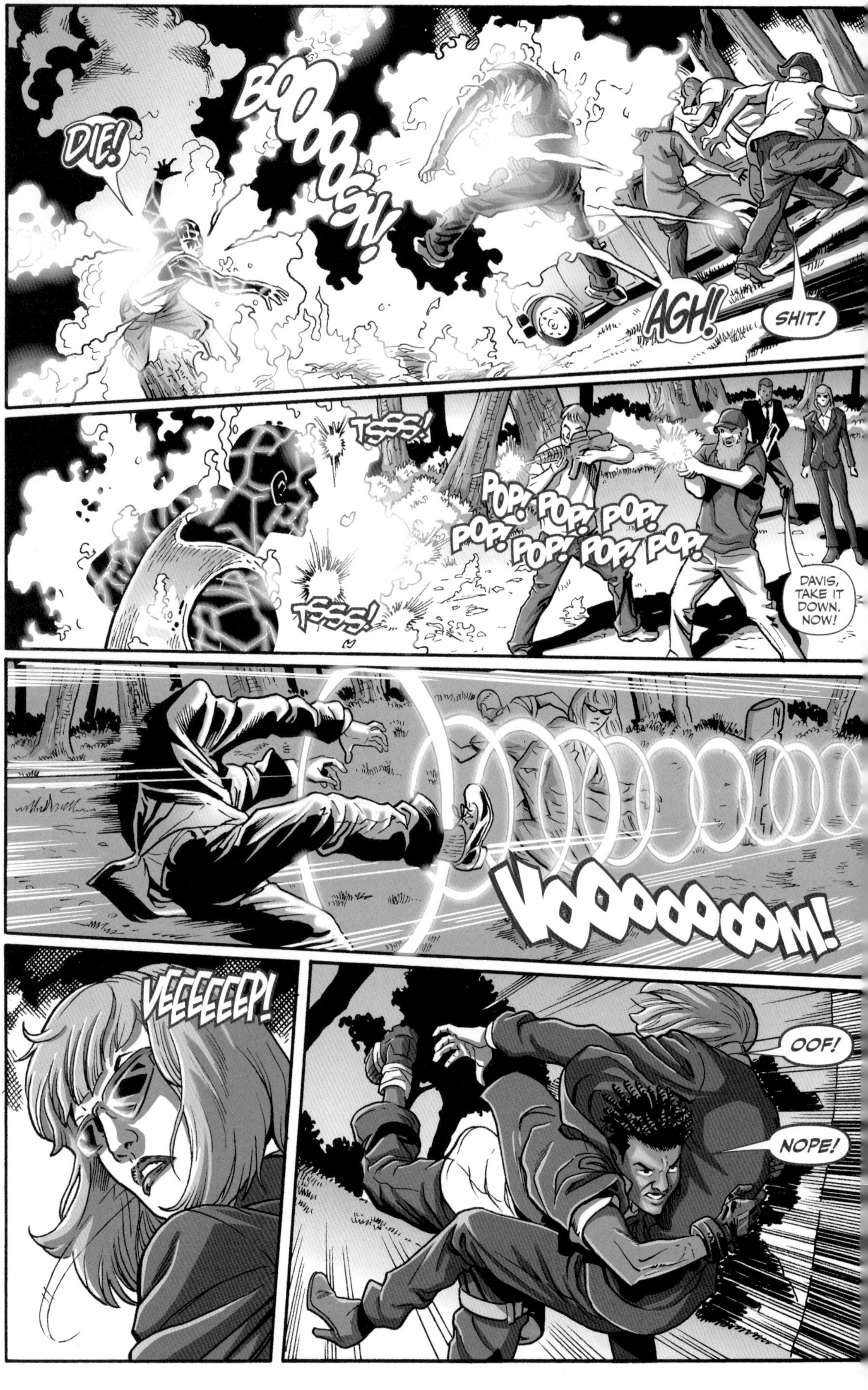
DIE!
BOOOOOSH!
AGH!
SHIT!
TSSS!
POP! POP! POP! POP! POP! POP! POP!
TSSS!
DAVIS, TAKE IT DOWN. NOW!
VOOOOOOOM!
VEEEEEEP!
OOF!
NOPE!

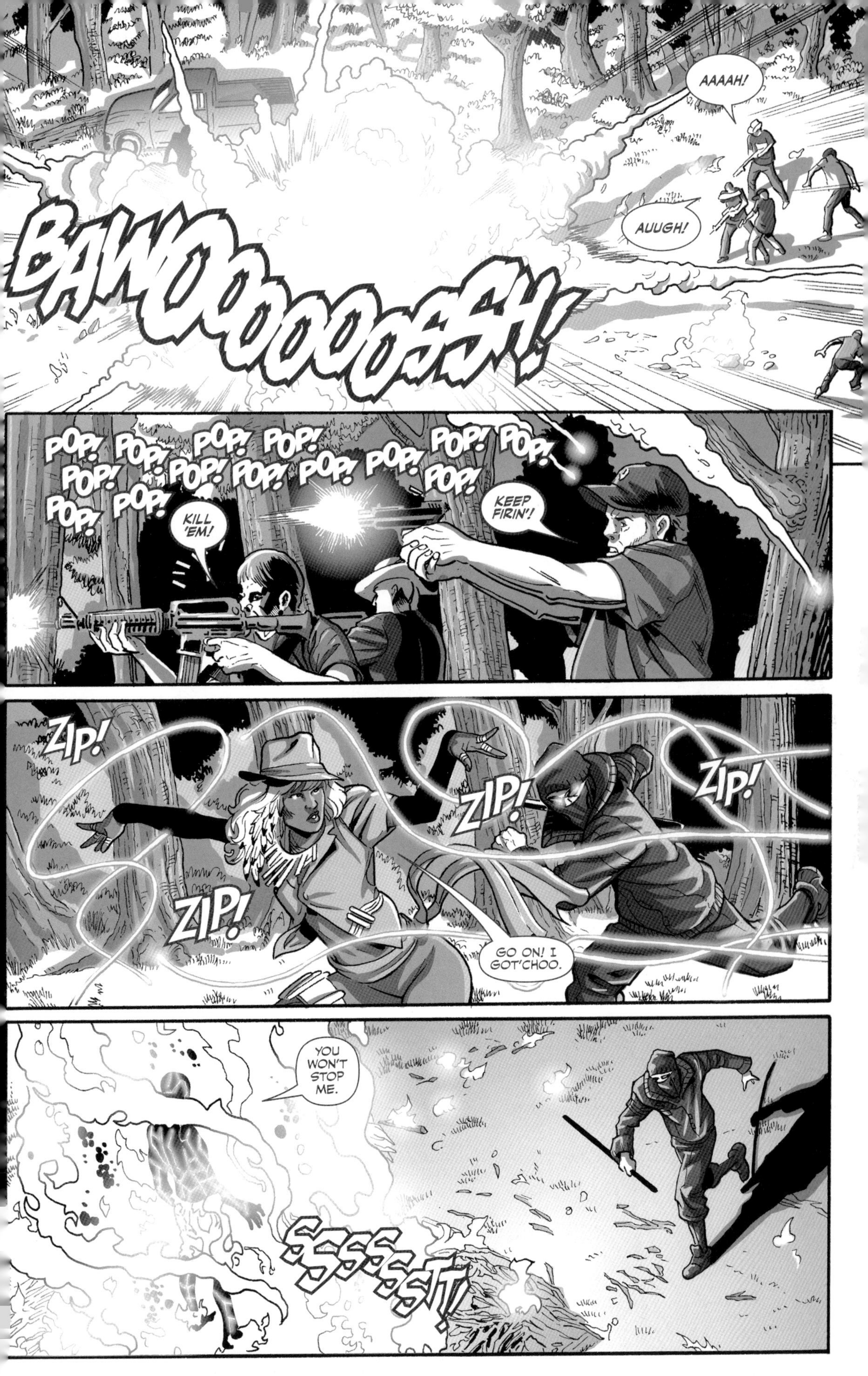
AAAAH!
AUUGH!
BAWOOOOOOSH!
POP! POP! POP! POP! POP! POP!
POP! POP! POP! POP! POP! POP!
POP! POP! POP!
KILL 'EM!
KEEP FIRIN'!
ZIP!
ZIP!
ZIP!
ZIP!
GO ON! I GOT'CHOO.
YOU WON'T STOP ME.
SSSSSST!

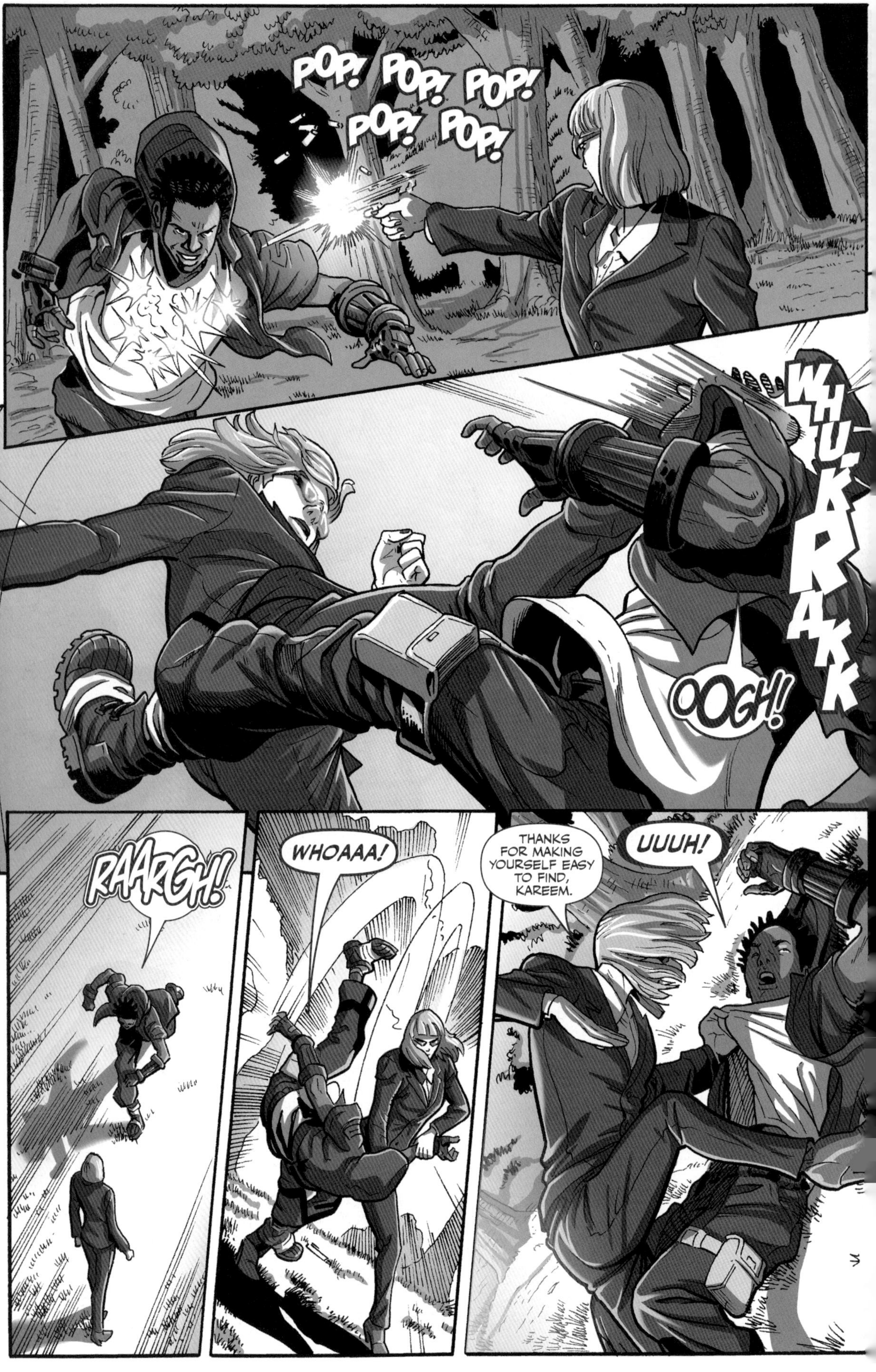
POP! POP! POP!
POP! POP!
WHUKARAKK
OOGH!
RAARGH!
WHOAAA!
THANKS FOR MAKING YOURSELF EASY TO FIND, KAREEM.
UUUH!

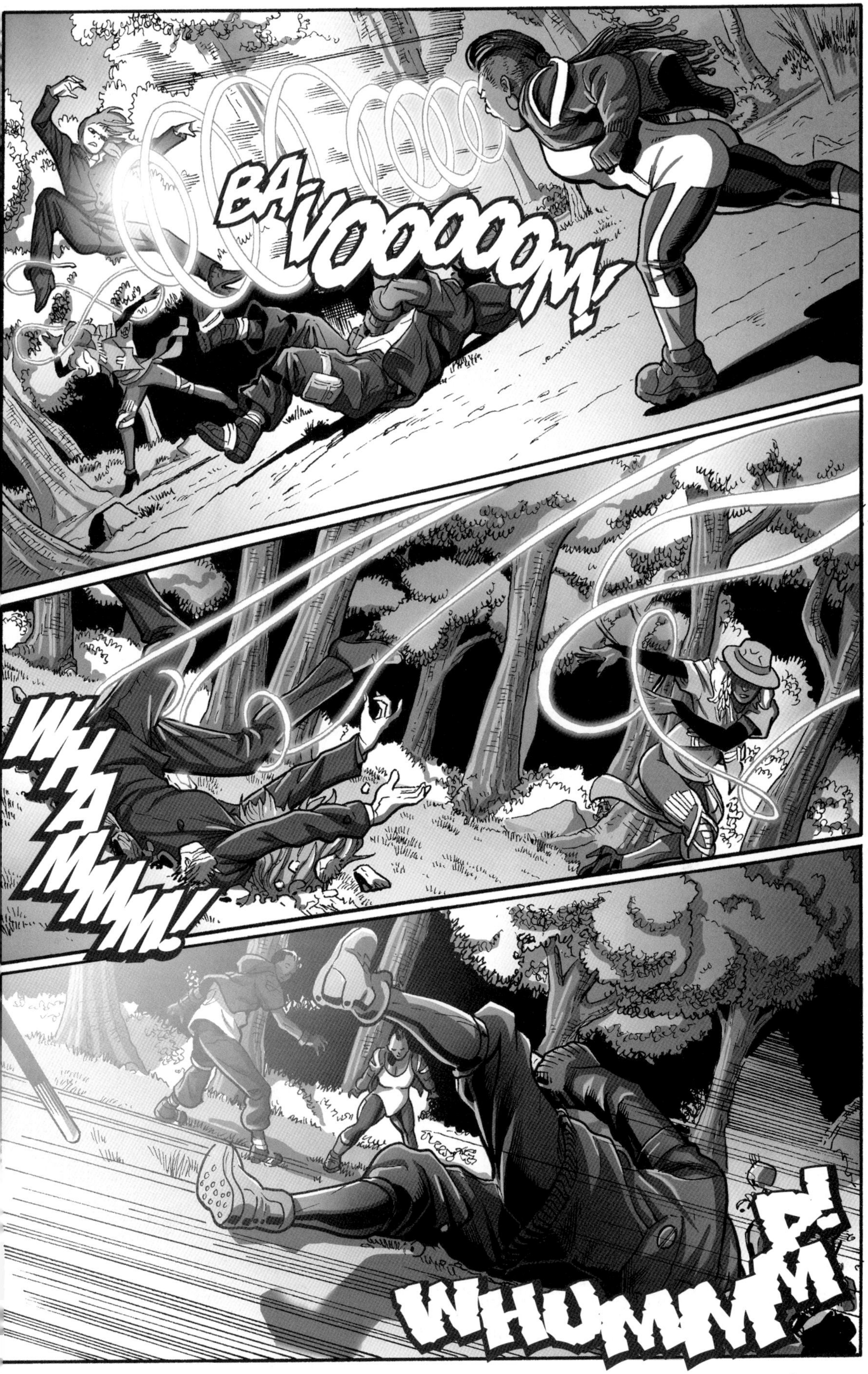
BA-VOOOOOM!
WHAMMMM!
WHUMMMP!

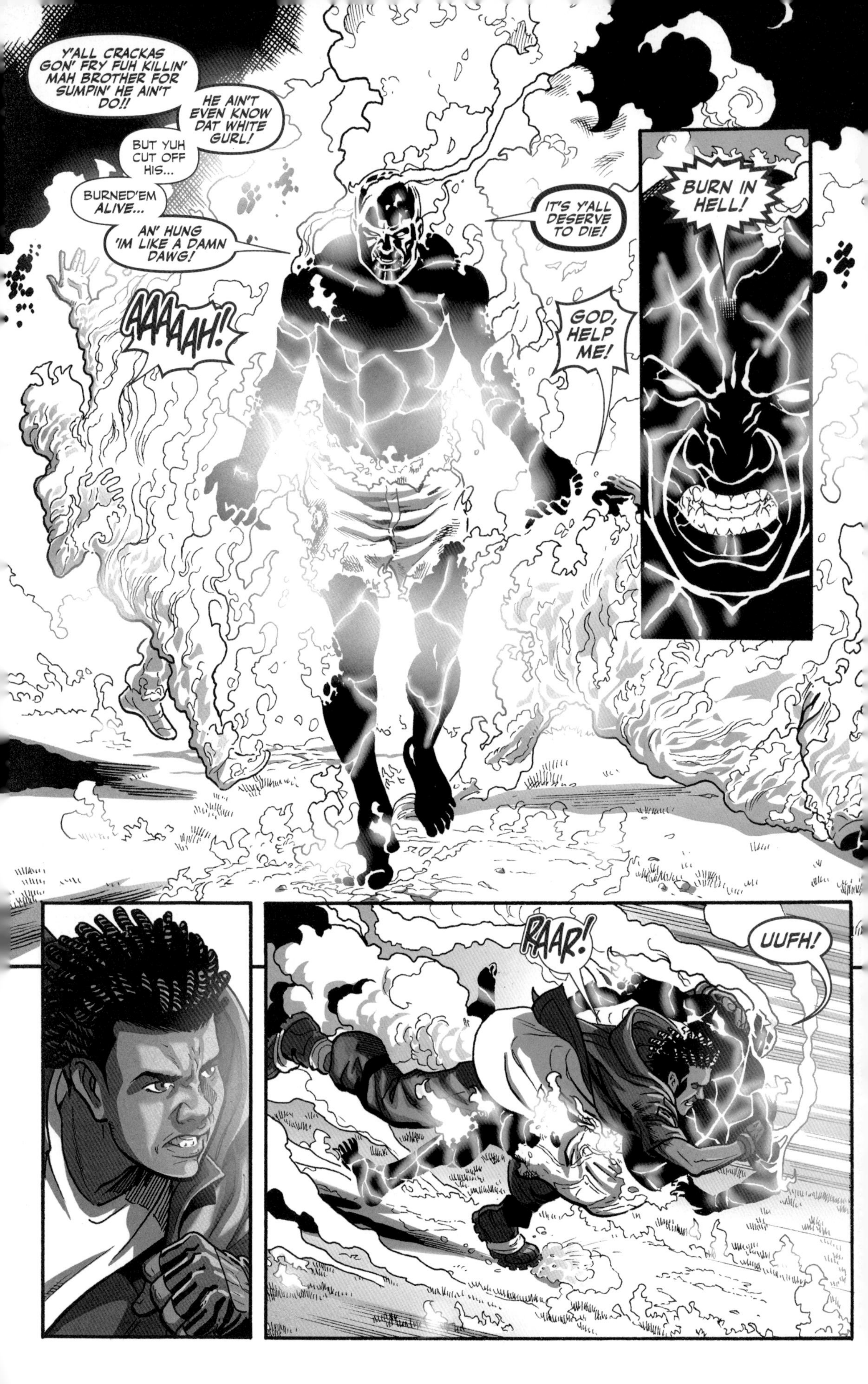
Y'ALL CRACKAS GON' FRY FUH KILLIN' MAH BROTHER FOR SUMPIN' HE AIN'T DO!!
HE AIN'T EVEN KNOW DAT WHITE GURL!
BUT YUH CUT OFF HIS...
BURNED'EM ALIVE...
AN' HUNG 'IM LIKE A DAMN DAWG!
IT'S Y'ALL DESERVE TO DIE!
AAAAAH!
GOD, HELP ME!
BURN IN HELL!
RAAR!
UUFH!

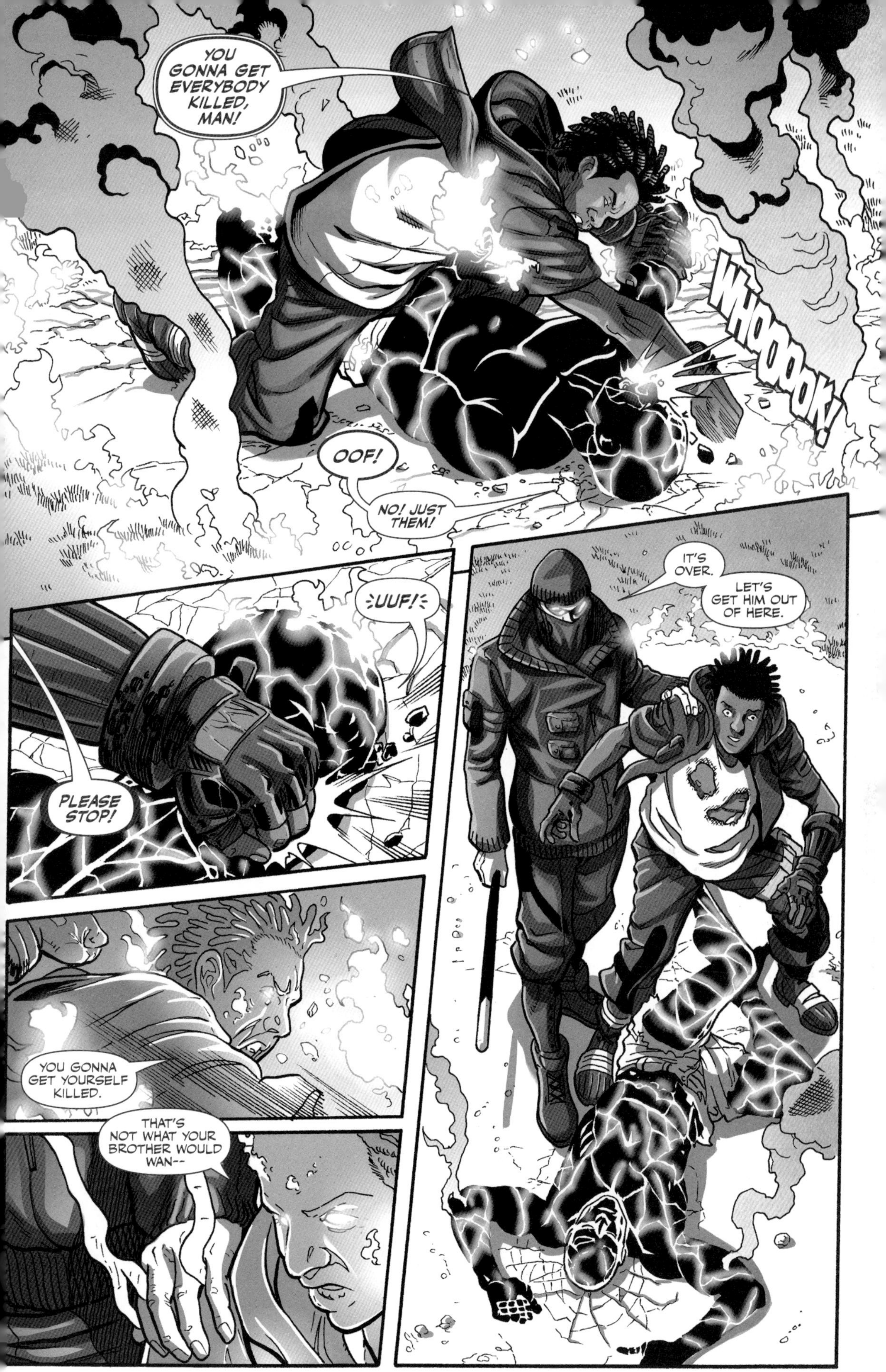
YOU GONNA GET EVERYBODY KILLED, MAN!
WHOOOOOK!
OOF!
NO! JUST THEM!
UUF!
PLEASE STOP!
YOU GONNA GET YOURSELF KILLED.
THAT'S NOT WHAT YOUR BROTHER WOULD WAN--
IT'S OVER.
LET'S GET HIM OUT OF HERE.

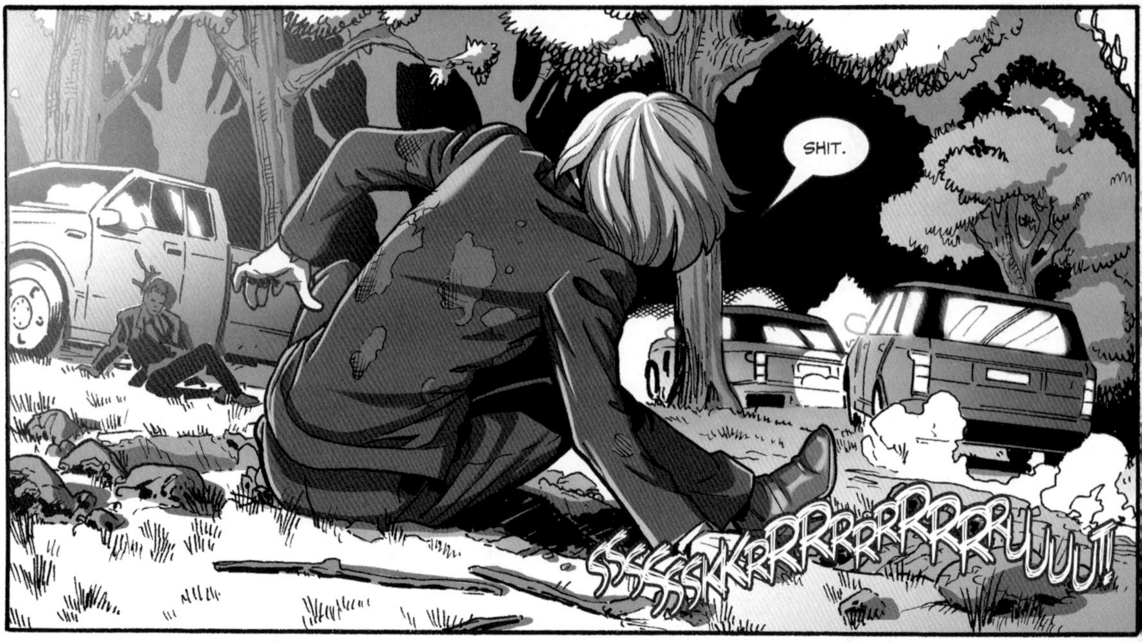
SHIT.
SSSSSSKKRRRRRRRRRRRUUUUT!

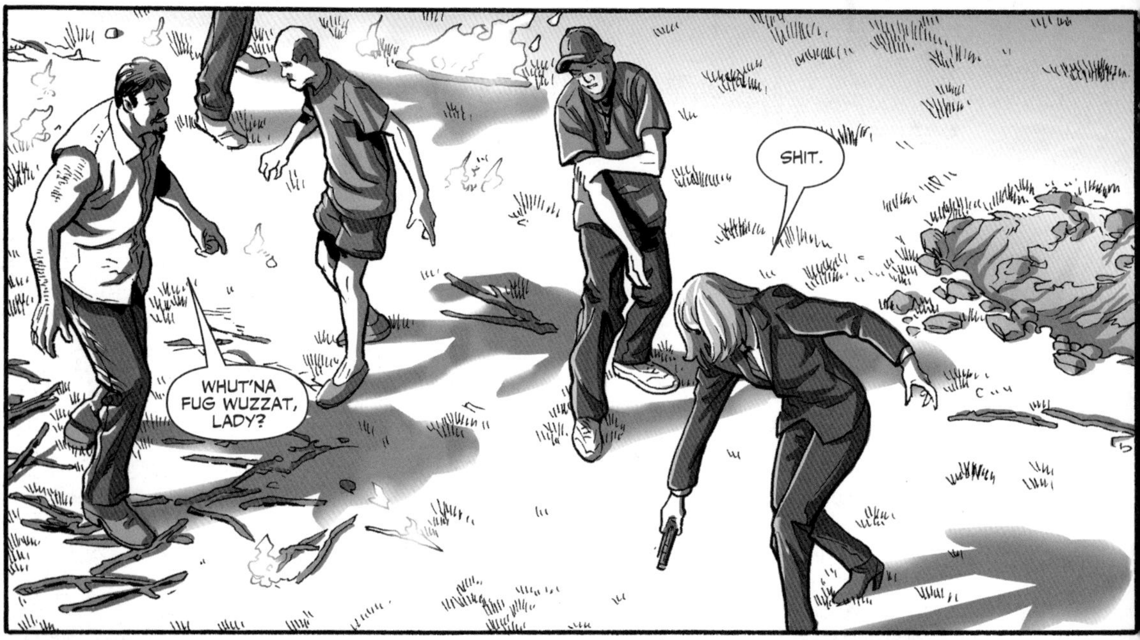
SHIT.
WHUT'NA FUG WUZZAT, LADY?

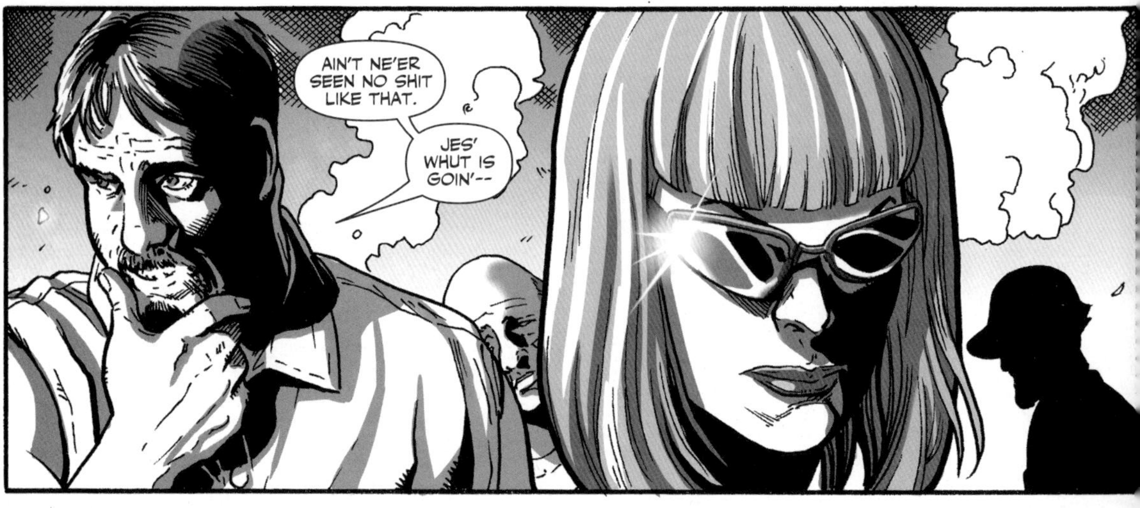
AIN'T NE'ER SEEN NO SHIT LIKE THAT.
JES' WHUT IS GOIN'--

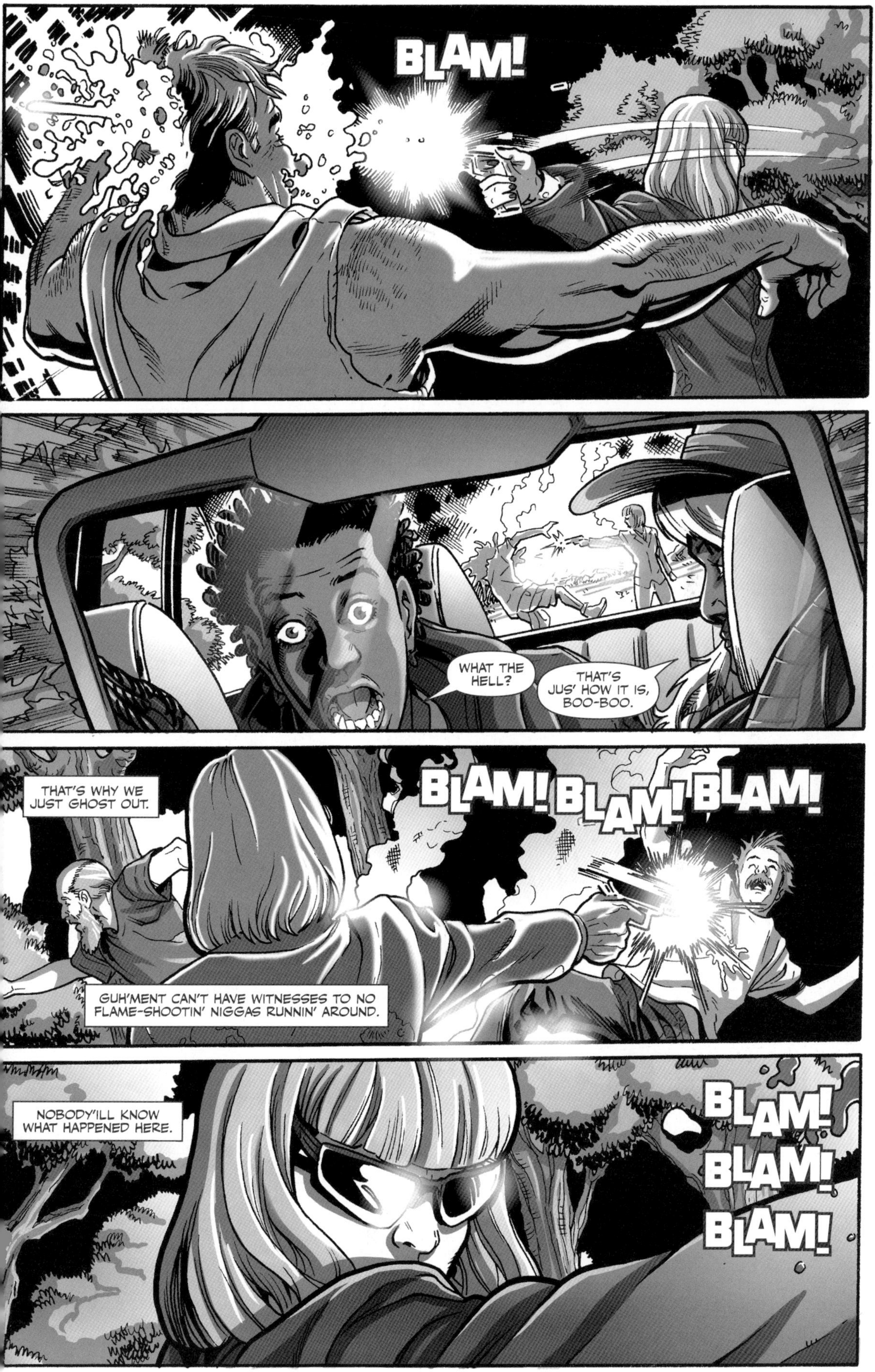
BLAM!
WHAT THE HELL?
THAT'S JUS' HOW IT IS, BOO-BOO.
THAT'S WHY WE JUST GHOST OUT.
BLAM! BLAM! BLAM!
GUH'MENT CAN'T HAVE WITNESSES TO NO FLAME-SHOOTIN' NIGGAS RUNNIN' AROUND.
NOBODY'LL KNOW WHAT HAPPENED HERE.
BLAM!
BLAM!
BLAM!

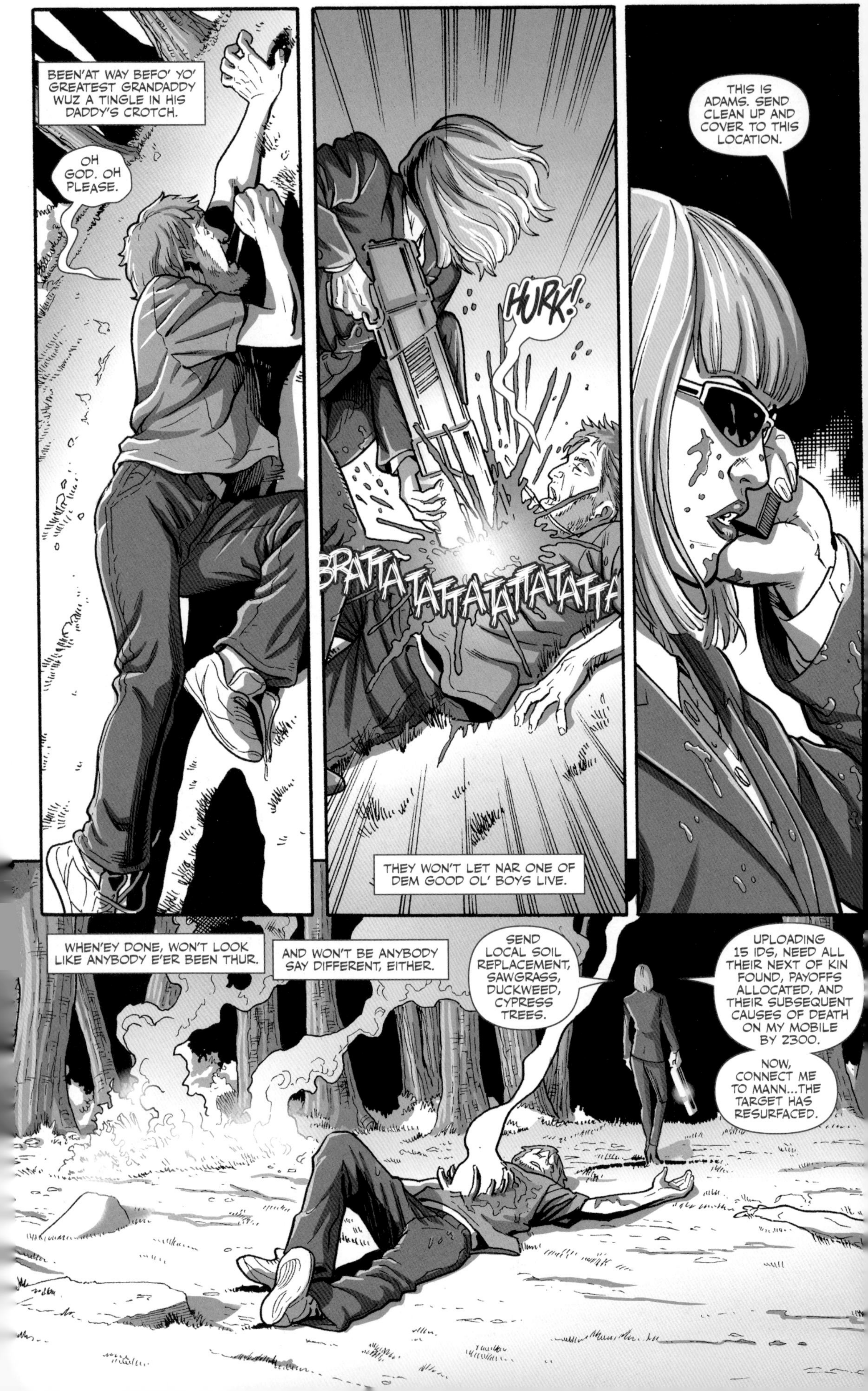
BEEN'AT WAY BEFO' YO' GREATEST GRANDADDY WUZ A TINGLE IN HIS DADDY'S CROTCH.
OH GOD. OH PLEASE.
HURK!
BRATTATATTATATTATATTA
THEY WON'T LET NAR ONE OF DEM GOOD OL' BOYS LIVE.
THIS IS ADAMS. SEND CLEAN UP AND COVER TO THIS LOCATION.
WHEN'EY DONE, WON'T LOOK LIKE ANYBODY E'ER BEEN THUR.
AND WON'T BE ANYBODY SAY DIFFERENT, EITHER.
SEND LOCAL SOIL REPLACEMENT, SAWGRASS, DUCKWEED, CYPRESS TREES.
UPLOADING 15 IDS, NEED ALL THEIR NEXT OF KIN FOUND, PAYOFFS ALLOCATED, AND THEIR SUBSEQUENT CAUSES OF DEATH ON MY MOBILE BY 2300.
NOW, CONNECT ME TO MANN...THE TARGET HAS RESURFACED.

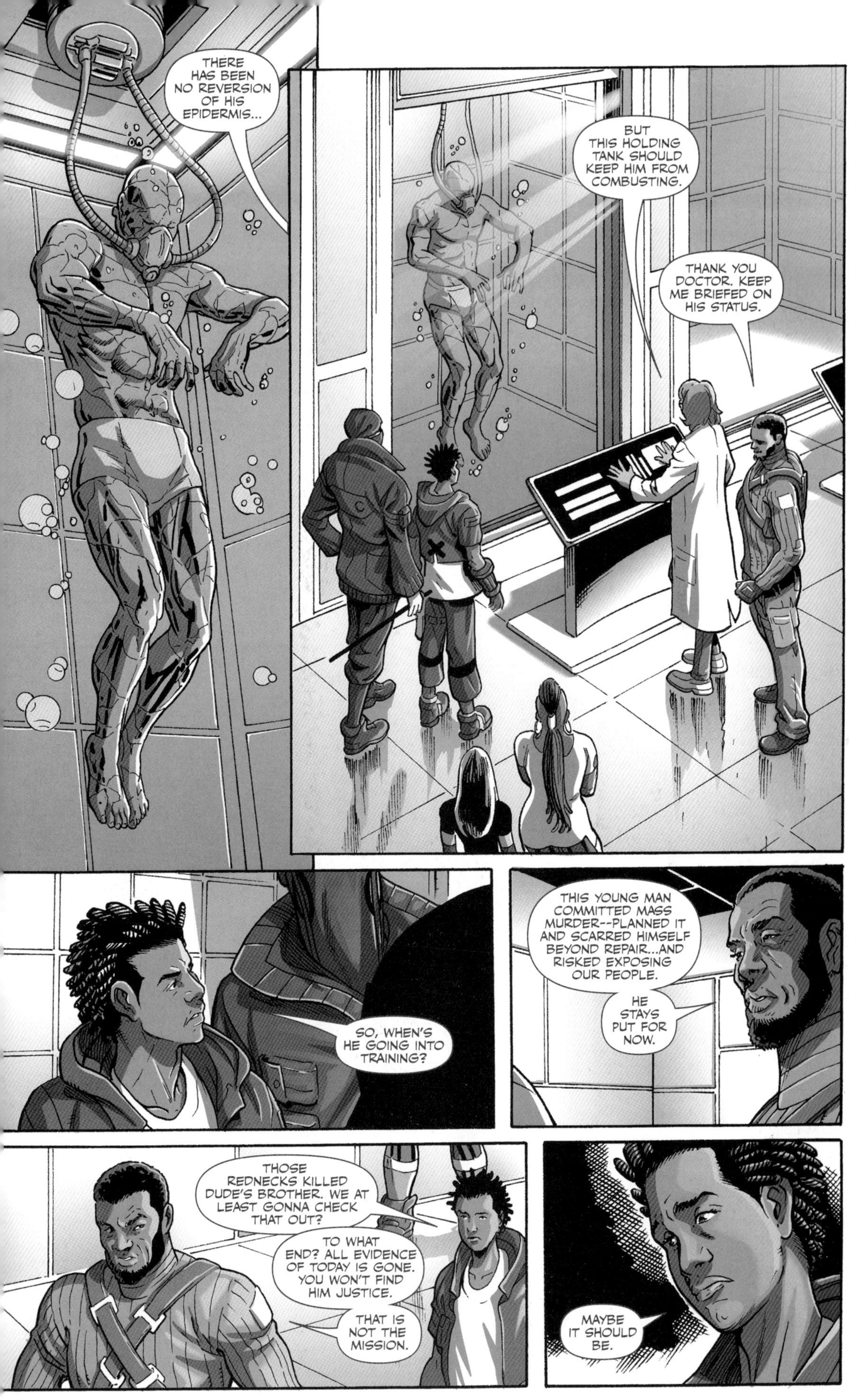
THERE HAS BEEN NO REVERSION OF HIS EPIDERMIS...
BUT THIS HOLDING TANK SHOULD KEEP HIM FROM COMBUSTING.
THANK YOU DOCTOR. KEEP ME BRIEFED ON HIS STATUS.
SO, WHEN'S HE GOING INTO TRAINING?
THIS YOUNG MAN COMMITTED MASS MURDER--PLANNED IT AND SCARRED HIMSELF BEYOND REPAIR...AND RISKED EXPOSING OUR PEOPLE.
HE STAYS PUT FOR NOW.
THOSE REDNECKS KILLED DUDE'S BROTHER. WE AT LEAST GONNA CHECK THAT OUT?
TO WHAT END? ALL EVIDENCE OF TODAY IS GONE. YOU WON'T FIND HIM JUSTICE.
THAT IS NOT THE MISSION.
MAYBE IT SHOULD BE.

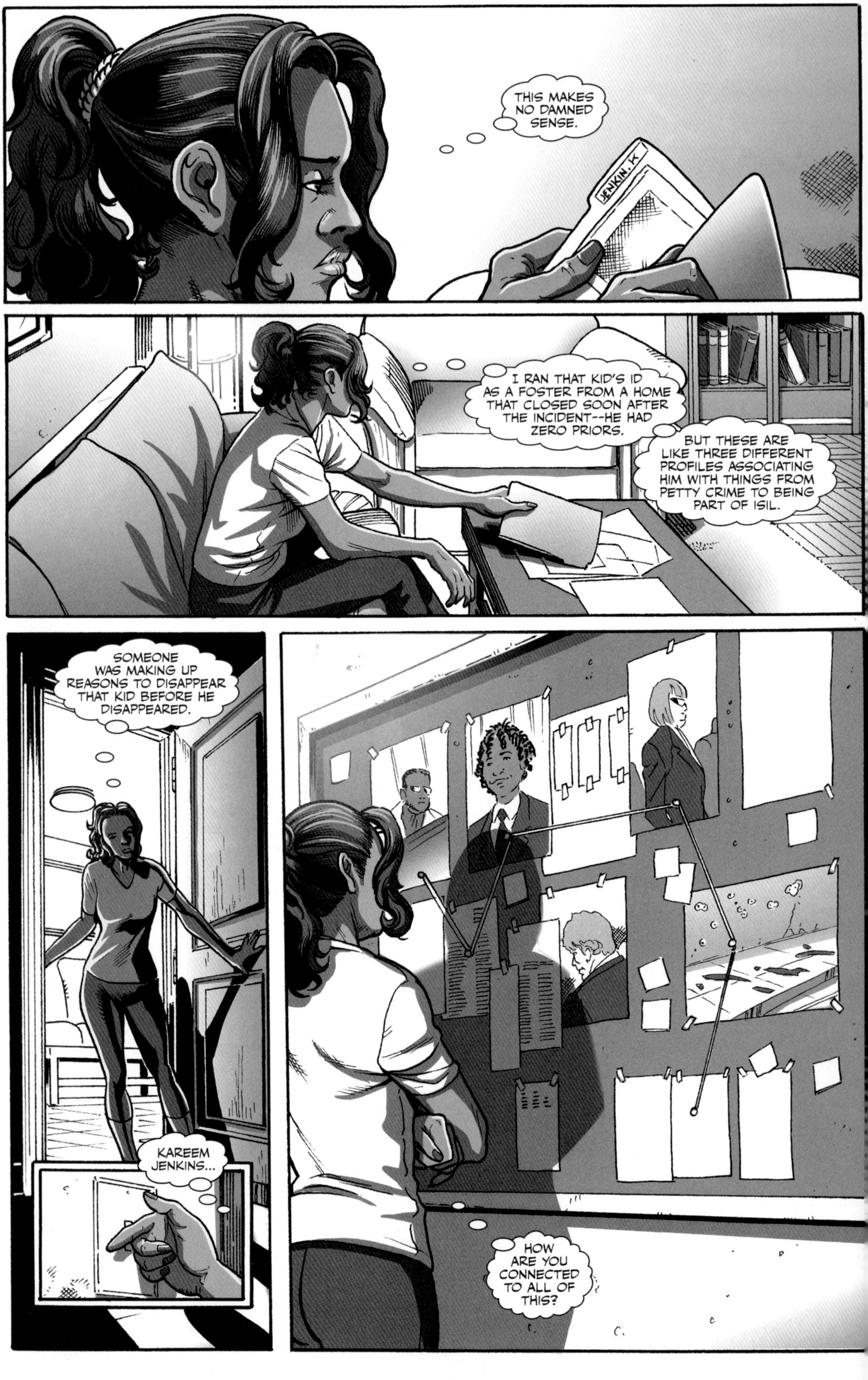
THIS MAKES NO DAMNED SENSE.
JENKIN, K
I RAN THAT KID'S ID AS A FOSTER FROM A HOME THAT CLOSED SOON AFTER THE INCIDENT--HE HAD ZERO PRIORS.
BUT THESE ARE LIKE THREE DIFFERENT PROFILES ASSOCIATING HIM WITH THINGS FROM PETTY CRIME TO BEING PART OF ISIL.
SOMEONE WAS MAKING UP REASONS TO DISAPPEAR THAT KID BEFORE HE DISAPPEARED.
KAREEM JENKINS...
HOW ARE YOU CONNECTED TO ALL OF THIS?

CHAPTER THREE

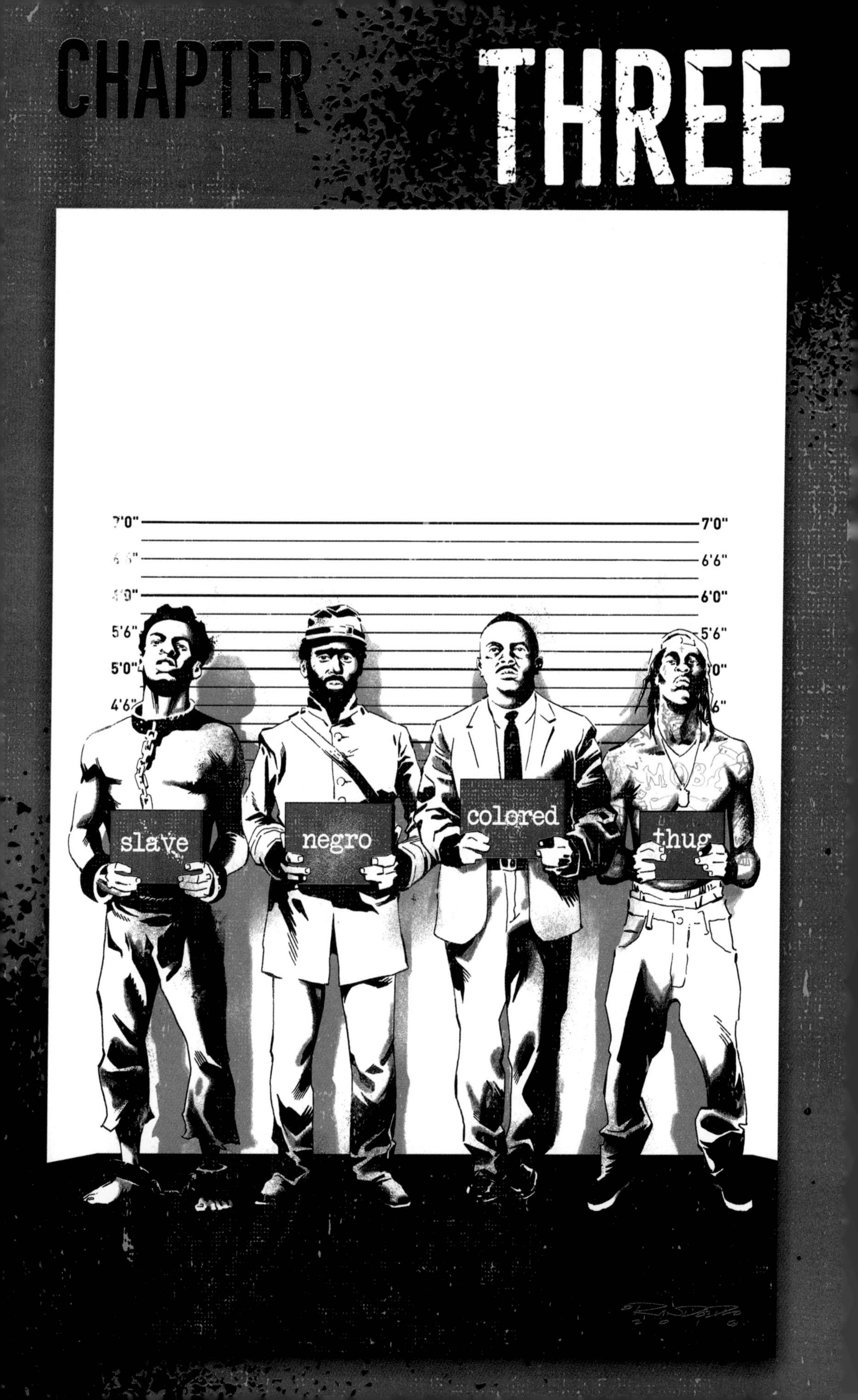

7'0"
6'6"
6'0"
5'6"
5'0"
4'6"
slave
negro
colored
thug

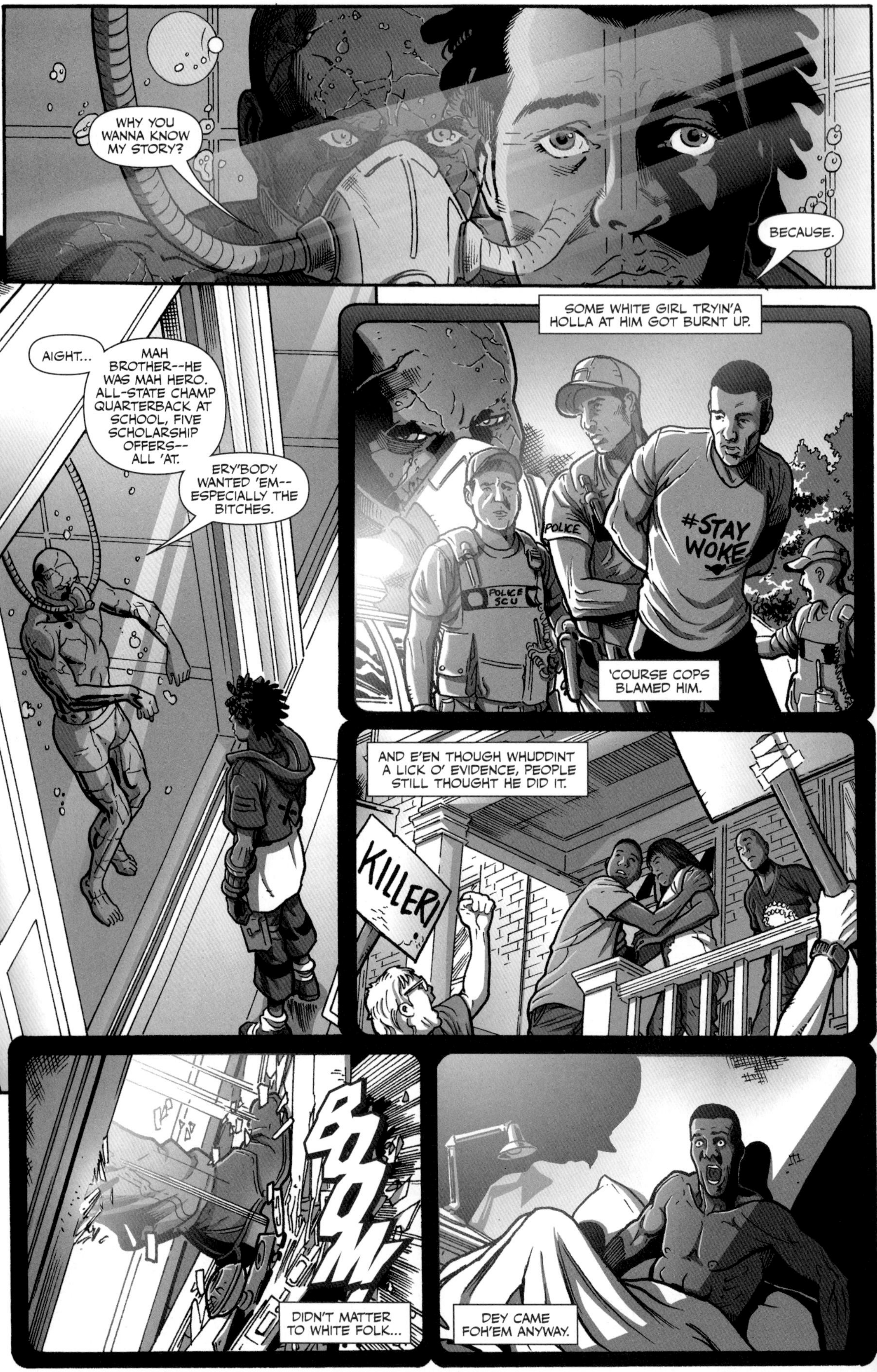
WHY YOU WANNA KNOW MY STORY?
BECAUSE.
AIGHT...
MAH BROTHER--HE WAS MAH HERO. ALL-STATE CHAMP QUARTERBACK AT SCHOOL, FIVE SCHOLARSHIP OFFERS-- ALL 'AT.
ERY'BODY WANTED 'EM-- ESPECIALLY THE BITCHES.
SOME WHITE GIRL TRYIN'A HOLLA AT HIM GOT BURNT UP.
POLICE
POLICE SCU
#STAY WOKE
'COURSE COPS BLAMED HIM.
AND E'EN THOUGH WHUDDINT A LICK O' EVIDENCE, PEOPLE STILL THOUGHT HE DID IT.
KILLER!
BOOM!
DIDN'T MATTER TO WHITE FOLK...
DEY CAME FOH'EM ANYWAY.

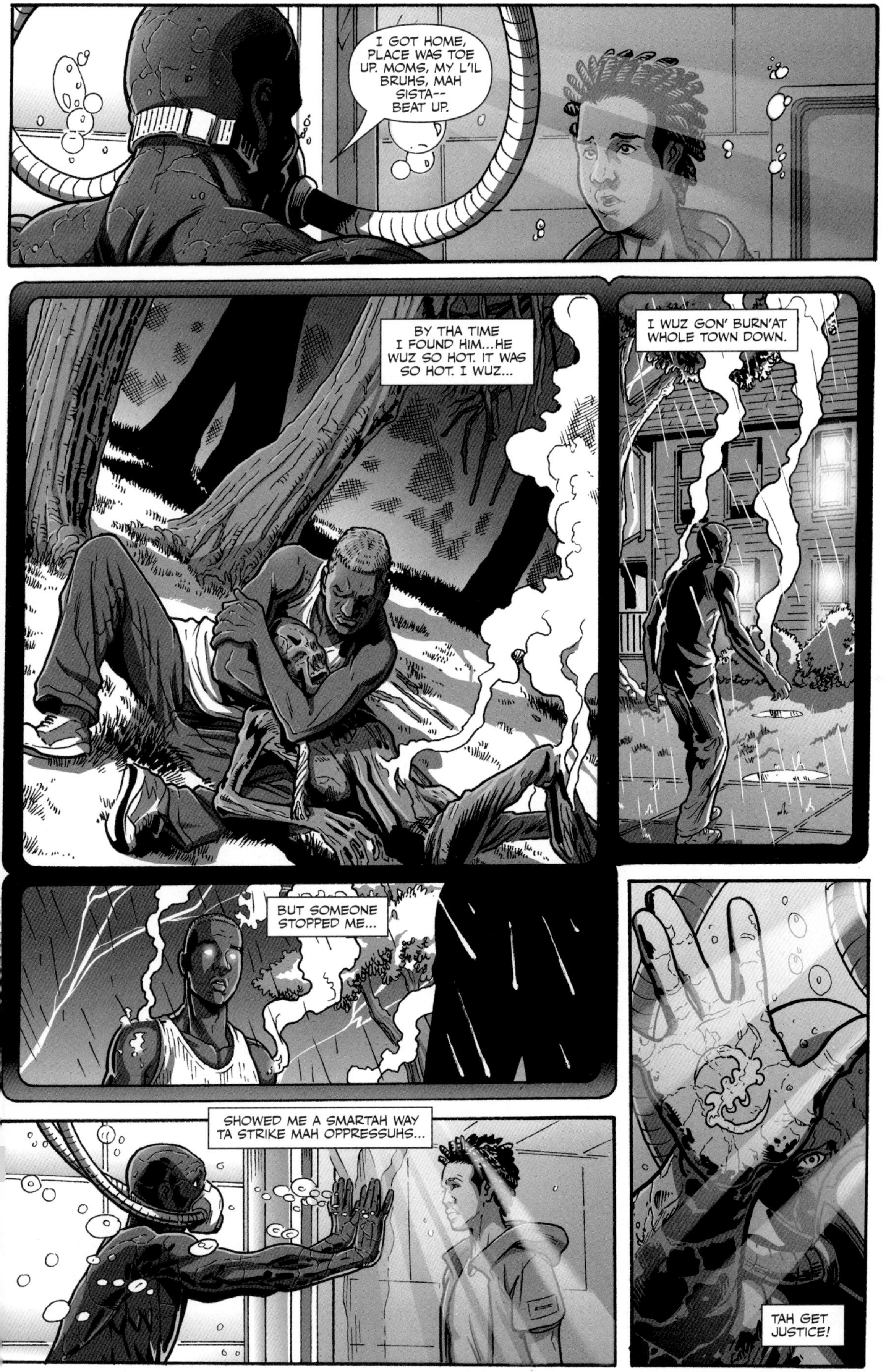
I GOT HOME, PLACE WAS TOE UP. MOMS, MY L'IL BRUHS, MAH SISTA-- BEAT UP.
BY THA TIME I FOUND HIM...HE WUZ SO HOT. IT WAS SO HOT. I WUZ...
I WUZ GON' BURN'AT WHOLE TOWN DOWN.
BUT SOMEONE STOPPED ME...
SHOWED ME A SMARTAH WAY TA STRIKE MAH OPPRESSUHS...
TAH GET JUSTICE!

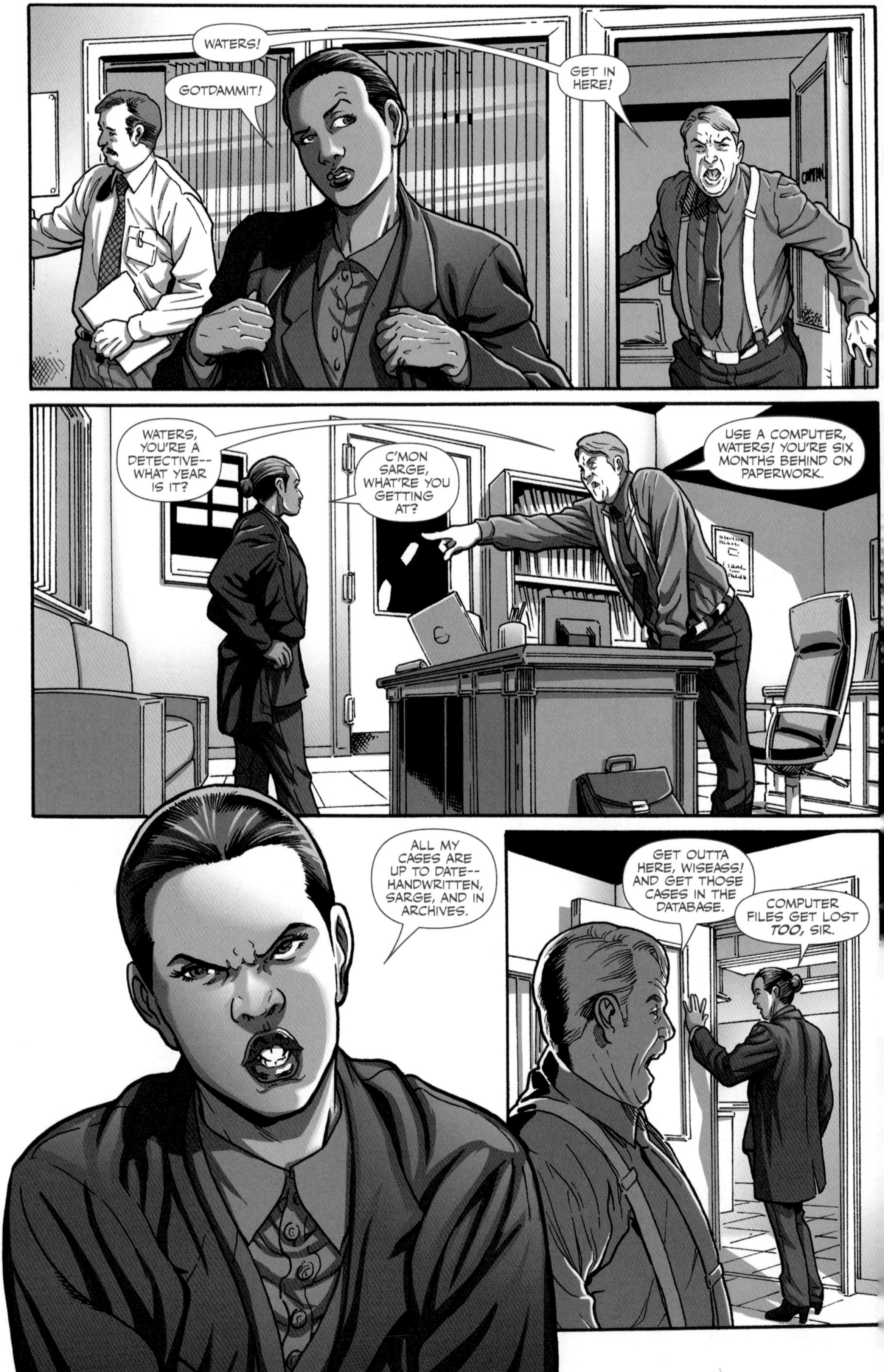
WATERS!
GOTDAMMIT!
GET IN HERE!
WATERS, YOU'RE A DETECTIVE-- WHAT YEAR IS IT?
C'MON SARGE, WHAT'RE YOU GETTING AT?
USE A COMPUTER, WATERS! YOU'RE SIX MONTHS BEHIND ON PAPERWORK.
ALL MY CASES ARE UP TO DATE-- HANDWRITTEN, SARGE, AND IN ARCHIVES.
GET OUTTA HERE, WISEASS! AND GET THOSE CASES IN THE DATABASE.
COMPUTER FILES GET LOST *TOO*, SIR.

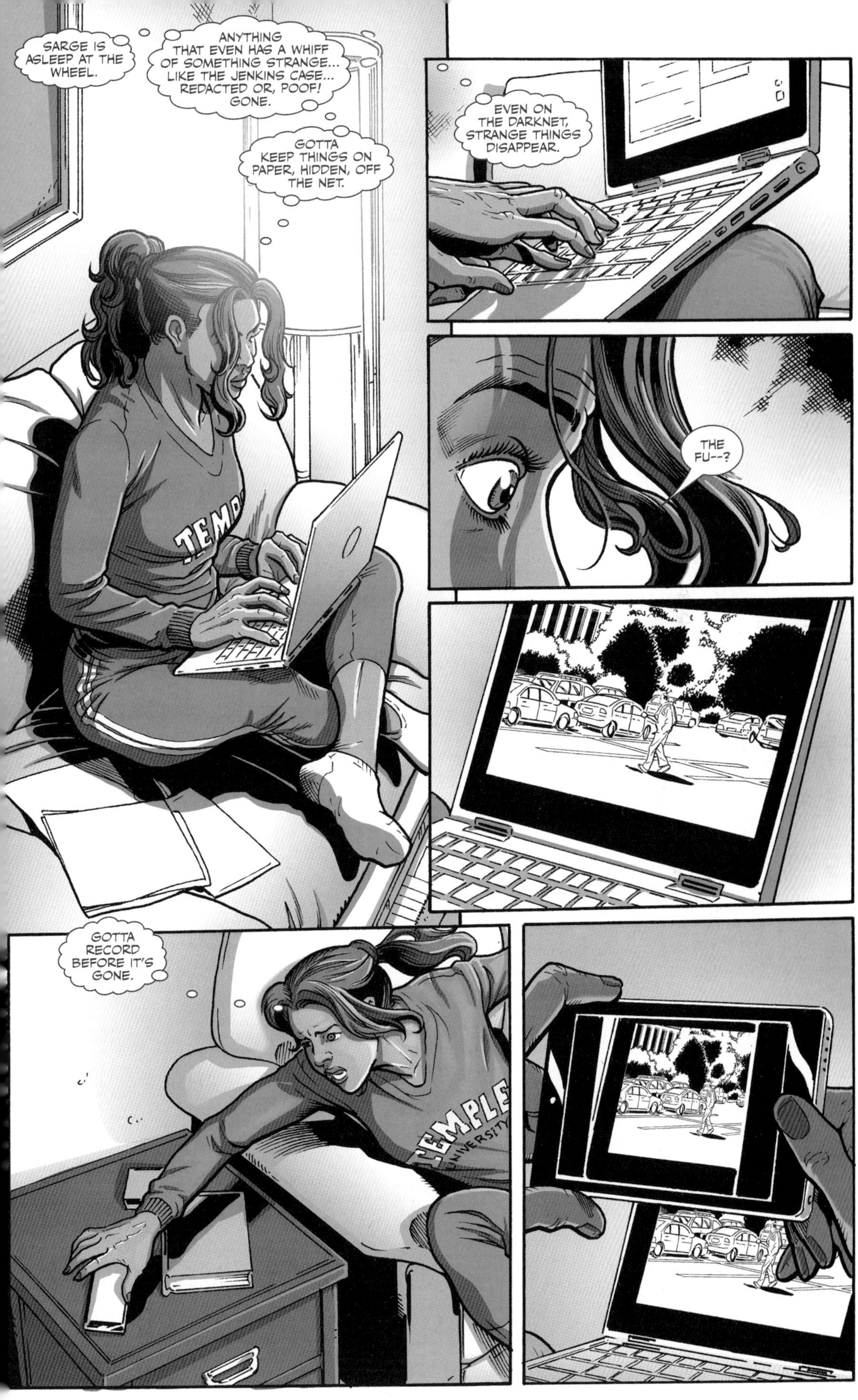
SARGE IS ASLEEP AT THE WHEEL.
ANYTHING THAT EVEN HAS A WHIFF OF SOMETHING STRANGE... LIKE THE JENKINS CASE... REDACTED OR, POOF! GONE.
GOTTA KEEP THINGS ON PAPER, HIDDEN, OFF THE NET.
EVEN ON THE DARKNET, STRANGE THINGS DISAPPEAR.
THE FU--?
GOTTA RECORD BEFORE IT'S GONE.

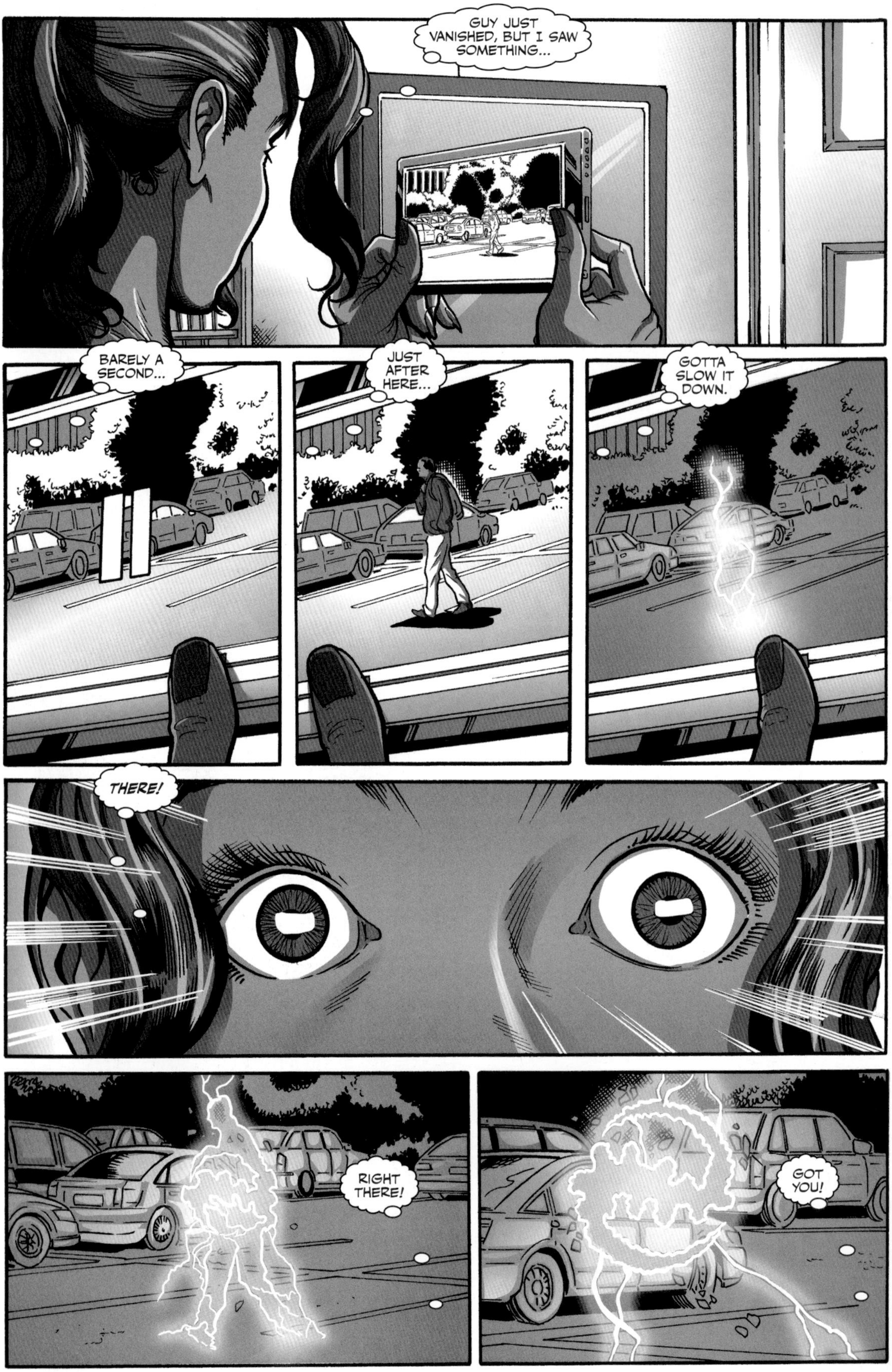
GUY JUST VANISHED, BUT I SAW SOMETHING...
BARELY A SECOND...
JUST AFTER HERE...
GOTTA SLOW IT DOWN.
THERE!
RIGHT THERE!
GOT YOU!

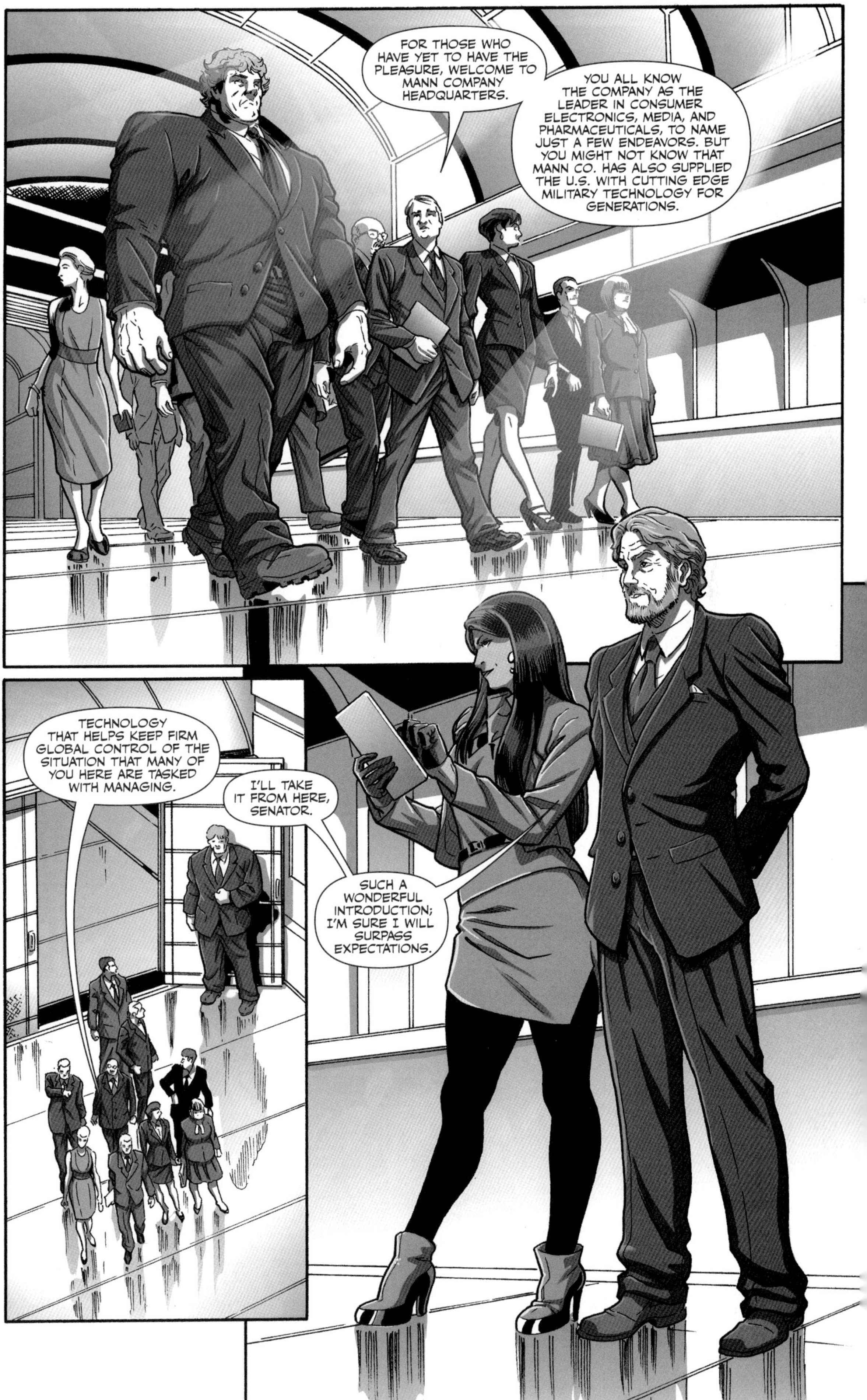
FOR THOSE WHO HAVE YET TO HAVE THE PLEASURE, WELCOME TO MANN COMPANY HEADQUARTERS.
YOU ALL KNOW THE COMPANY AS THE LEADER IN CONSUMER ELECTRONICS, MEDIA, AND PHARMACEUTICALS, TO NAME JUST A FEW ENDEAVORS. BUT YOU MIGHT NOT KNOW THAT MANN CO. HAS ALSO SUPPLIED THE U.S. WITH CUTTING EDGE MILITARY TECHNOLOGY FOR GENERATIONS.
TECHNOLOGY THAT HELPS KEEP FIRM GLOBAL CONTROL OF THE SITUATION THAT MANY OF YOU HERE ARE TASKED WITH MANAGING.
I'LL TAKE IT FROM HERE, SENATOR.
SUCH A WONDERFUL INTRODUCTION; I'M SURE I WILL SURPASS EXPECTATIONS.

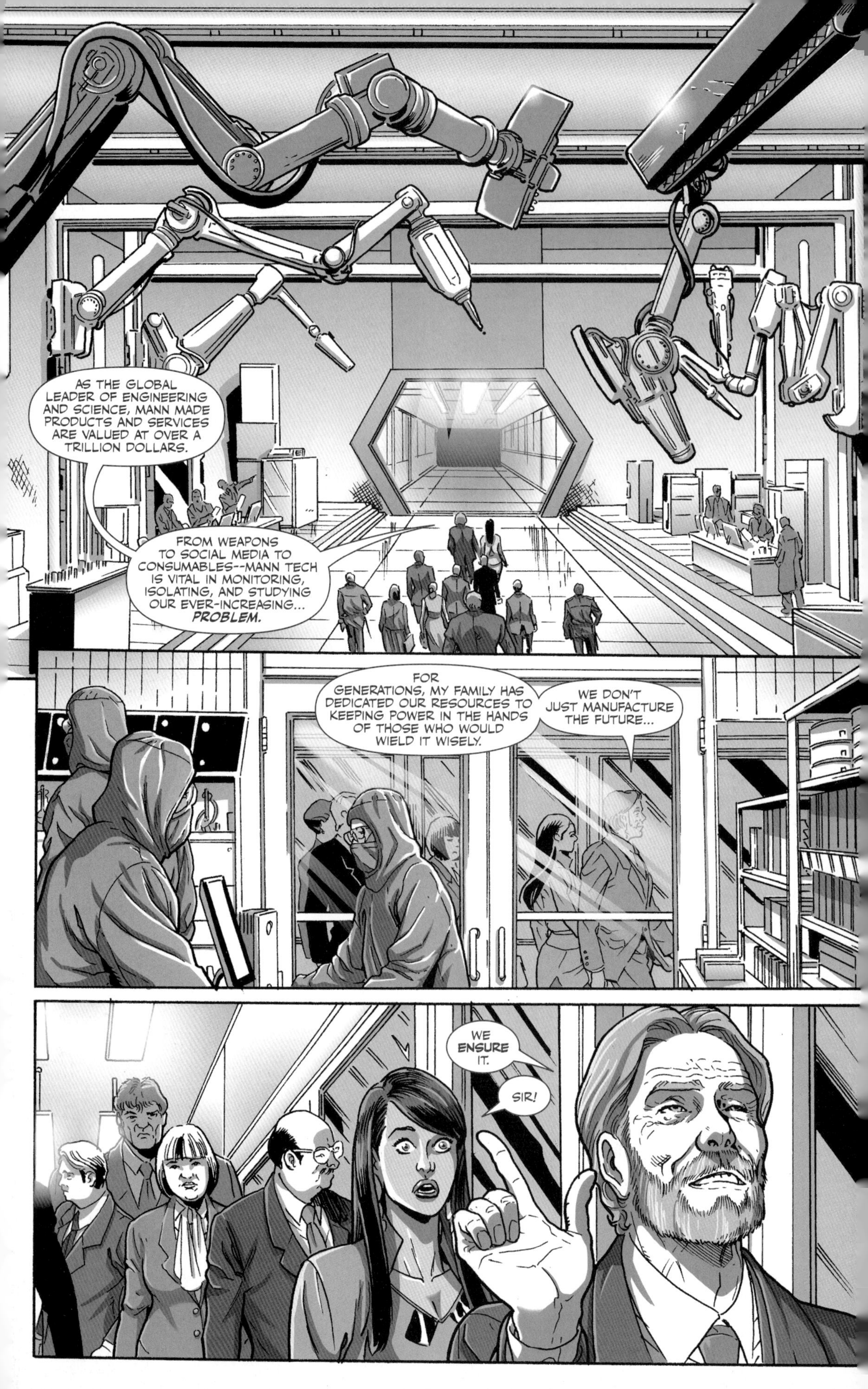
AS THE GLOBAL LEADER OF ENGINEERING AND SCIENCE, MANN MADE PRODUCTS AND SERVICES ARE VALUED AT OVER A TRILLION DOLLARS.
FROM WEAPONS TO SOCIAL MEDIA TO CONSUMABLES--MANN TECH IS VITAL IN MONITORING, ISOLATING, AND STUDYING OUR EVER-INCREASING... PROBLEM.
FOR GENERATIONS, MY FAMILY HAS DEDICATED OUR RESOURCES TO KEEPING POWER IN THE HANDS OF THOSE WHO WOULD WIELD IT WISELY.
WE DON'T JUST MANUFACTURE THE FUTURE...
WE ENSURE IT.
SIR!

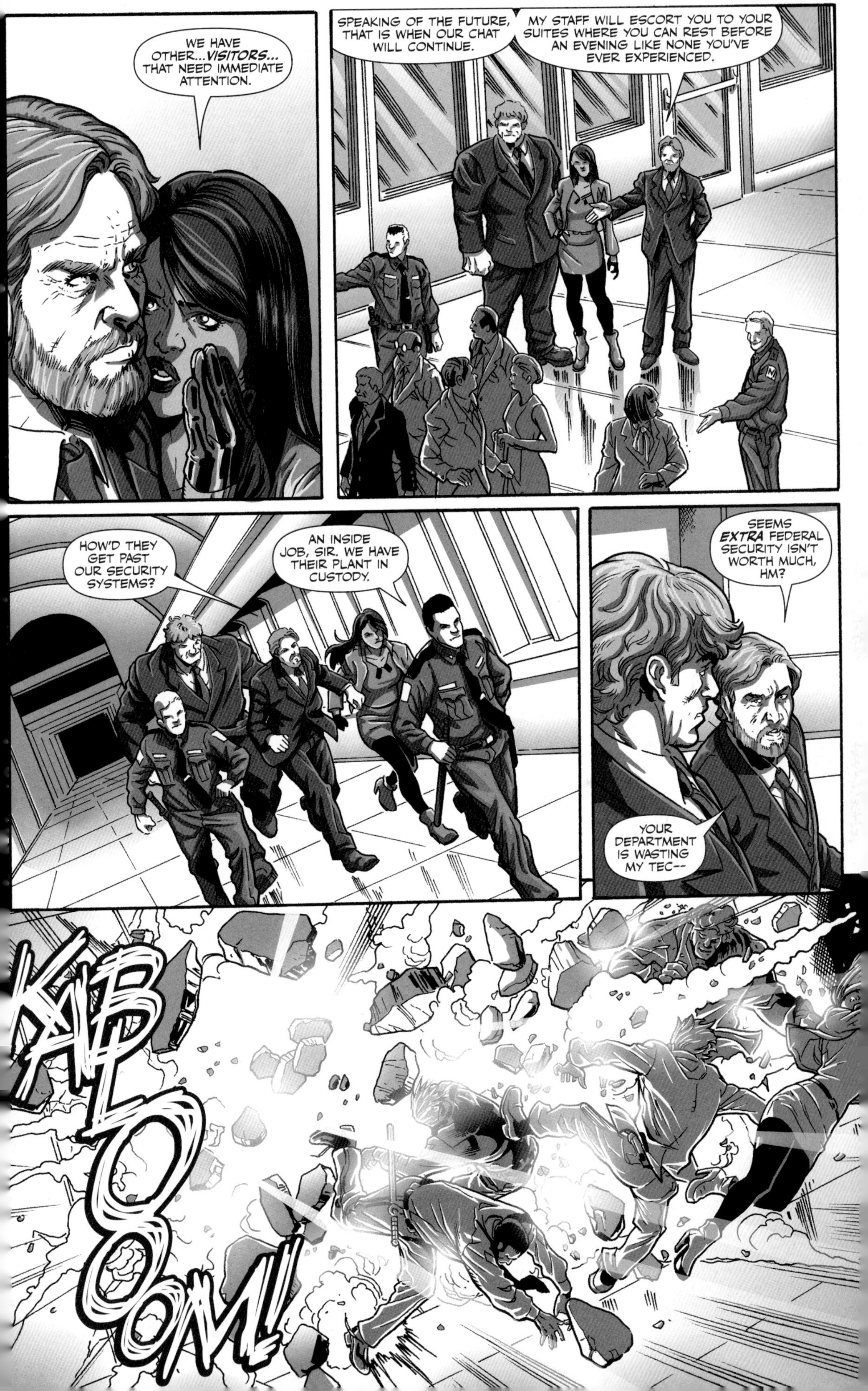
WE HAVE OTHER... VISITORS... THAT NEED IMMEDIATE ATTENTION.
SPEAKING OF THE FUTURE, THAT IS WHEN OUR CHAT WILL CONTINUE.
MY STAFF WILL ESCORT YOU TO YOUR SUITES WHERE YOU CAN REST BEFORE AN EVENING LIKE NONE YOU'VE EVER EXPERIENCED.
HOW'D THEY GET PAST OUR SECURITY SYSTEMS?
AN INSIDE JOB, SIR. WE HAVE THEIR PLANT IN CUSTODY.
SEEMS EXTRA FEDERAL SECURITY ISN'T WORTH MUCH, HM?
YOUR DEPARTMENT IS WASTING MY TEC--
KABLOOOM!

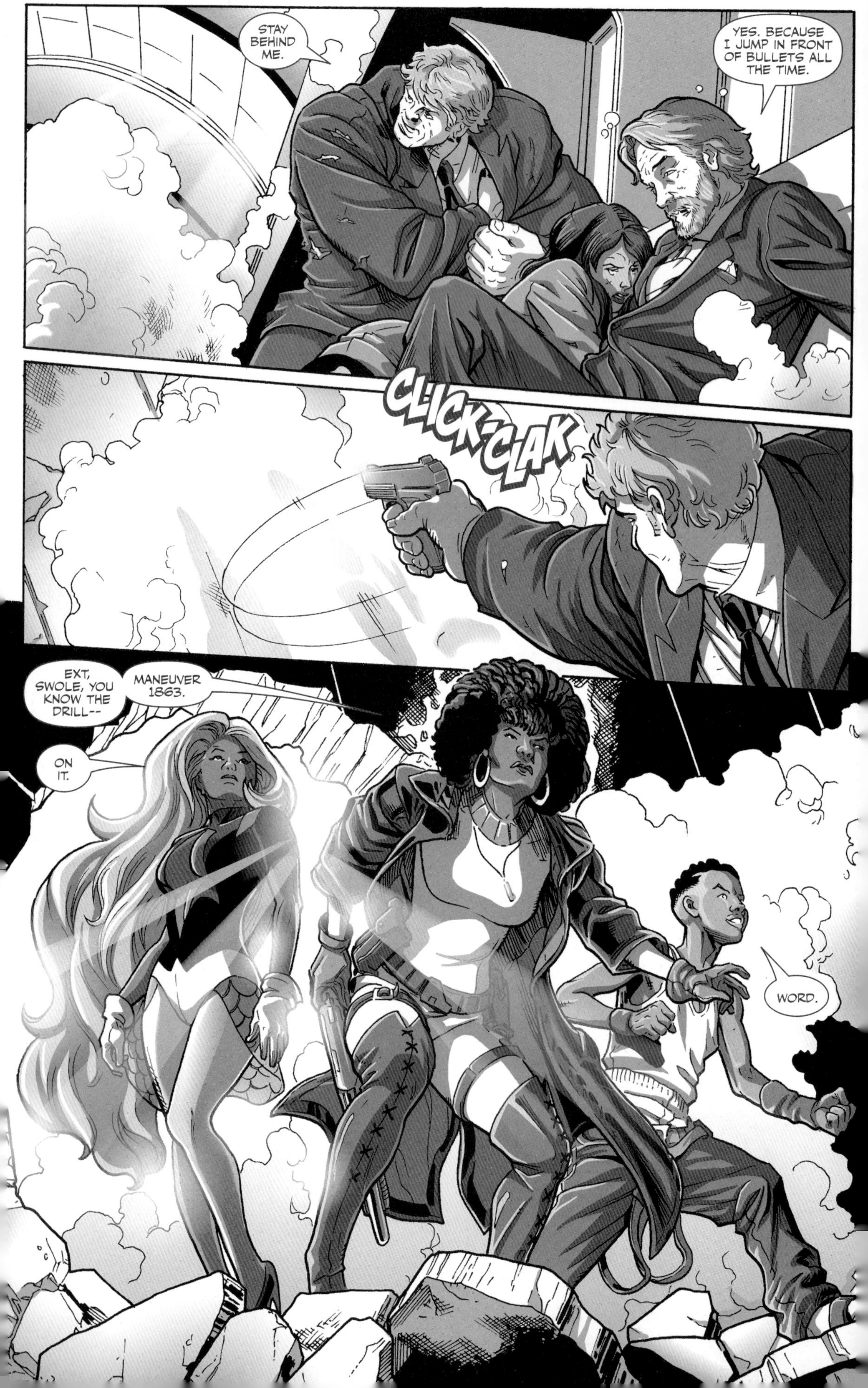
STAY BEHIND ME.
YES. BECAUSE I JUMP IN FRONT OF BULLETS ALL THE TIME.
CLICK-CLAK
EXT, SWOLE, YOU KNOW THE DRILL--
MANEUVER 1863.
ON IT.
WORD.

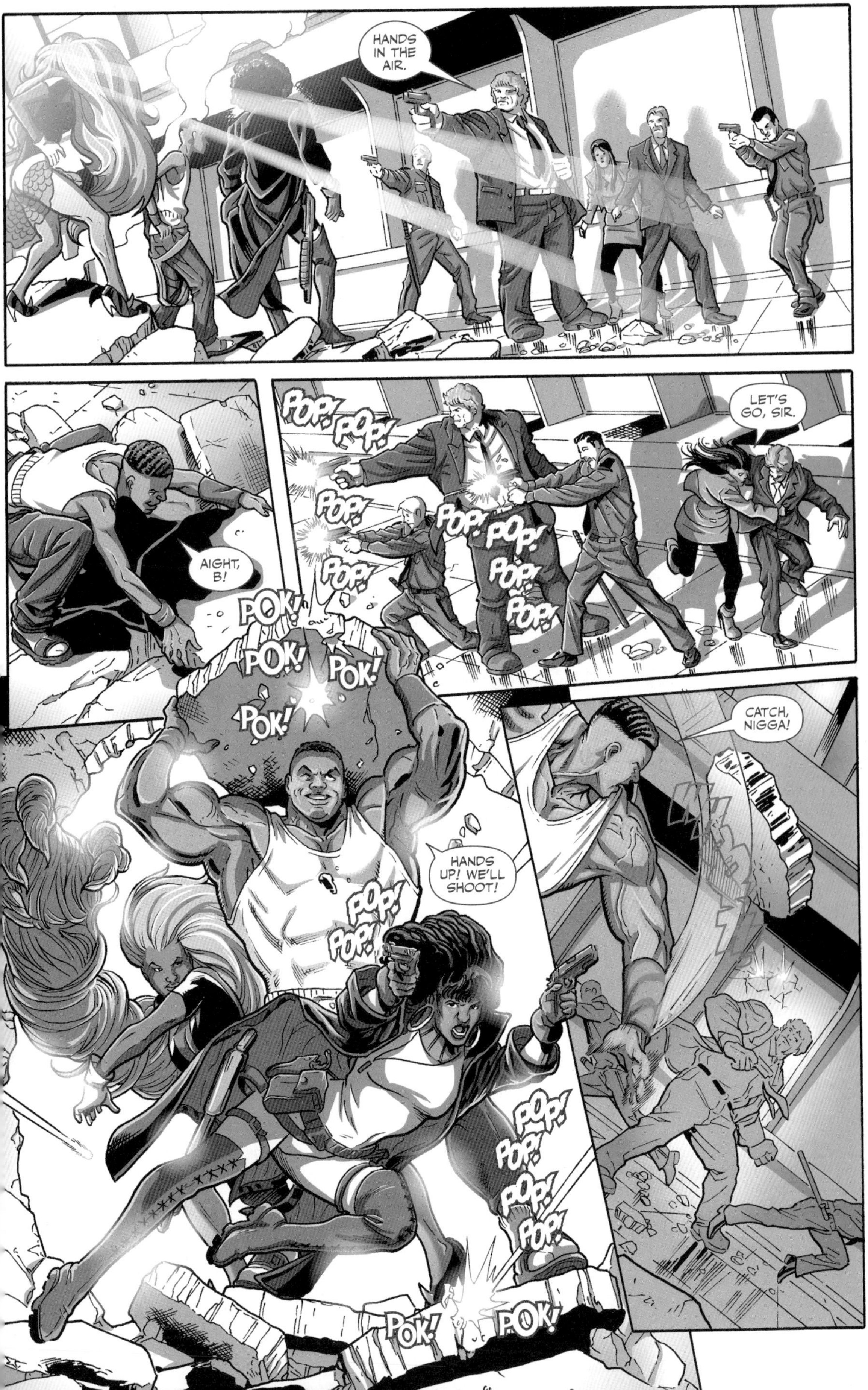
HANDS IN THE AIR.
AIGHT, B!
POP! POP!
POP!
POP! POP!
POP!
POP! POP!
LET'S GO, SIR.
POK!
POK!
POK!
POK!
HANDS UP! WE'LL SHOOT!
POP! POP!
POP! POP! POP! POP!
POK! POK!
CATCH, NIGGA!

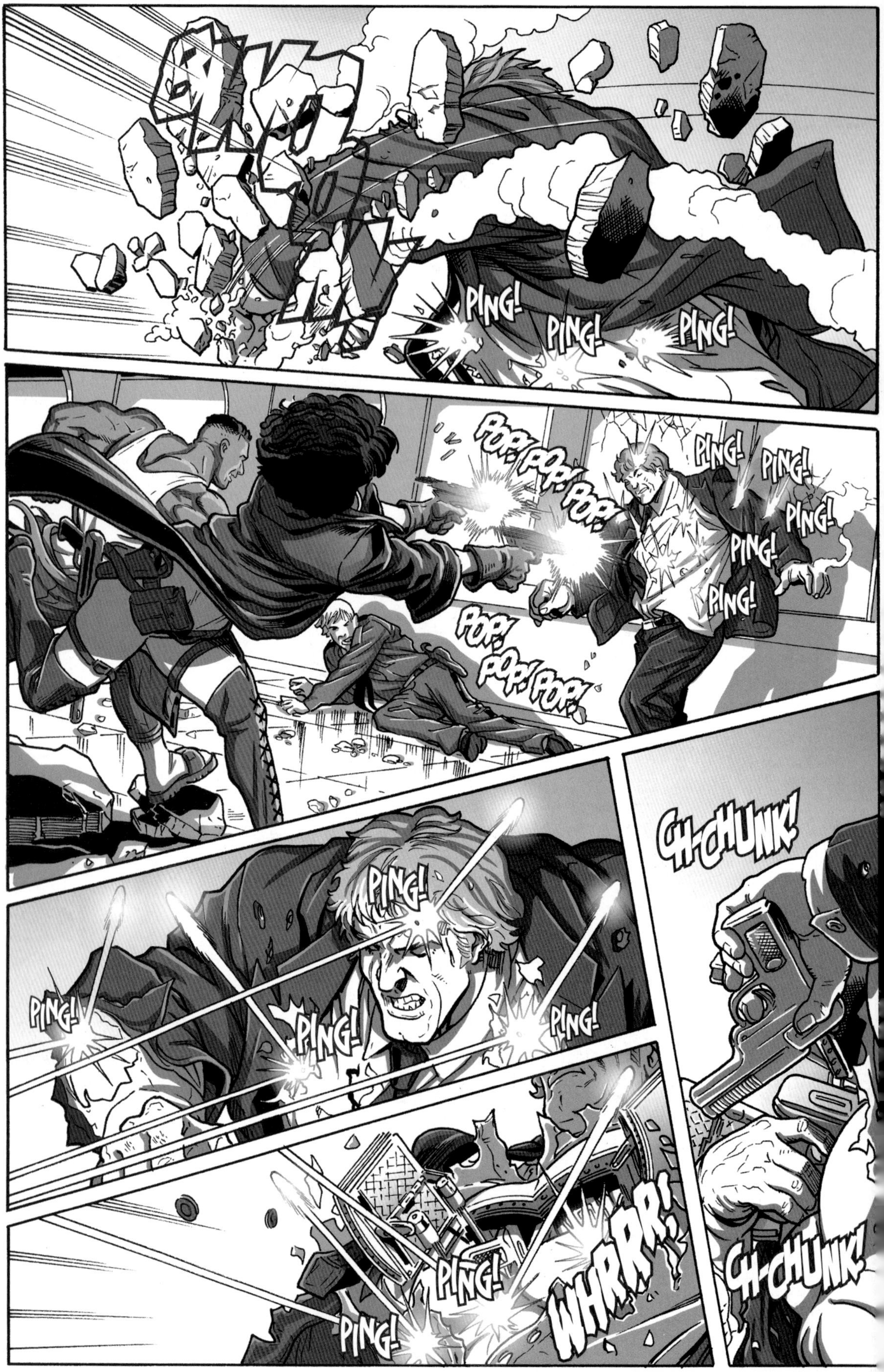
PING!
PING!
PING!
POP! POP! POP!
PING!
PING!
PING!
PING!
PING!
POP!
POP! POP!
PING!
PING!
PING!
PING!
CH-CHUNK!
PING!
PING!
WHRRR!
CH-CHUNK!

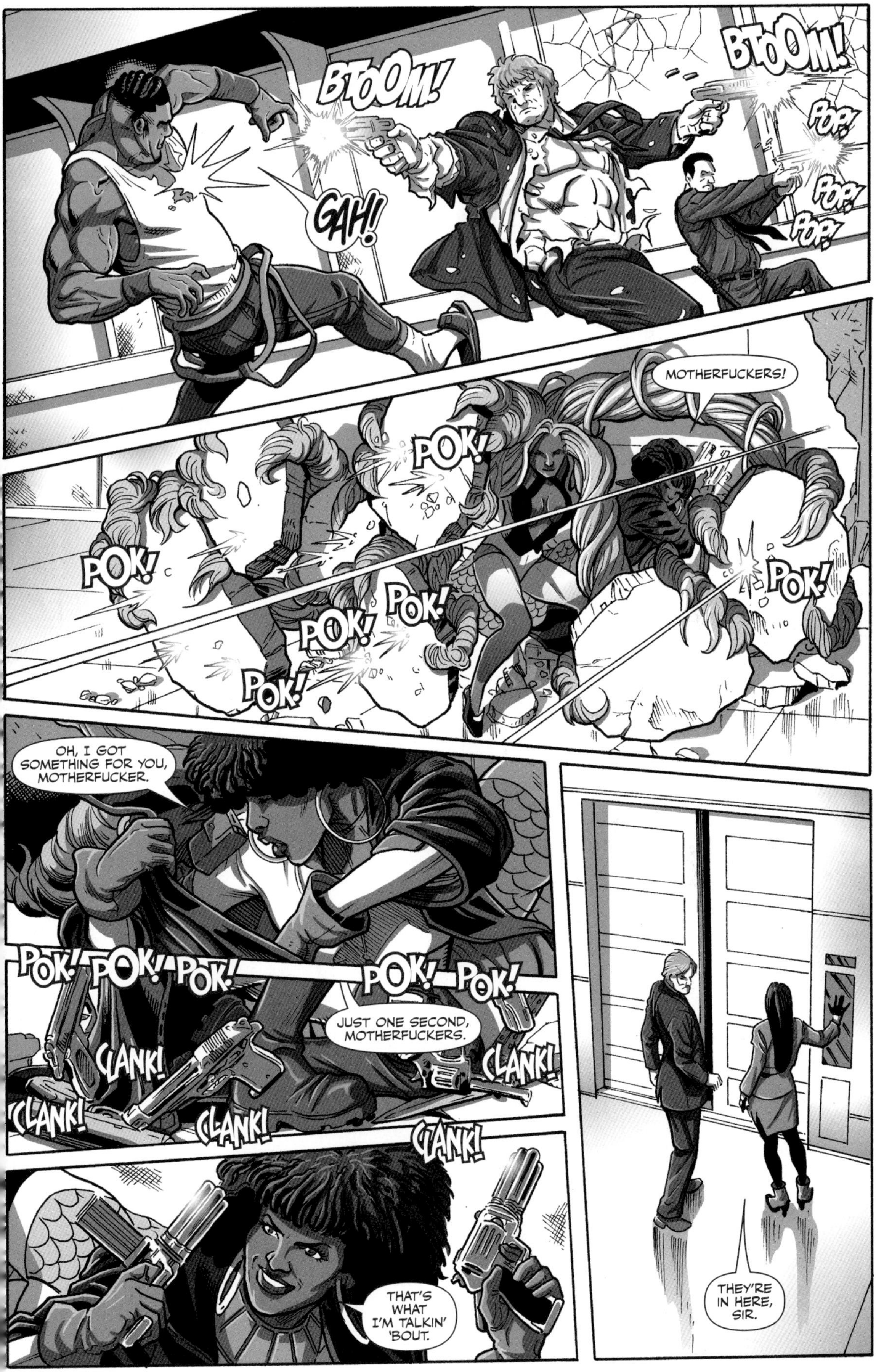
BTOOM!
BTOOM!
GAH!
POP!
POP!
POP!
MOTHERFUCKERS!
POK!
POK!
POK!
POK!
POK!
POK!
OH, I GOT SOMETHING FOR YOU, MOTHERFUCKER.
POK! POK! POK! POK! POK!
JUST ONE SECOND, MOTHERFUCKERS.
CLANK!
CLANK!
CLANK!
CLANK!
CLANK!
THAT'S WHAT I'M TALKIN' 'BOUT.
THEY'RE IN HERE, SIR.

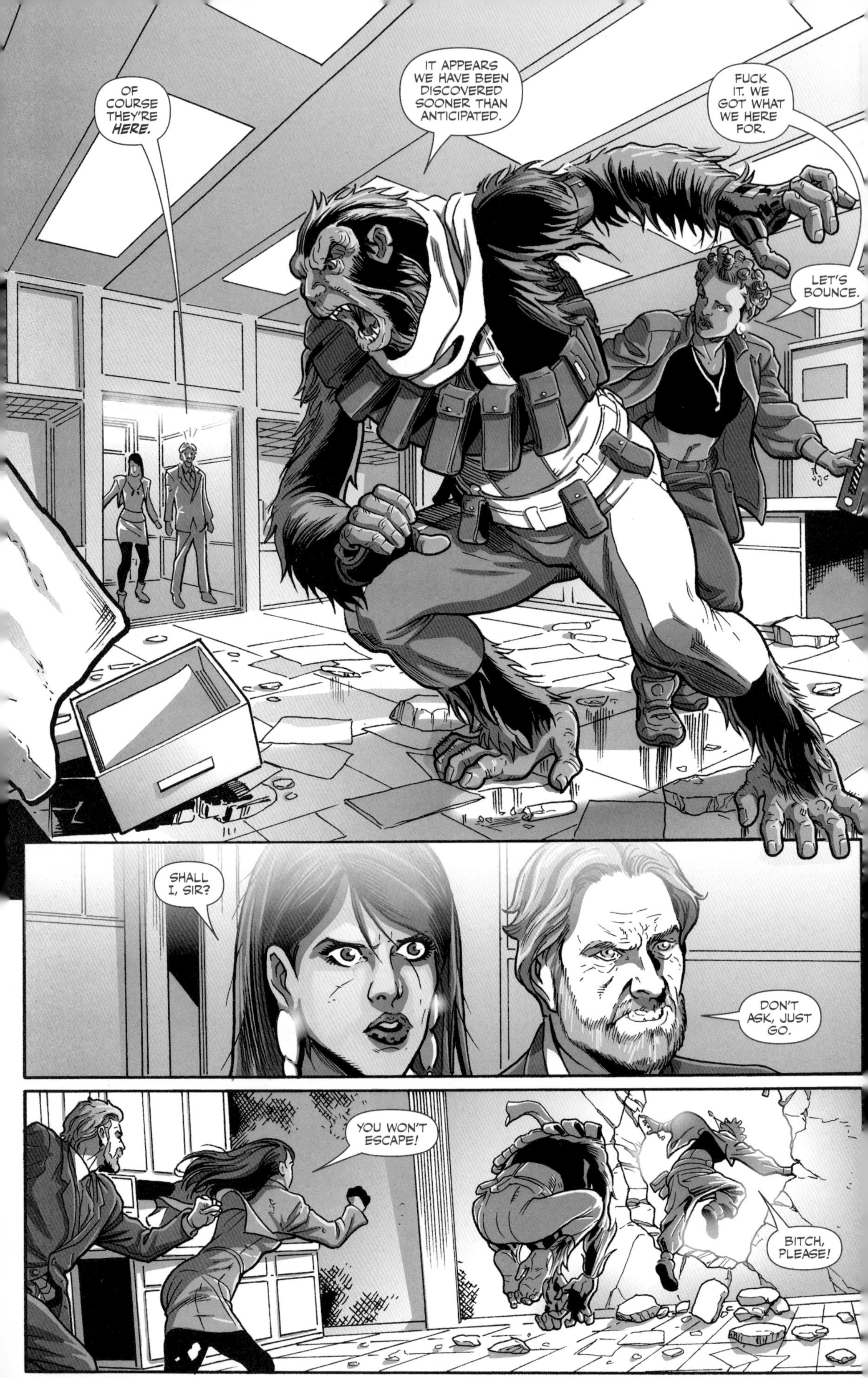
OF COURSE THEY'RE *HERE.*
IT APPEARS WE HAVE BEEN DISCOVERED SOONER THAN ANTICIPATED.
FUCK IT. WE GOT WHAT WE HERE FOR.
LET'S BOUNCE.
SHALL I, SIR?
DON'T ASK, JUST GO.
YOU WON'T ESCAPE!
BITCH, PLEASE!

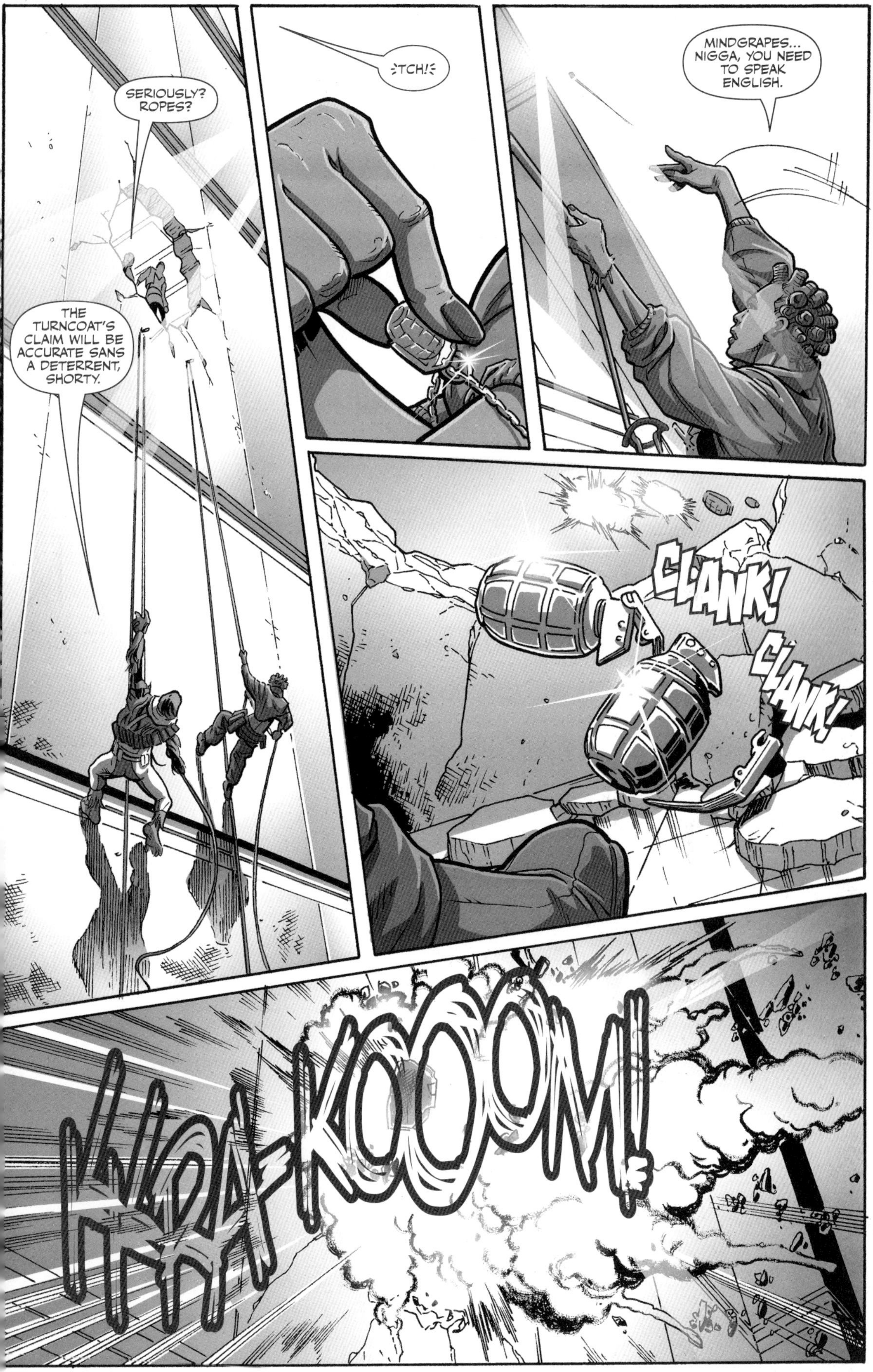

SERIOUSLY? ROPES?
THE TURNCOAT'S CLAIM WILL BE ACCURATE SANS A DETERRENT, SHORTY.
TCH!
MINDGRAPES... NIGGA, YOU NEED TO SPEAK ENGLISH.
CLANK!
CLANK!
KOOOM!

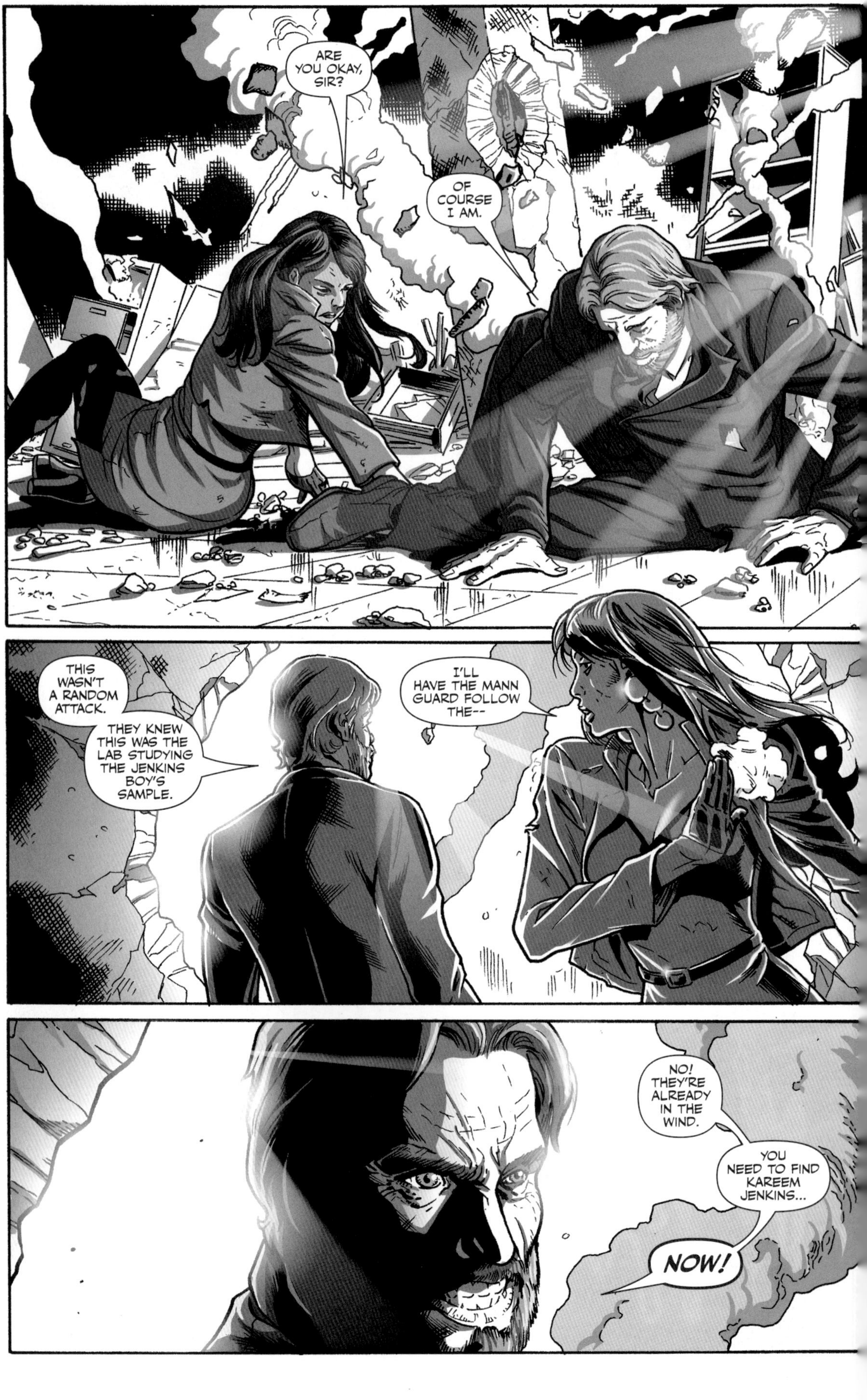
ARE YOU OKAY, SIR?
OF COURSE I AM.
THIS WASN'T A RANDOM ATTACK.
THEY KNEW THIS WAS THE LAB STUDYING THE JENKINS BOY'S SAMPLE.
I'LL HAVE THE MANN GUARD FOLLOW THE--
NO! THEY'RE ALREADY IN THE WIND.
YOU NEED TO FIND KAREEM JENKINS...
NOW!

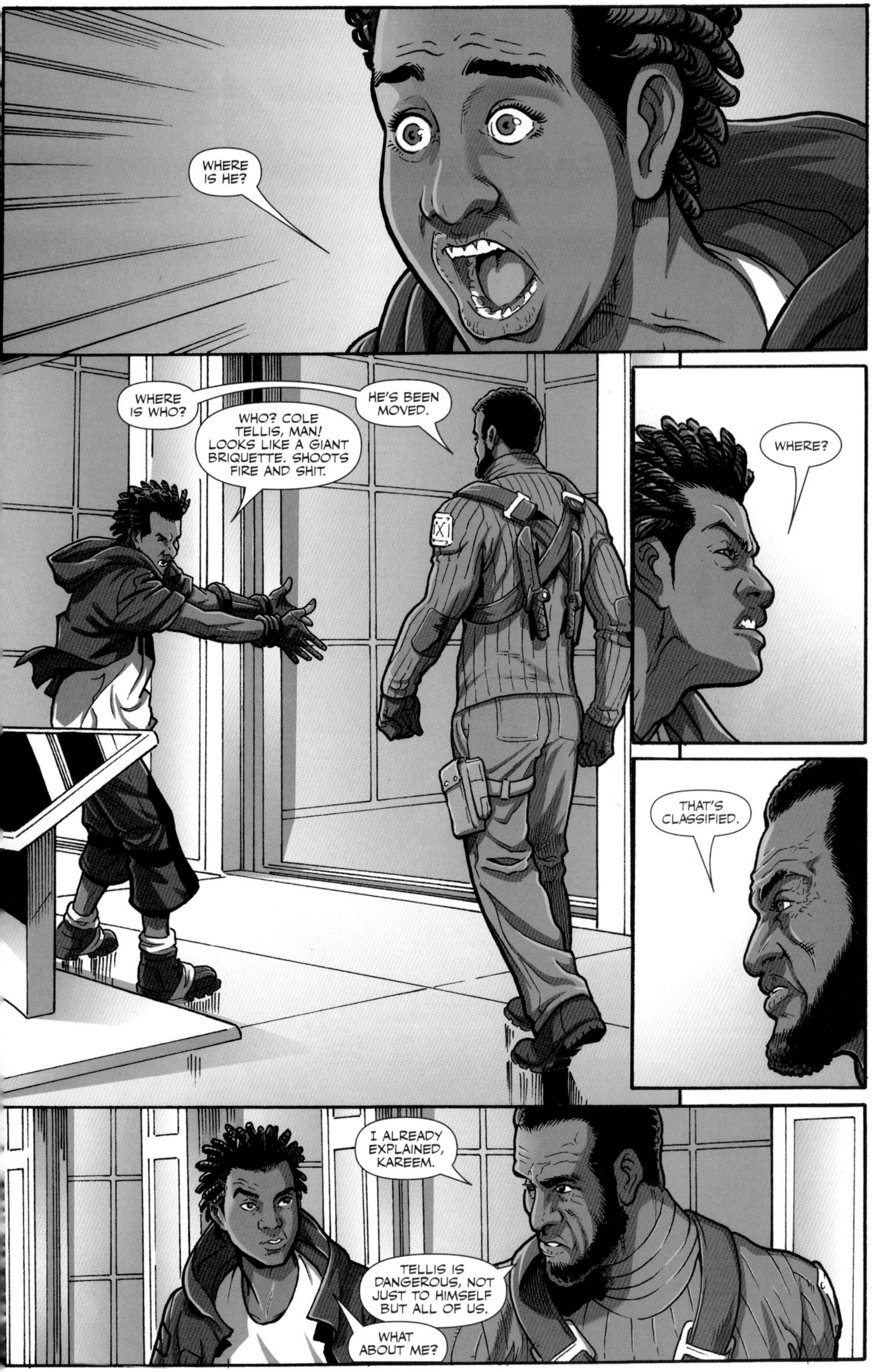
WHERE IS HE?
WHERE IS WHO?
HE'S BEEN MOVED.
WHO? COLE TELLIS, MAN! LOOKS LIKE A GIANT BRIQUETTE. SHOOTS FIRE AND SHIT.
WHERE?
THAT'S CLASSIFIED.
I ALREADY EXPLAINED, KAREEM.
TELLIS IS DANGEROUS, NOT JUST TO HIMSELF BUT ALL OF US.
WHAT ABOUT ME?

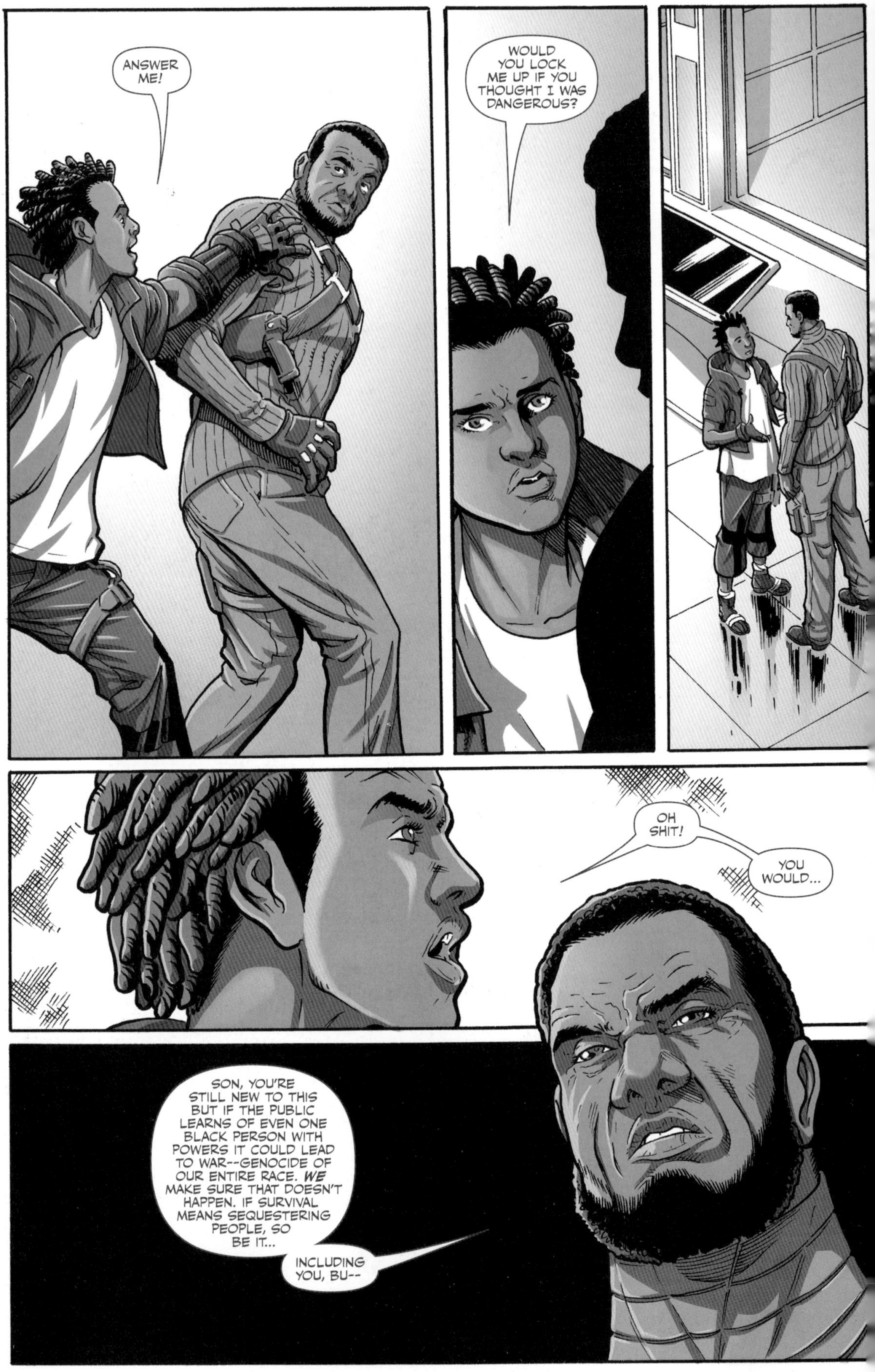
ANSWER ME!
WOULD YOU LOCK ME UP IF YOU THOUGHT I WAS DANGEROUS?
OH SHIT!
YOU WOULD...
SON, YOU'RE STILL NEW TO THIS BUT IF THE PUBLIC LEARNS OF EVEN ONE BLACK PERSON WITH POWERS IT COULD LEAD TO WAR--GENOCIDE OF OUR ENTIRE RACE. *WE* MAKE SURE THAT DOESN'T HAPPEN. IF SURVIVAL MEANS SEQUESTERING PEOPLE, SO BE IT...
INCLUDING YOU, BU--

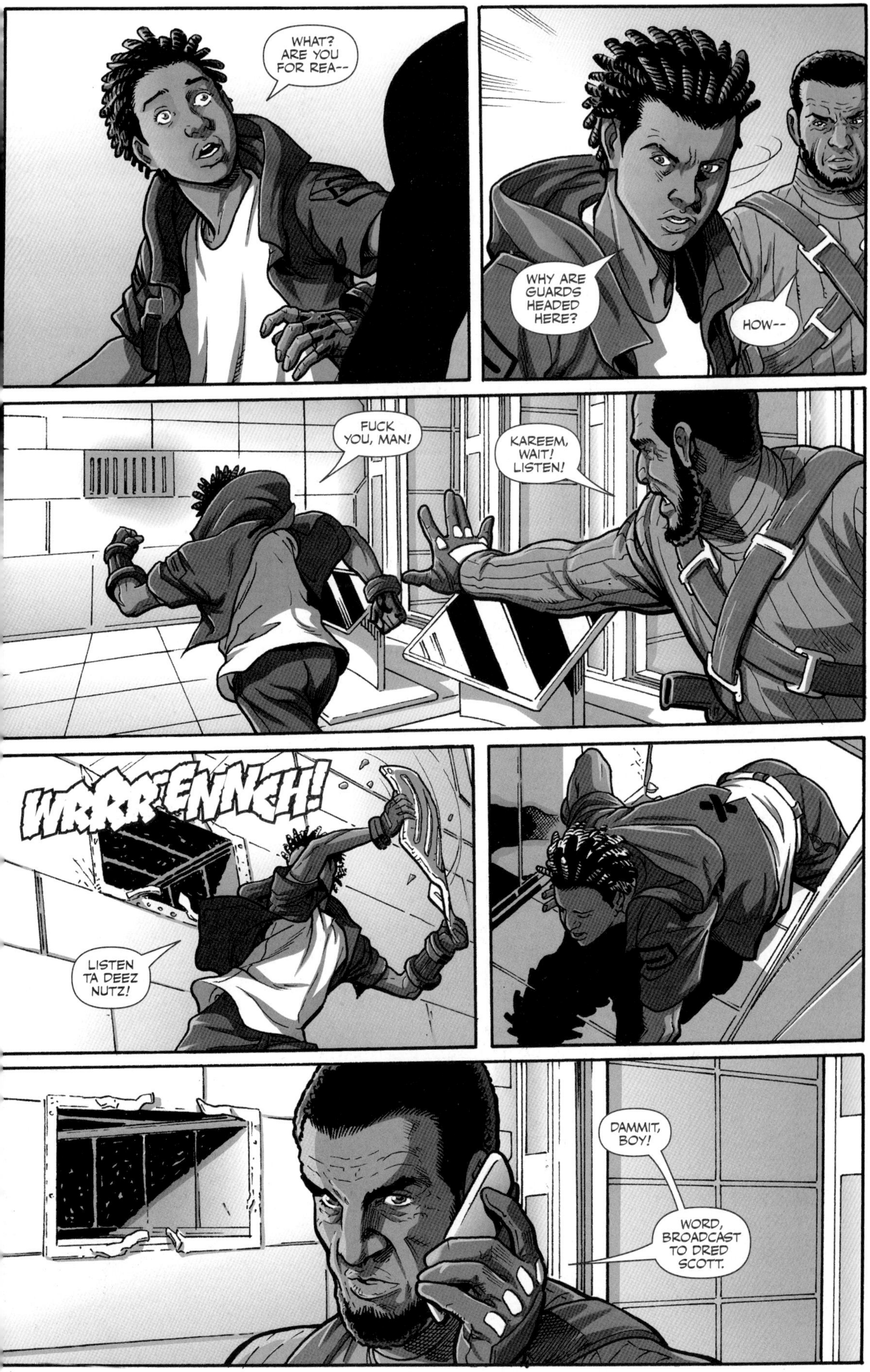
WHAT? ARE YOU FOR REA--
WHY ARE GUARDS HEADED HERE?
HOW--
FUCK YOU, MAN!
KAREEM, WAIT! LISTEN!
WRRRRENNCH!
LISTEN TA DEEZ NUTZ!
DAMMIT, BOY!
WORD, BROADCAST TO DRED SCOTT.

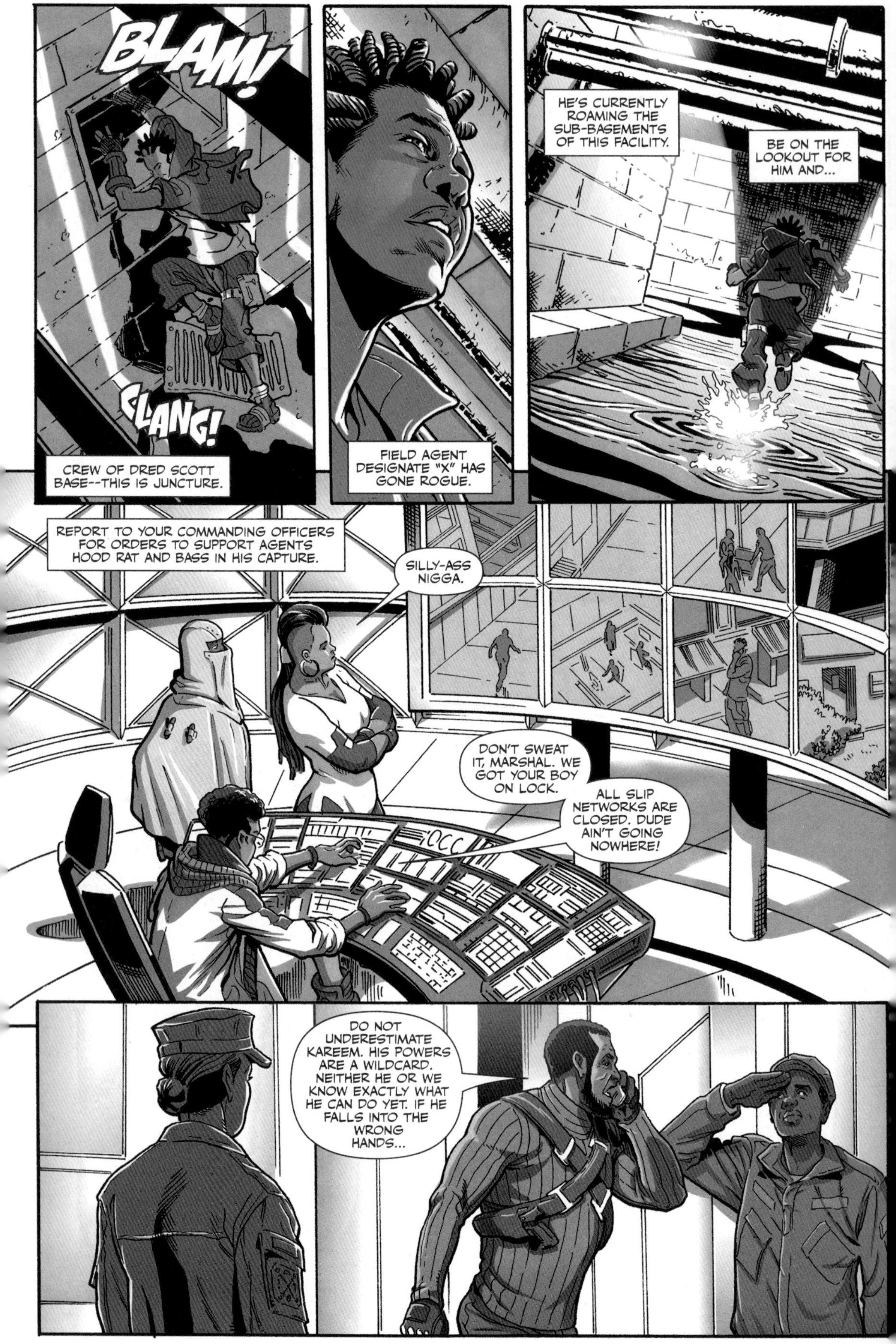
BLAM!
CLANG!
CREW OF DRED SCOTT BASE--THIS IS JUNCTURE.
FIELD AGENT DESIGNATE "X" HAS GONE ROGUE.
HE'S CURRENTLY ROAMING THE SUB-BASEMENTS OF THIS FACILITY.
BE ON THE LOOKOUT FOR HIM AND...
REPORT TO YOUR COMMANDING OFFICERS FOR ORDERS TO SUPPORT AGENTS HOOD RAT AND BASS IN HIS CAPTURE.
SILLY-ASS NIGGA.
DON'T SWEAT IT, MARSHAL. WE GOT YOUR BOY ON LOCK.
ALL SLIP NETWORKS ARE CLOSED. DUDE AIN'T GOING NOWHERE!
DO NOT UNDERESTIMATE KAREEM. HIS POWERS ARE A WILDCARD. NEITHER HE OR WE KNOW EXACTLY WHAT HE CAN DO YET. IF HE FALLS INTO THE WRONG HANDS...

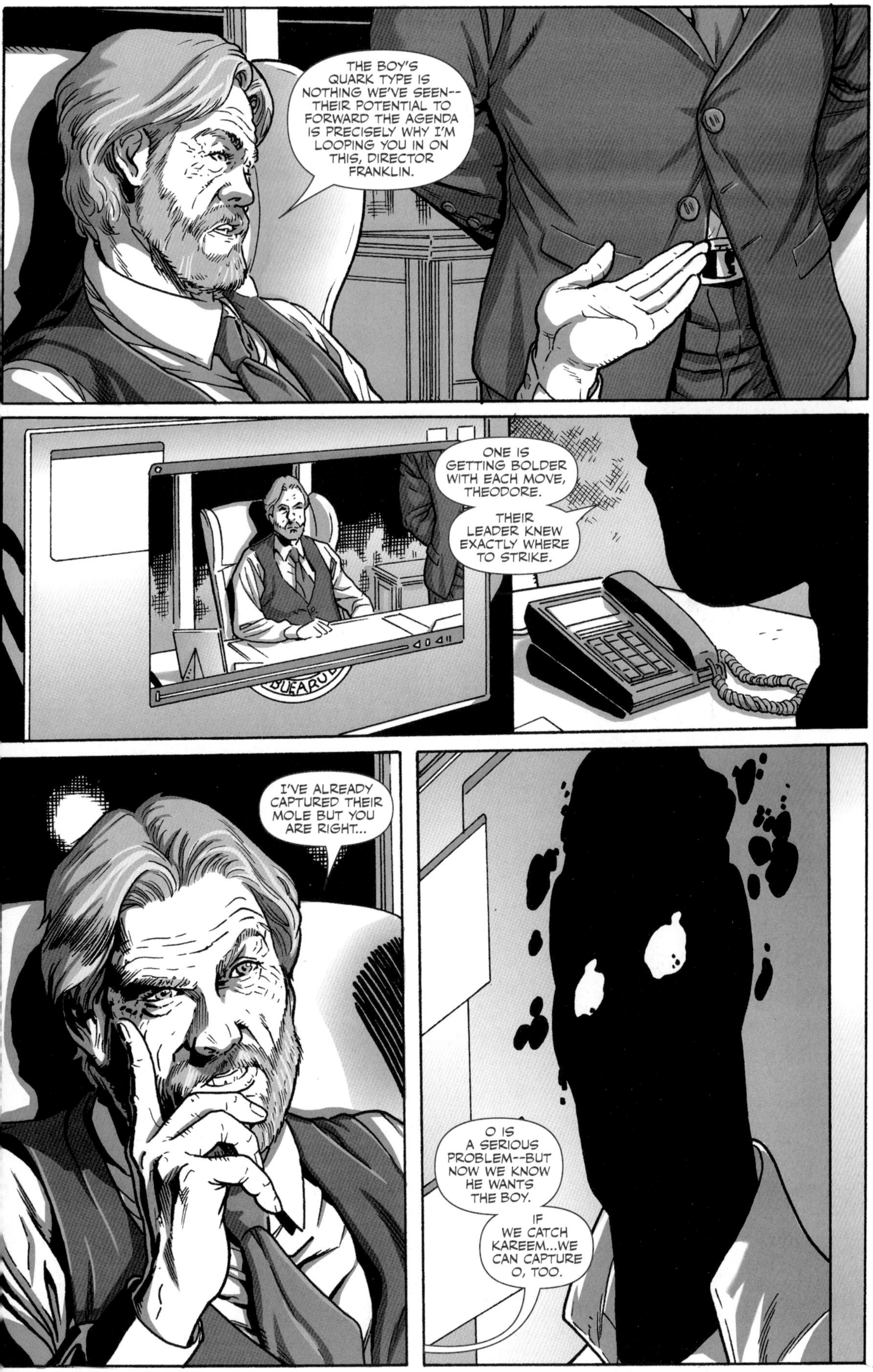
THE BOY'S QUARK TYPE IS NOTHING WE'VE SEEN--THEIR POTENTIAL TO FORWARD THE AGENDA IS PRECISELY WHY I'M LOOPING YOU IN ON THIS, DIRECTOR FRANKLIN.
ONE IS GETTING BOLDER WITH EACH MOVE, THEODORE.
THEIR LEADER KNEW EXACTLY WHERE TO STRIKE.
I'VE ALREADY CAPTURED THEIR MOLE BUT YOU ARE RIGHT...
O IS A SERIOUS PROBLEM--BUT NOW WE KNOW HE WANTS THE BOY.
IF WE CATCH KAREEM...WE CAN CAPTURE O, TOO.

CHAPTER FOUR

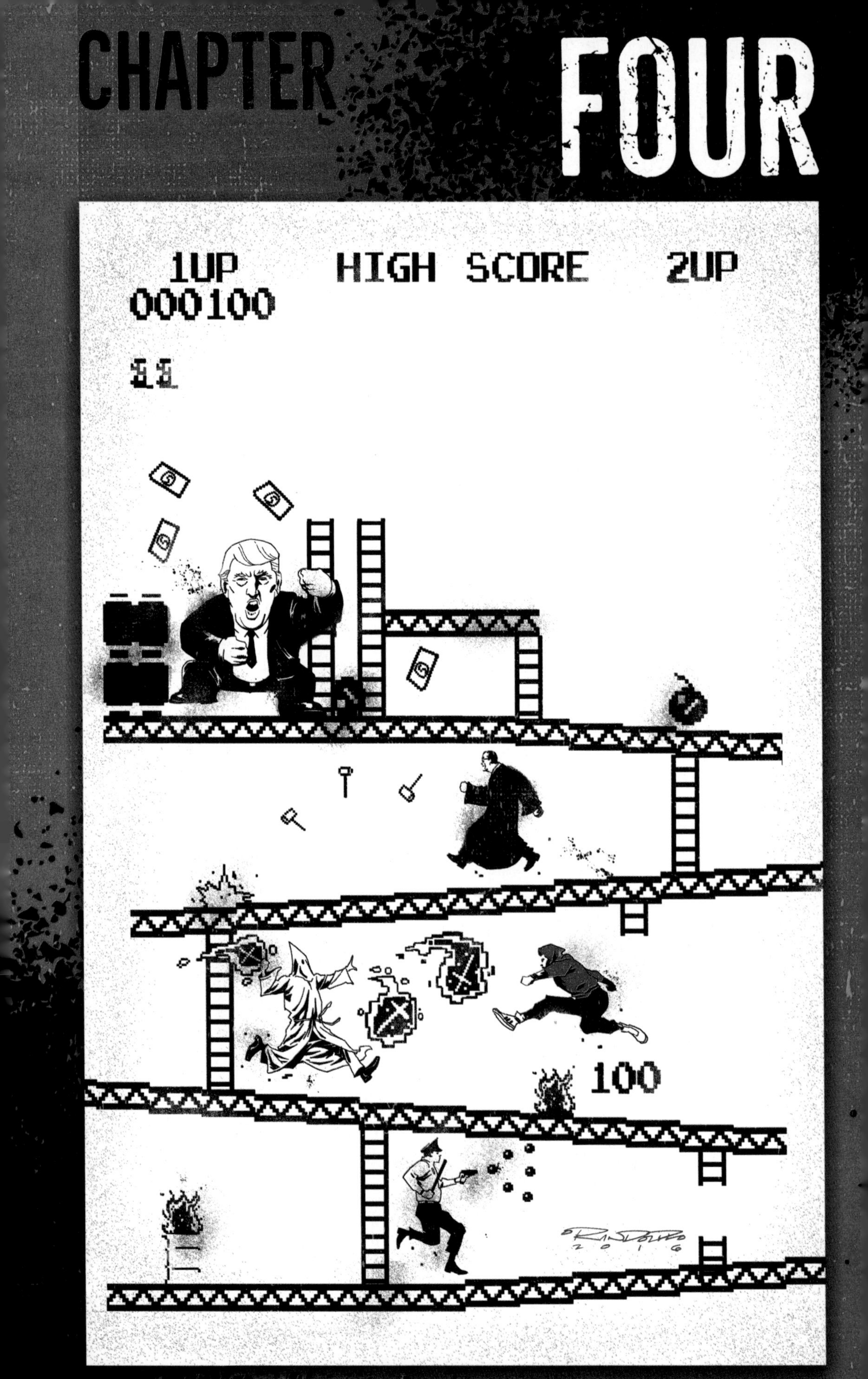

1UP
HIGH SCORE
2UP
000100
100
RANDOLPH 2016

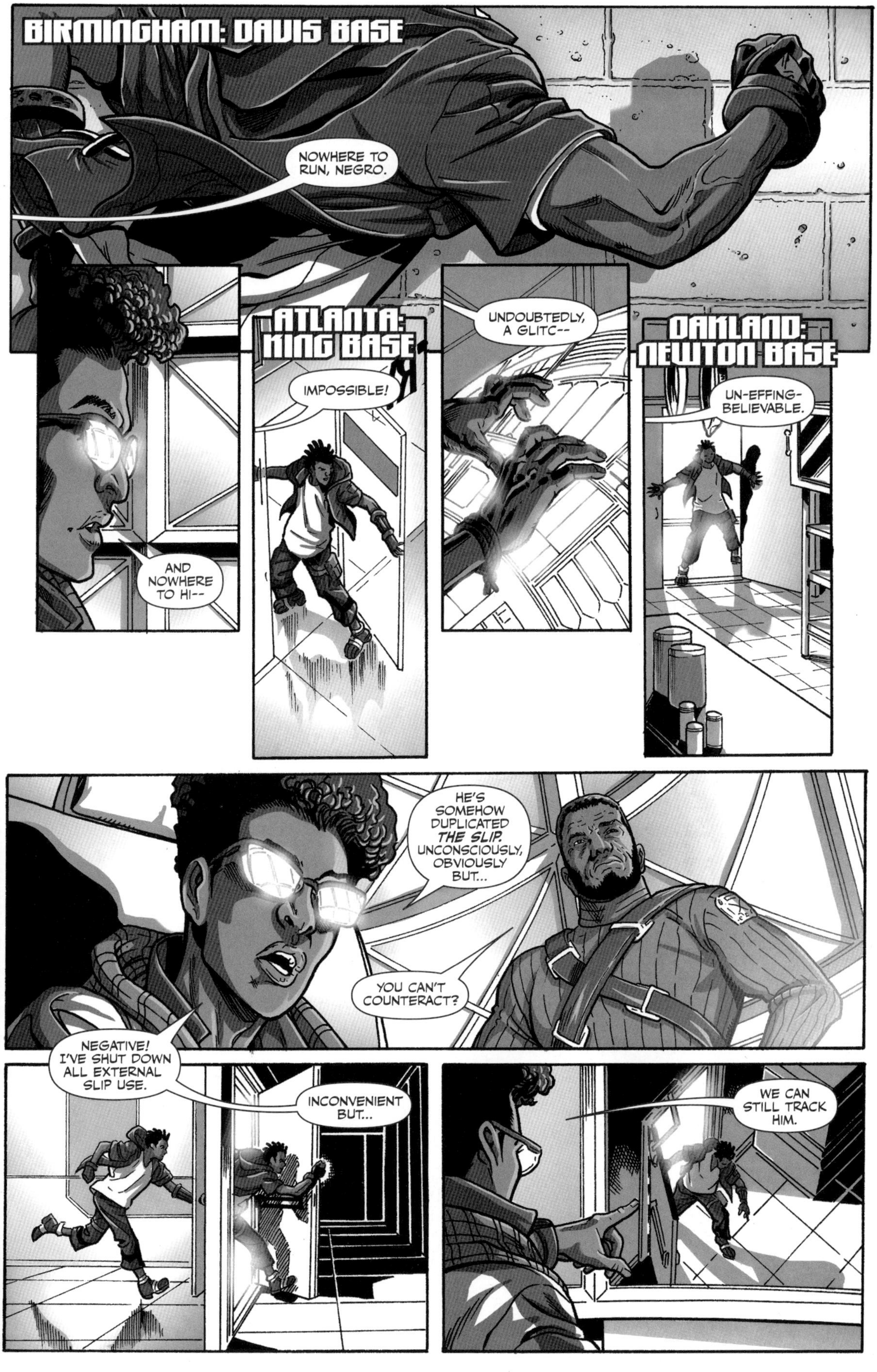
BIRMINGHAM: DAVIS BASE
NOWHERE TO RUN, NEGRO.
AND NOWHERE TO HI--
ATLANTA: KING BASE
IMPOSSIBLE!
UNDOUBTEDLY, A GLITC--
OAKLAND: NEWTON BASE
UN-EFFING-BELIEVABLE.
HE'S SOMEHOW DUPLICATED THE SLIP. UNCONSCIOUSLY, OBVIOUSLY BUT...
YOU CAN'T COUNTERACT?
NEGATIVE! I'VE SHUT DOWN ALL EXTERNAL SLIP USE.
INCONVENIENT BUT...
WE CAN STILL TRACK HIM.

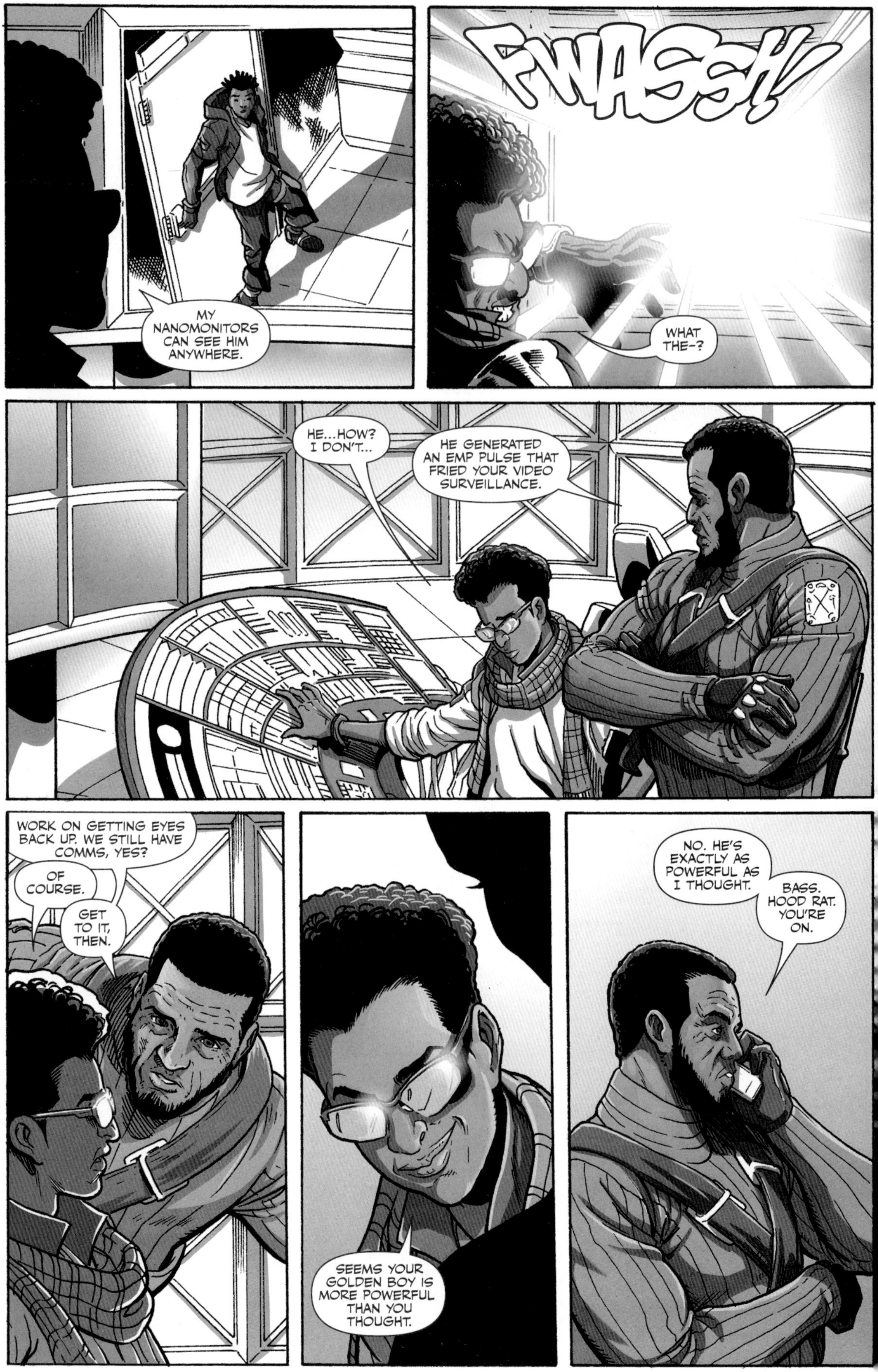
MY NANOMONITORS CAN SEE HIM ANYWHERE.
FWASSH!!
WHAT THE-?
HE...HOW? I DON'T...
HE GENERATED AN EMP PULSE THAT FRIED YOUR VIDEO SURVEILLANCE.
WORK ON GETTING EYES BACK UP. WE STILL HAVE COMMS, YES?
OF COURSE.
GET TO IT, THEN.
SEEMS YOUR GOLDEN BOY IS MORE POWERFUL THAN YOU THOUGHT.
NO. HE'S EXACTLY AS POWERFUL AS I THOUGHT.
BASS. HOOD RAT. YOU'RE ON.

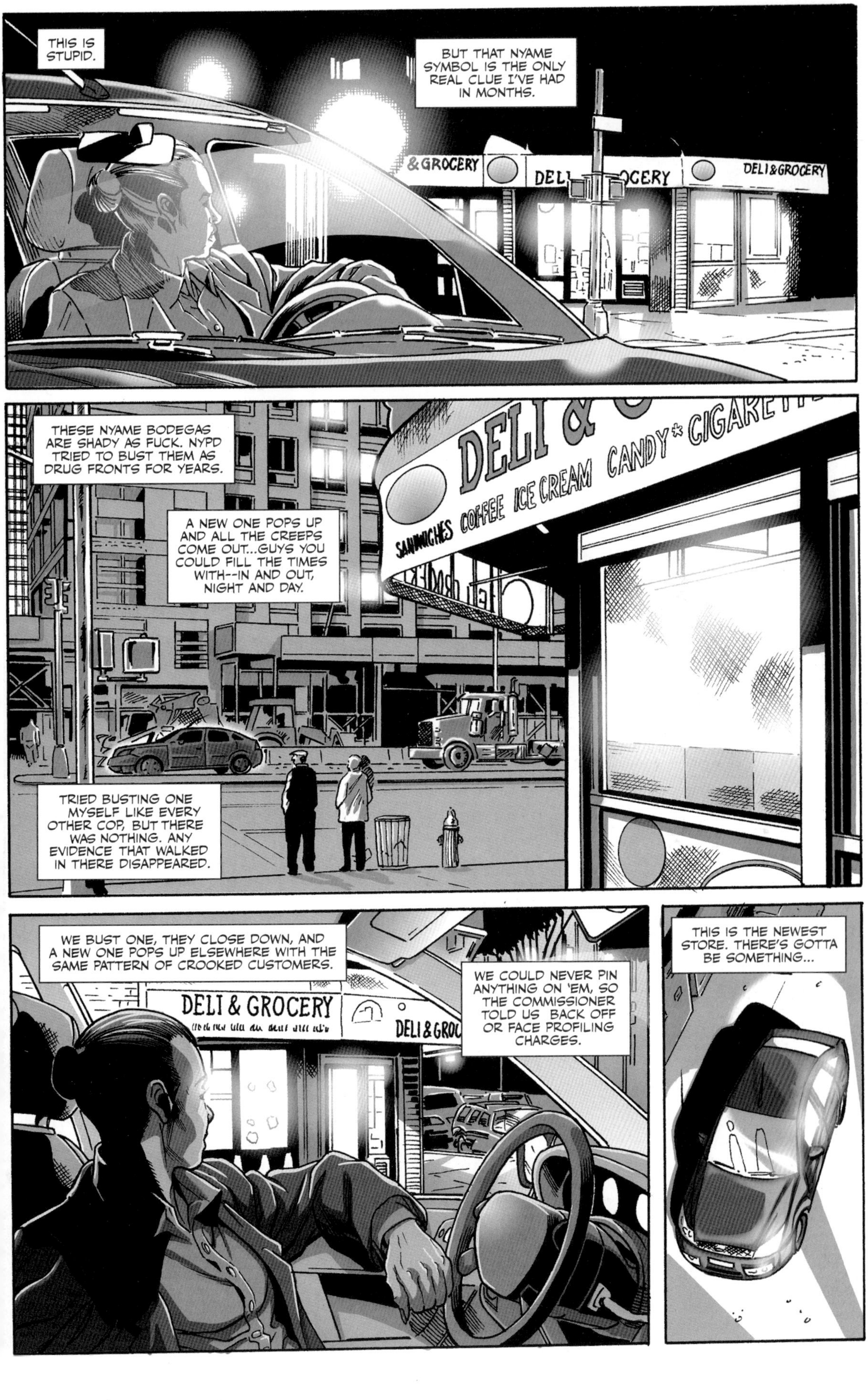
THIS IS STUPID.
BUT THAT NYAME SYMBOL IS THE ONLY REAL CLUE I'VE HAD IN MONTHS.
& GROCERY
DELI & GROCERY
DELI & GROCERY
THESE NYAME BODEGAS ARE SHADY AS FUCK. NYPD TRIED TO BUST THEM AS DRUG FRONTS FOR YEARS.
DELI & C
SANDWICHES COFFEE ICE CREAM CANDY* CIGARETTES
A NEW ONE POPS UP AND ALL THE CREEPS COME OUT...GUYS YOU COULD FILL THE TIMES WITH--IN AND OUT, NIGHT AND DAY.
TRIED BUSTING ONE MYSELF LIKE EVERY OTHER COP, BUT THERE WAS NOTHING. ANY EVIDENCE THAT WALKED IN THERE DISAPPEARED.
WE BUST ONE, THEY CLOSE DOWN, AND A NEW ONE POPS UP ELSEWHERE WITH THE SAME PATTERN OF CROOKED CUSTOMERS.
DELI & GROCERY
DELI & GROC
WE COULD NEVER PIN ANYTHING ON 'EM, SO THE COMMISSIONER TOLD US BACK OFF OR FACE PROFILING CHARGES.
THIS IS THE NEWEST STORE. THERE'S GOTTA BE SOMETHING...

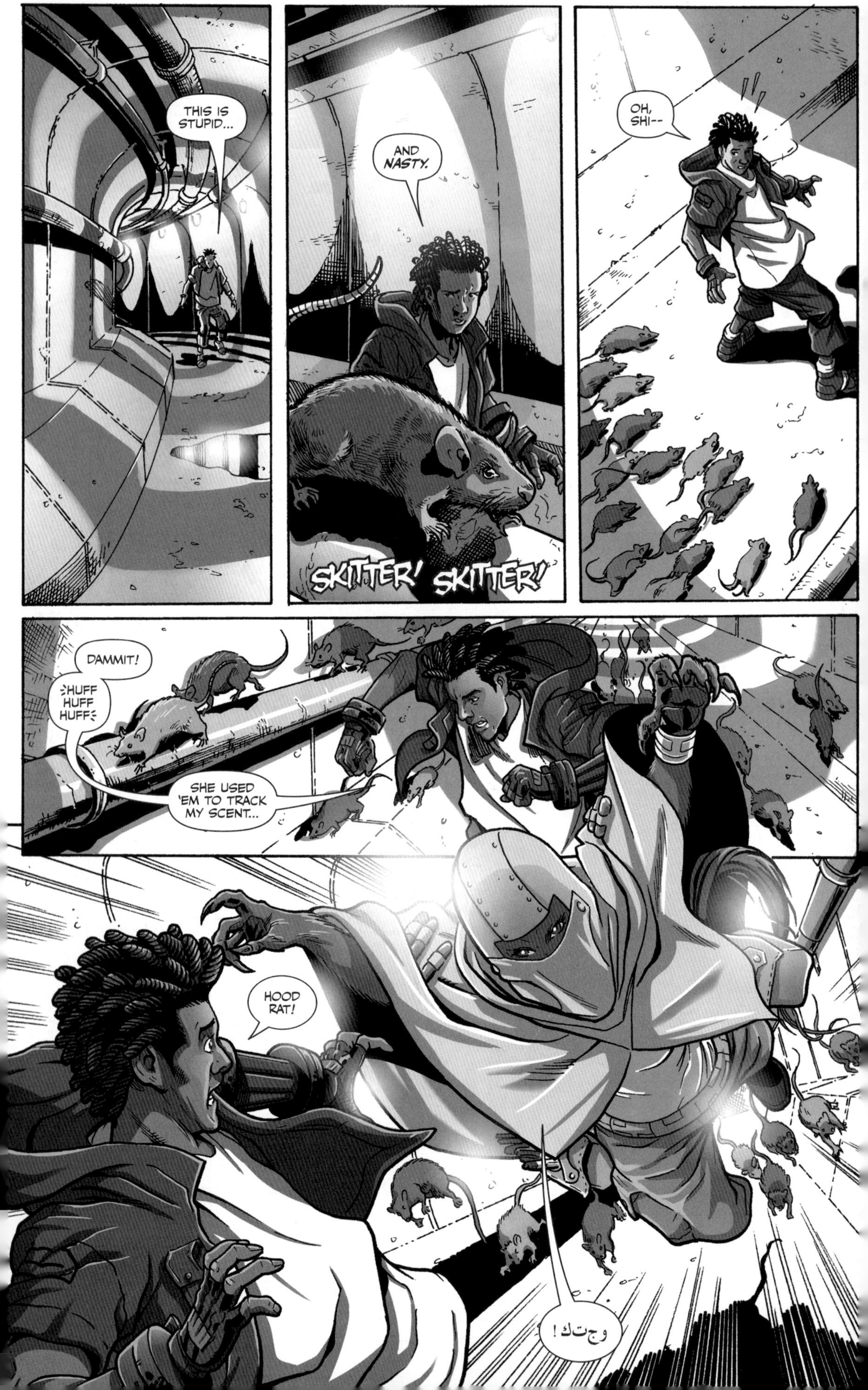
THIS IS STUPID...
AND NASTY.
SKITTER! SKITTER!
OH, SHI--
DAMMIT!
HUFF HUFF HUFF
SHE USED 'EM TO TRACK MY SCENT...
HOOD RAT!
وجتك !

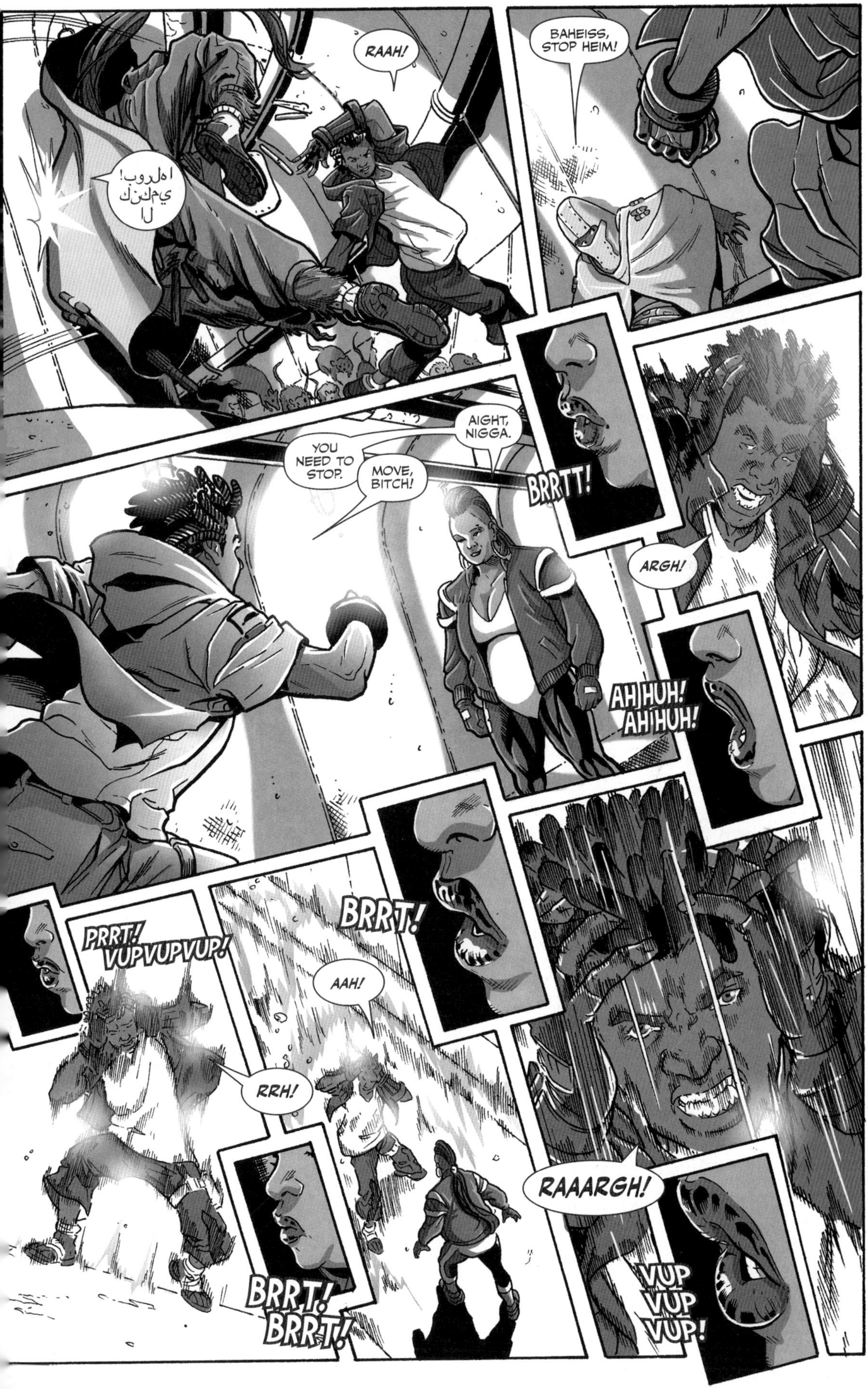
RAAH!
بورلها!
يمكنك
لا
BAHEISS, STOP HEIM!
AIGHT, NIGGA.
YOU NEED TO STOP.
MOVE, BITCH!
BRRTT!
ARGH!
AH HUH! AH HUH!
PRRT! VUPVUPVUP!
BRRT!
AAH!
RRH!
BRRT! BRRT!
RAAARGH!
VUP VUP VUP!

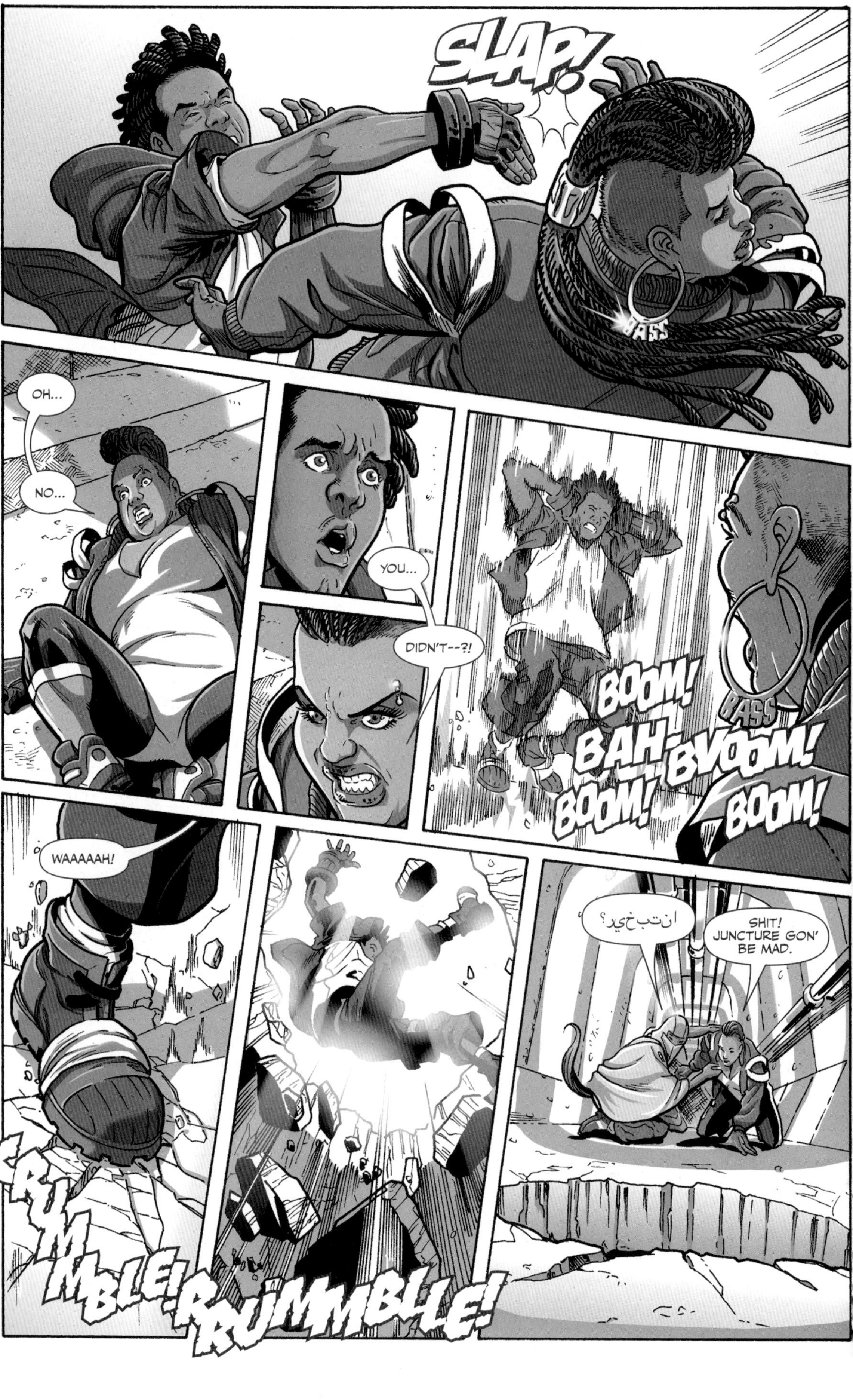
SLAP!
OH...
NO...
YOU...
DIDN'T--?!
BASS
BOOM!
BAH-BOOM!
BVOOM!
BOOM!
WAAAAAH!
CRUMBLE!
RUMMBLLE!
ان تبخير؟
SHIT! JUNCTURE GON' BE MAD.

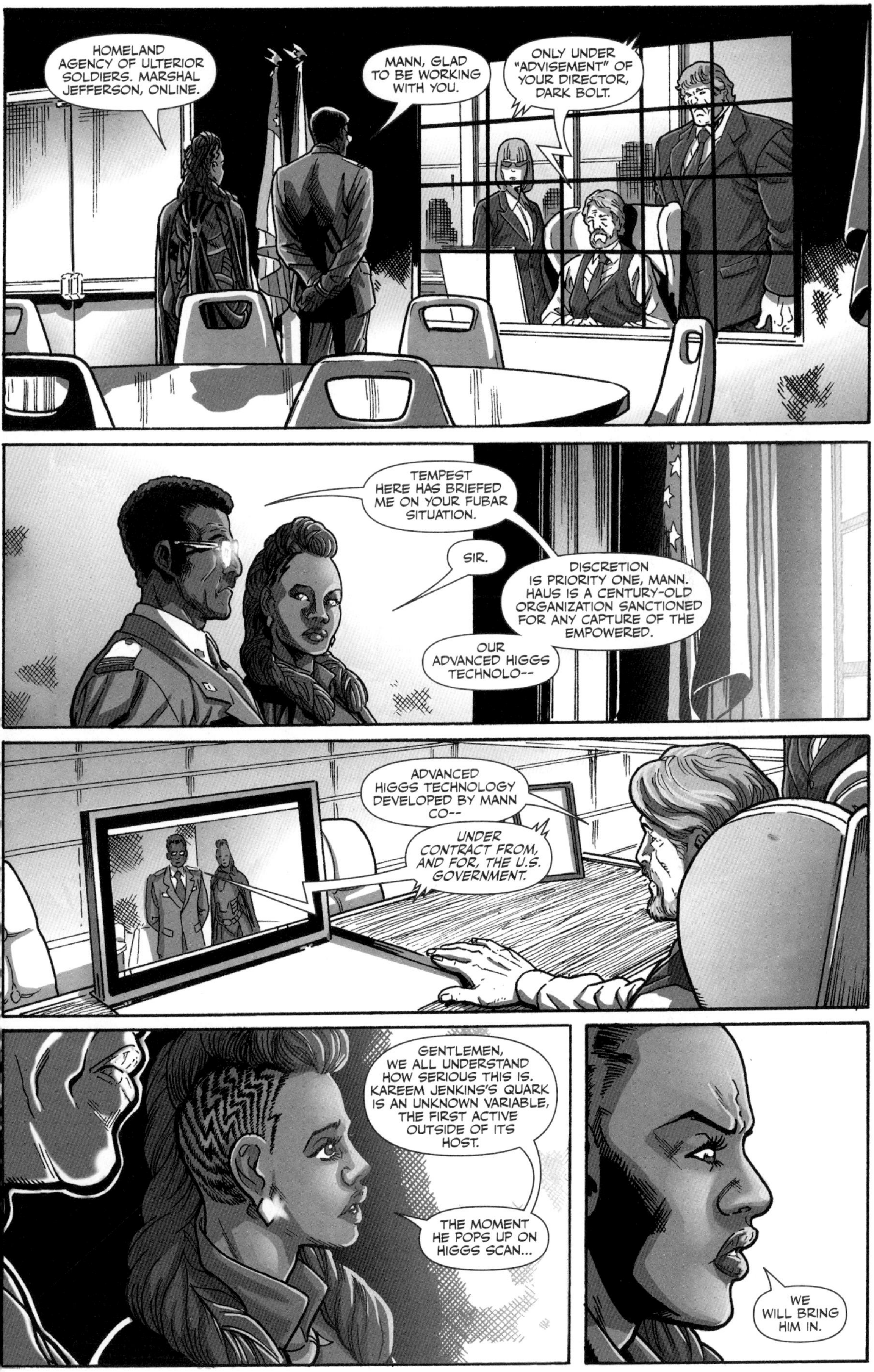
HOMELAND AGENCY OF ULTERIOR SOLDIERS. MARSHAL JEFFERSON, ONLINE.
MANN, GLAD TO BE WORKING WITH YOU.
ONLY UNDER "ADVISEMENT" OF YOUR DIRECTOR, DARK BOLT.
TEMPEST HERE HAS BRIEFED ME ON YOUR FUBAR SITUATION.
SIR.
DISCRETION IS PRIORITY ONE, MANN. HAUS IS A CENTURY-OLD ORGANIZATION SANCTIONED FOR ANY CAPTURE OF THE EMPOWERED.
OUR ADVANCED HIGGS TECHNOLO--
ADVANCED HIGGS TECHNOLOGY DEVELOPED BY MANN CO--
UNDER CONTRACT FROM, AND FOR, THE U.S. GOVERNMENT.
GENTLEMEN, WE ALL UNDERSTAND HOW SERIOUS THIS IS. KAREEM JENKINS'S QUARK IS AN UNKNOWN VARIABLE, THE FIRST ACTIVE OUTSIDE OF ITS HOST.
THE MOMENT HE POPS UP ON HIGGS SCAN...
WE WILL BRING HIM IN.

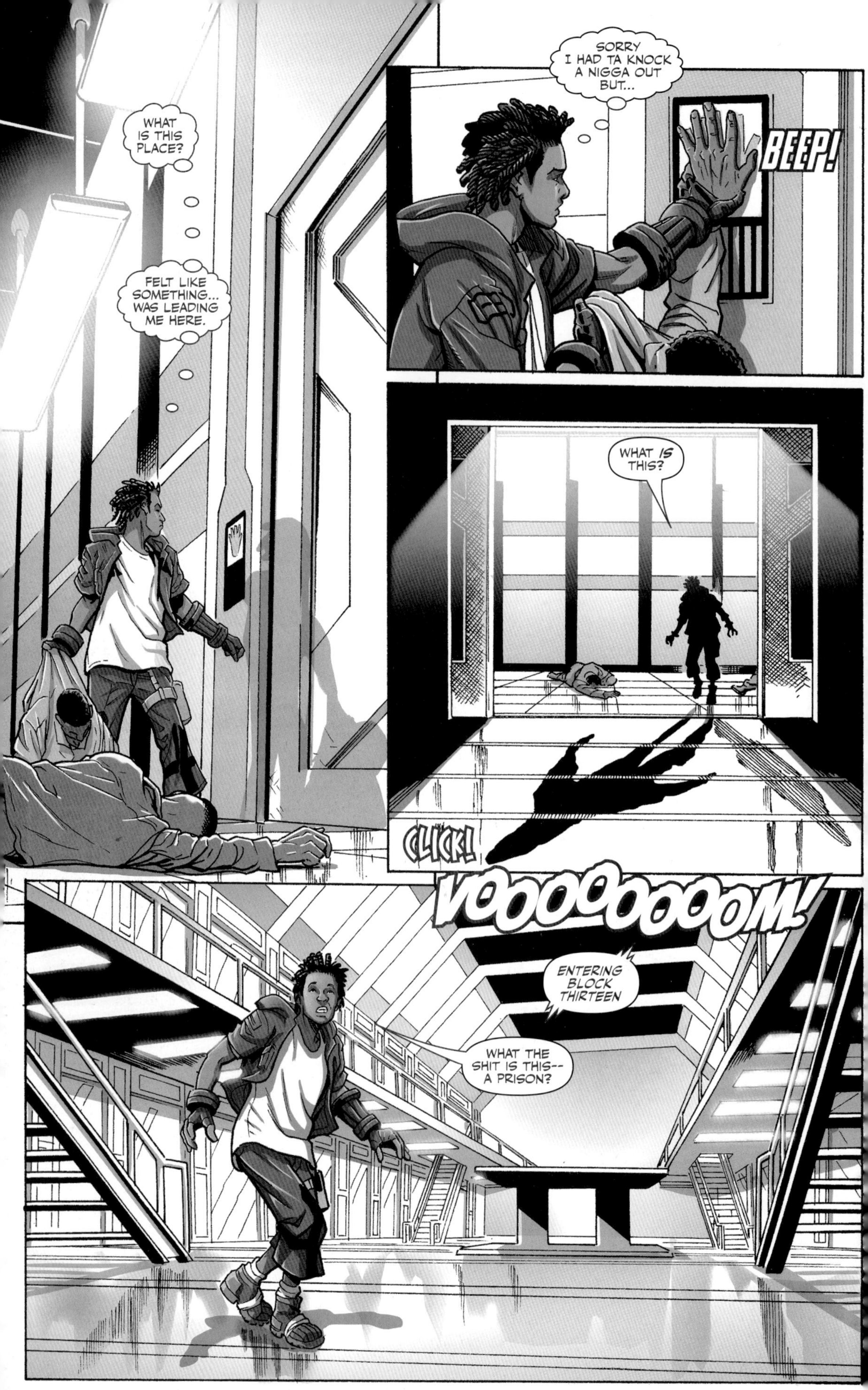
WHAT IS THIS PLACE?
FELT LIKE SOMETHING... WAS LEADING ME HERE.
SORRY I HAD TA KNOCK A NIGGA OUT BUT...
BEEP!
WHAT *IS* THIS?
CLICK!
VOOOOOOOOM!
ENTERING BLOCK THIRTEEN
WHAT THE SHIT IS THIS-- A PRISON?

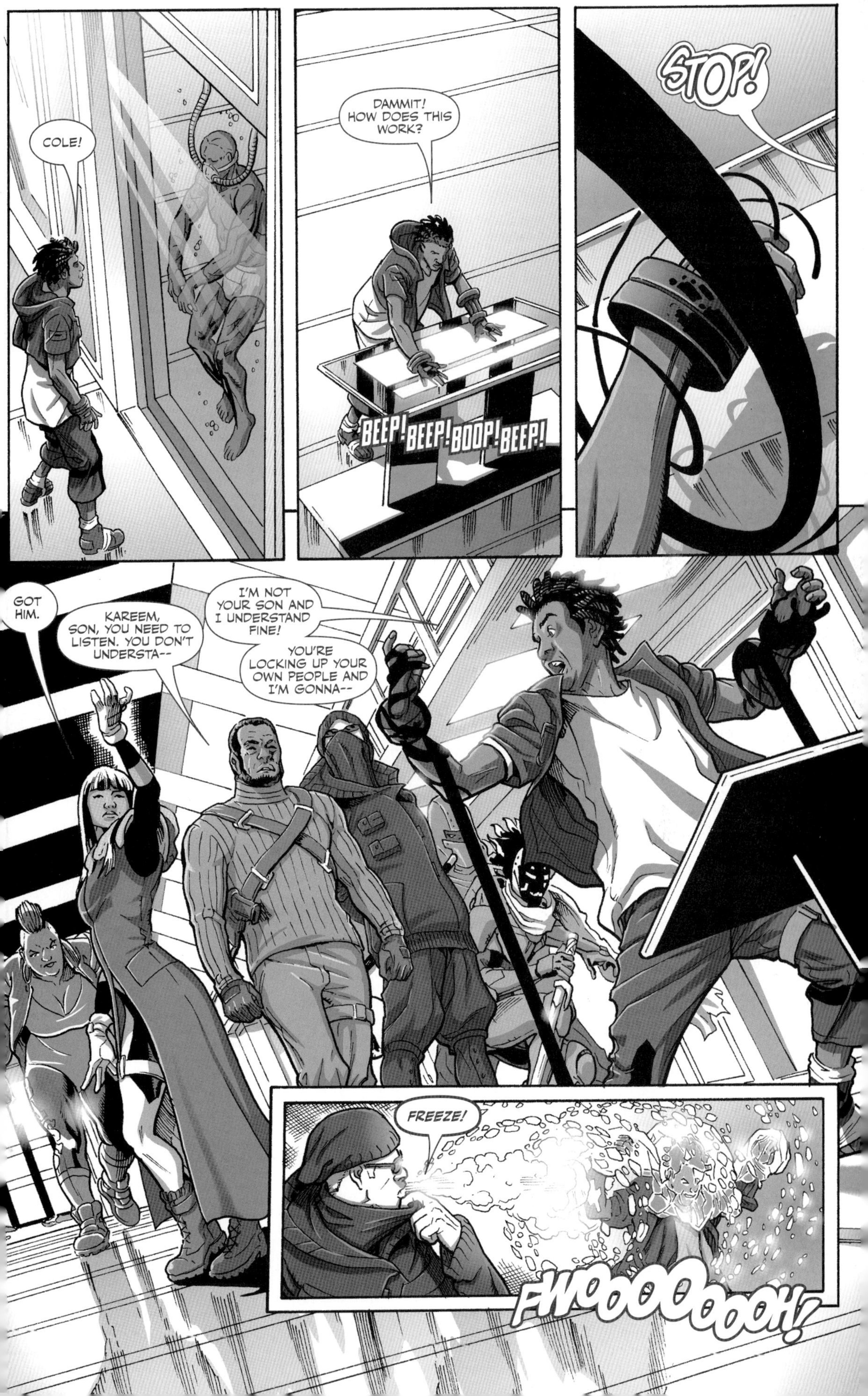
COLE!
DAMMIT! HOW DOES THIS WORK?
BEEP! BEEP! BOOP! BEEP!
STOP!
GOT HIM.
KAREEM, SON, YOU NEED TO LISTEN. YOU DON'T UNDERSTA--
I'M NOT YOUR SON AND I UNDERSTAND FINE!
YOU'RE LOCKING UP YOUR OWN PEOPLE AND I'M GONNA--
FREEZE!
FWOOOOOOOOH!

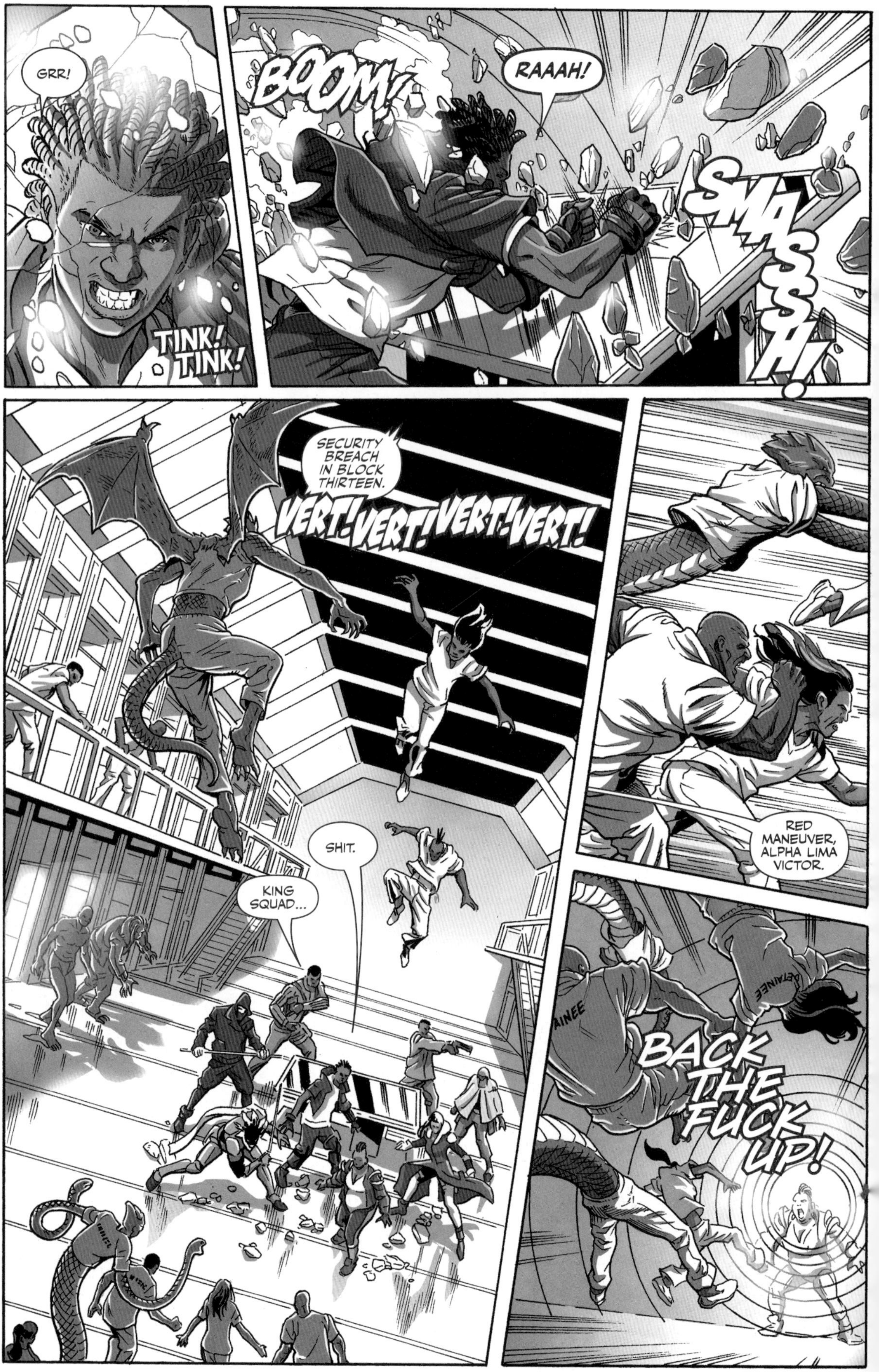
GRR!
TINK! TINK!
BOOM!
RAAAH!
SMASSH!
SECURITY BREACH IN BLOCK THIRTEEN.
VERT! VERT! VERT! VERT!
SHIT.
KING SQUAD...
RED MANEUVER, ALPHA LIMA VICTOR.
BACK THE FUCK UP!

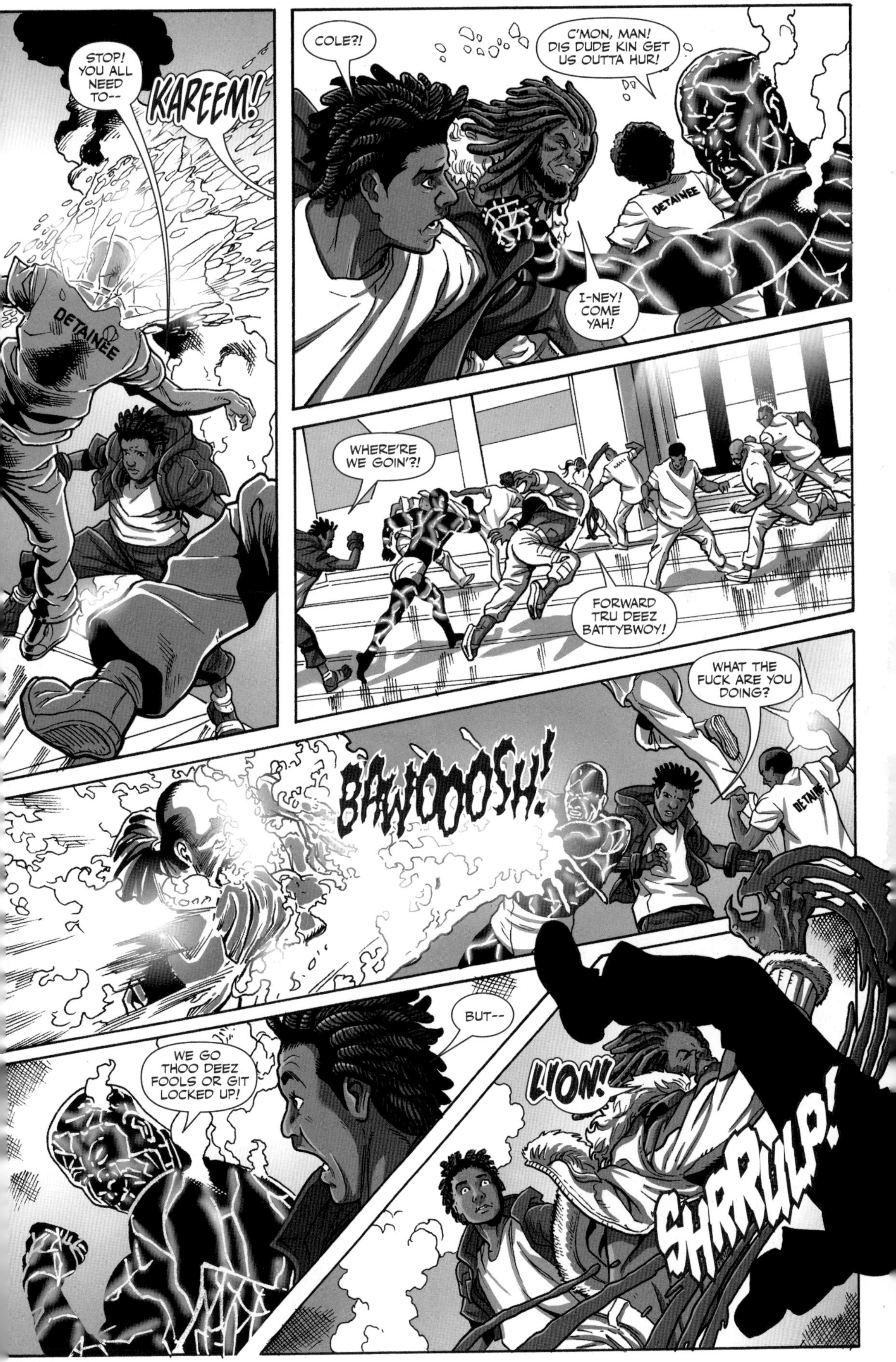
STOP! YOU ALL NEED TO--
KAREEM!
COLE?!
C'MON, MAN! DIS DUDE KIN GET US OUTTA HUR!
I-NEY! COME YAH!
WHERE'RE WE GOIN'?!
FORWARD TRU DEEZ BATTYBWOY!
WHAT THE FUCK ARE YOU DOING?
BAWOOOSH!
BUT--
WE GO THOO DEEZ FOOLS OR GIT LOCKED UP!
LION!
SHRRULP!

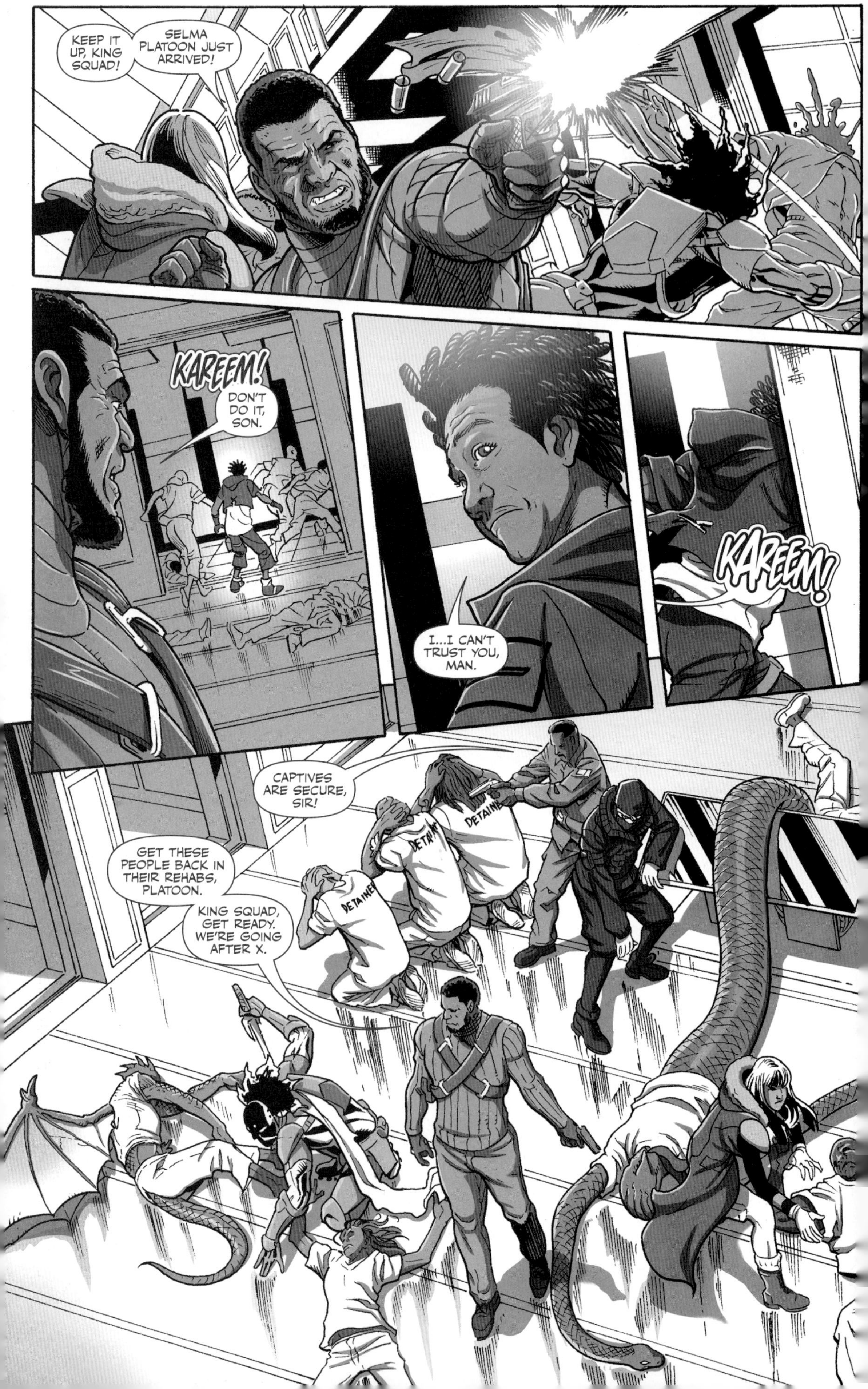
KEEP IT UP, KING SQUAD!
SELMA PLATOON JUST ARRIVED!
KAREEM!
DON'T DO IT, SON.
I...I CAN'T TRUST YOU, MAN.
KAREEM!
CAPTIVES ARE SECURE, SIR!
GET THESE PEOPLE BACK IN THEIR REHABS, PLATOON.
KING SQUAD, GET READY. WE'RE GOING AFTER X.
DETAINEE

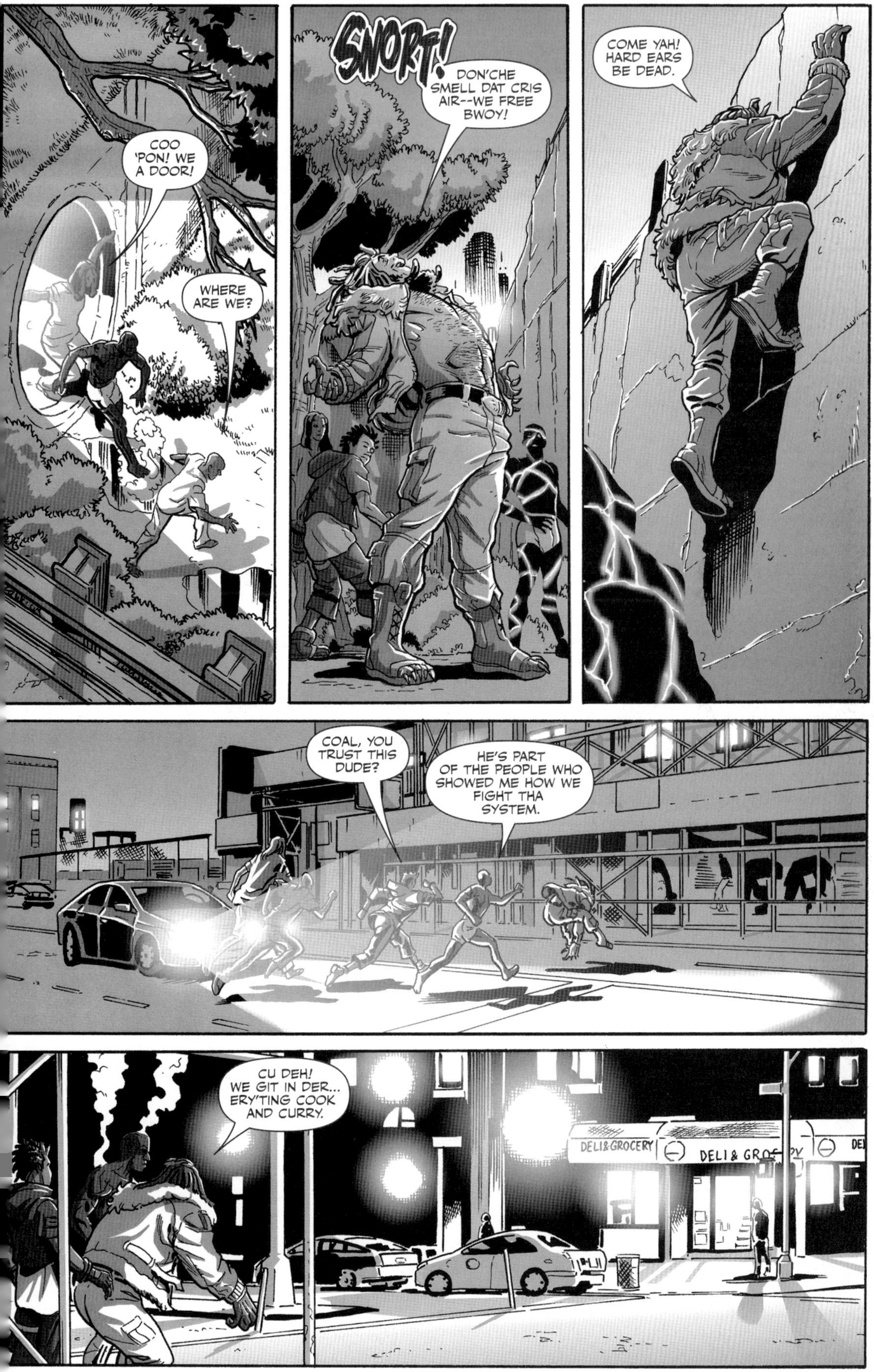
COO 'PON! WE A DOOR!
WHERE ARE WE?
SNORT!
DON'CHE SMELL DAT CRIS AIR--WE FREE BWOY!
COME YAH! HARD EARS BE DEAD.
COAL, YOU TRUST THIS DUDE?
HE'S PART OF THE PEOPLE WHO SHOWED ME HOW WE FIGHT THA SYSTEM.
CU DEH! WE GIT IN DER... ERY'TING COOK AND CURRY.
DELI & GROCERY
DELI & GRO

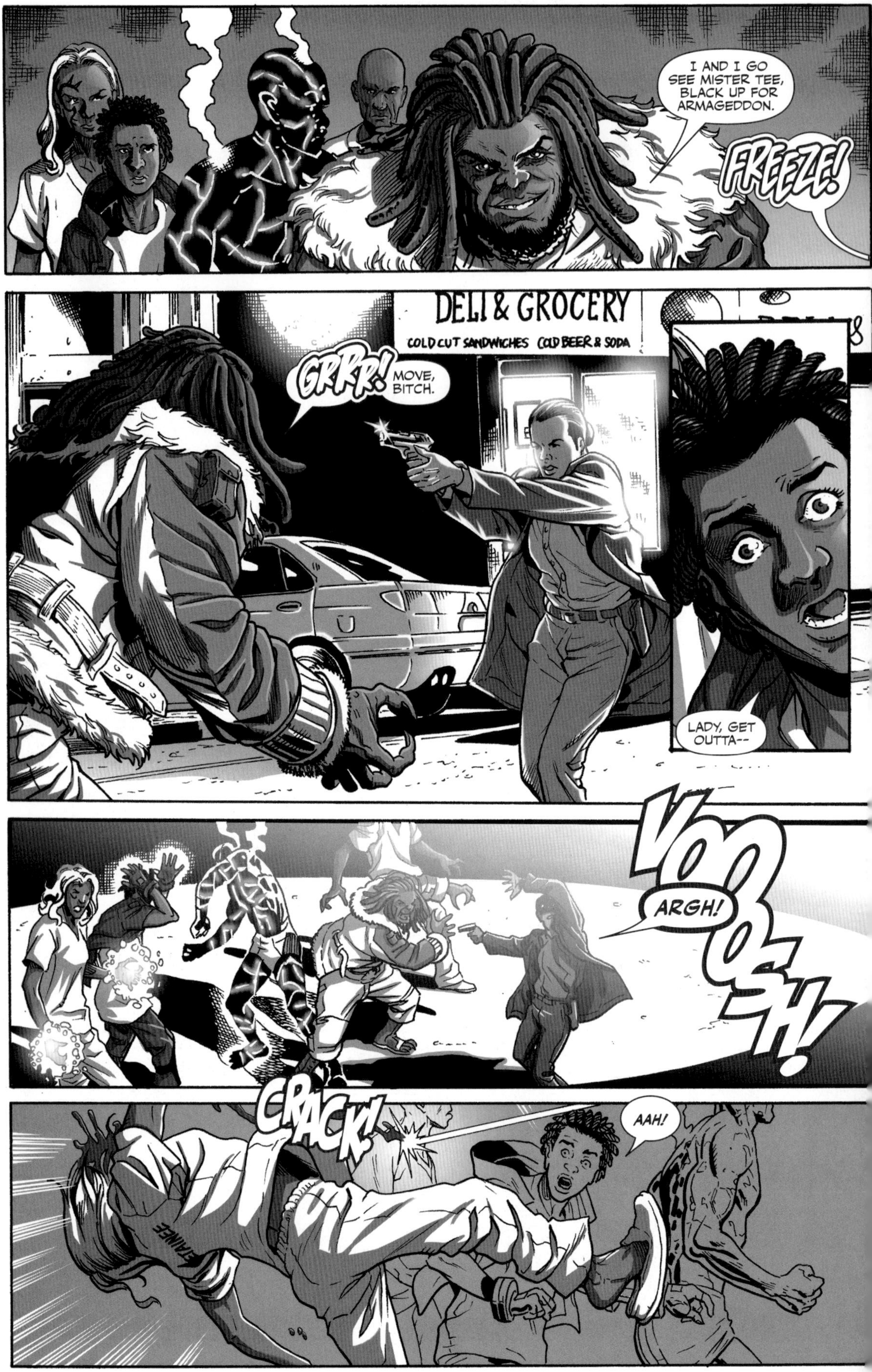
I AND I GO SEE MISTER TEE, BLACK UP FOR ARMAGEDDON.
FREEZE!
DELI & GROCERY
COLD CUT SANDWICHES COLD BEER & SODA
GRRR!
MOVE, BITCH.
LADY, GET OUTTA--
VOOOSH!
ARGH!
CRACK!
AAH!

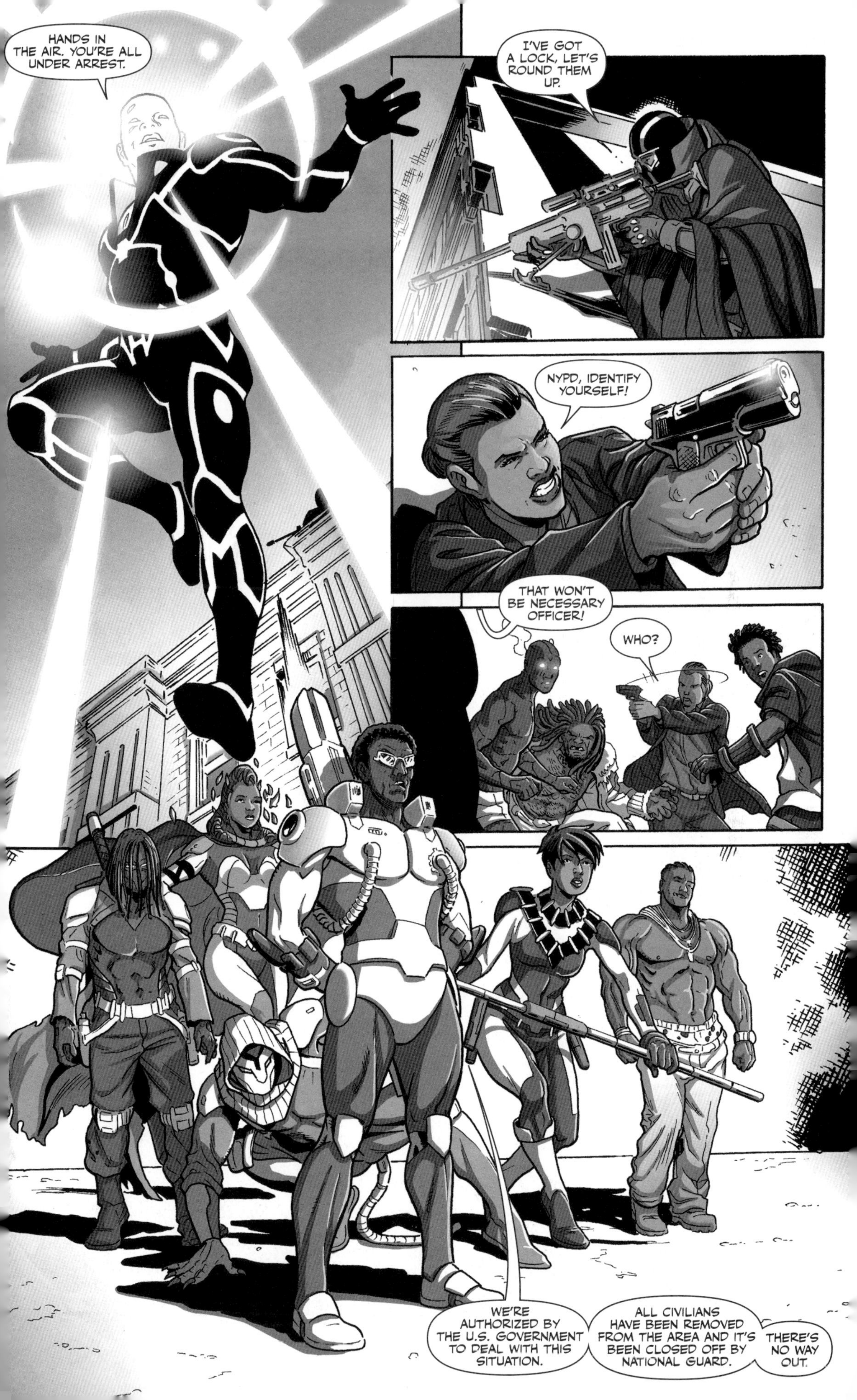
HANDS IN THE AIR. YOU'RE ALL UNDER ARREST.
I'VE GOT A LOCK, LET'S ROUND THEM UP.
NYPD, IDENTIFY YOURSELF!
THAT WON'T BE NECESSARY OFFICER!
WHO?
WE'RE AUTHORIZED BY THE U.S. GOVERNMENT TO DEAL WITH THIS SITUATION.
ALL CIVILIANS HAVE BEEN REMOVED FROM THE AREA AND IT'S BEEN CLOSED OFF BY NATIONAL GUARD.
THERE'S NO WAY OUT.

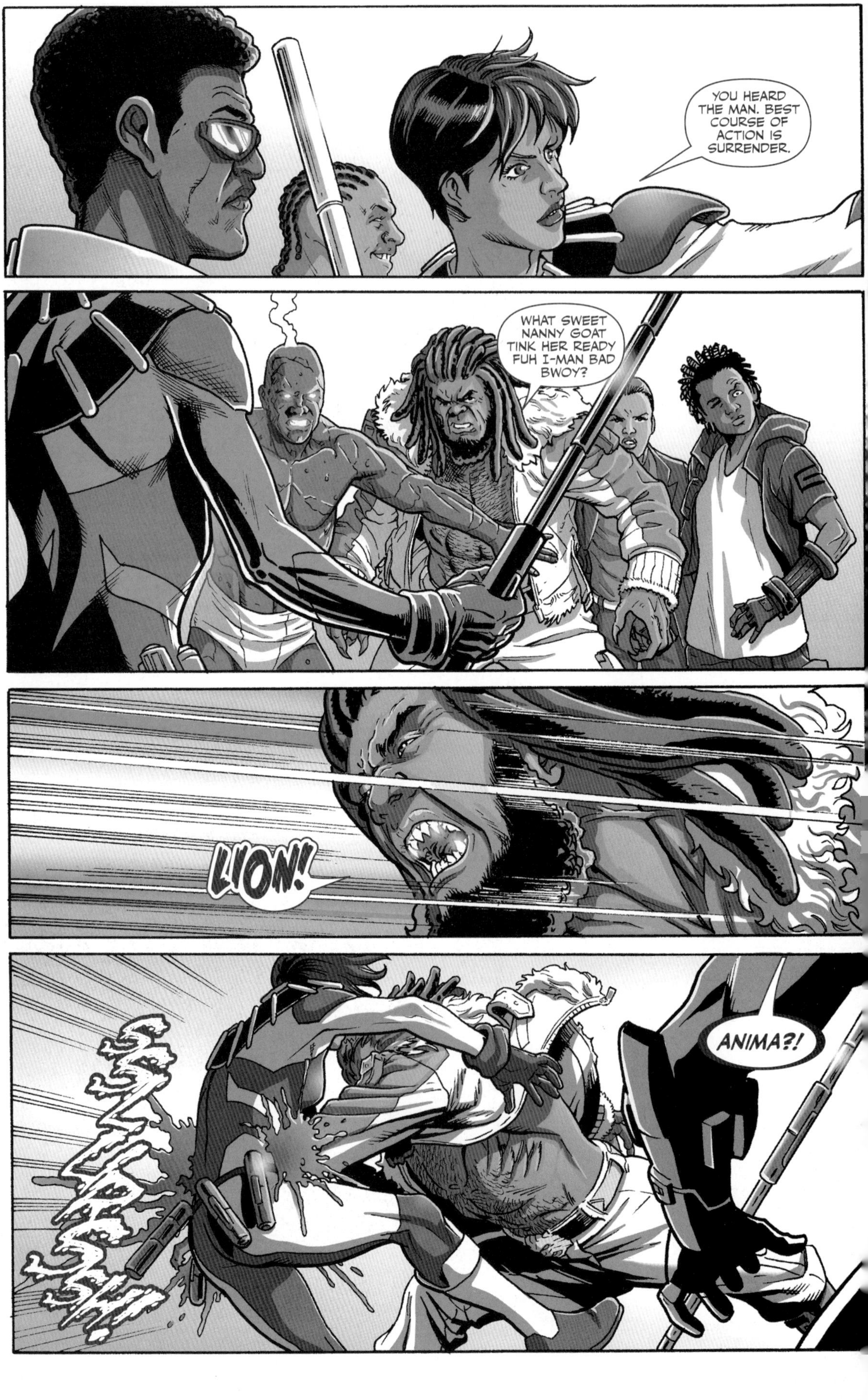
YOU HEARD THE MAN. BEST COURSE OF ACTION IS SURRENDER.
WHAT SWEET NANNY GOAT TINK HER READY FUH I-MAN BAD BWOY?
LION!
ANIMA?!

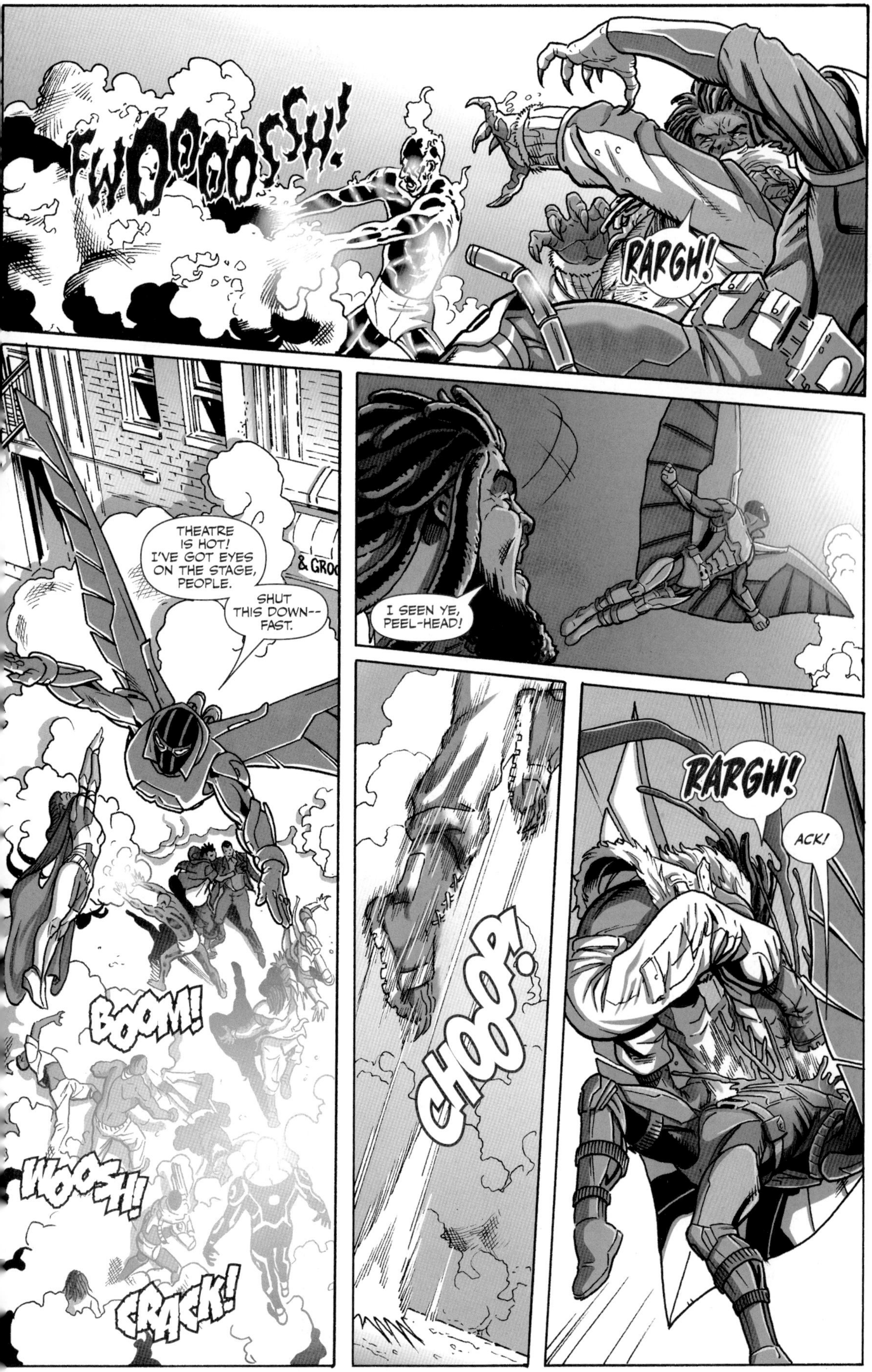
FWOOOOSH!
RARGH!
THEATRE IS HOT! I'VE GOT EYES ON THE STAGE, PEOPLE.
SHUT THIS DOWN--FAST.
& GROC
BOOM!
WOOSH!
CRACK!
I SEEN YE, PEEL-HEAD!
CHOOOP!
RARGH!
ACK!

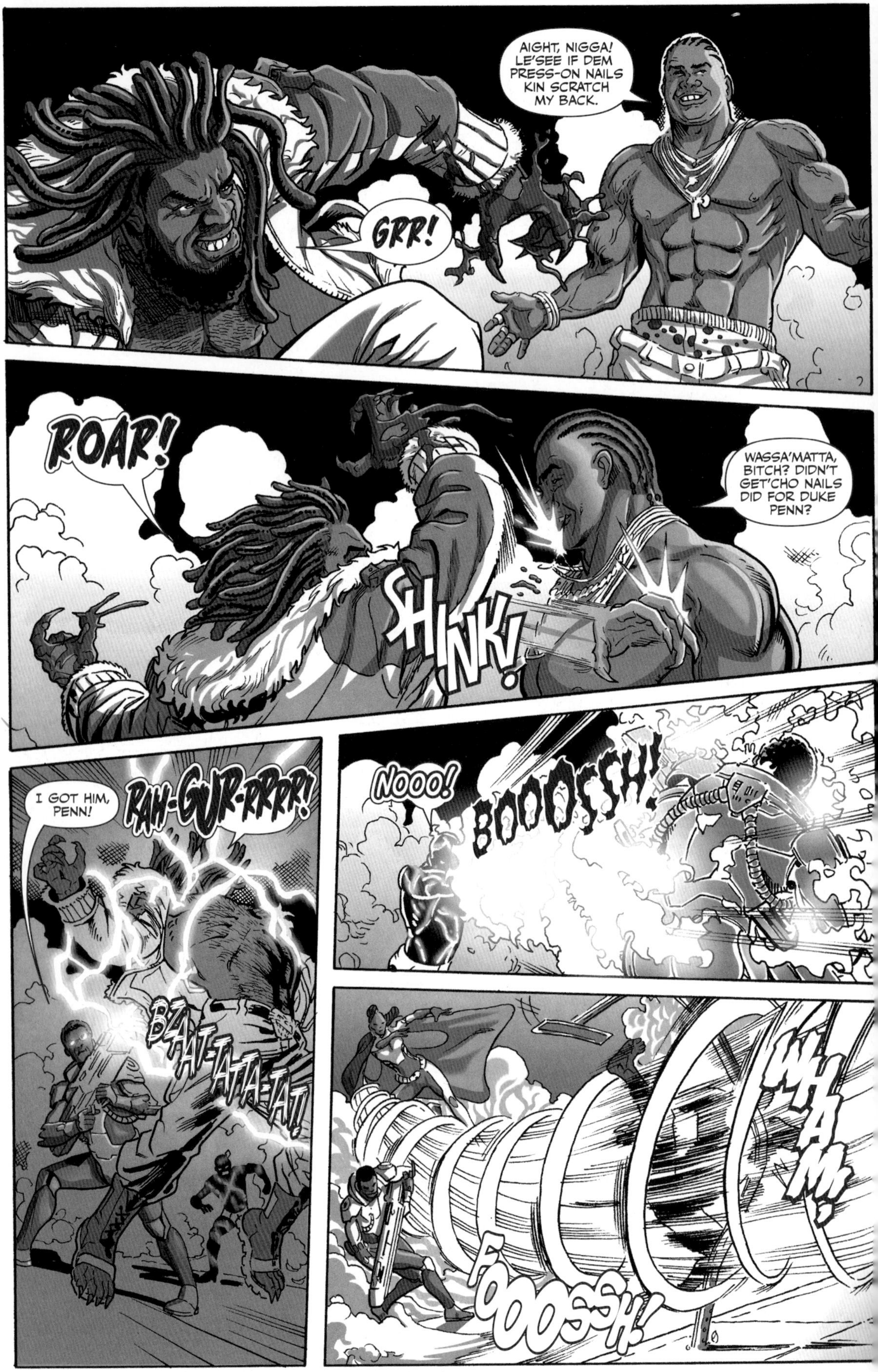
AIGHT, NIGGA! LE'SEE IF DEM PRESS-ON NAILS KIN SCRATCH MY BACK.
GRR!
ROAR!
WASSA'MATTA, BITCH? DIDN'T GET'CHO NAILS DID FOR DUKE PENN?
SHINK!
I GOT HIM, PENN!
RAH-GUR-RRRR!
BZAAT-TATA-TAT!
NOOO!
BOOOSSH!
WHAM!
FOOOSSH!

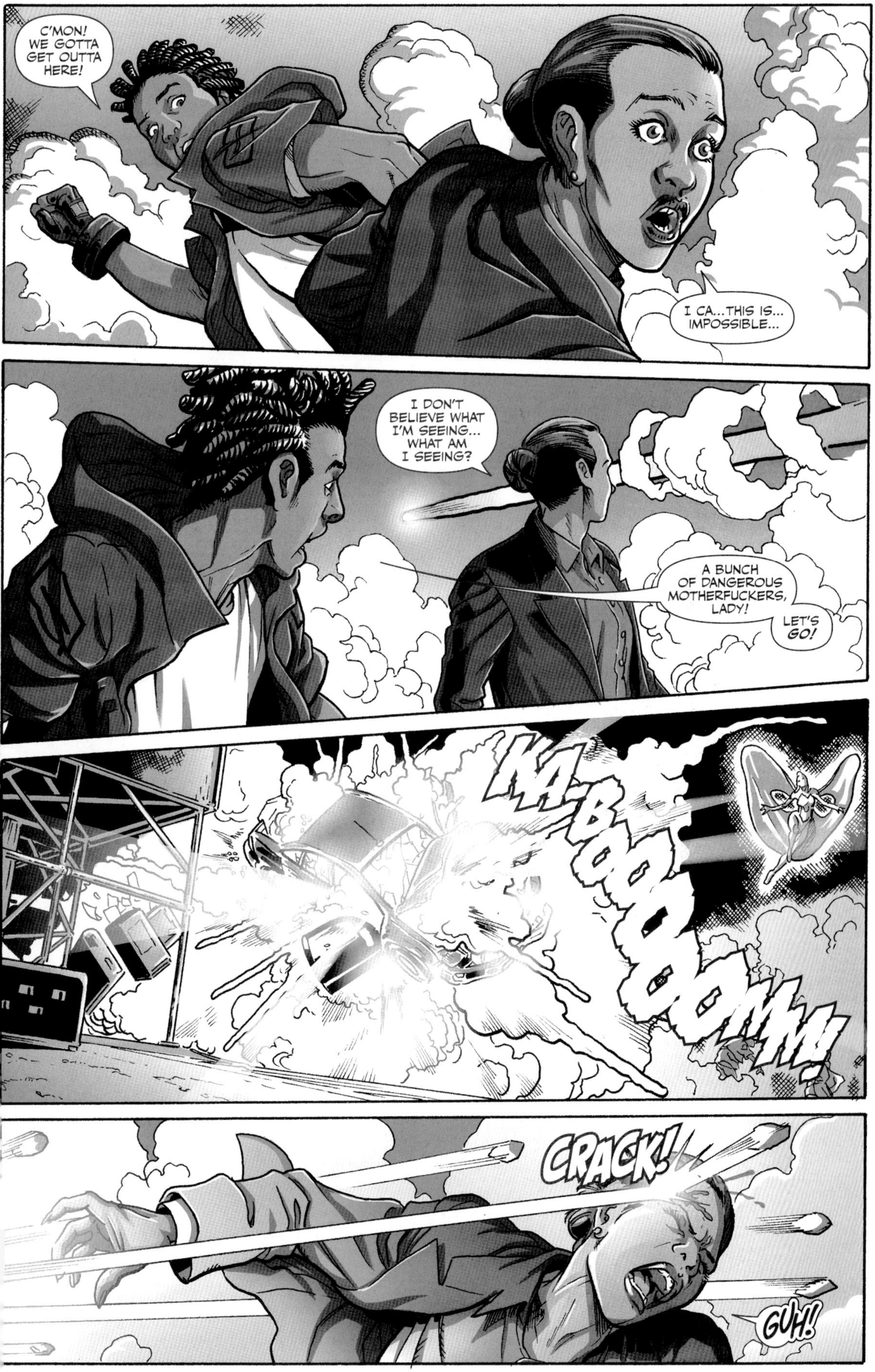
C'MON! WE GOTTA GET OUTTA HERE!
I CA...THIS IS... IMPOSSIBLE...
I DON'T BELIEVE WHAT I'M SEEING... WHAT AM I SEEING?
A BUNCH OF DANGEROUS MOTHERFUCKERS, LADY!
LET'S GO!
KA-BOOOOOOMM!
CRACK!
GUH!

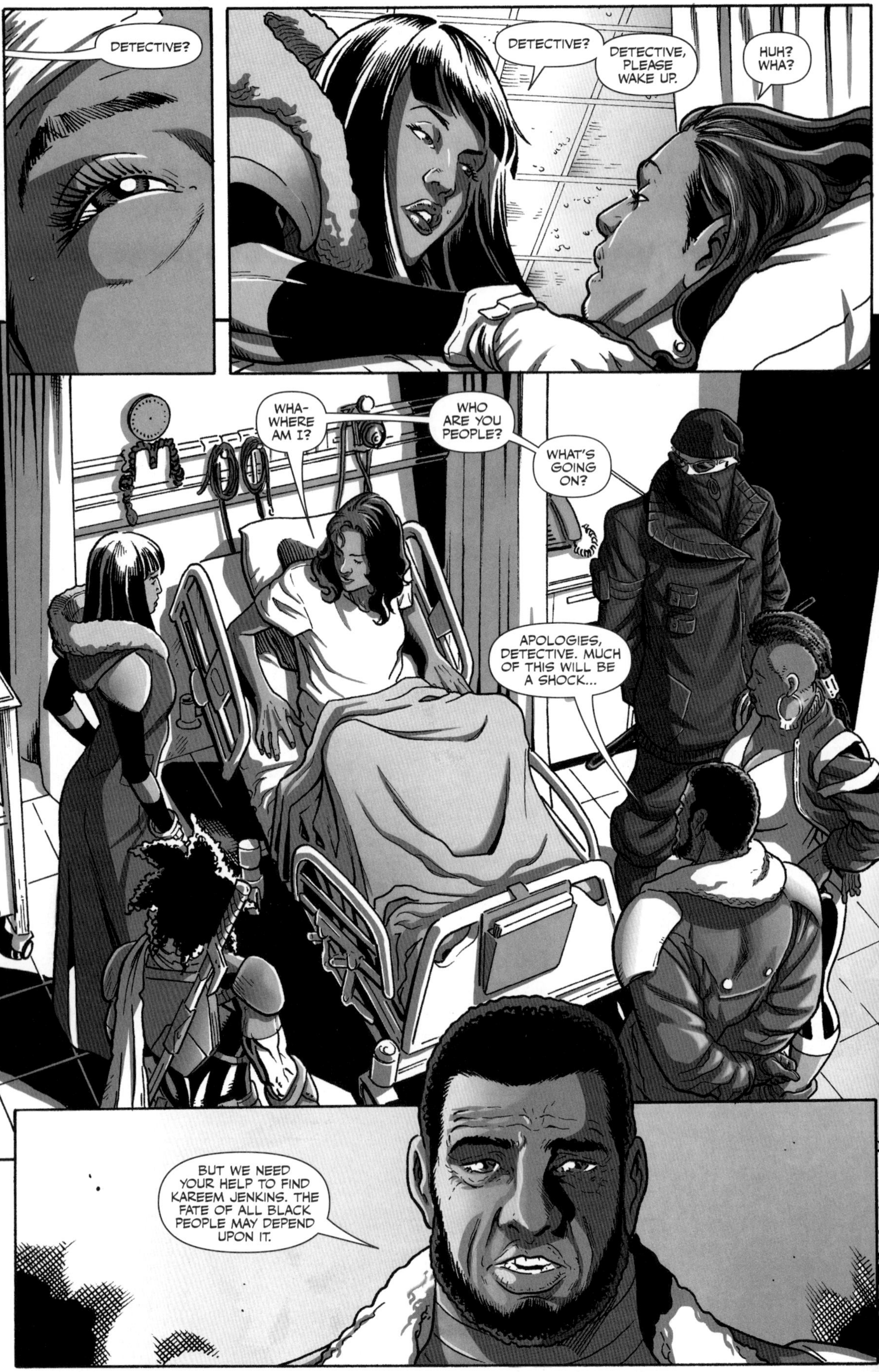
DETECTIVE?
DETECTIVE?
DETECTIVE, PLEASE WAKE UP.
HUH? WHA?
WHA- WHERE AM I?
WHO ARE YOU PEOPLE?
WHAT'S GOING ON?
APOLOGIES, DETECTIVE. MUCH OF THIS WILL BE A SHOCK...
BUT WE NEED YOUR HELP TO FIND KAREEM JENKINS. THE FATE OF ALL BLACK PEOPLE MAY DEPEND UPON IT.

CHAPTER FIVE

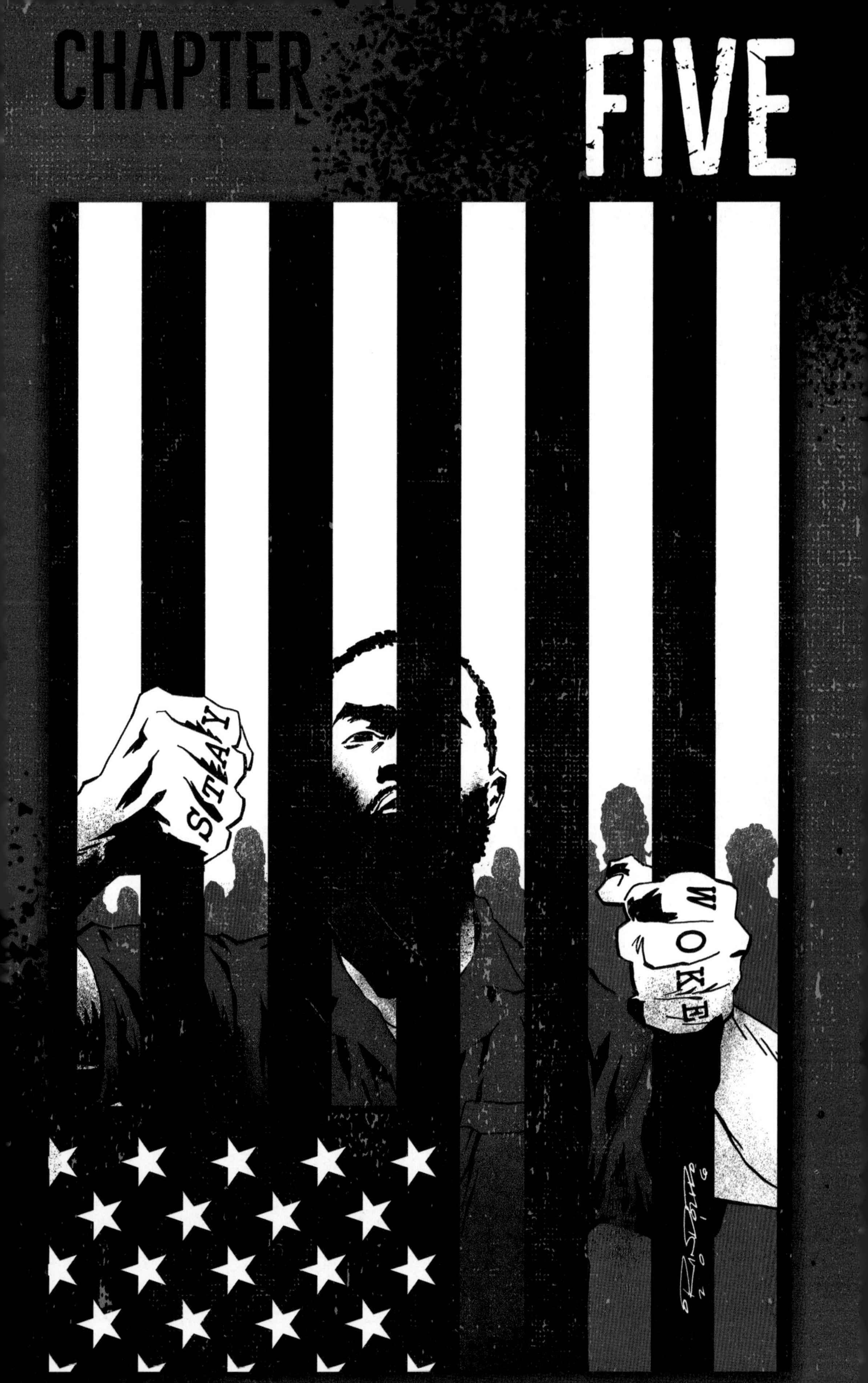
STAY
WOKE

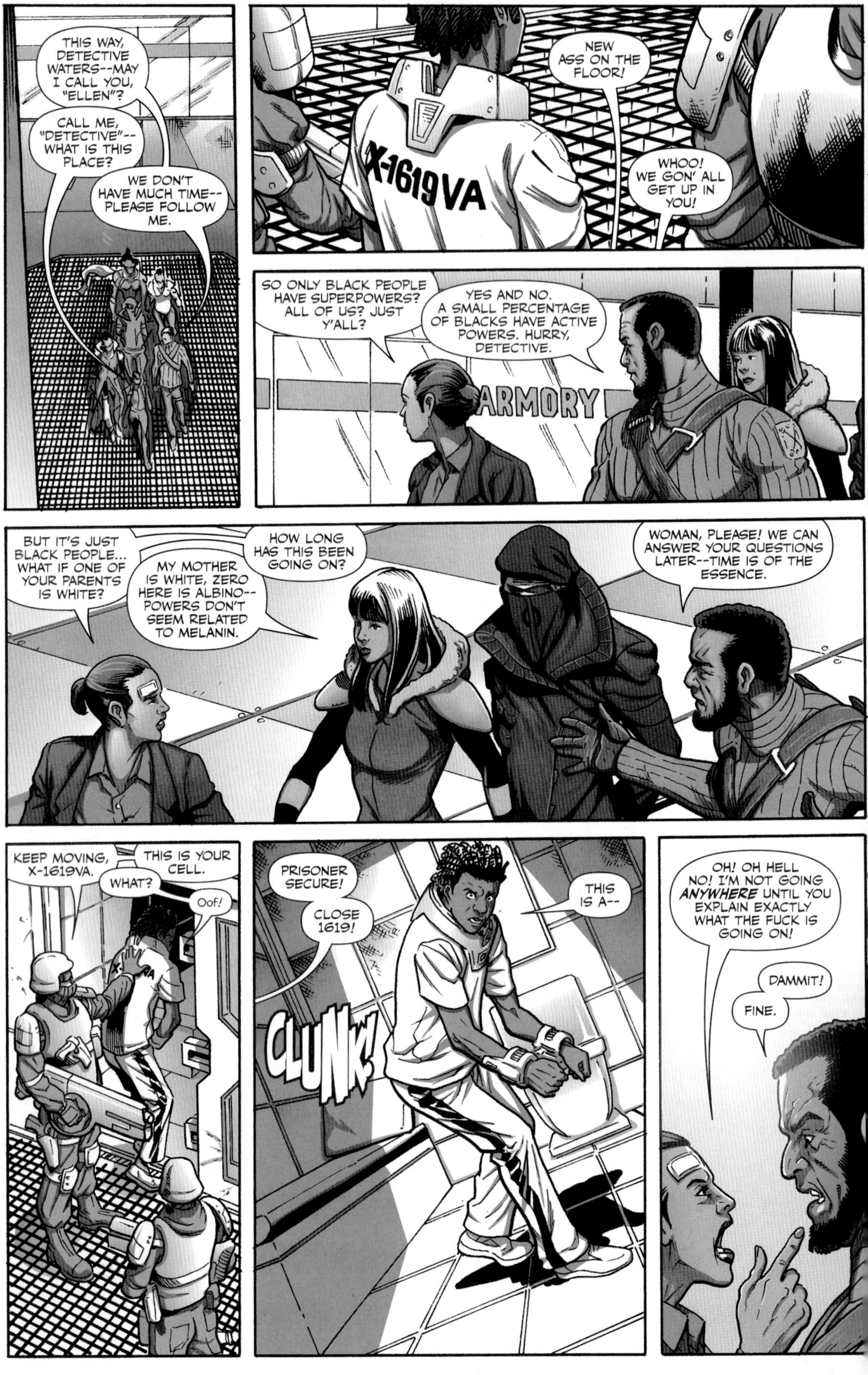
THIS WAY, DETECTIVE WATERS--MAY I CALL YOU, "ELLEN"?
CALL ME, "DETECTIVE"-- WHAT IS THIS PLACE?
WE DON'T HAVE MUCH TIME-- PLEASE FOLLOW ME.
X-1619VA
NEW ASS ON THE FLOOR!
WHOO! WE GON' ALL GET UP IN YOU!
SO ONLY BLACK PEOPLE HAVE SUPERPOWERS? ALL OF US? JUST Y'ALL?
YES AND NO. A SMALL PERCENTAGE OF BLACKS HAVE ACTIVE POWERS. HURRY, DETECTIVE.
ARMORY
BUT IT'S JUST BLACK PEOPLE... WHAT IF ONE OF YOUR PARENTS IS WHITE?
MY MOTHER IS WHITE, ZERO HERE IS ALBINO-- POWERS DON'T SEEM RELATED TO MELANIN.
HOW LONG HAS THIS BEEN GOING ON?
WOMAN, PLEASE! WE CAN ANSWER YOUR QUESTIONS LATER--TIME IS OF THE ESSENCE.
KEEP MOVING, X-1619VA.
THIS IS YOUR CELL.
WHAT?
Oof!
PRISONER SECURE!
CLOSE 1619!
THIS IS A--
CLUNK!
OH! OH HELL NO! I'M NOT GOING ANYWHERE UNTIL YOU EXPLAIN EXACTLY WHAT THE FUCK IS GOING ON!
DAMMIT!
FINE.

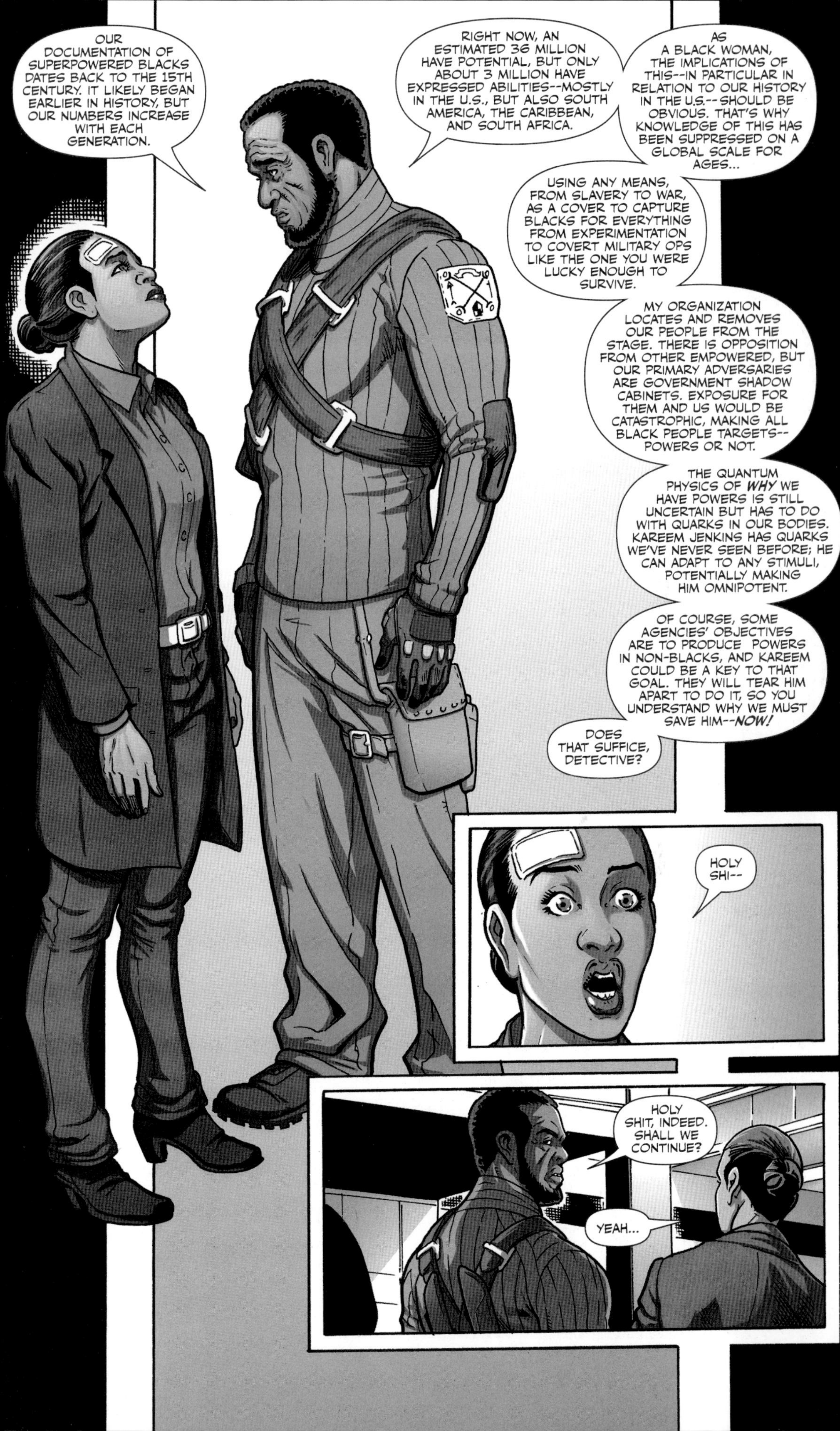
OUR DOCUMENTATION OF SUPERPOWERED BLACKS DATES BACK TO THE 15TH CENTURY. IT LIKELY BEGAN EARLIER IN HISTORY, BUT OUR NUMBERS INCREASE WITH EACH GENERATION.
RIGHT NOW, AN ESTIMATED 36 MILLION HAVE POTENTIAL, BUT ONLY ABOUT 3 MILLION HAVE EXPRESSED ABILITIES--MOSTLY IN THE U.S., BUT ALSO SOUTH AMERICA, THE CARIBBEAN, AND SOUTH AFRICA.
AS A BLACK WOMAN, THE IMPLICATIONS OF THIS--IN PARTICULAR IN RELATION TO OUR HISTORY IN THE U.S.--SHOULD BE OBVIOUS. THAT'S WHY KNOWLEDGE OF THIS HAS BEEN SUPPRESSED ON A GLOBAL SCALE FOR AGES...
USING ANY MEANS, FROM SLAVERY TO WAR, AS A COVER TO CAPTURE BLACKS FOR EVERYTHING FROM EXPERIMENTATION TO COVERT MILITARY OPS LIKE THE ONE YOU WERE LUCKY ENOUGH TO SURVIVE.
MY ORGANIZATION LOCATES AND REMOVES OUR PEOPLE FROM THE STAGE. THERE IS OPPOSITION FROM OTHER EMPOWERED, BUT OUR PRIMARY ADVERSARIES ARE GOVERNMENT SHADOW CABINETS. EXPOSURE FOR THEM AND US WOULD BE CATASTROPHIC, MAKING ALL BLACK PEOPLE TARGETS--POWERS OR NOT.
THE QUANTUM PHYSICS OF *WHY* WE HAVE POWERS IS STILL UNCERTAIN BUT HAS TO DO WITH QUARKS IN OUR BODIES. KAREEM JENKINS HAS QUARKS WE'VE NEVER SEEN BEFORE; HE CAN ADAPT TO ANY STIMULI, POTENTIALLY MAKING HIM OMNIPOTENT.
OF COURSE, SOME AGENCIES' OBJECTIVES ARE TO PRODUCE POWERS IN NON-BLACKS, AND KAREEM COULD BE A KEY TO THAT GOAL. THEY WILL TEAR HIM APART TO DO IT, SO YOU UNDERSTAND WHY WE MUST SAVE HIM--*NOW!*
DOES THAT SUFFICE, DETECTIVE?
HOLY SHI--
HOLY SHIT, INDEED. SHALL WE CONTINUE?
YEAH...

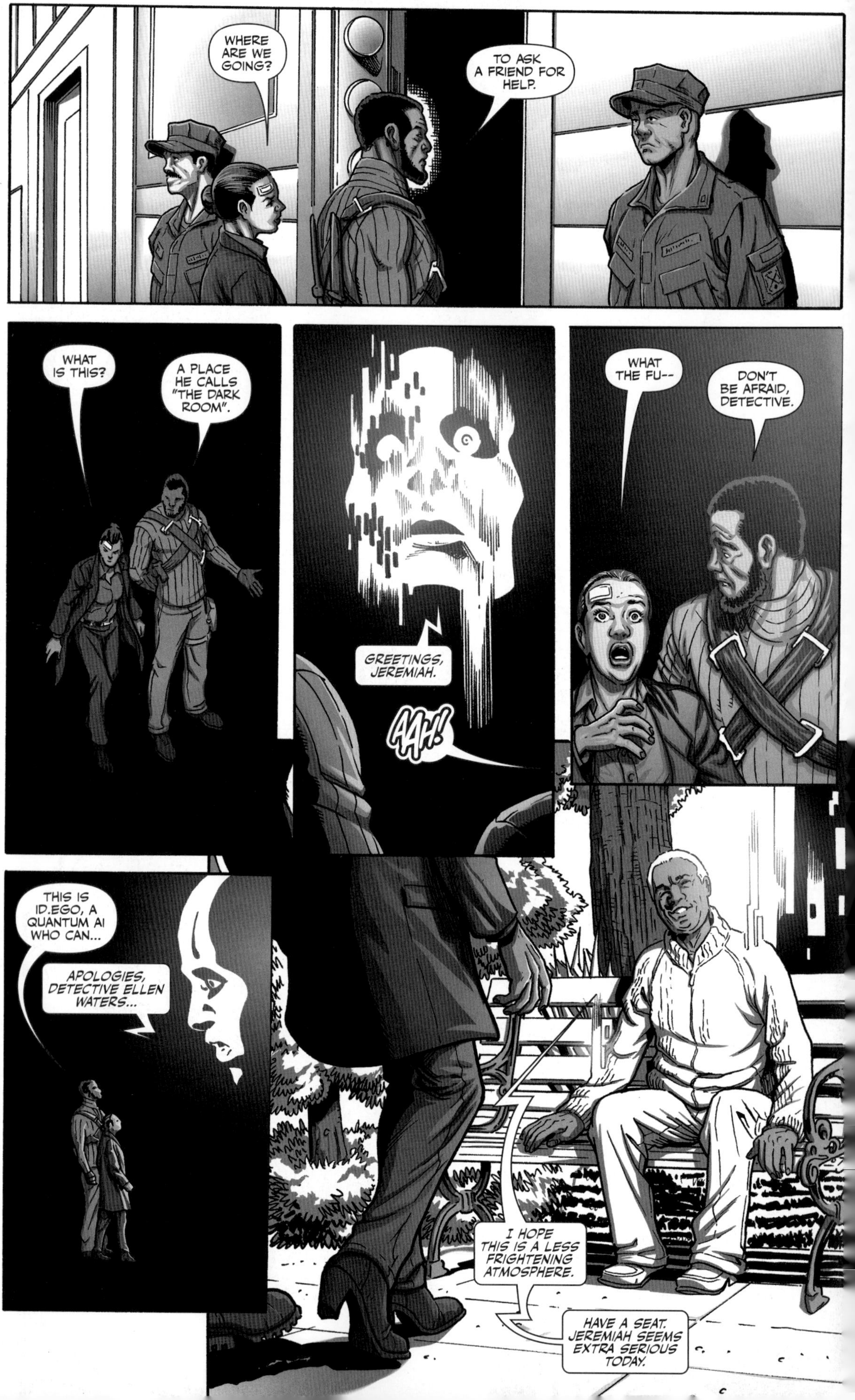

WHERE ARE WE GOING?
TO ASK A FRIEND FOR HELP.
WHAT IS THIS?
A PLACE HE CALLS "THE DARK ROOM".
GREETINGS, JEREMIAH.
AAH!
WHAT THE FU--
DON'T BE AFRAID, DETECTIVE.
THIS IS ID.EGO, A QUANTUM AI WHO CAN...
APOLOGIES, DETECTIVE ELLEN WATERS...
I HOPE THIS IS A LESS FRIGHTENING ATMOSPHERE.
HAVE A SEAT. JEREMIAH SEEMS EXTRA SERIOUS TODAY.

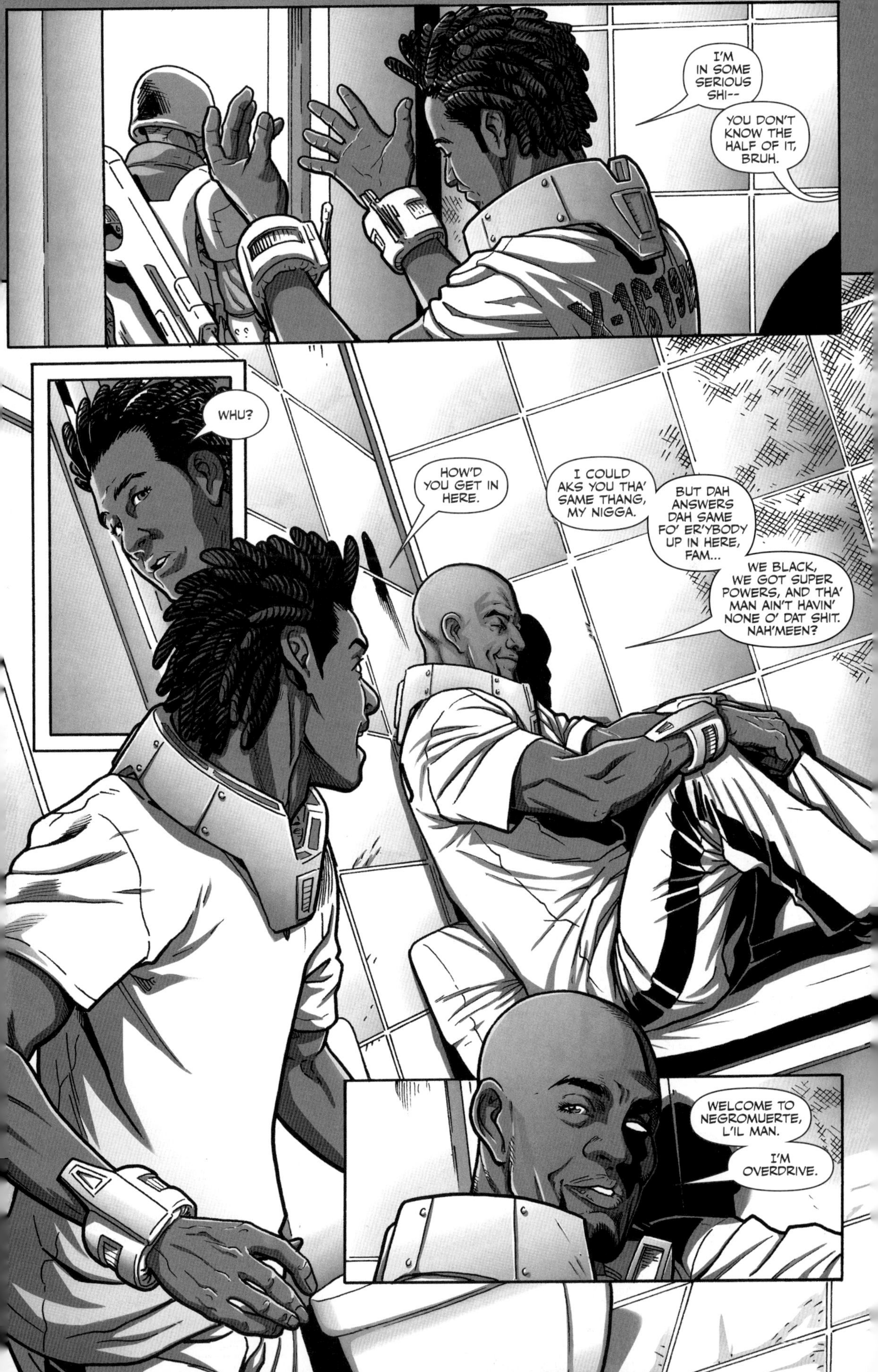
I'M IN SOME SERIOUS SHI--
YOU DON'T KNOW THE HALF OF IT, BRUH.
WHU?
HOW'D YOU GET IN HERE.
I COULD AKS YOU THA' SAME THANG, MY NIGGA.
BUT DAH ANSWERS DAH SAME FO' ER'YBODY UP IN HERE, FAM...
WE BLACK, WE GOT SUPER POWERS, AND THA' MAN AIN'T HAVIN' NONE O' DAT SHIT. NAH'MEEN?
WELCOME TO NEGROMUERTE, L'IL MAN.
I'M OVERDRIVE.

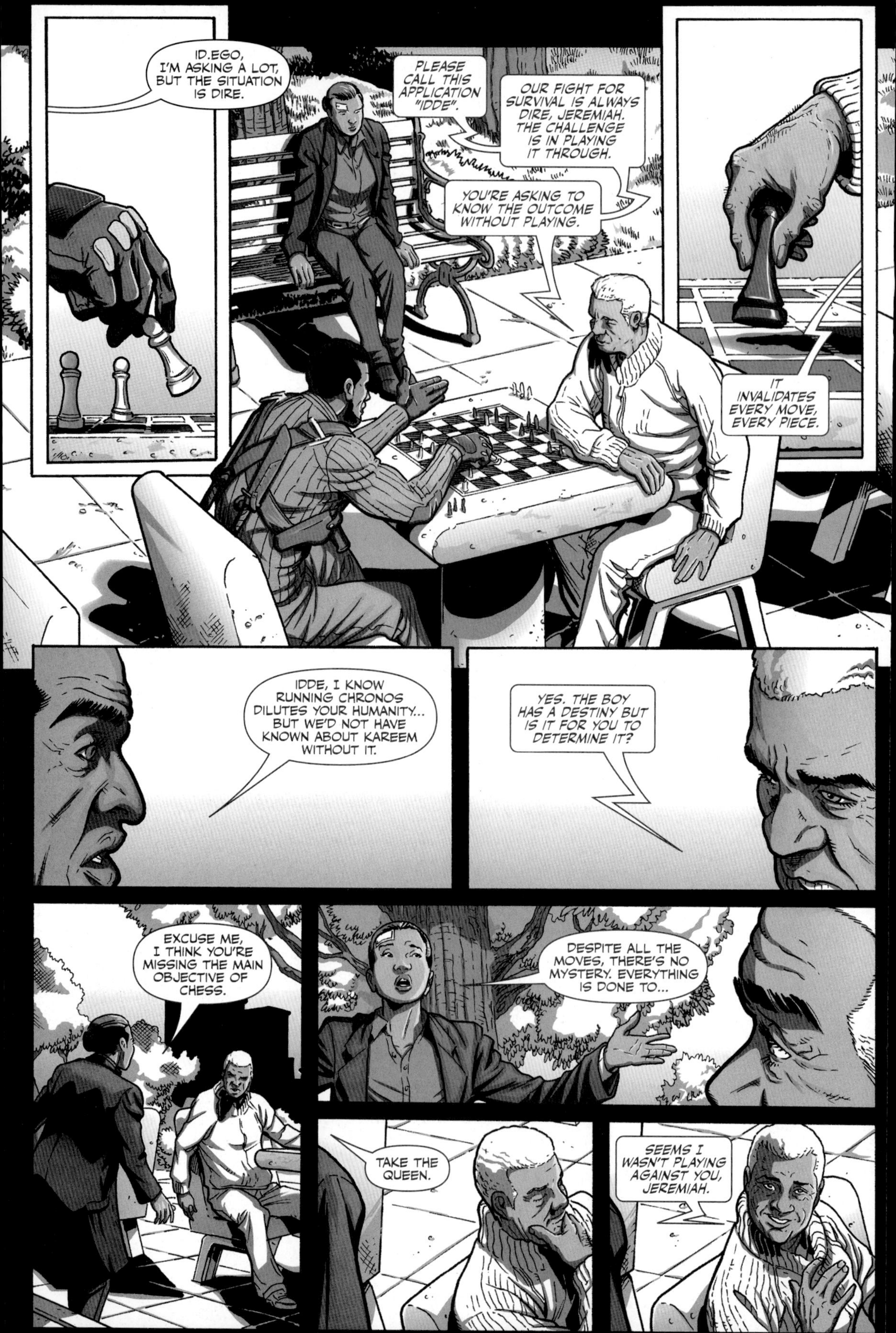
ID.EGO, I'M ASKING A LOT, BUT THE SITUATION IS DIRE.
PLEASE CALL THIS APPLICATION "IDDE".
OUR FIGHT FOR SURVIVAL IS ALWAYS DIRE, JEREMIAH. THE CHALLENGE IS IN PLAYING IT THROUGH.
YOU'RE ASKING TO KNOW THE OUTCOME WITHOUT PLAYING.
IT INVALIDATES EVERY MOVE, EVERY PIECE.
IDDE, I KNOW RUNNING CHRONOS DILUTES YOUR HUMANITY... BUT WE'D NOT HAVE KNOWN ABOUT KAREEM WITHOUT IT.
YES. THE BOY HAS A DESTINY BUT IS IT FOR YOU TO DETERMINE IT?
EXCUSE ME, I THINK YOU'RE MISSING THE MAIN OBJECTIVE OF CHESS.
DESPITE ALL THE MOVES, THERE'S NO MYSTERY. EVERYTHING IS DONE TO...
TAKE THE QUEEN.
SEEMS I WASN'T PLAYING AGAINST YOU, JEREMIAH.

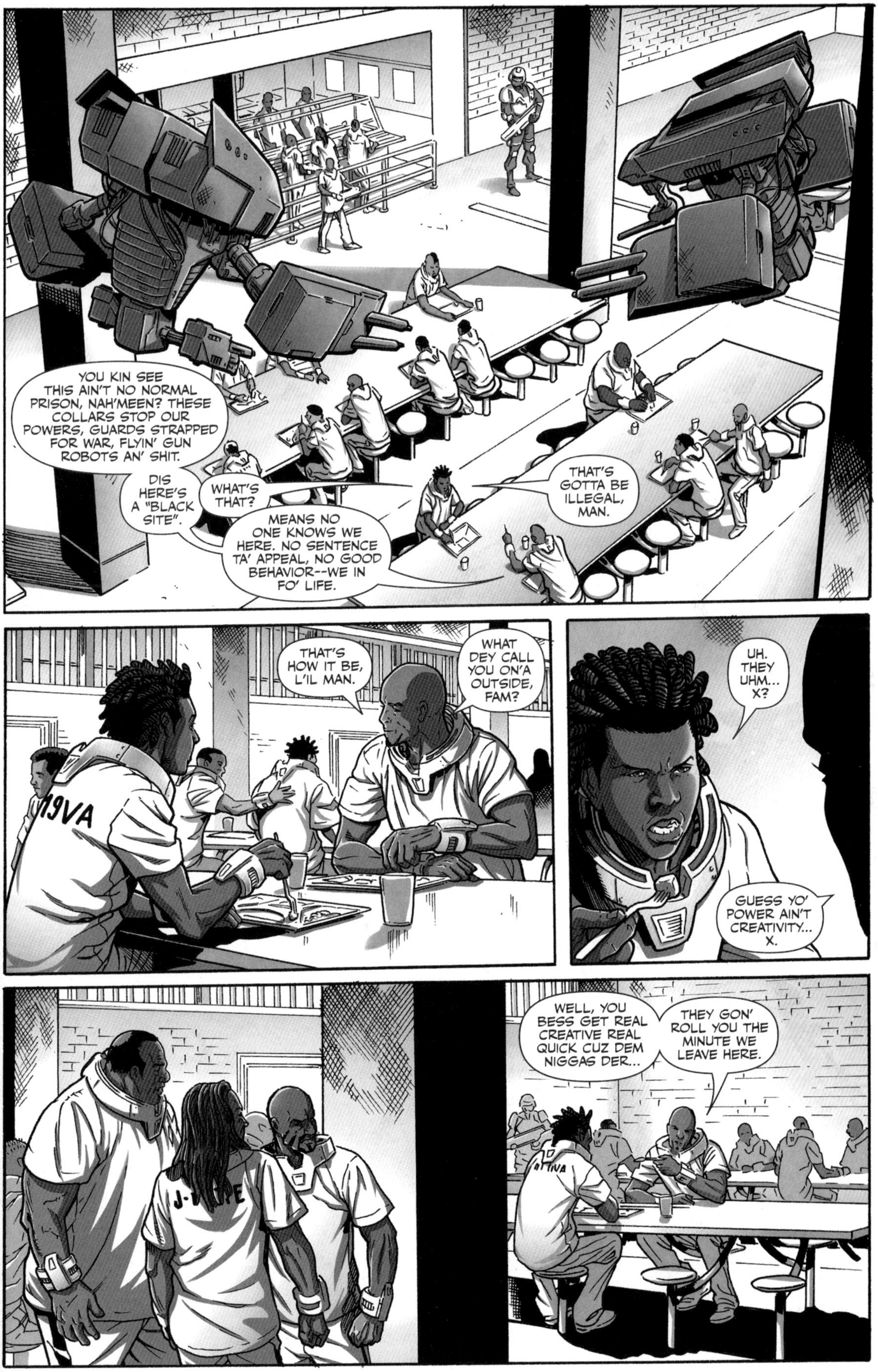
YOU KIN SEE THIS AIN'T NO NORMAL PRISON, NAH'MEEN? THESE COLLARS STOP OUR POWERS, GUARDS STRAPPED FOR WAR, FLYIN' GUN ROBOTS AN' SHIT.
THAT'S GOTTA BE ILLEGAL, MAN.
DIS HERE'S A "BLACK SITE".
WHAT'S THAT?
MEANS NO ONE KNOWS WE HERE. NO SENTENCE TA' APPEAL, NO GOOD BEHAVIOR--WE IN FO' LIFE.
19VA
THAT'S HOW IT BE, L'IL MAN.
WHAT DEY CALL YOU ON'A OUTSIDE, FAM?
UH. THEY UHM... X?
GUESS YO' POWER AIN'T CREATIVITY... X.
WELL, YOU BESS GET REAL CREATIVE REAL QUICK CUZ DEM NIGGAS DER...
THEY GON' ROLL YOU THE MINUTE WE LEAVE HERE.

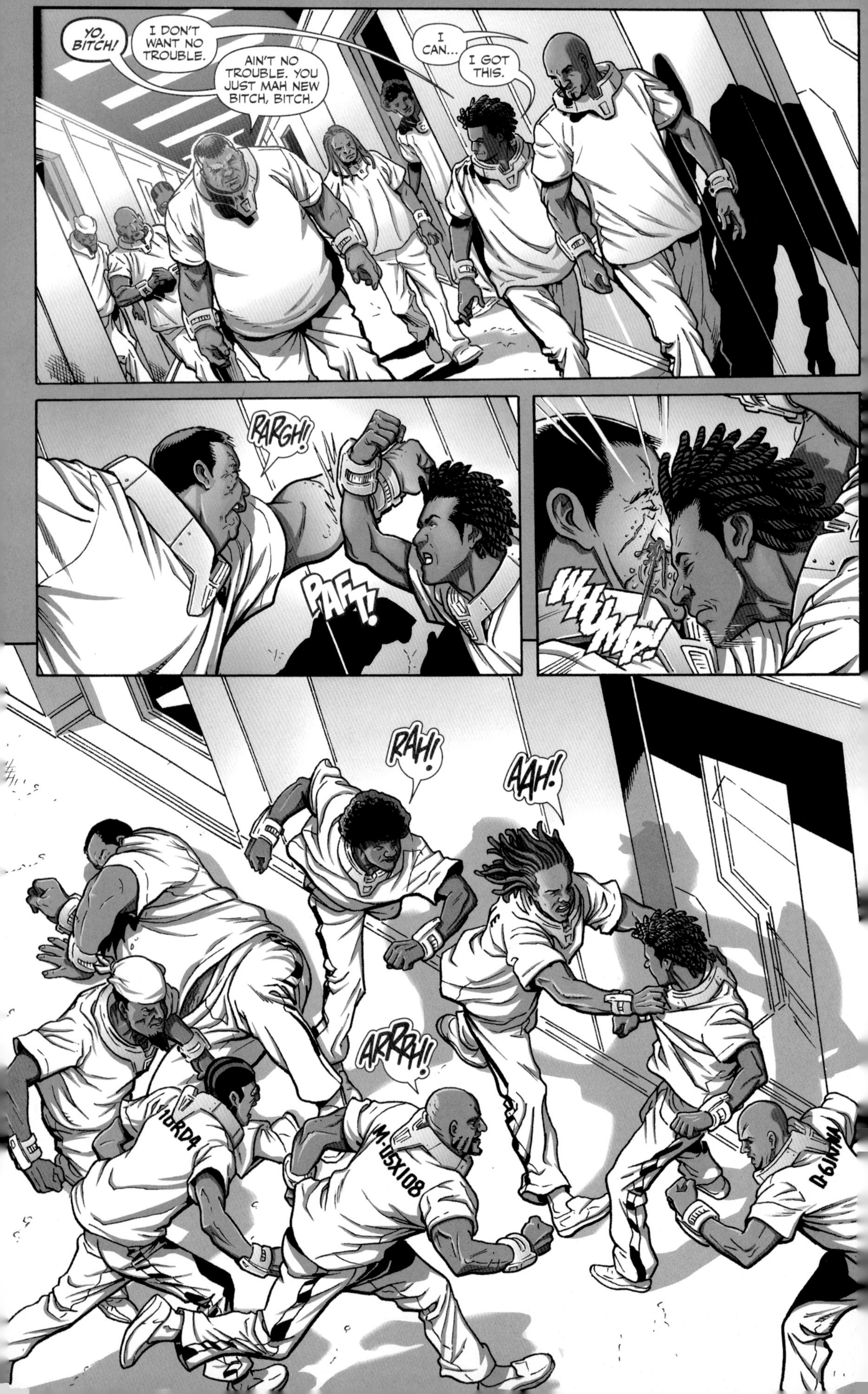
YO, BITCH!
I DON'T WANT NO TROUBLE.
AIN'T NO TROUBLE. YOU JUST MAH NEW BITCH, BITCH.
I CAN...
I GOT THIS.
RARGH!
PAFF!
WHUMP!
RAH!
AAH!
ARRRH!

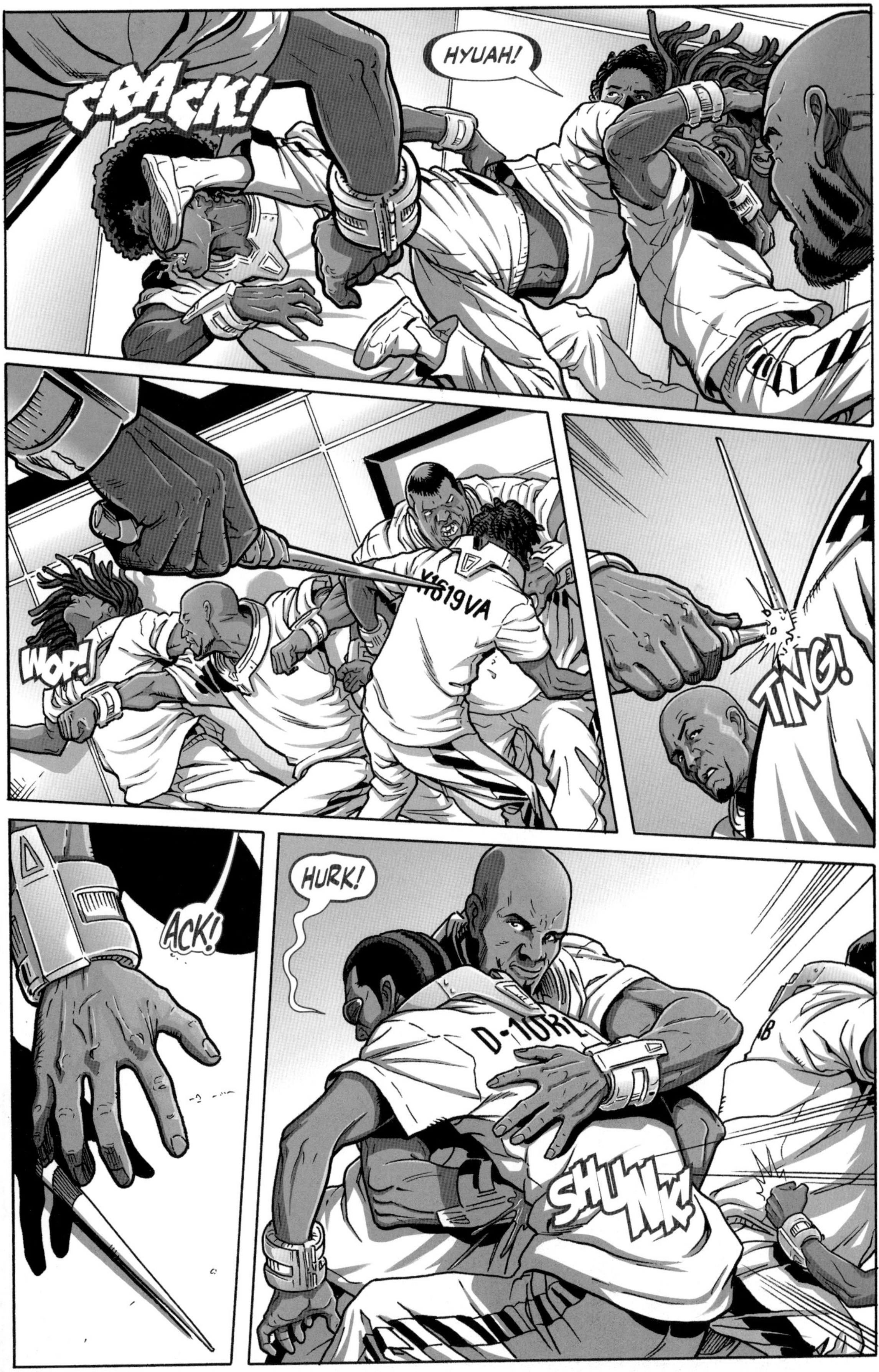
CRACK!
HYUAH!
X1619VA
WOP!
TING!
ACK!
HURK!
D-10RL
SHUNK!

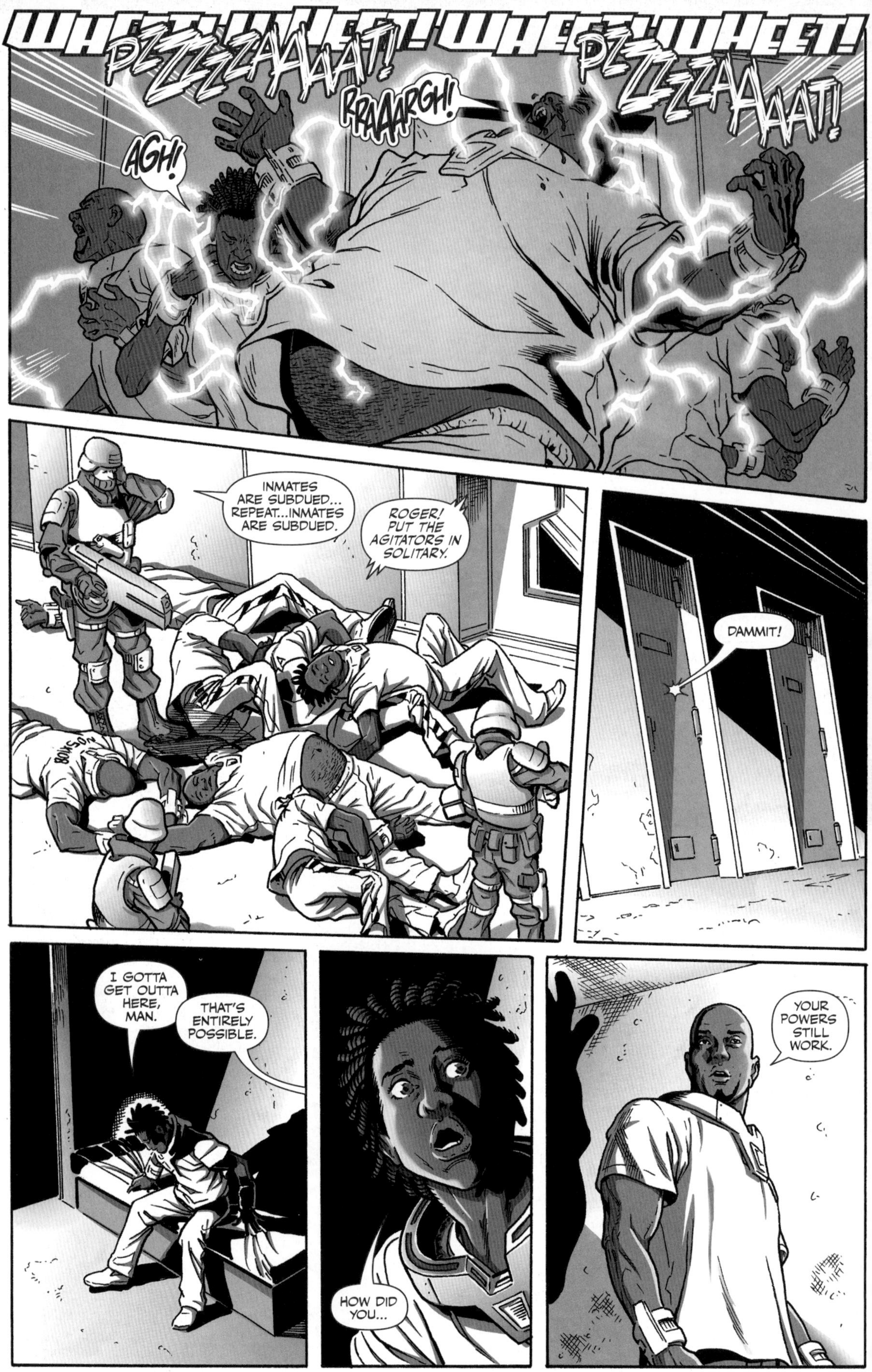
WHEET! WHEET!
PZZZZZAAAAAT!
RRAAARGH!
PZZZZZAAAAAT!
AGH!
INMATES ARE SUBDUED... REPEAT...INMATES ARE SUBDUED.
ROGER! PUT THE AGITATORS IN SOLITARY.
DAMMIT!
I GOTTA GET OUTTA HERE, MAN.
THAT'S ENTIRELY POSSIBLE.
HOW DID YOU...
YOUR POWERS STILL WORK.

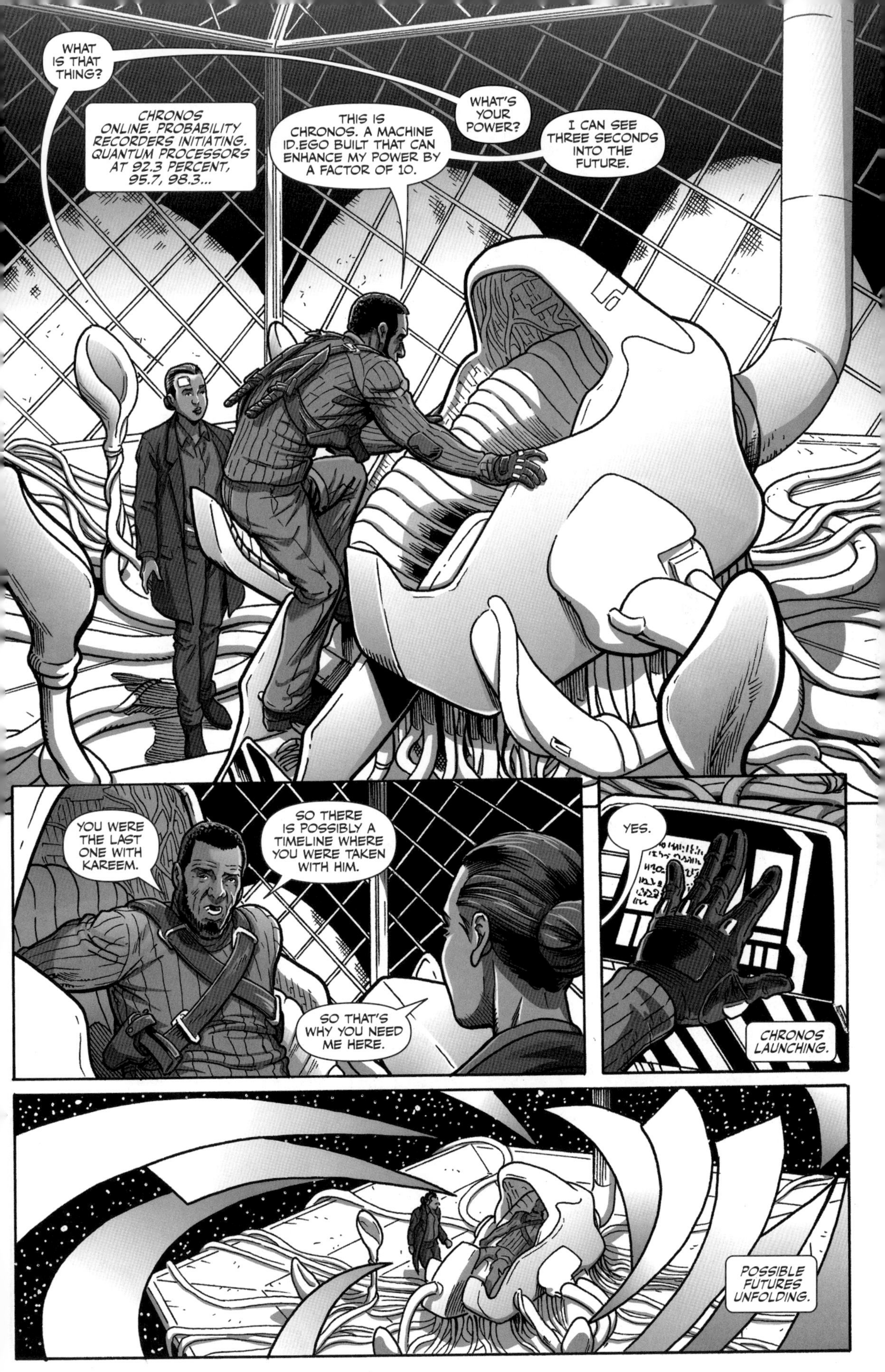
WHAT IS THAT THING?
CHRONOS ONLINE. PROBABILITY RECORDERS INITIATING. QUANTUM PROCESSORS AT 92.3 PERCENT, 95.7, 98.3...
THIS IS CHRONOS. A MACHINE ID.EGO BUILT THAT CAN ENHANCE MY POWER BY A FACTOR OF 10.
WHAT'S YOUR POWER?
I CAN SEE THREE SECONDS INTO THE FUTURE.
YOU WERE THE LAST ONE WITH KAREEM.
SO THERE IS POSSIBLY A TIMELINE WHERE YOU WERE TAKEN WITH HIM.
SO THAT'S WHY YOU NEED ME HERE.
YES.
CHRONOS LAUNCHING.
POSSIBLE FUTURES UNFOLDING.

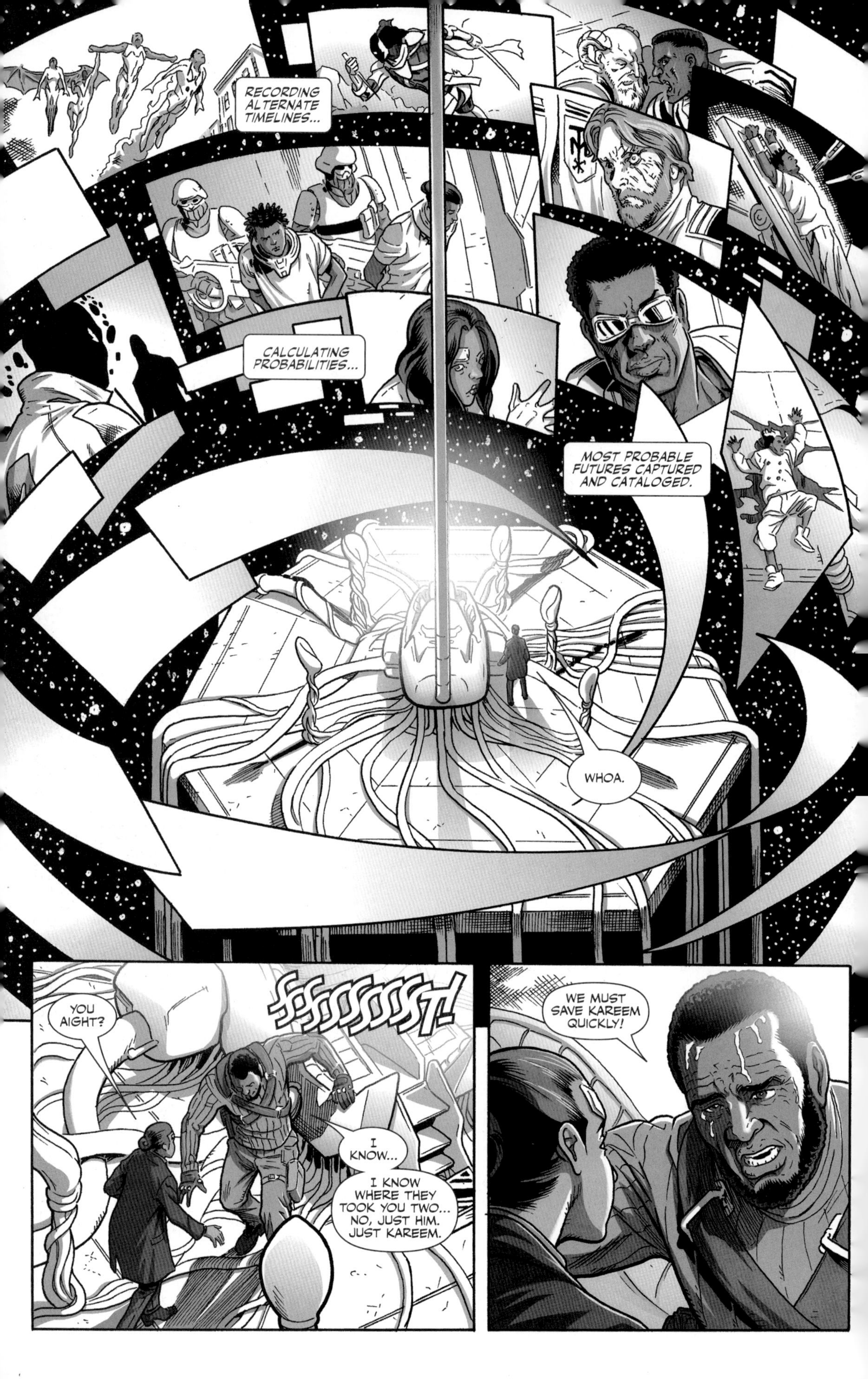
RECORDING ALTERNATE TIMELINES...
CALCULATING PROBABILITIES...
MOST PROBABLE FUTURES CAPTURED AND CATALOGED.
WHOA.
SSSSSSST!
YOU AIGHT?
I KNOW...
I KNOW WHERE THEY TOOK YOU TWO... NO, JUST HIM. JUST KAREEM.
WE MUST SAVE KAREEM QUICKLY!

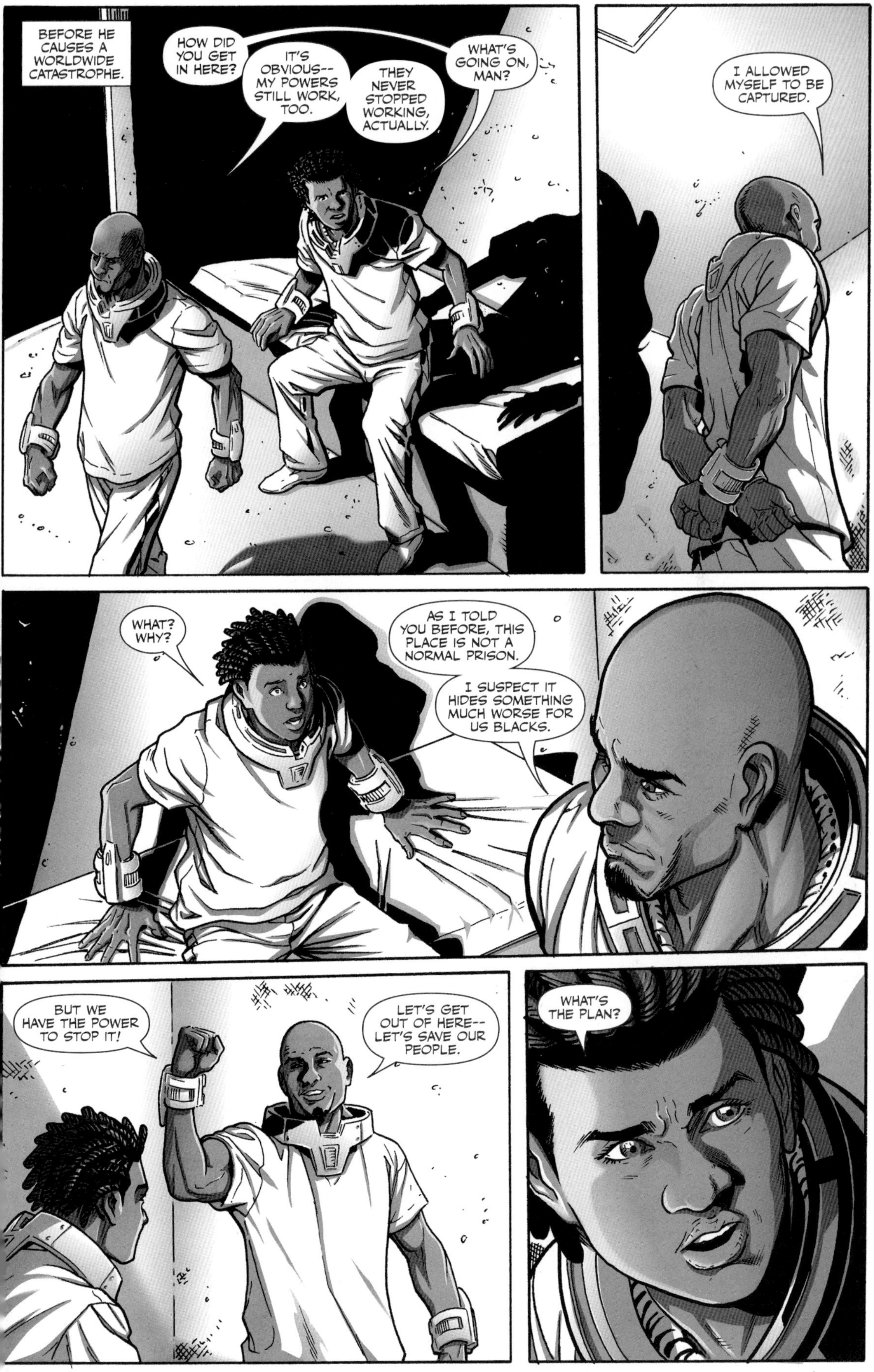
BEFORE HE CAUSES A WORLDWIDE CATASTROPHE.
HOW DID YOU GET IN HERE?
IT'S OBVIOUS-- MY POWERS STILL WORK, TOO.
THEY NEVER STOPPED WORKING, ACTUALLY.
WHAT'S GOING ON, MAN?
I ALLOWED MYSELF TO BE CAPTURED.
WHAT? WHY?
AS I TOLD YOU BEFORE, THIS PLACE IS NOT A NORMAL PRISON.
I SUSPECT IT HIDES SOMETHING MUCH WORSE FOR US BLACKS.
BUT WE HAVE THE POWER TO STOP IT!
LET'S GET OUT OF HERE-- LET'S SAVE OUR PEOPLE.
WHAT'S THE PLAN?

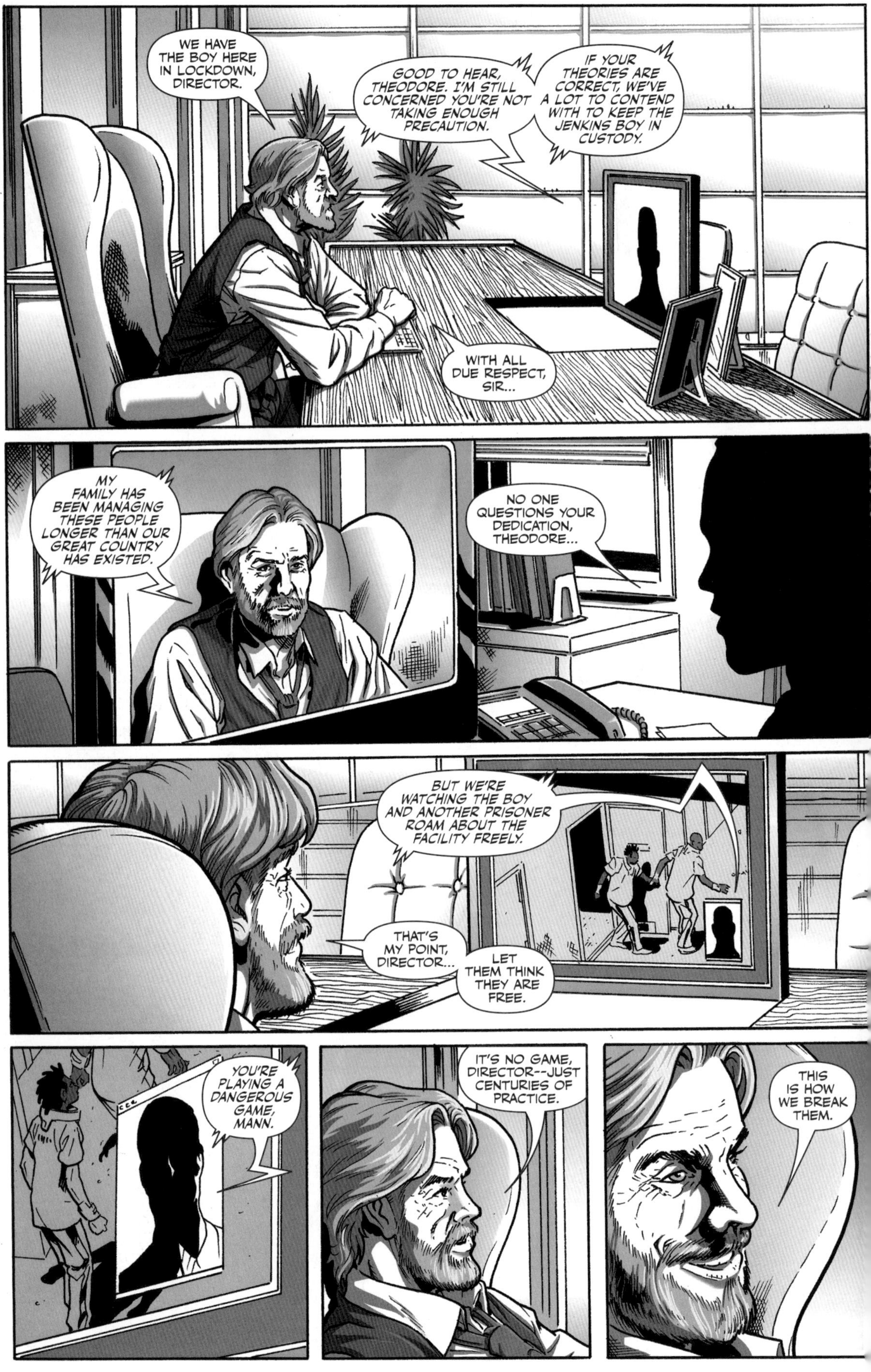
WE HAVE THE BOY HERE IN LOCKDOWN, DIRECTOR.
GOOD TO HEAR, THEODORE. I'M STILL CONCERNED YOU'RE NOT TAKING ENOUGH PRECAUTION.
IF YOUR THEORIES ARE CORRECT, WE'VE A LOT TO CONTEND WITH TO KEEP THE JENKINS BOY IN CUSTODY.
WITH ALL DUE RESPECT, SIR...
MY FAMILY HAS BEEN MANAGING THESE PEOPLE LONGER THAN OUR GREAT COUNTRY HAS EXISTED.
NO ONE QUESTIONS YOUR DEDICATION, THEODORE...
BUT WE'RE WATCHING THE BOY AND ANOTHER PRISONER ROAM ABOUT THE FACILITY FREELY.
THAT'S MY POINT, DIRECTOR...
LET THEM THINK THEY ARE FREE.
YOU'RE PLAYING A DANGEROUS GAME, MANN.
IT'S NO GAME, DIRECTOR--JUST CENTURIES OF PRACTICE.
THIS IS HOW WE BREAK THEM.

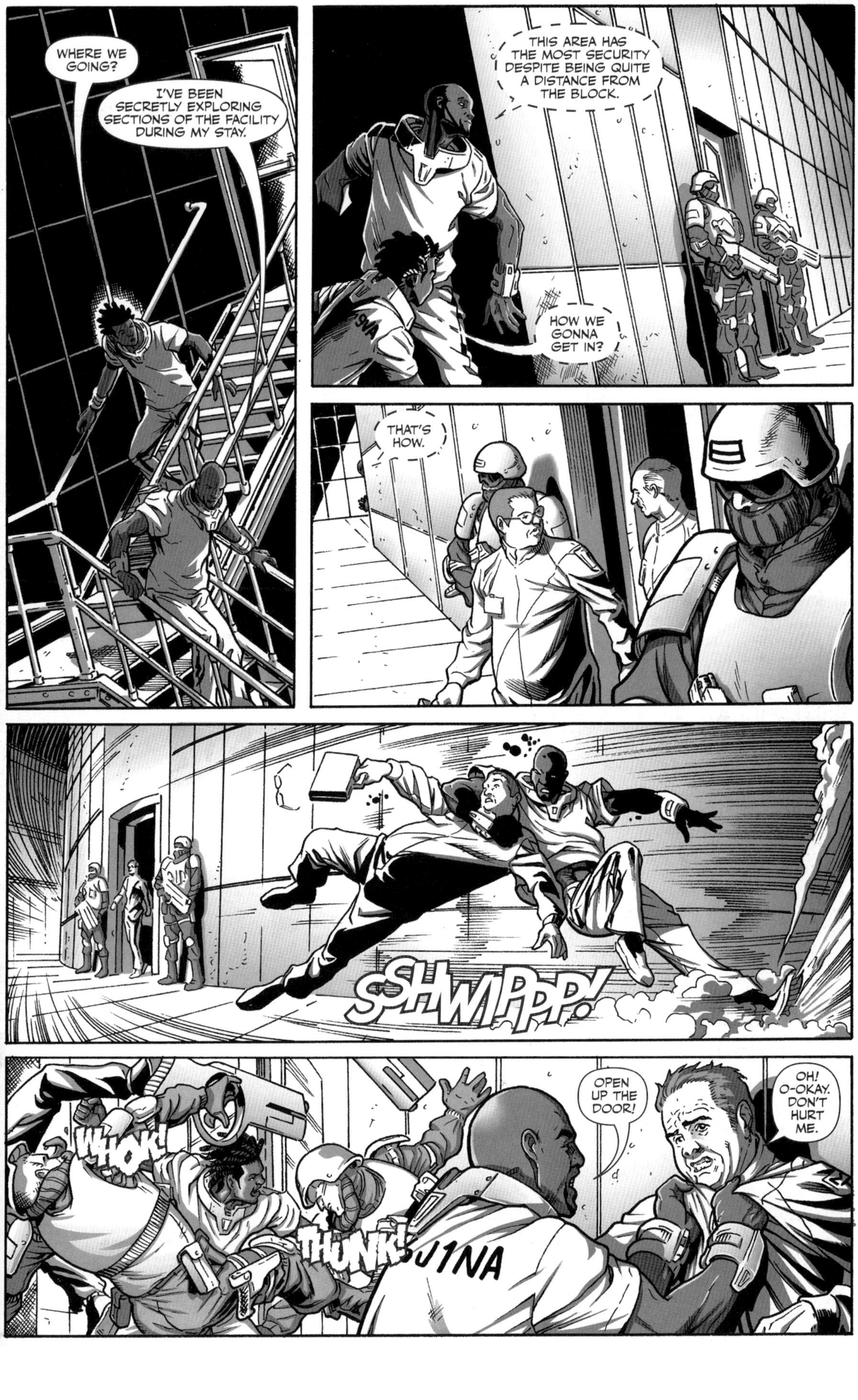
WHERE WE GOING?
I'VE BEEN SECRETLY EXPLORING SECTIONS OF THE FACILITY DURING MY STAY.
THIS AREA HAS THE MOST SECURITY DESPITE BEING QUITE A DISTANCE FROM THE BLOCK.
HOW WE GONNA GET IN?
THAT'S HOW.
SSHWIPPP!
WHOK!
THUNK!
J1NA
OPEN UP THE DOOR!
OH! O-OKAY. DON'T HURT ME.

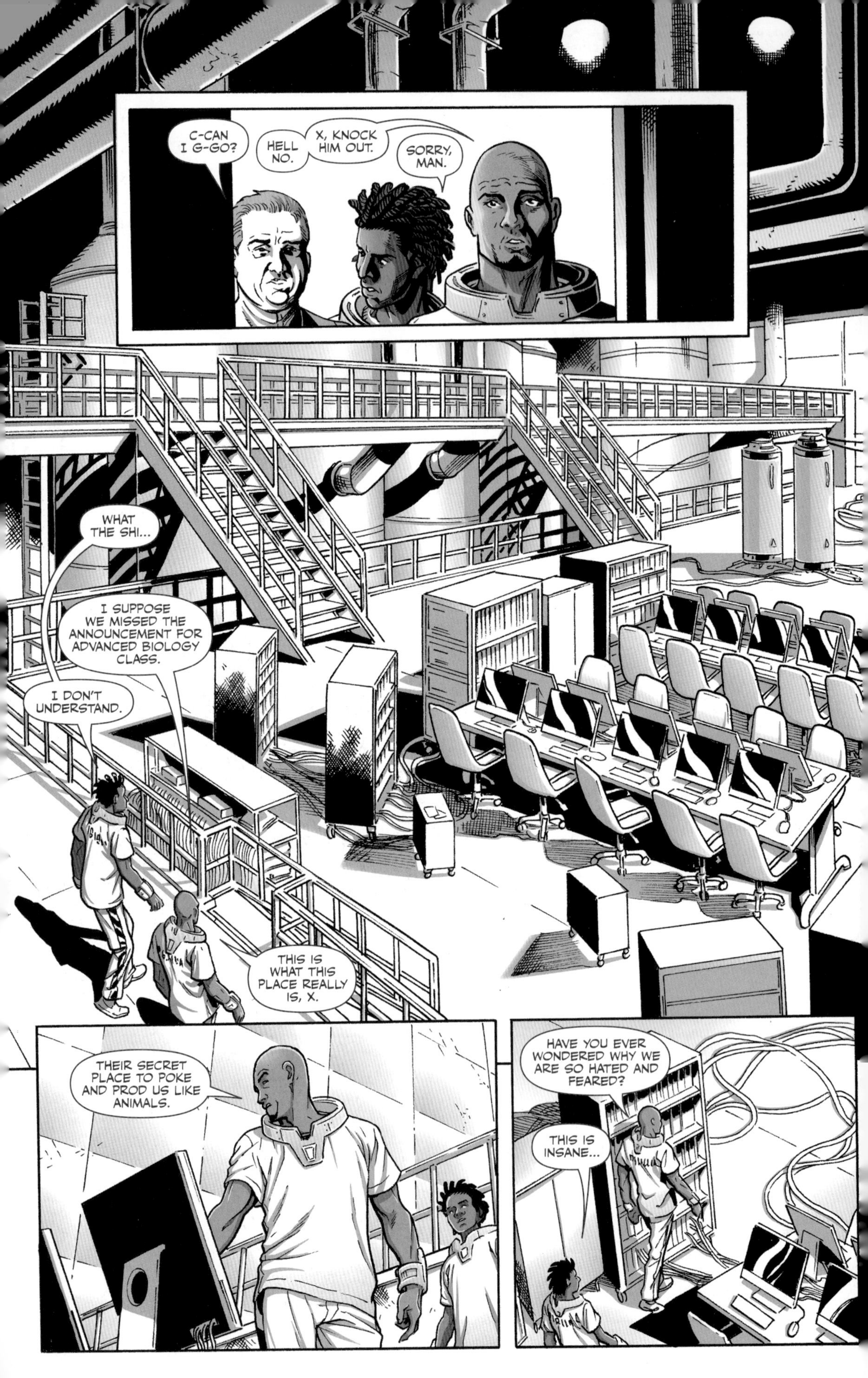
C-CAN I G-GO?
HELL NO.
X, KNOCK HIM OUT.
SORRY, MAN.
WHAT THE SHI...
I SUPPOSE WE MISSED THE ANNOUNCEMENT FOR ADVANCED BIOLOGY CLASS.
I DON'T UNDERSTAND.
THIS IS WHAT THIS PLACE REALLY IS, X.
THEIR SECRET PLACE TO POKE AND PROD US LIKE ANIMALS.
HAVE YOU EVER WONDERED WHY WE ARE SO HATED AND FEARED?
THIS IS INSANE...

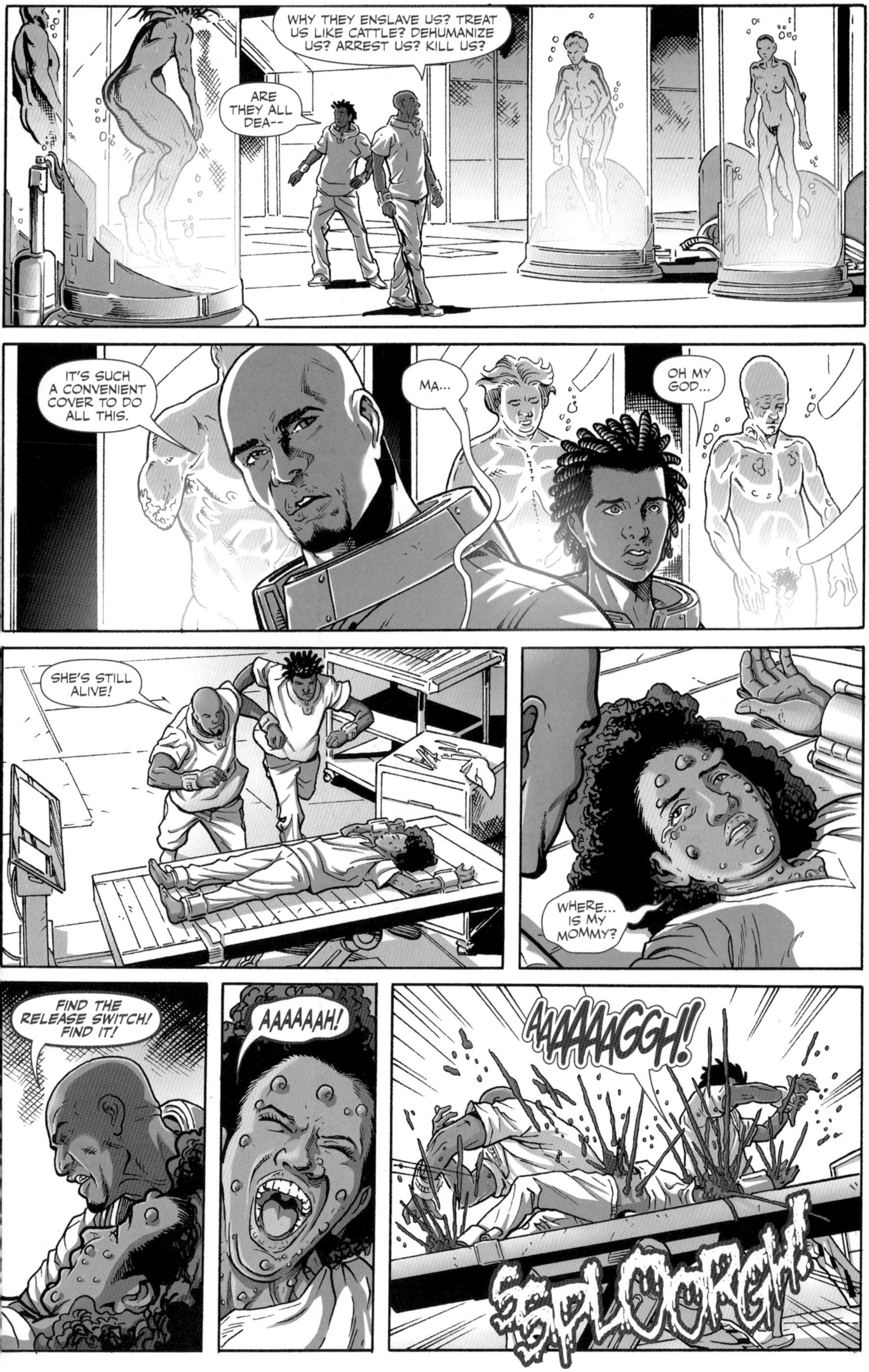
WHY THEY ENSLAVE US? TREAT US LIKE CATTLE? DEHUMANIZE US? ARREST US? KILL US?
ARE THEY ALL DEA--
IT'S SUCH A CONVENIENT COVER TO DO ALL THIS.
MA...
OH MY GOD...
SHE'S STILL ALIVE!
WHERE... IS MY MOMMY?
FIND THE RELEASE SWITCH! FIND IT!
AAAAAAH!
AAAAAAGGH!
SPLOORCH!

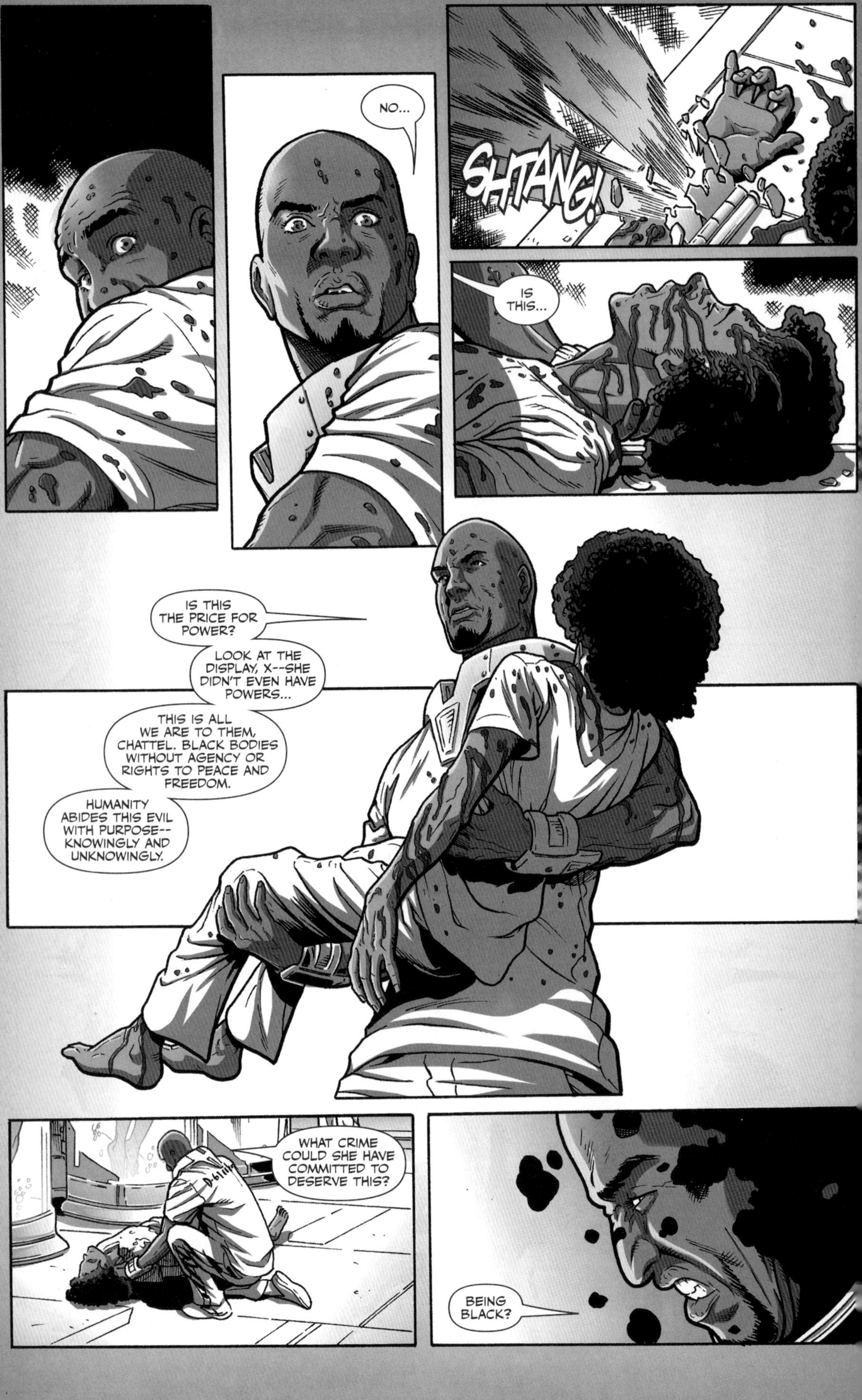
NO...
SHTANG!
IS THIS...
IS THIS THE PRICE FOR POWER?
LOOK AT THE DISPLAY, X--SHE DIDN'T EVEN HAVE POWERS...
THIS IS ALL WE ARE TO THEM, CHATTEL. BLACK BODIES WITHOUT AGENCY OR RIGHTS TO PEACE AND FREEDOM.
HUMANITY ABIDES THIS EVIL WITH PURPOSE-- KNOWINGLY AND UNKNOWINGLY.
WHAT CRIME COULD SHE HAVE COMMITTED TO DESERVE THIS?
BEING BLACK?

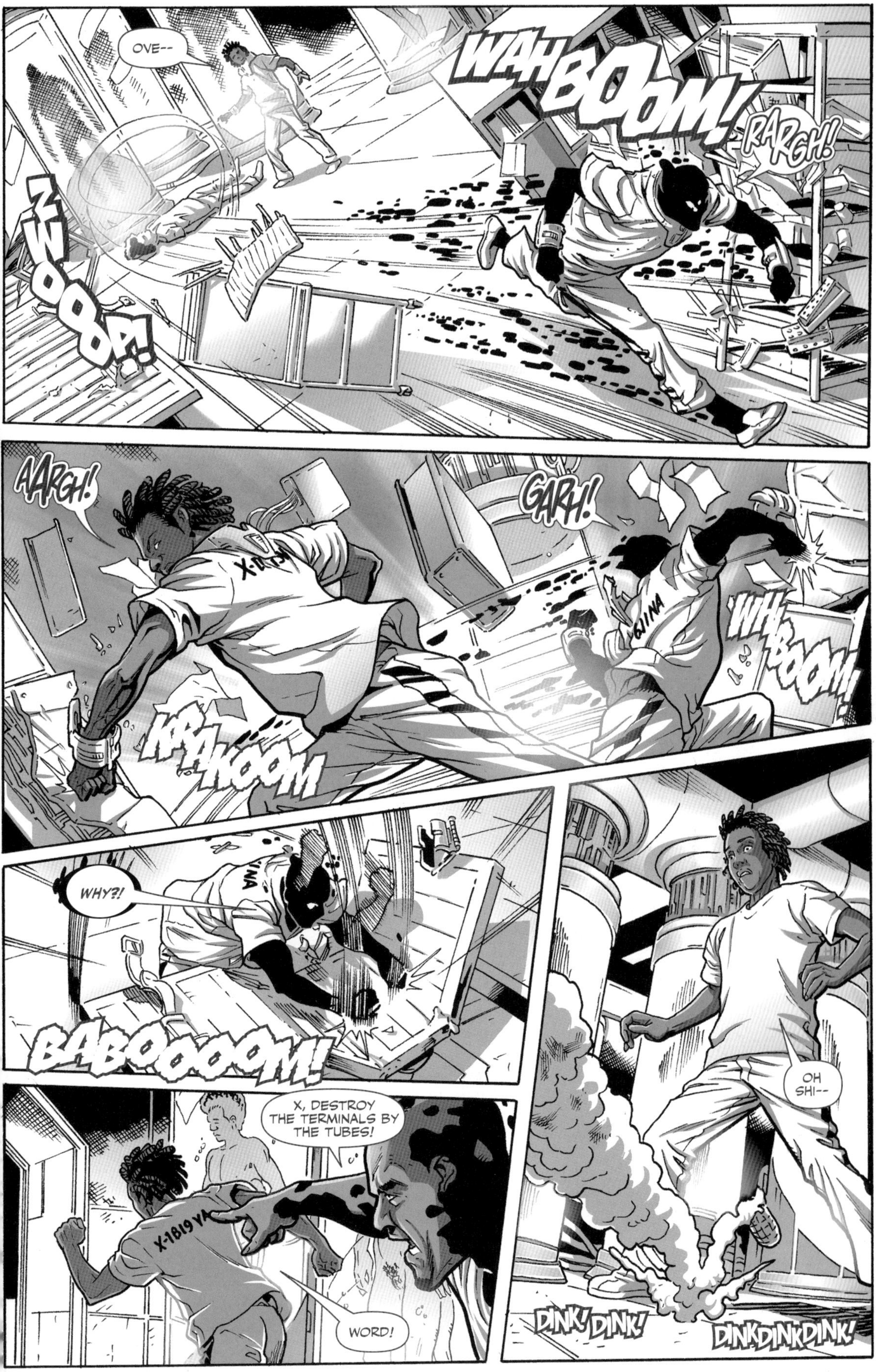
OVE--
WAHBOOM!
RARGH!
ZWOOOP!
AARGH!
GARH!
WHABOOM!
KRAKOOM
WHY?!
BABOOOOOM!
OH SHI--
X, DESTROY THE TERMINALS BY THE TUBES!
WORD!
DINK! DINK!
DINKDINKDINK!

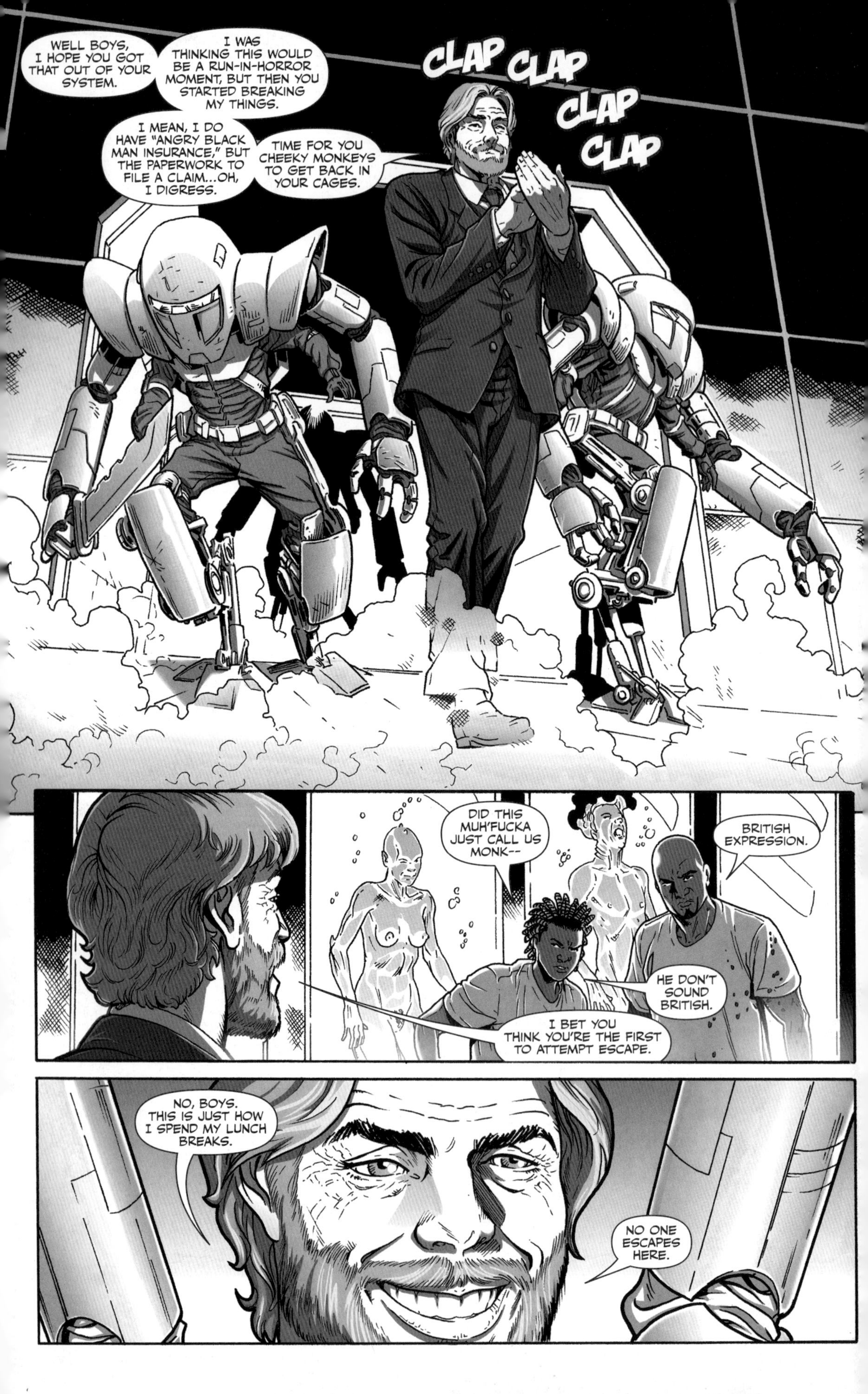
WELL BOYS, I HOPE YOU GOT THAT OUT OF YOUR SYSTEM.
I WAS THINKING THIS WOULD BE A RUN-IN-HORROR MOMENT, BUT THEN YOU STARTED BREAKING MY THINGS.
CLAP CLAP CLAP CLAP
I MEAN, I DO HAVE "ANGRY BLACK MAN INSURANCE," BUT THE PAPERWORK TO FILE A CLAIM...OH, I DIGRESS.
TIME FOR YOU CHEEKY MONKEYS TO GET BACK IN YOUR CAGES.
DID THIS MUH'FUCKA JUST CALL US MONK--
BRITISH EXPRESSION.
HE DON'T SOUND BRITISH.
I BET YOU THINK YOU'RE THE FIRST TO ATTEMPT ESCAPE.
NO, BOYS. THIS IS JUST HOW I SPEND MY LUNCH BREAKS.
NO ONE ESCAPES HERE.

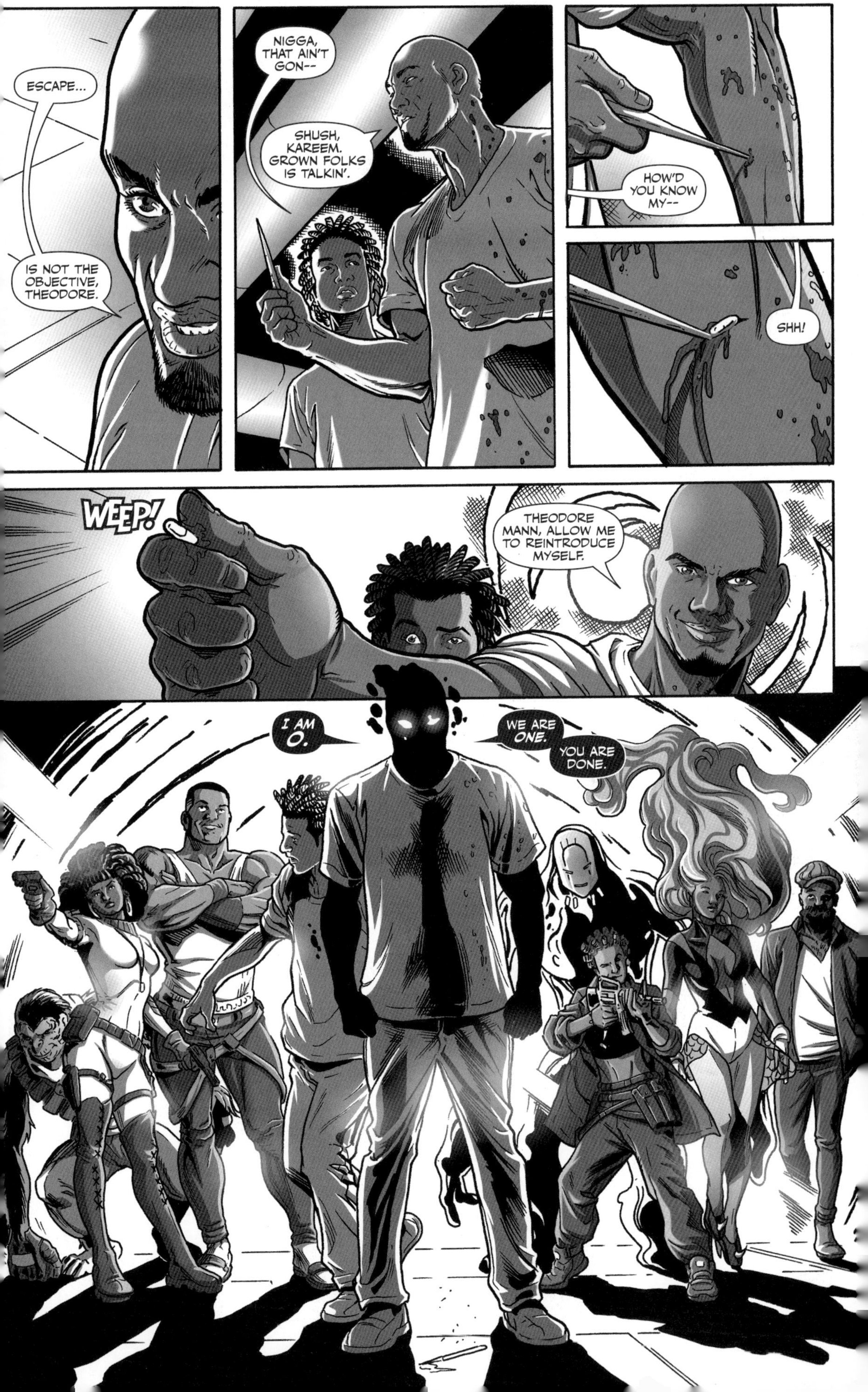
ESCAPE...
IS NOT THE OBJECTIVE, THEODORE.
NIGGA, THAT AIN'T GON--
SHUSH, KAREEM. GROWN FOLKS IS TALKIN'.
HOW'D YOU KNOW MY--
SHH!
WEEP!
THEODORE MANN, ALLOW ME TO REINTRODUCE MYSELF.
I AM O.
WE ARE ONE.
YOU ARE DONE.

CHAPTER SIX

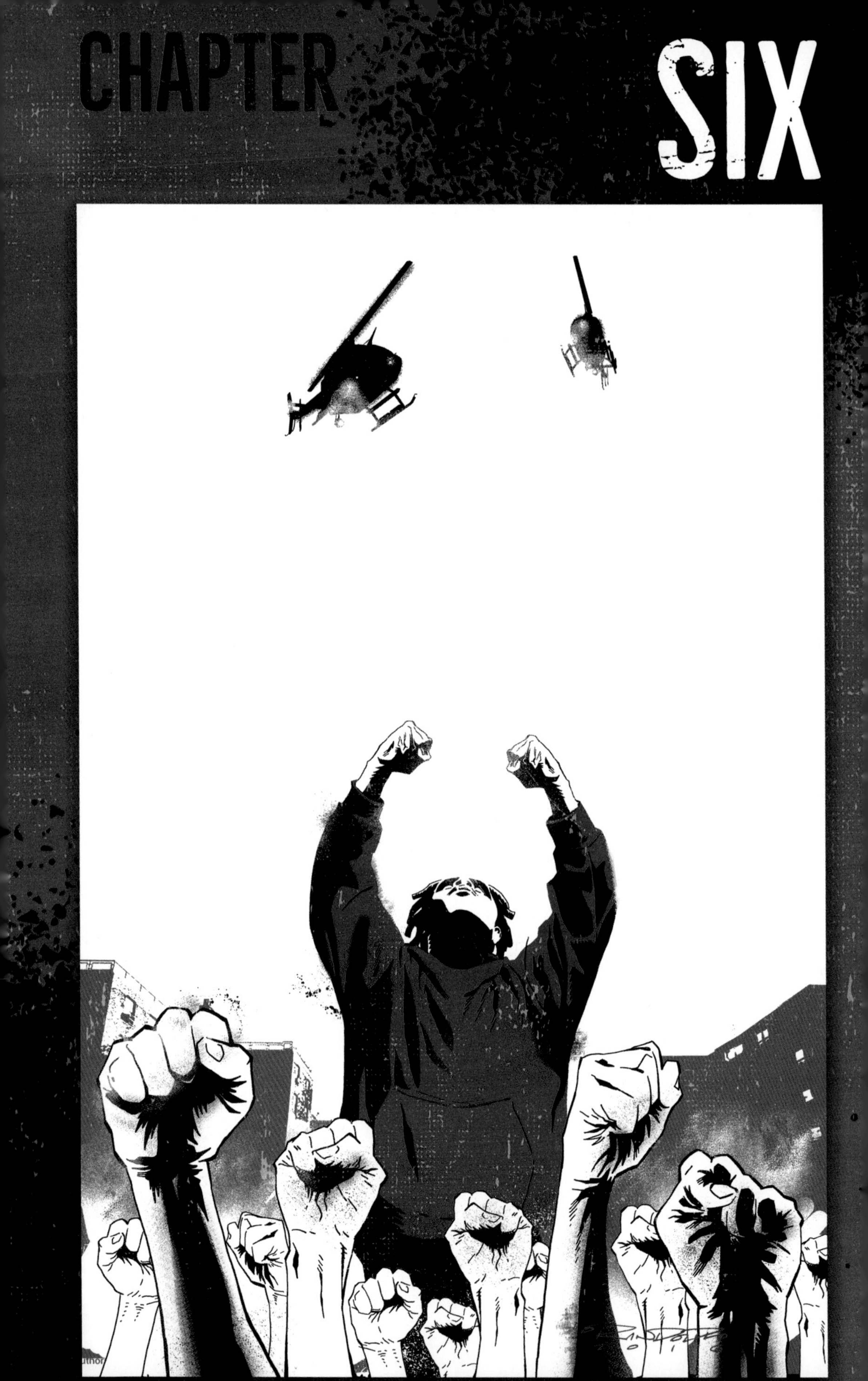

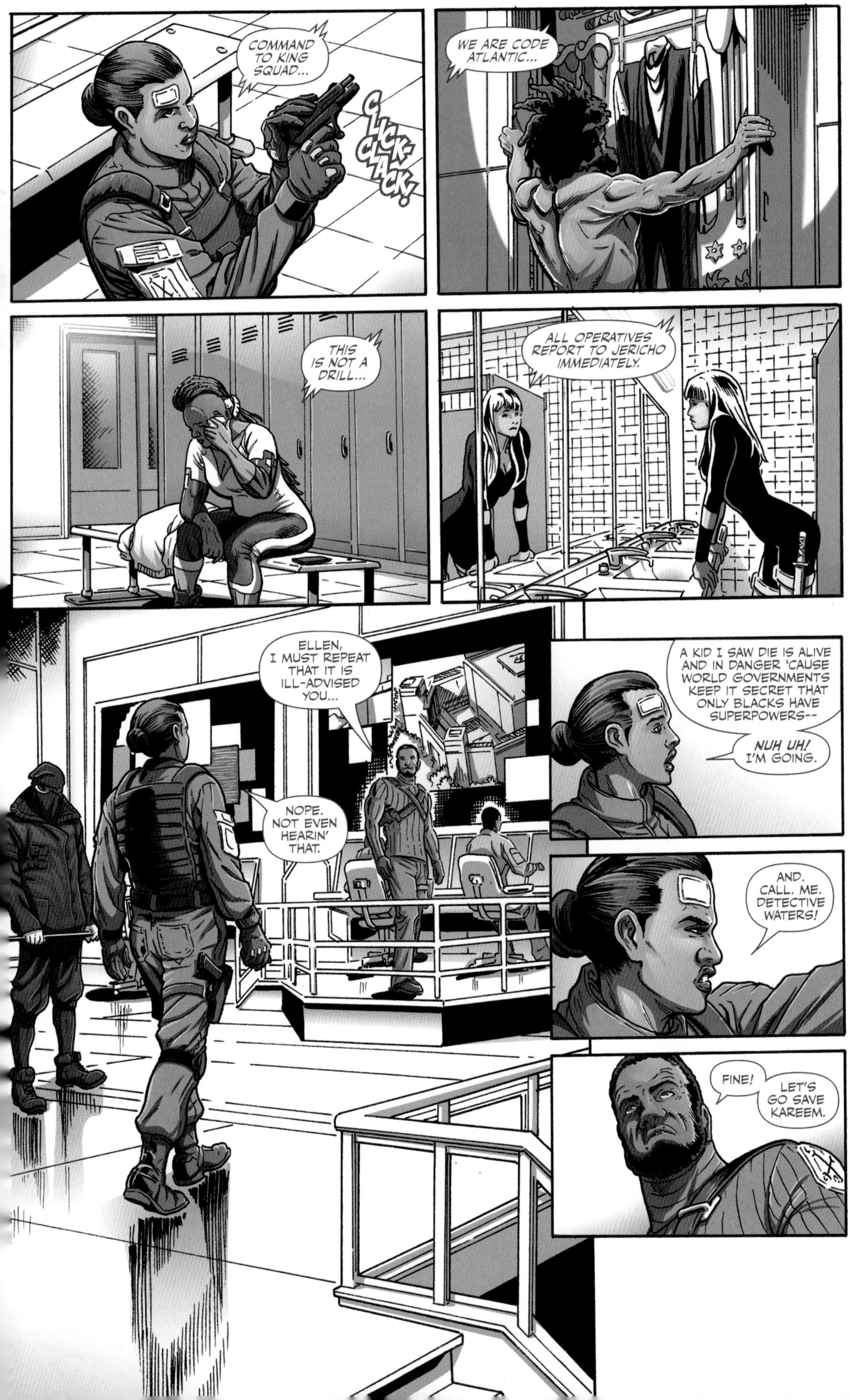
COMMAND TO KING SQUAD...
CLICK CLACK!
WE ARE CODE ATLANTIC...
THIS IS NOT A DRILL...
ALL OPERATIVES REPORT TO JERICHO IMMEDIATELY.
ELLEN, I MUST REPEAT THAT IT IS ILL-ADVISED YOU...
NOPE. NOT EVEN HEARIN' THAT.
A KID I SAW DIE IS ALIVE AND IN DANGER 'CAUSE WORLD GOVERNMENTS KEEP IT SECRET THAT ONLY BLACKS HAVE SUPERPOWERS--
NUH UH! I'M GOING.
AND. CALL. ME. DETECTIVE WATERS!
FINE!
LET'S GO SAVE KAREEM.

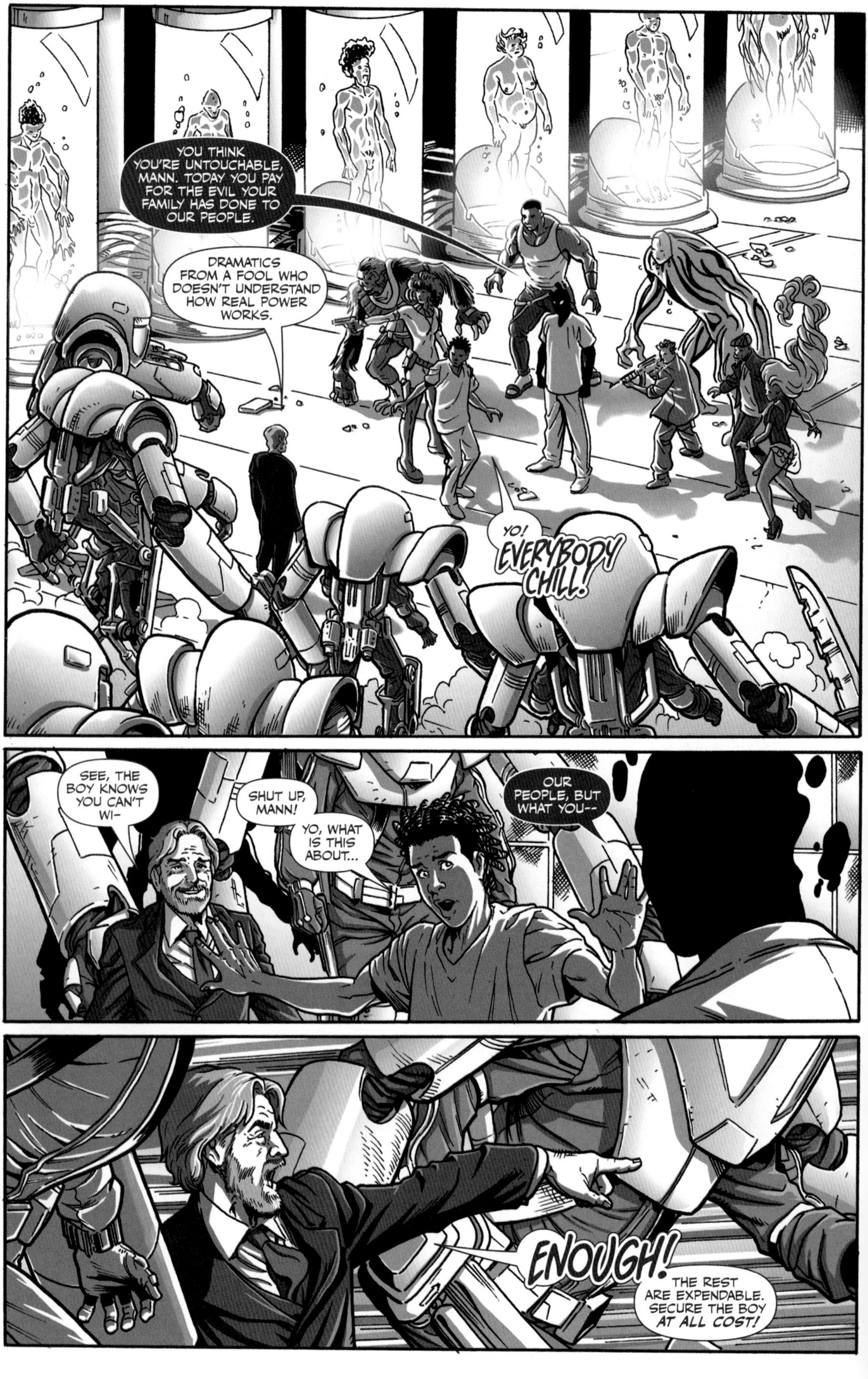

YOU THINK YOU'RE UNTOUCHABLE, MANN. TODAY YOU PAY FOR THE EVIL YOUR FAMILY HAS DONE TO OUR PEOPLE.
DRAMATICS FROM A FOOL WHO DOESN'T UNDERSTAND HOW REAL POWER WORKS.
YO! EVERYBODY CHILL!
SEE, THE BOY KNOWS YOU CAN'T WI-
SHUT UP, MANN!
YO, WHAT IS THIS ABOUT...
OUR PEOPLE, BUT WHAT YOU--
ENOUGH!
THE REST ARE EXPENDABLE. SECURE THE BOY AT ALL COST!

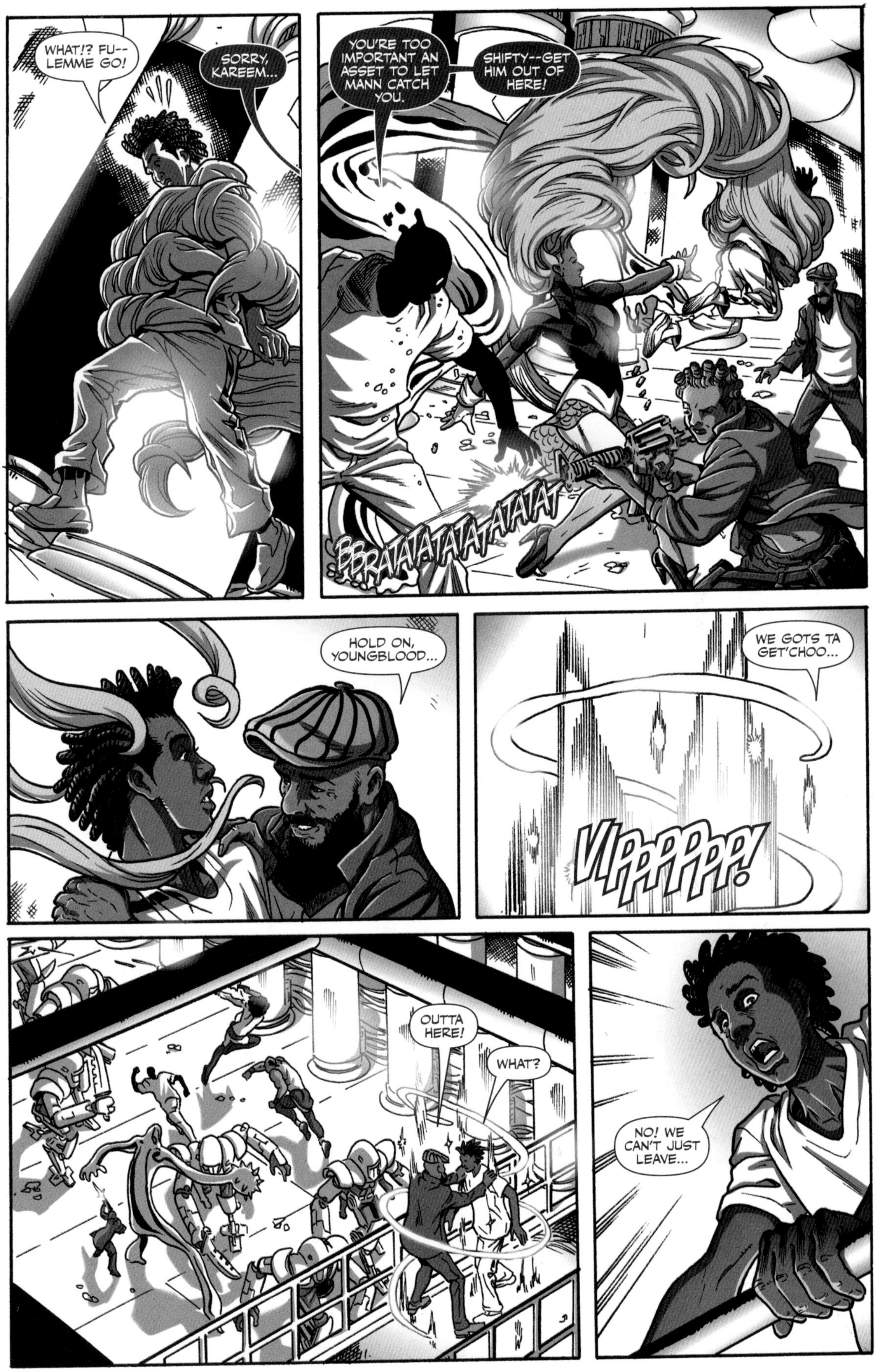
WHAT!? FU--
LEMME GO!
SORRY,
KAREEM...
YOU'RE TOO
IMPORTANT AN
ASSET TO LET
MANN CATCH
YOU.
SHIFTY--GET
HIM OUT OF
HERE!
BBRATATATATATATAT
HOLD ON,
YOUNGBLOOD...
WE GOTS TA
GET'CHOO...
VIPPPPPP!
OUTTA
HERE!
WHAT?
NO! WE
CAN'T JUST
LEAVE...

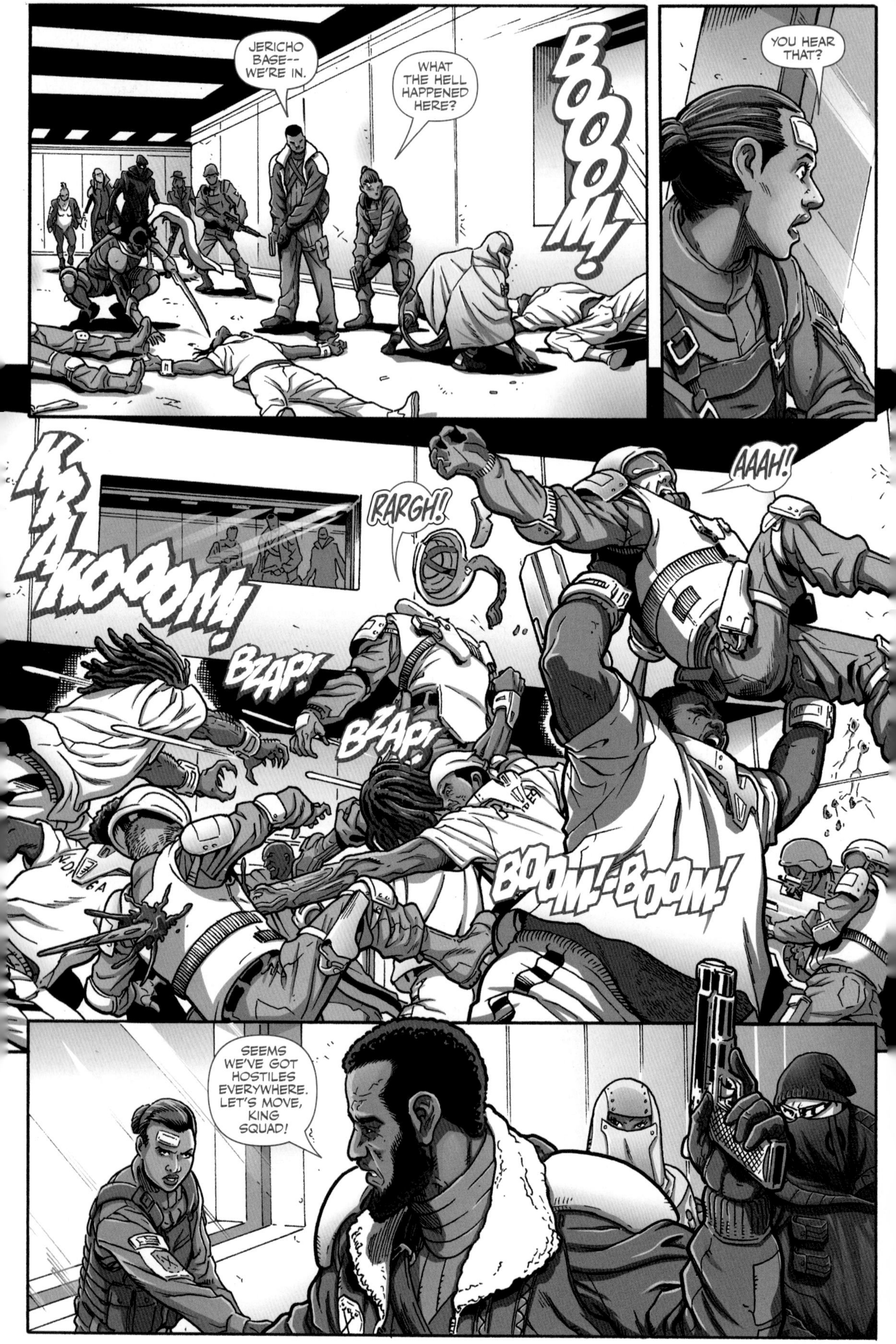

JERICHO BASE-- WE'RE IN.
WHAT THE HELL HAPPENED HERE?
BOOOOM!
YOU HEAR THAT?
KRAKOOOOM!
RARGH!
AAAH!
BZAP!
BZAP!
BOOM! BOOM!
SEEMS WE'VE GOT HOSTILES EVERYWHERE. LET'S MOVE, KING SQUAD!

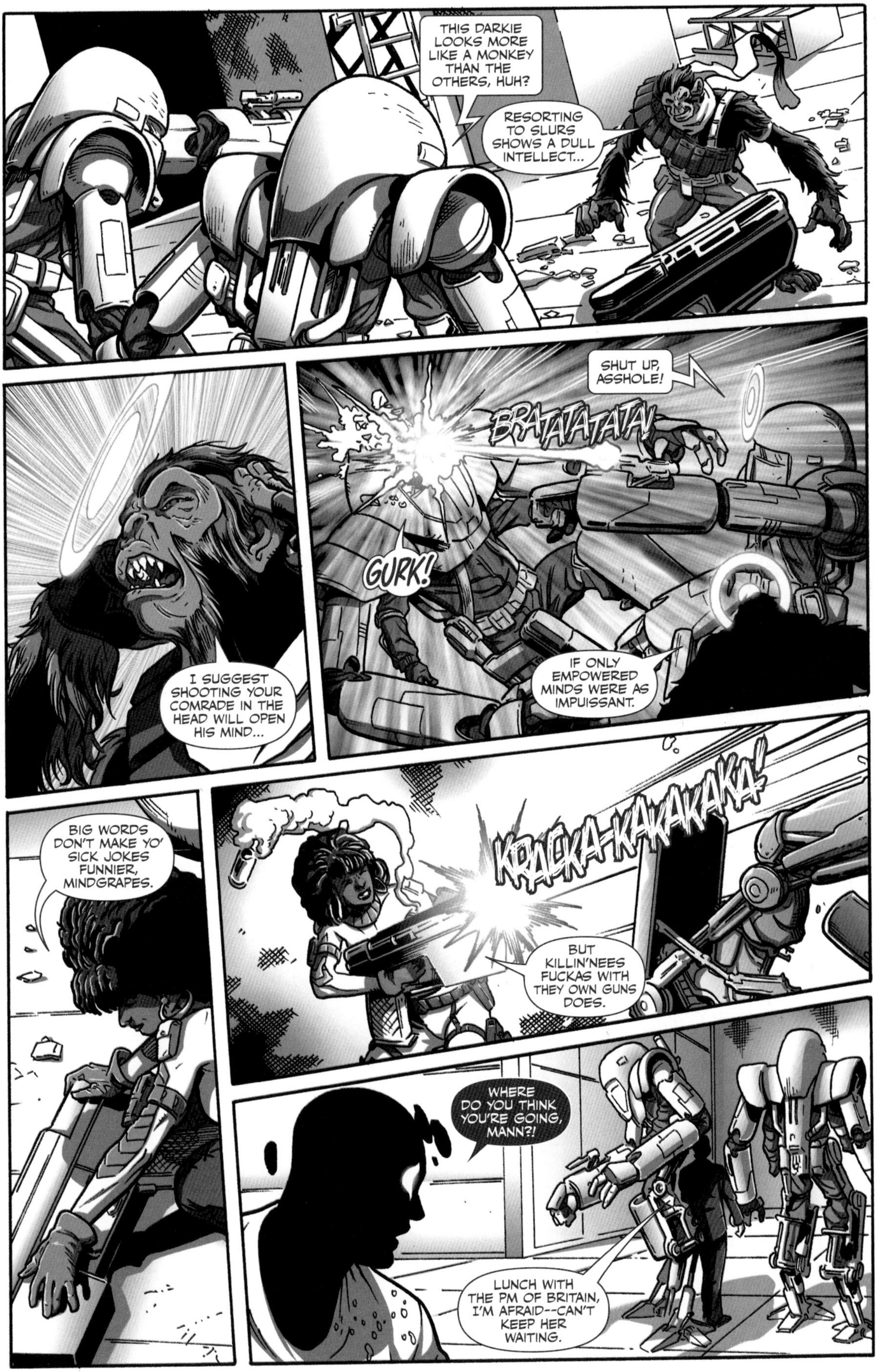

THIS DARKIE LOOKS MORE LIKE A MONKEY THAN THE OTHERS, HUH?
RESORTING TO SLURS SHOWS A DULL INTELLECT...
I SUGGEST SHOOTING YOUR COMRADE IN THE HEAD WILL OPEN HIS MIND...
SHUT UP, ASSHOLE!
BRATATATATA!
GURK!
IF ONLY EMPOWERED MINDS WERE AS IMPUISSANT.
BIG WORDS DON'T MAKE YO' SICK JOKES FUNNIER, MINDGRAPES.
KRACKA-KAKAKAKA!
BUT KILLIN'NEES FUCKAS WITH THEY OWN GUNS DOES.
WHERE DO YOU THINK YOU'RE GOING, MANN?!
LUNCH WITH THE PM OF BRITAIN, I'M AFRAID--CAN'T KEEP HER WAITING.

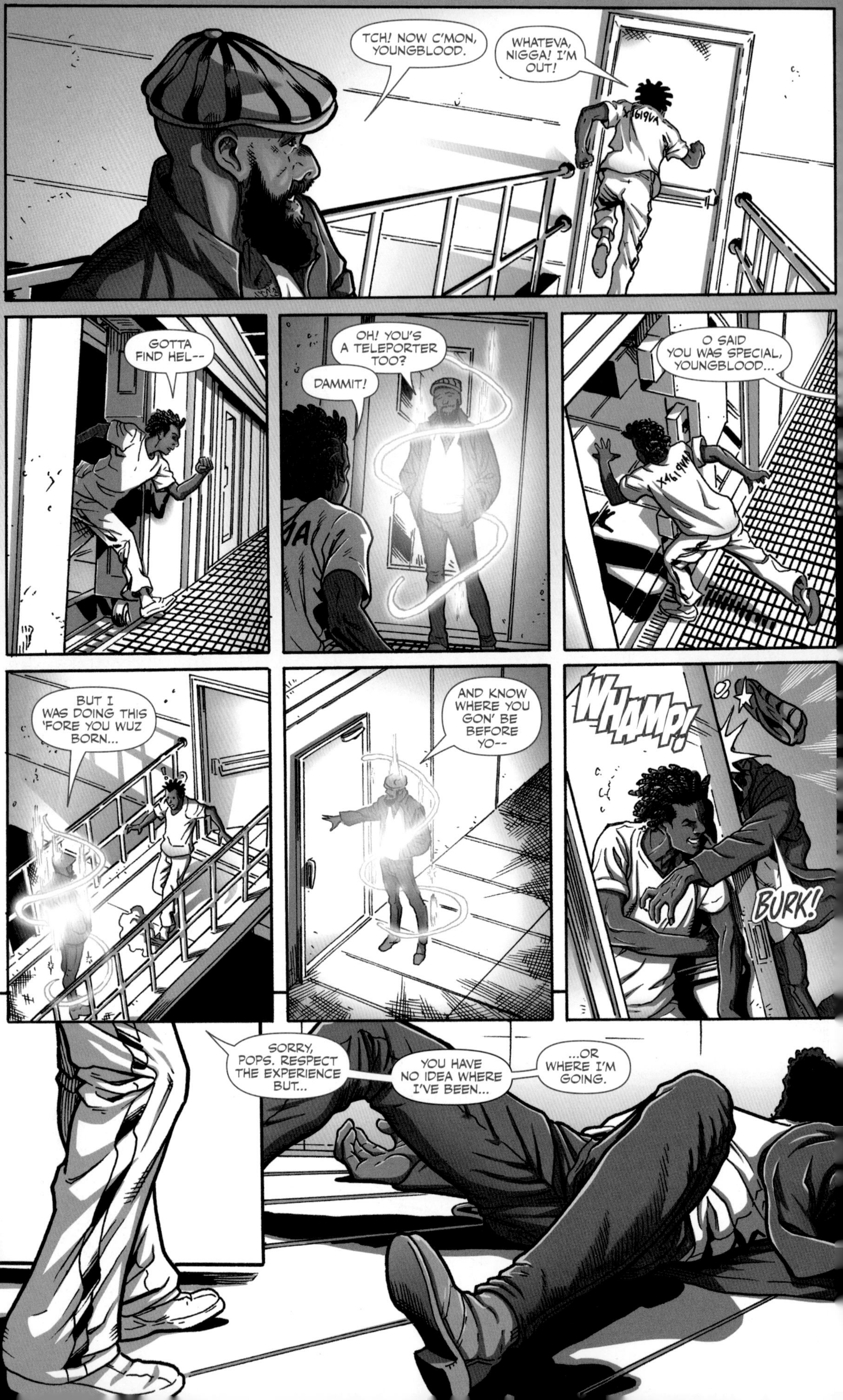
TCH! NOW C'MON, YOUNGBLOOD.
WHATEVA, NIGGA! I'M OUT!
GOTTA FIND HEL--
OH! YOU'S A TELEPORTER TOO?
DAMMIT!
O SAID YOU WAS SPECIAL, YOUNGBLOOD...
BUT I WAS DOING THIS 'FORE YOU WUZ BORN...
AND KNOW WHERE YOU GON' BE BEFORE YO--
WHAMP!
BURK!
SORRY, POPS. RESPECT THE EXPERIENCE BUT...
YOU HAVE NO IDEA WHERE I'VE BEEN...
...OR WHERE I'M GOING.

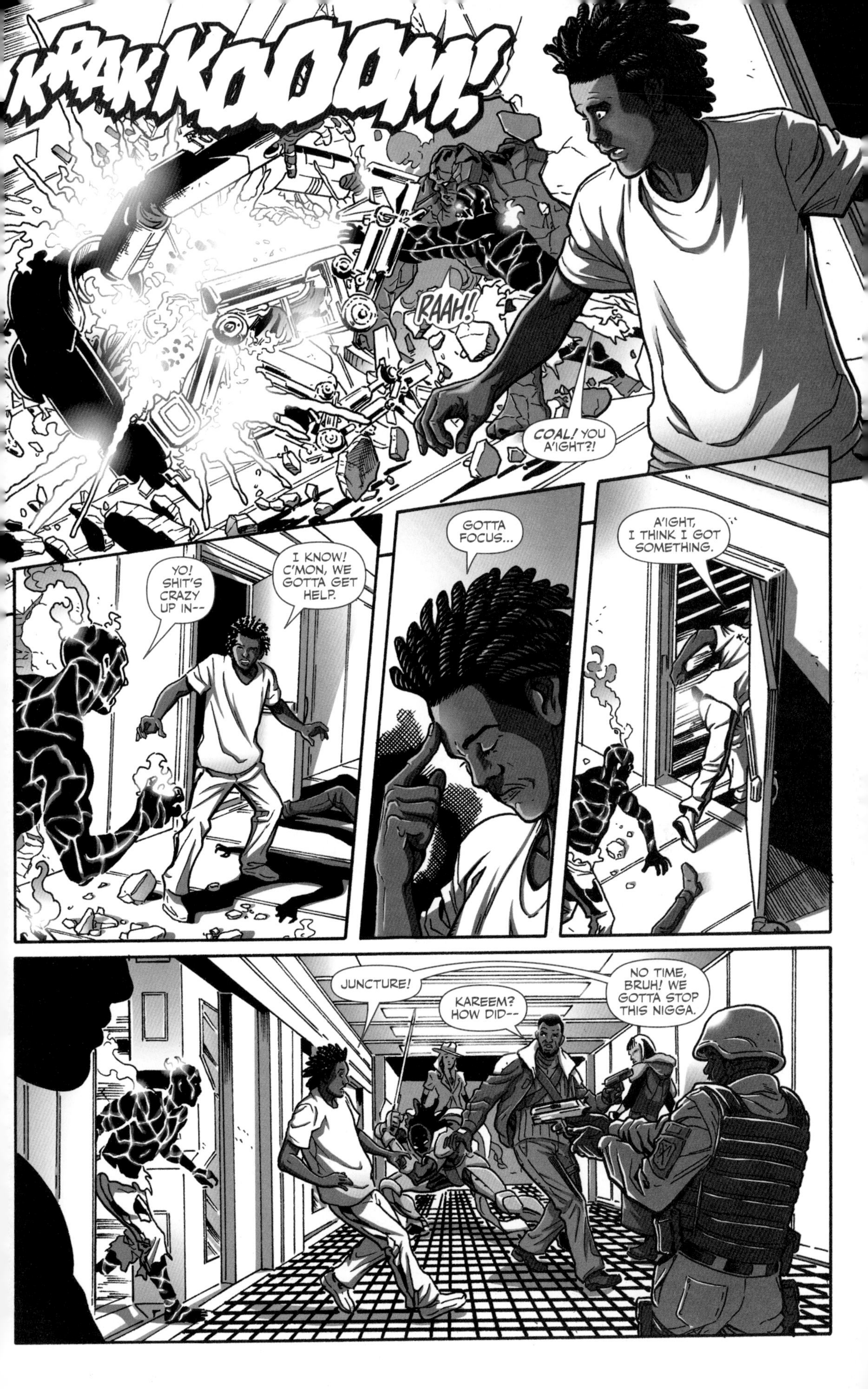

KRAK KOOOM!
RAAH!
COAL! YOU A'IGHT?!
YO! SHIT'S CRAZY UP IN--
I KNOW! C'MON, WE GOTTA GET HELP.
GOTTA FOCUS...
A'IGHT, I THINK I GOT SOMETHING.
JUNCTURE!
KAREEM? HOW DID--
NO TIME, BRUH! WE GOTTA STOP THIS NIGGA.

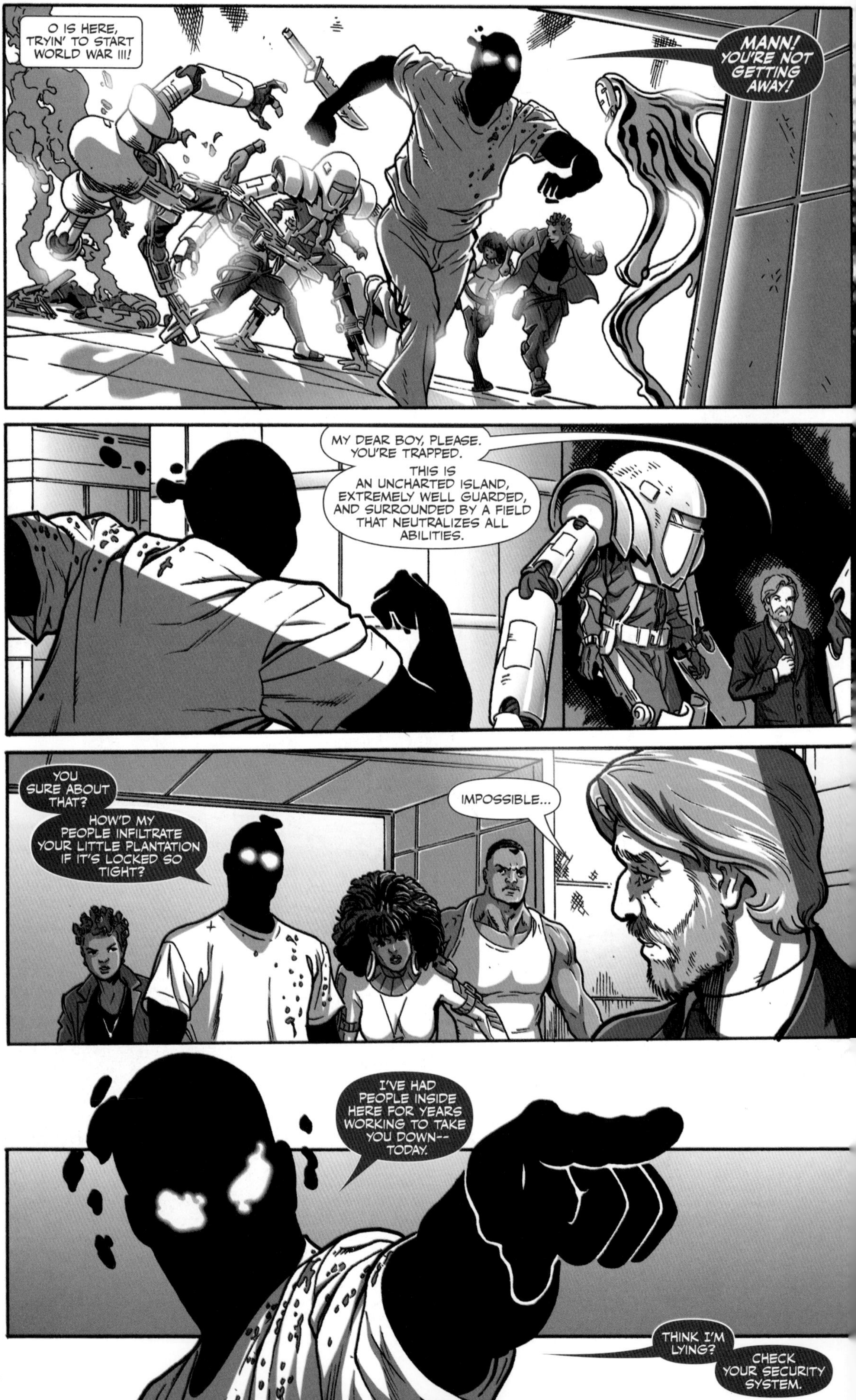
O IS HERE, TRYIN' TO START WORLD WAR III!
MANN! YOU'RE NOT GETTING AWAY!
MY DEAR BOY, PLEASE. YOU'RE TRAPPED.
THIS IS AN UNCHARTED ISLAND, EXTREMELY WELL GUARDED, AND SURROUNDED BY A FIELD THAT NEUTRALIZES ALL ABILITIES.
YOU SURE ABOUT THAT?
HOW'D MY PEOPLE INFILTRATE YOUR LITTLE PLANTATION IF IT'S LOCKED SO TIGHT?
IMPOSSIBLE...
I'VE HAD PEOPLE INSIDE HERE FOR YEARS WORKING TO TAKE YOU DOWN-- TODAY.
THINK I'M LYING?
CHECK YOUR SECURITY SYSTEM.

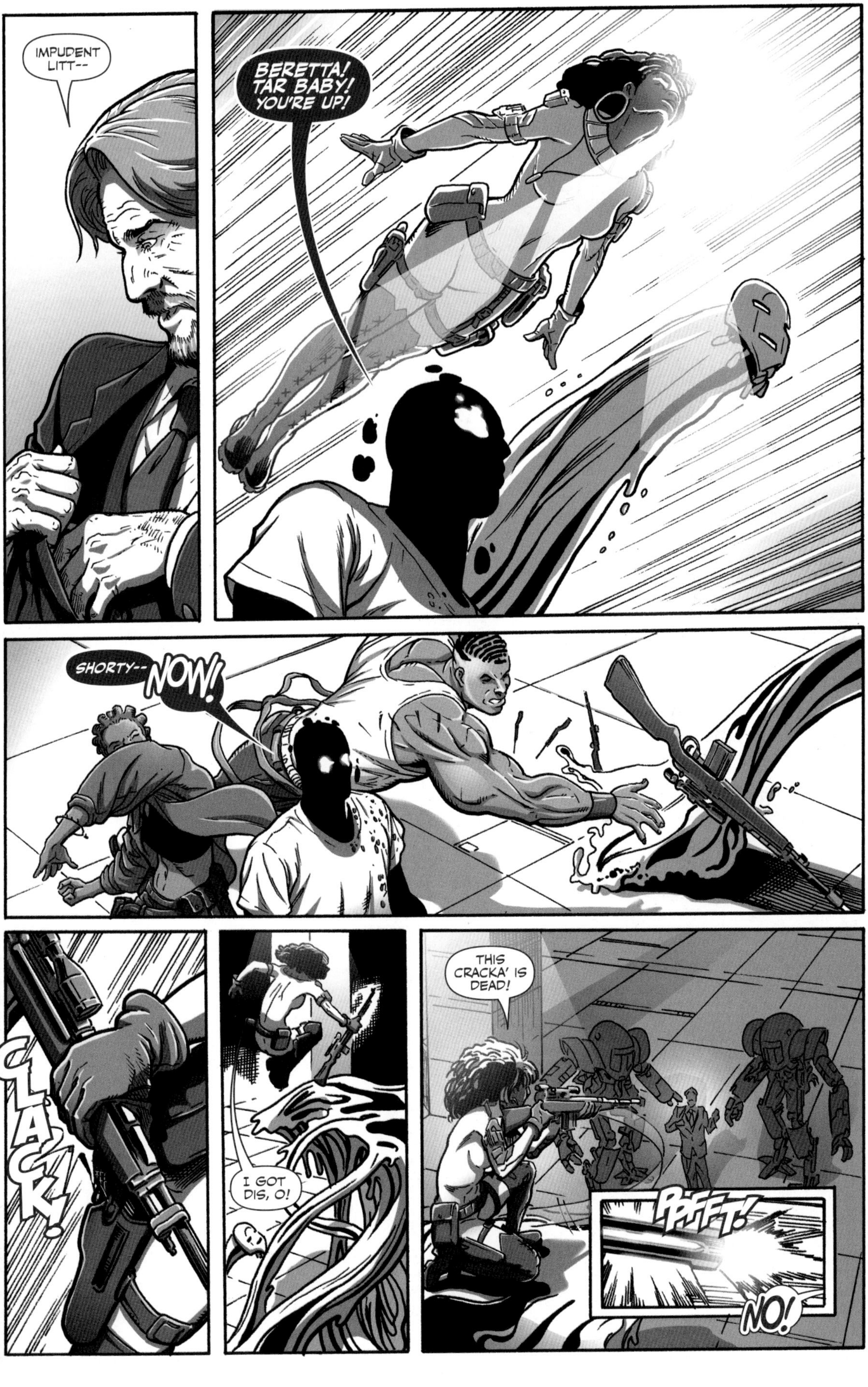

IMPUDENT LITT--
BERETTA! TAR BABY! YOU'RE UP!
SHORTY--NOW!
CLACK!
I GOT DIS, O!
THIS CRACKA' IS DEAD!
PFFT!
NO!

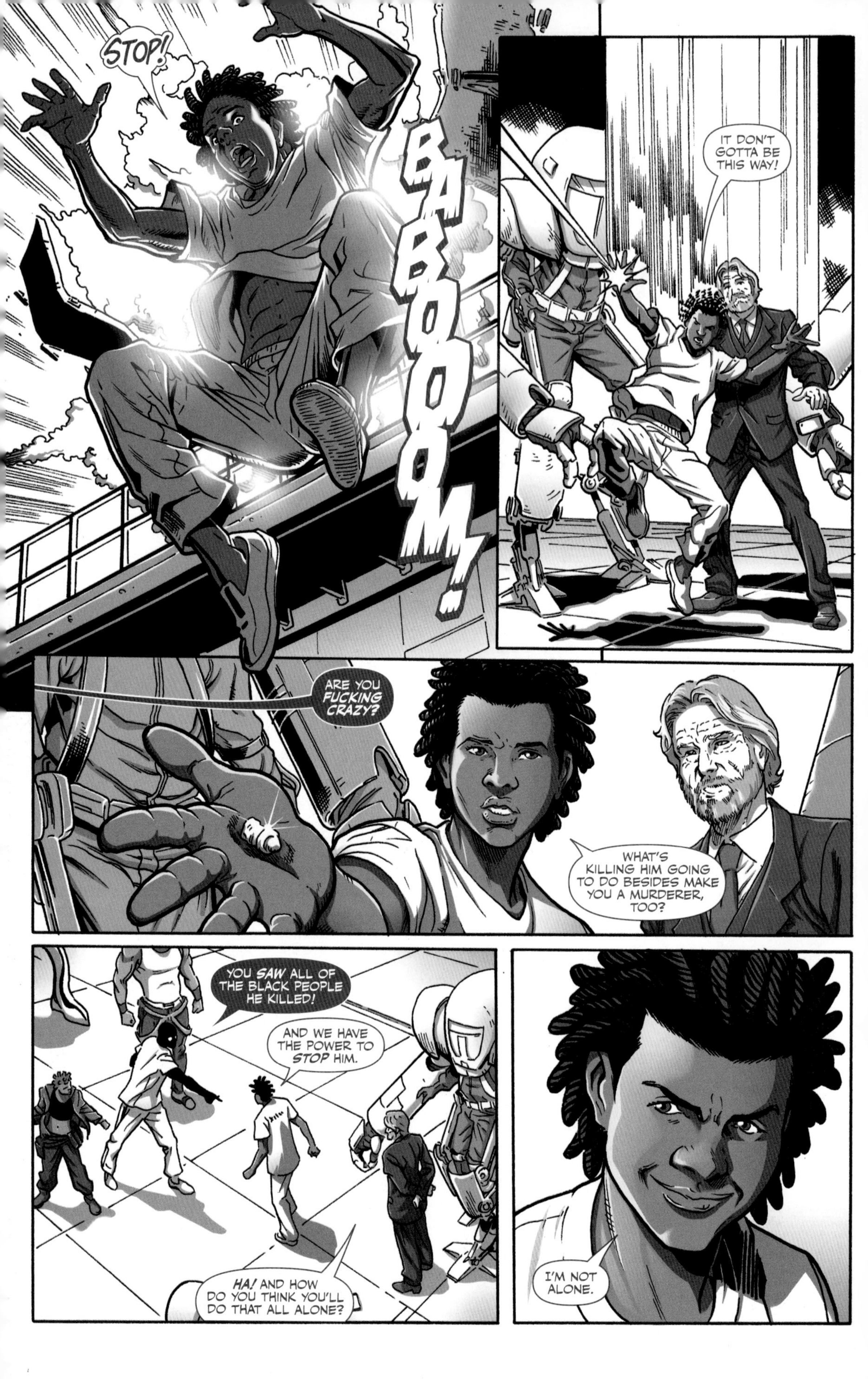
STOP!
BABOOOOM!
IT DON'T GOTTA BE THIS WAY!
ARE YOU FUCKING CRAZY?
WHAT'S KILLING HIM GOING TO DO BESIDES MAKE YOU A MURDERER, TOO?
YOU SAW ALL OF THE BLACK PEOPLE HE KILLED!
AND WE HAVE THE POWER TO STOP HIM.
HA! AND HOW DO YOU THINK YOU'LL DO THAT ALL ALONE?
I'M NOT ALONE.

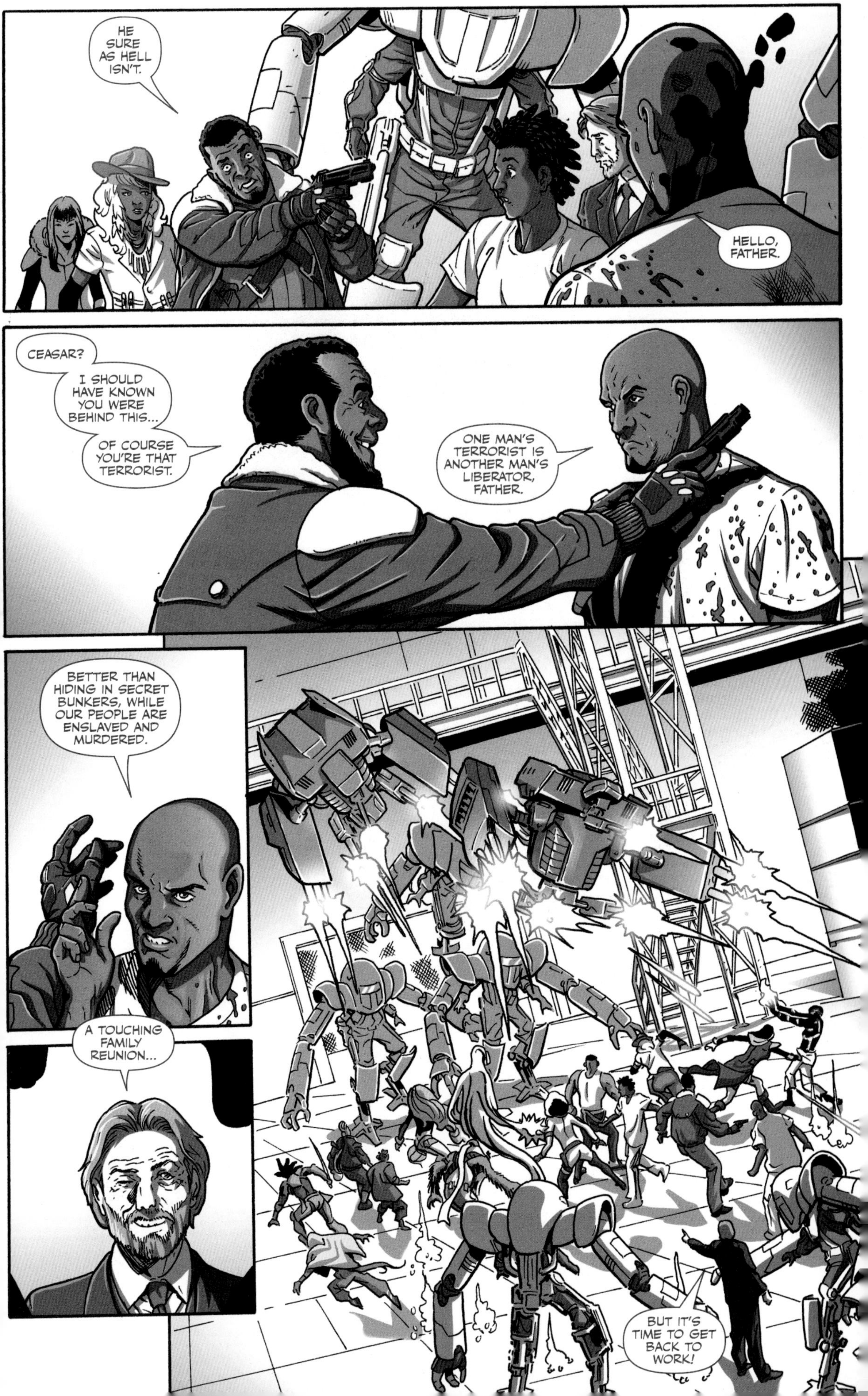
HE SURE AS HELL ISN'T.
HELLO, FATHER.
CEASAR?
I SHOULD HAVE KNOWN YOU WERE BEHIND THIS...
OF COURSE YOU'RE THAT TERRORIST.
ONE MAN'S TERRORIST IS ANOTHER MAN'S LIBERATOR, FATHER.
BETTER THAN HIDING IN SECRET BUNKERS, WHILE OUR PEOPLE ARE ENSLAVED AND MURDERED.
A TOUCHING FAMILY REUNION...
BUT IT'S TIME TO GET BACK TO WORK!

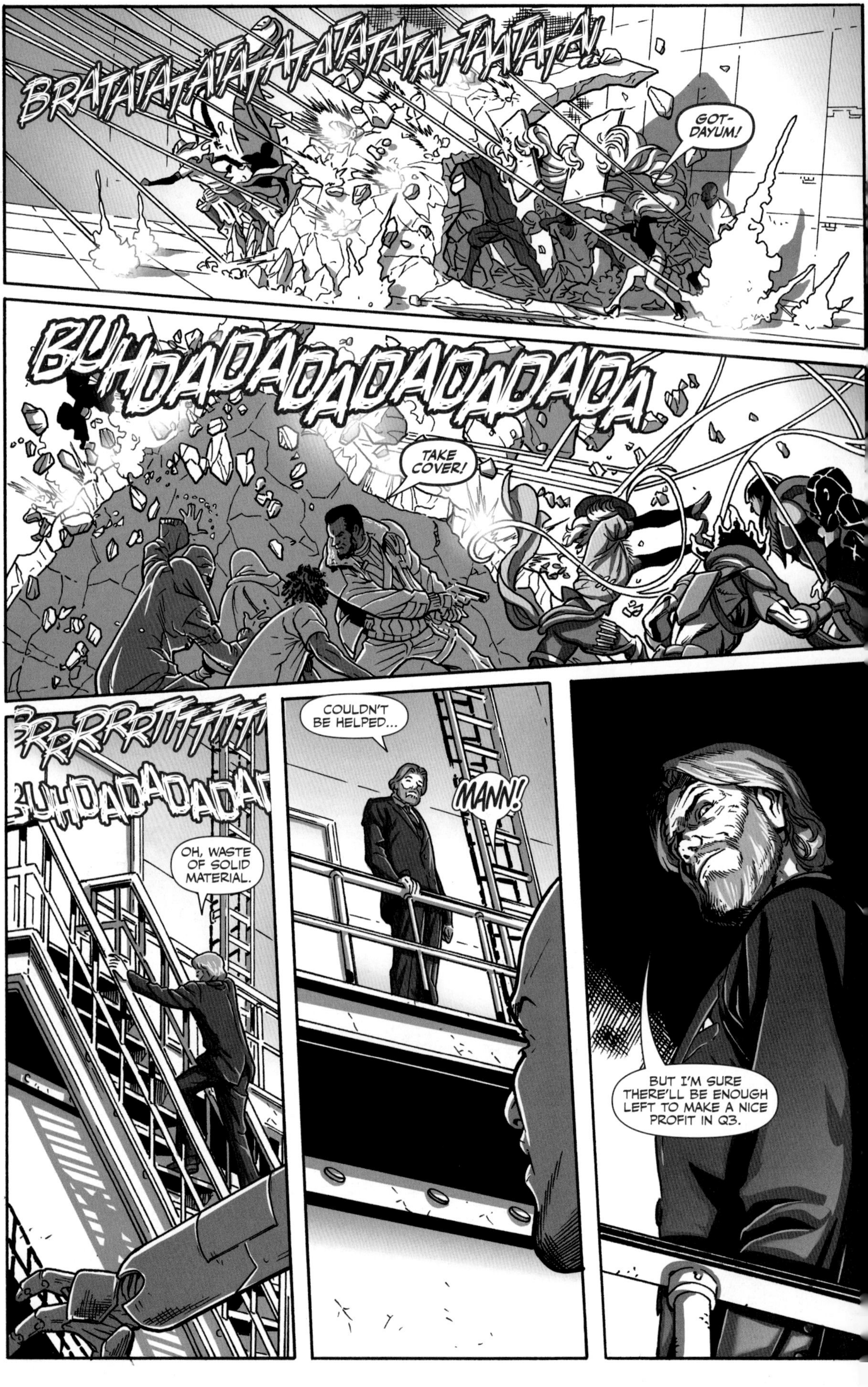
BRATATATATATATATATATATAATATA!
GOT-DAYUM!
BUHDADADADADADADA
TAKE COVER!
BRRRRTTTTTTT
BUHDADADADAD
OH, WASTE OF SOLID MATERIAL.
COULDN'T BE HELPED...
MANN!
BUT I'M SURE THERE'LL BE ENOUGH LEFT TO MAKE A NICE PROFIT IN Q3.

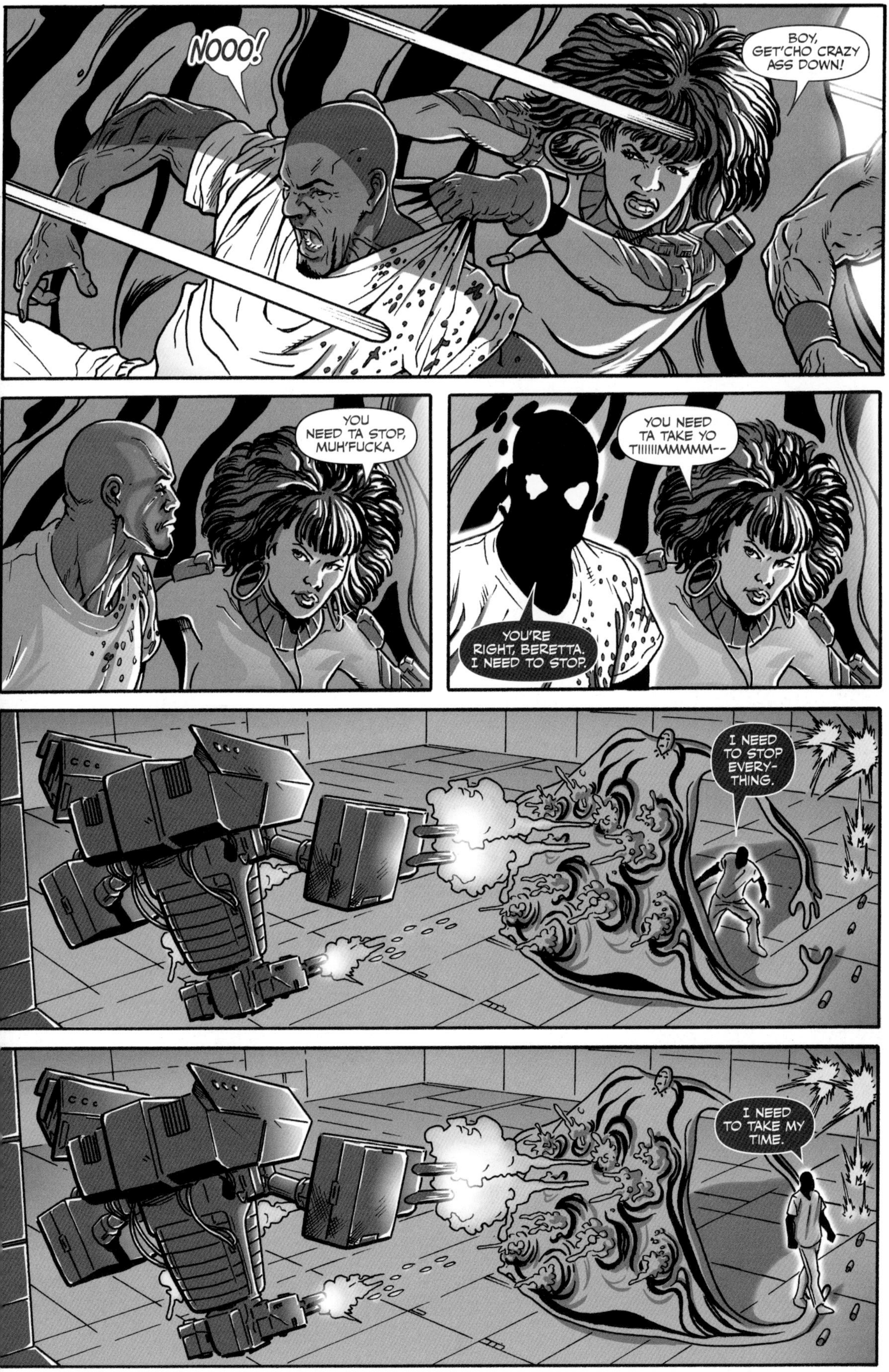
NOOO!
BOY, GET'CHO CRAZY ASS DOWN!
YOU NEED TA STOP, MUH'FUCKA.
YOU NEED TA TAKE YO TIIIIIMMMMM--
YOU'RE RIGHT, BERETTA. I NEED TO STOP.
I NEED TO STOP EVERY-THING.
I NEED TO TAKE MY TIME.

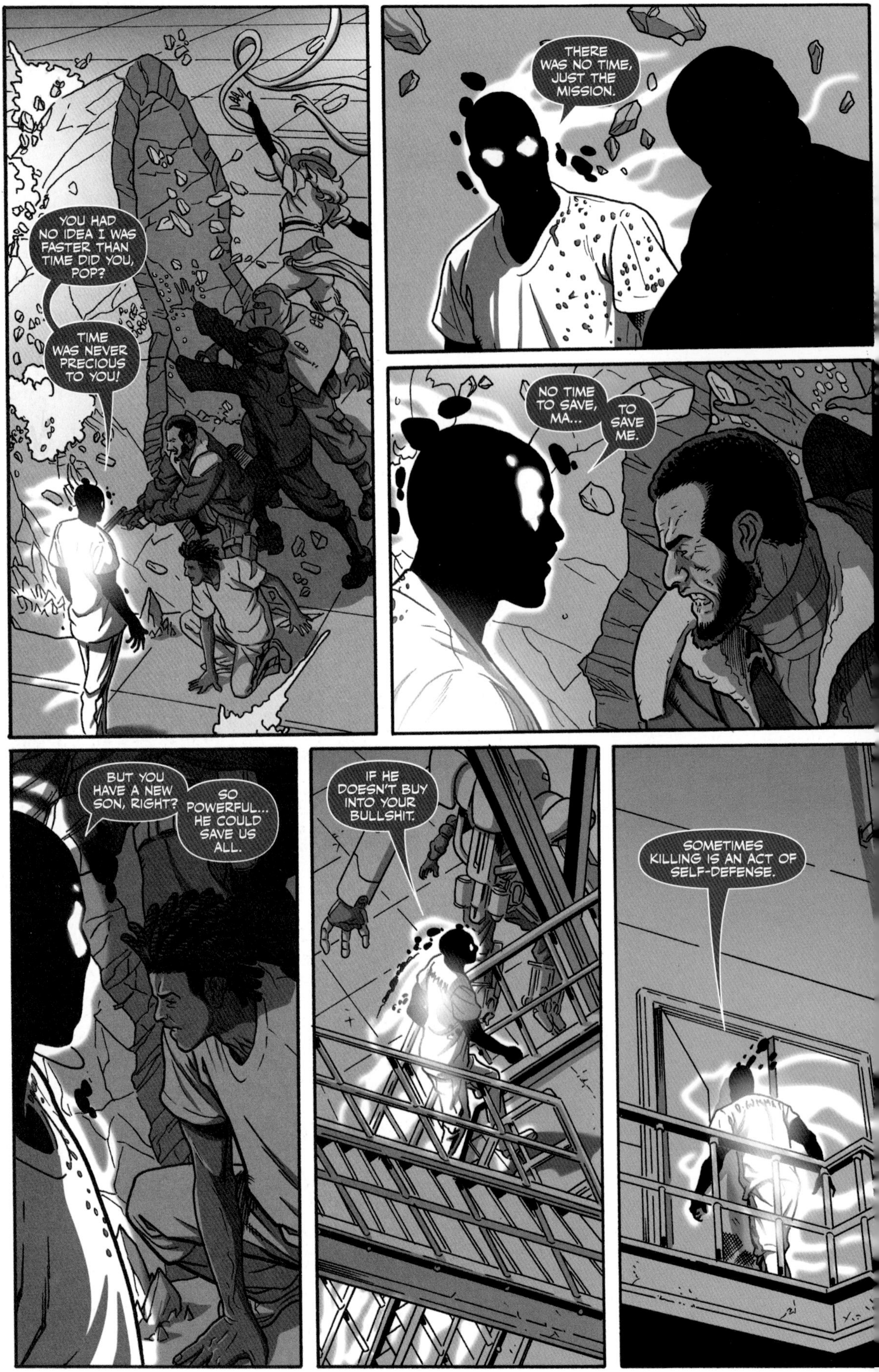
YOU HAD NO IDEA I WAS FASTER THAN TIME DID YOU, POP?
TIME WAS NEVER PRECIOUS TO YOU!
THERE WAS NO TIME, JUST THE MISSION.
NO TIME TO SAVE, MA...
TO SAVE ME.
BUT YOU HAVE A NEW SON, RIGHT?
SO POWERFUL... HE COULD SAVE US ALL.
IF HE DOESN'T BUY INTO YOUR BULLSHIT.
SOMETIMES KILLING IS AN ACT OF SELF-DEFENSE.

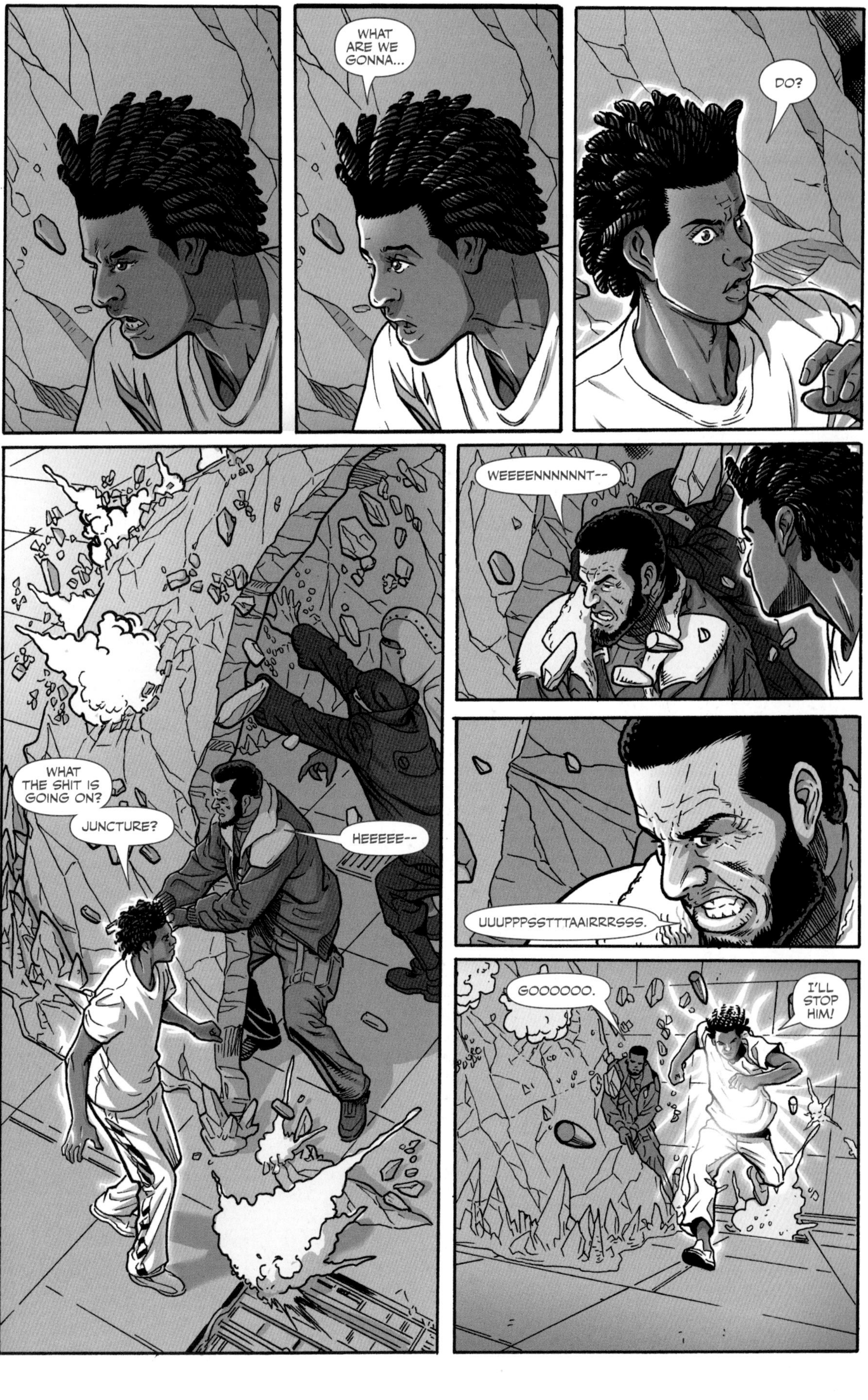
WHAT ARE WE GONNA...
DO?
WHAT THE SHIT IS GOING ON?
JUNCTURE?
HEEEEE--
WEEEENNNNNNT--
UUUPPPSSTTTAAIRRRSSS.
GOOOOOO.
I'LL STOP HIM!

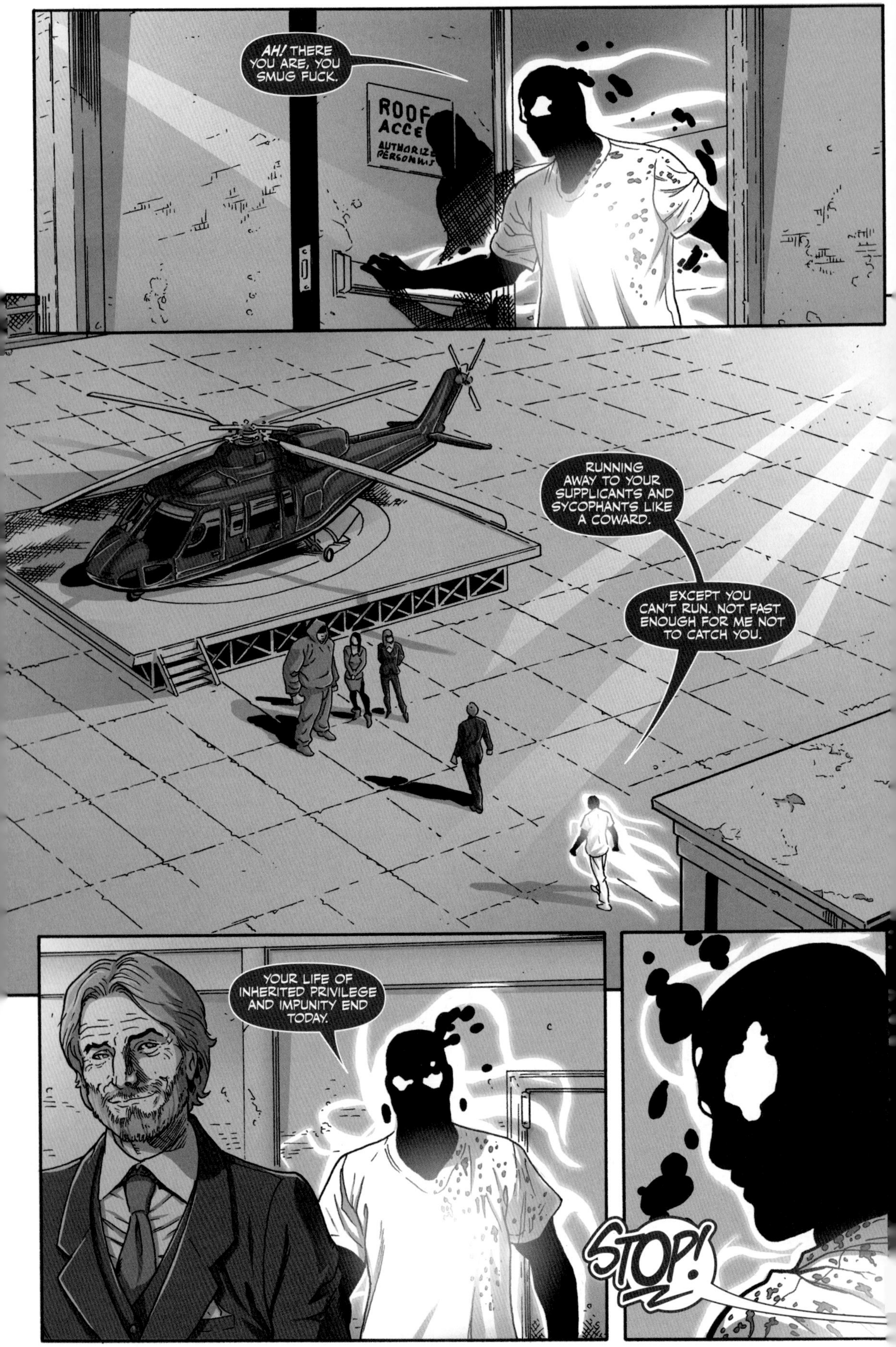

AH! THERE YOU ARE, YOU SMUG FUCK.
ROOF ACCE AUTHORIZE PERSONNE
RUNNING AWAY TO YOUR SUPPLICANTS AND SYCOPHANTS LIKE A COWARD.
EXCEPT YOU CAN'T RUN. NOT FAST ENOUGH FOR ME NOT TO CATCH YOU.
YOUR LIFE OF INHERITED PRIVILEGE AND IMPUNITY END TODAY.
STOP!

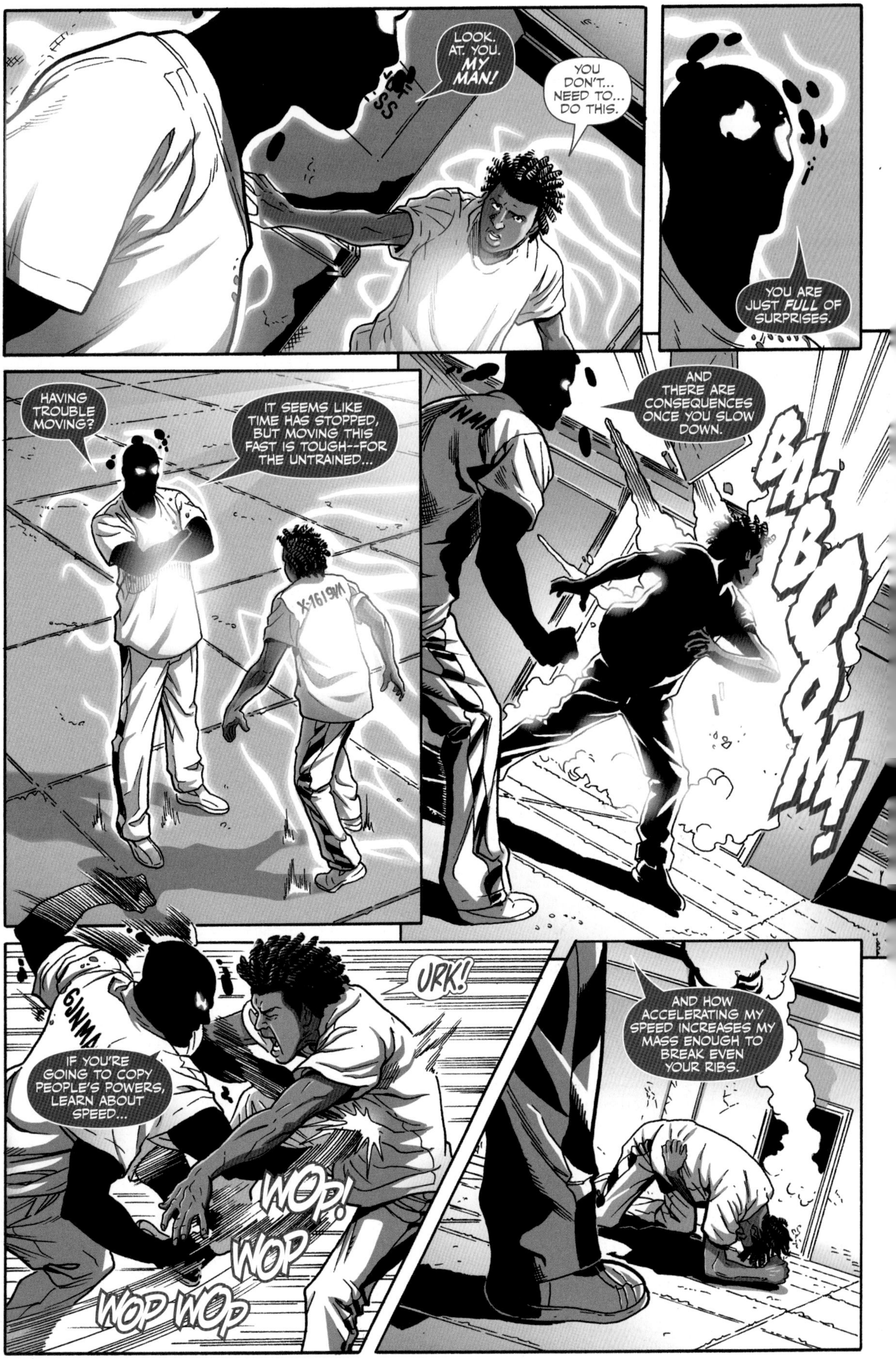
LOOK. AT. YOU. MY MAN!
YOU DON'T... NEED TO... DO THIS.
YOU ARE JUST FULL OF SURPRISES.
HAVING TROUBLE MOVING?
IT SEEMS LIKE TIME HAS STOPPED, BUT MOVING THIS FAST IS TOUGH--FOR THE UNTRAINED...
AND THERE ARE CONSEQUENCES ONCE YOU SLOW DOWN.
BA-BOOM!
URK!
IF YOU'RE GOING TO COPY PEOPLE'S POWERS, LEARN ABOUT SPEED...
WOP!
WOP
WOP WOP
AND HOW ACCELERATING MY SPEED INCREASES MY MASS ENOUGH TO BREAK EVEN YOUR RIBS.

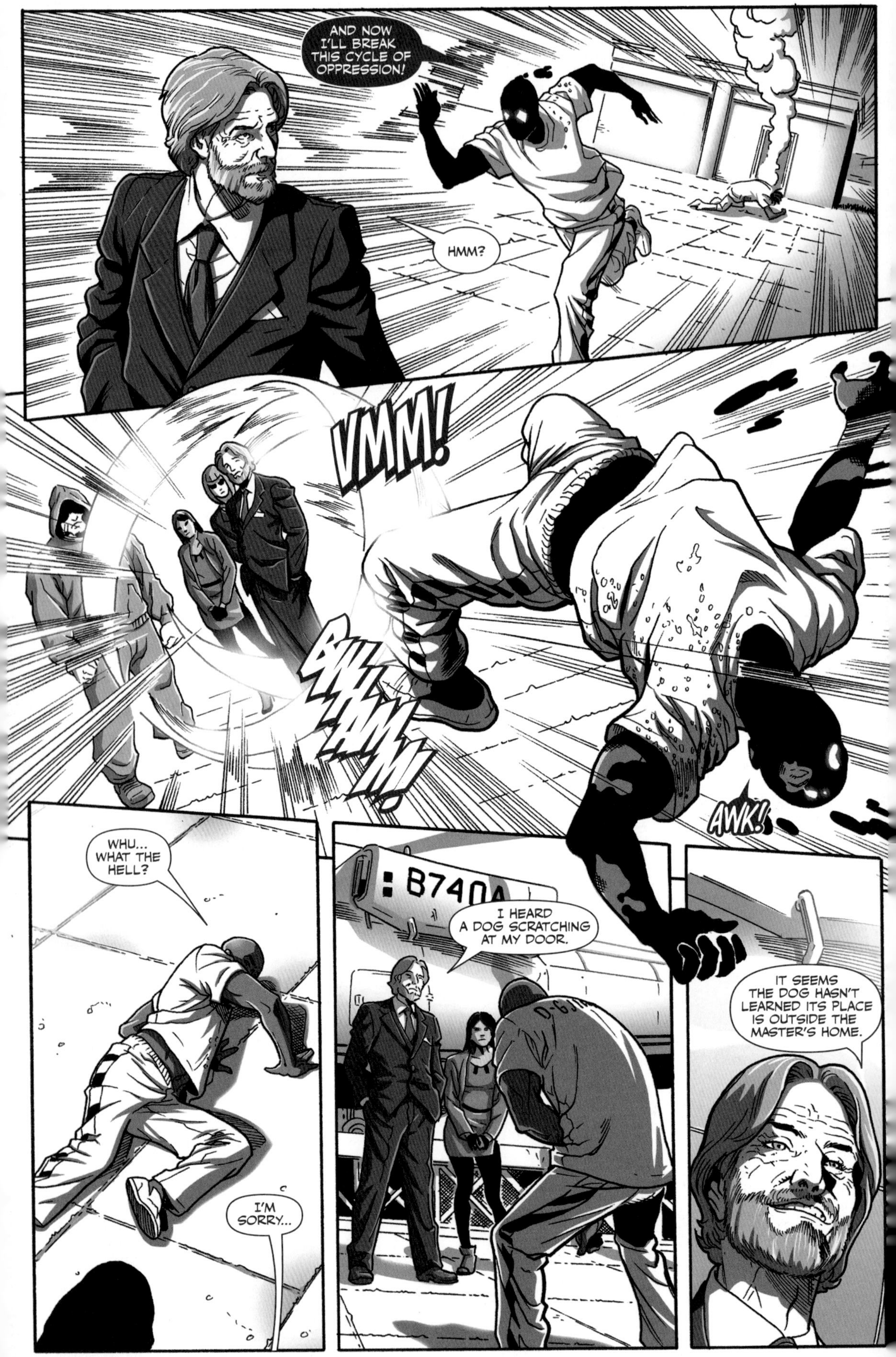
AND NOW I'LL BREAK THIS CYCLE OF OPPRESSION!
HMM?
VMM!
BWHAM!
AWK!
WHU... WHAT THE HELL?
I'M SORRY...
B740A
I HEARD A DOG SCRATCHING AT MY DOOR.
IT SEEMS THE DOG HASN'T LEARNED ITS PLACE IS OUTSIDE THE MASTER'S HOME.

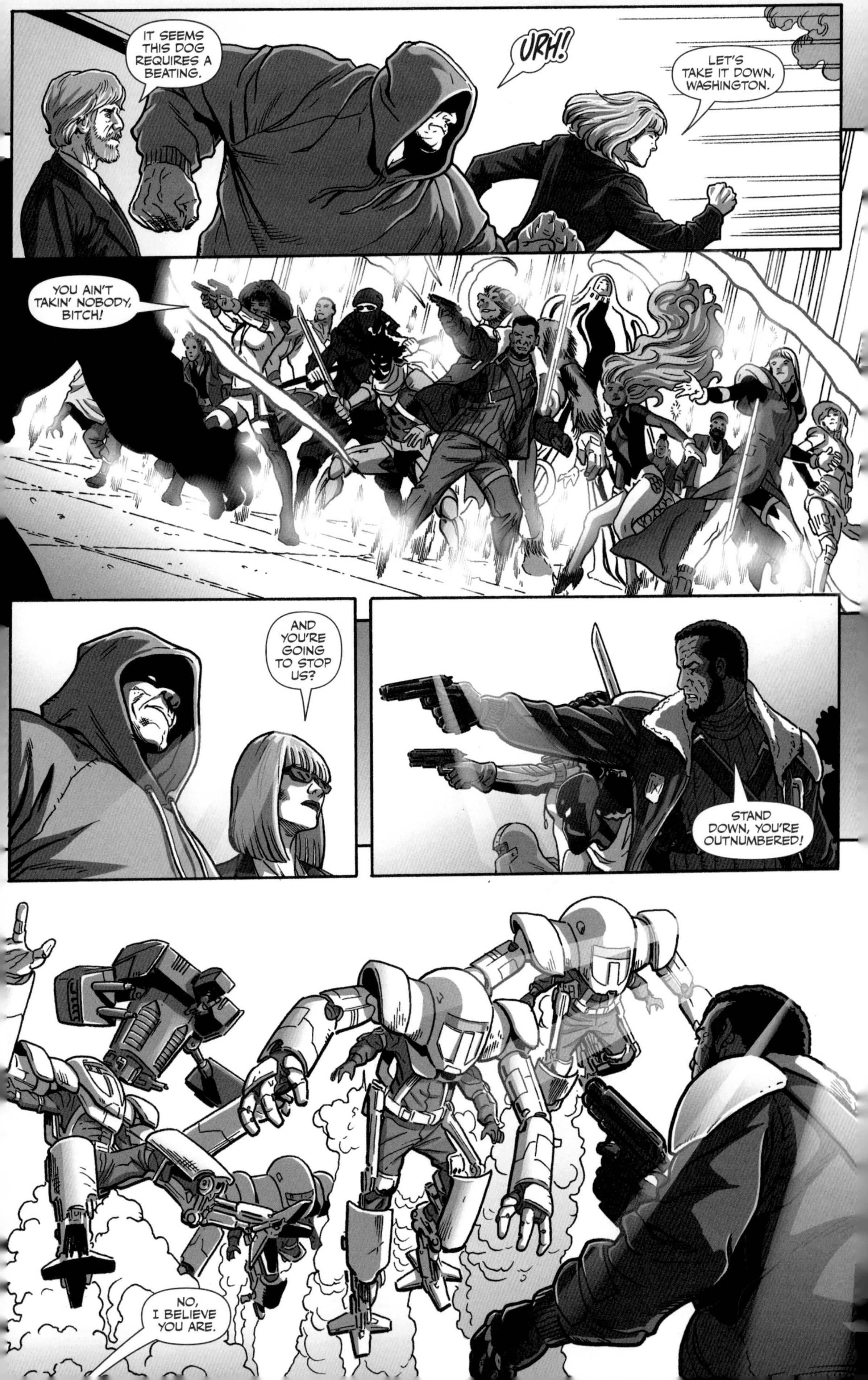
IT SEEMS THIS DOG REQUIRES A BEATING.
URH!
LET'S TAKE IT DOWN, WASHINGTON.
YOU AIN'T TAKIN' NOBODY, BITCH!
AND YOU'RE GOING TO STOP US?
STAND DOWN, YOU'RE OUTNUMBERED!
NO, I BELIEVE YOU ARE.

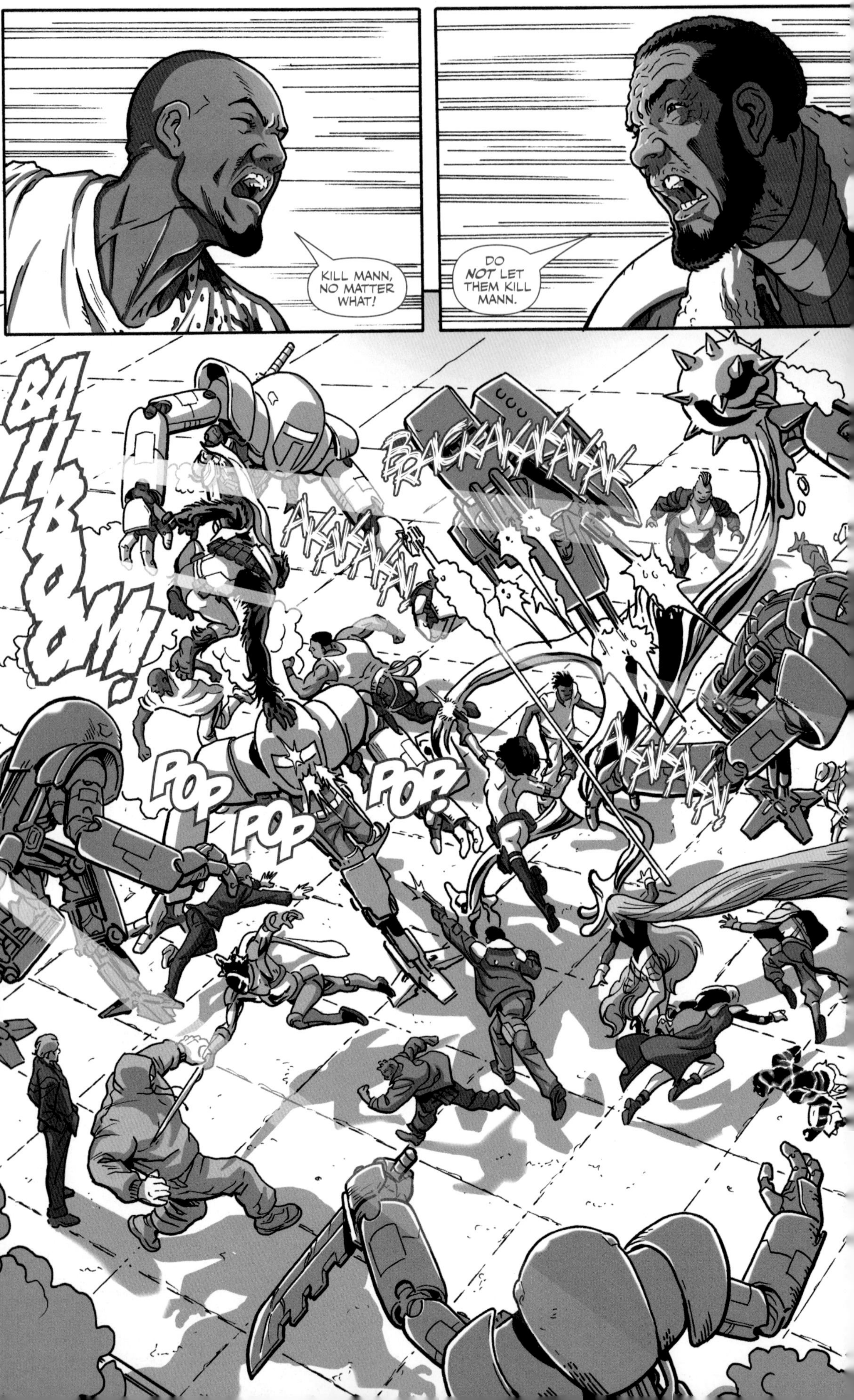
KILL MANN, NO MATTER WHAT!
DO *NOT* LET THEM KILL MANN.
BAHBOOM!
BRACKAKAKAKAKAK
AKAKAKAKAK
POP
POP
POP
AKAKAKAKAK

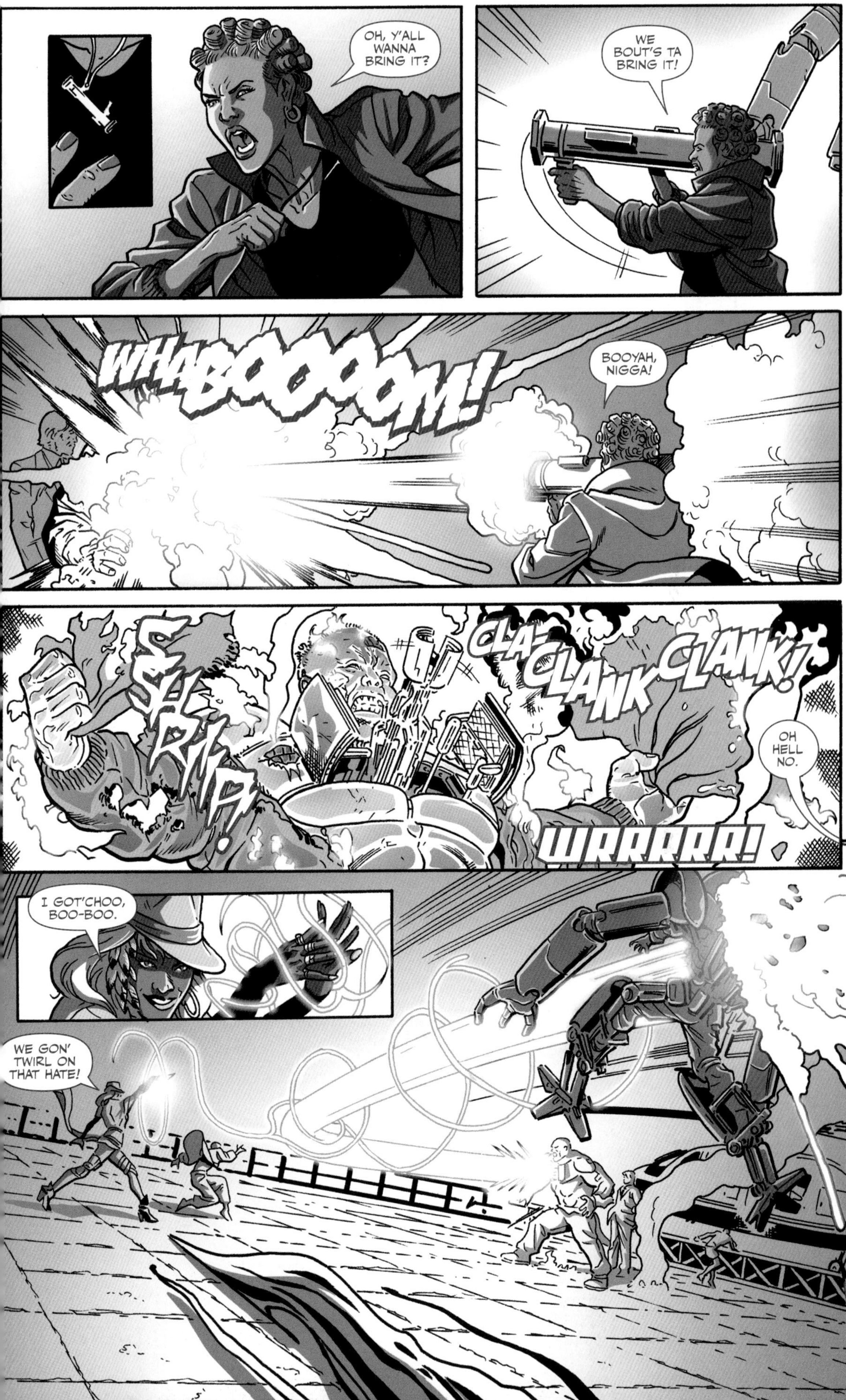
OH, Y'ALL WANNA BRING IT?
WE BOUT'S TA BRING IT!
WHABOOOOM!
BOOYAH, NIGGA!
CLA-CLANK CLANK CLANK!
OH HELL NO.
WRRRRR!
I GOT'CHOO, BOO-BOO.
WE GON' TWIRL ON THAT HATE!

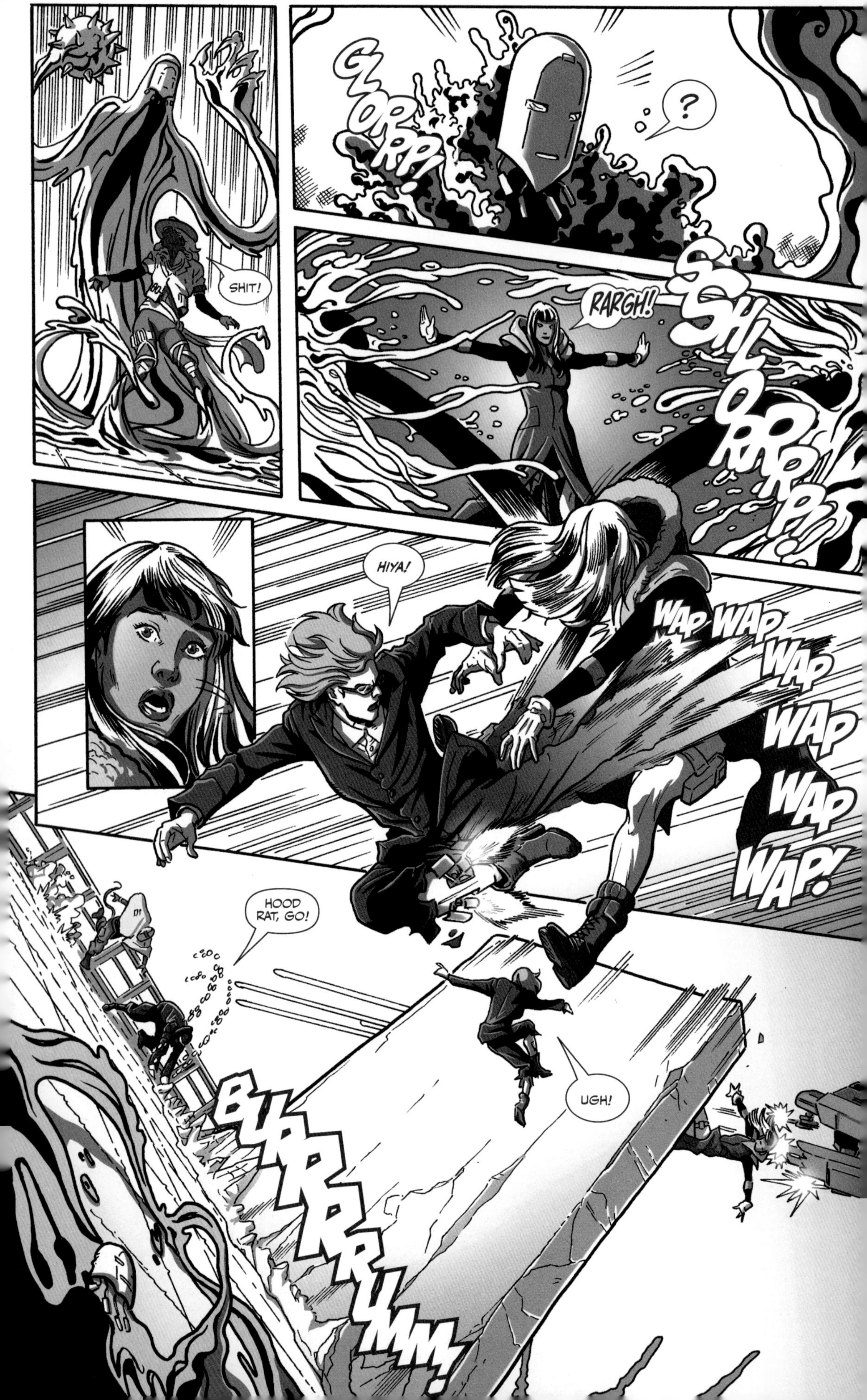
SHIT!
GLORRP!
?
RARGH!
SHLORRRRP!!
HIYA!
WAP WAP WAP WAP WAP WAP!
HOOD RAT, GO!
UGH!
BUDRRRUMMM!

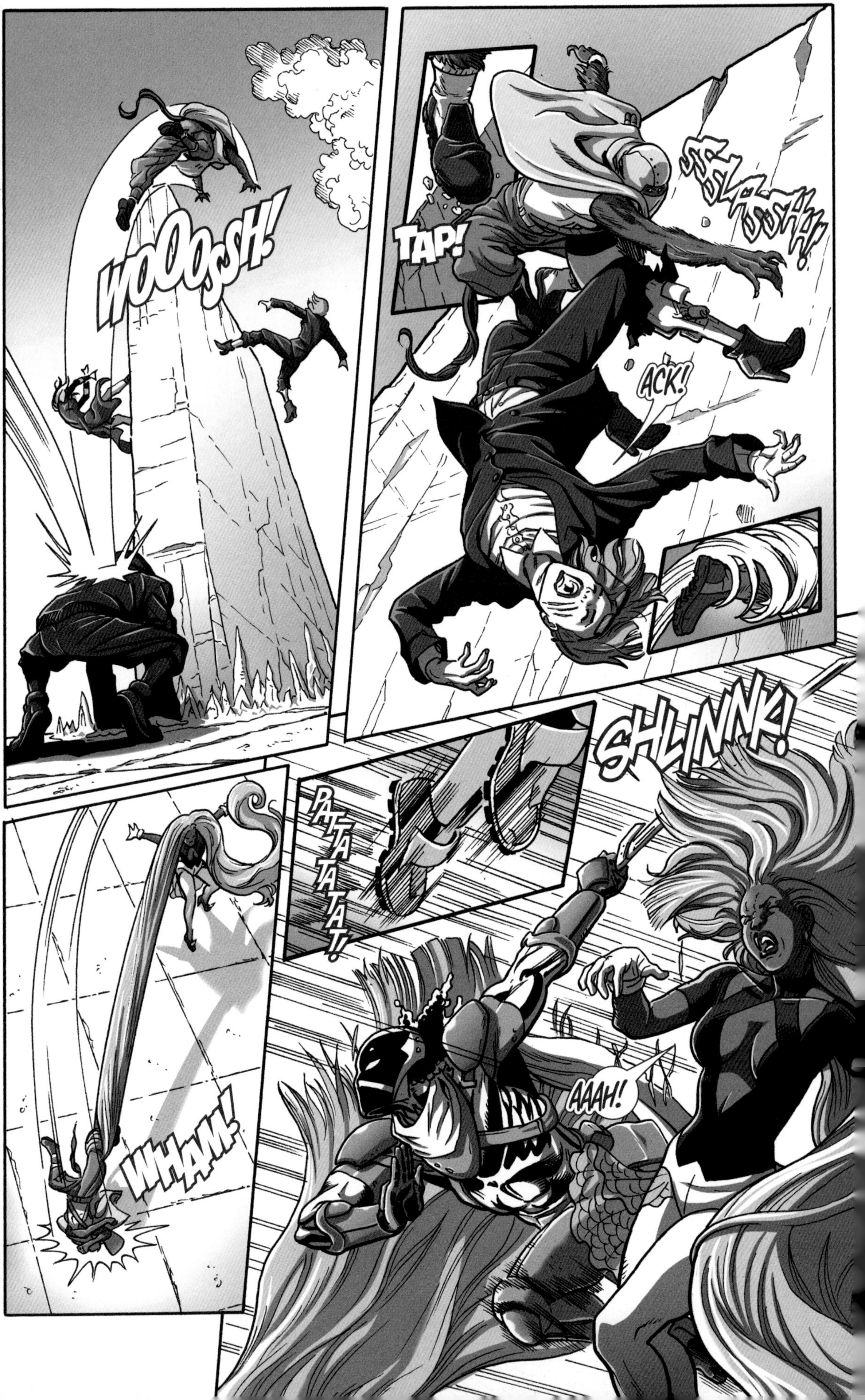
WOOOSSH!
TAP!
SSSLASSSH!
ACK!
SHLINNK!
PATATATAT!
WHAM!
AAAH!

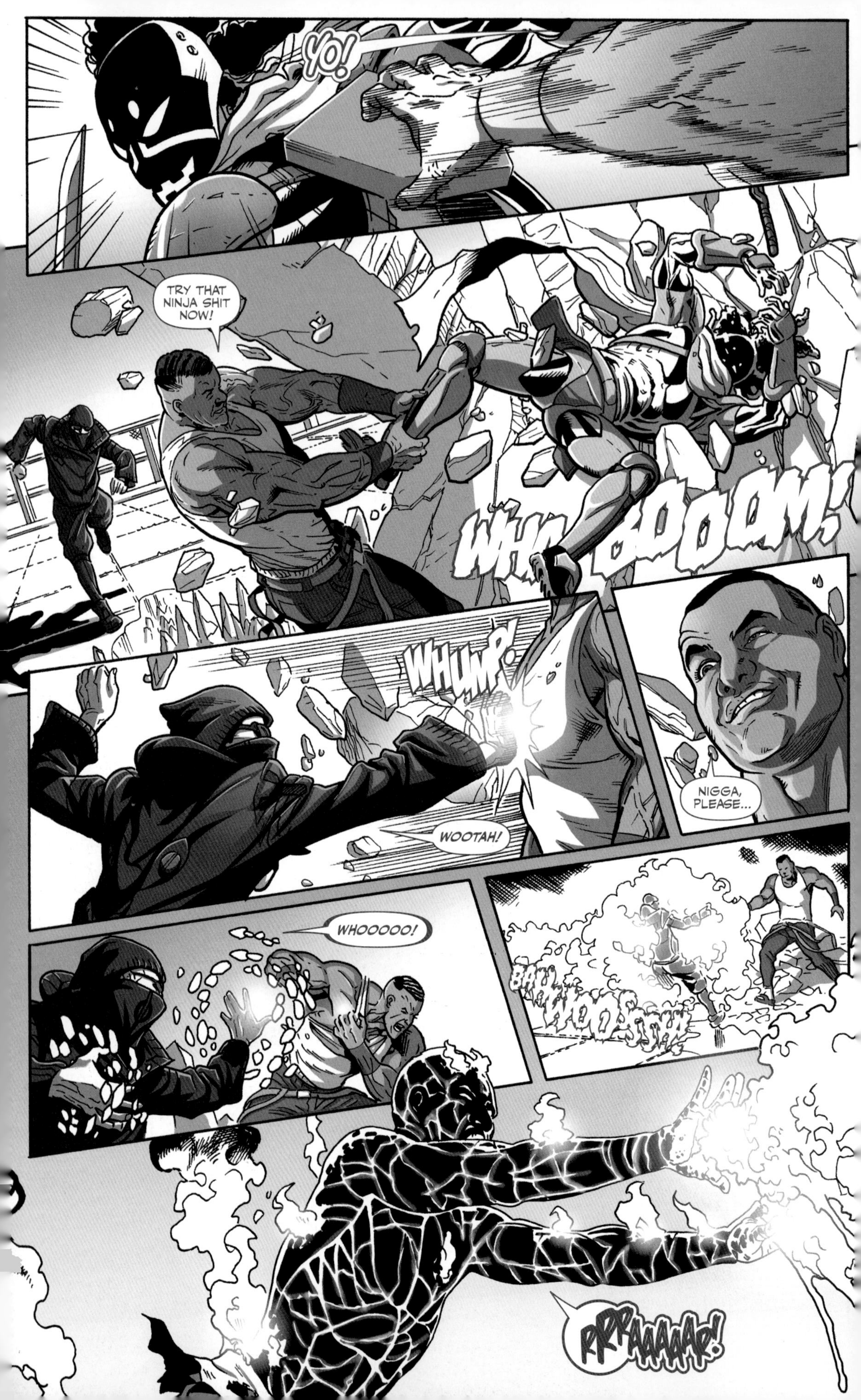
YO!
TRY THAT NINJA SHIT NOW!
BOOOM!
WHUMP!
WOOTAH!
NIGGA, PLEASE...
WHOOOOO!
RRRAAAAAR!

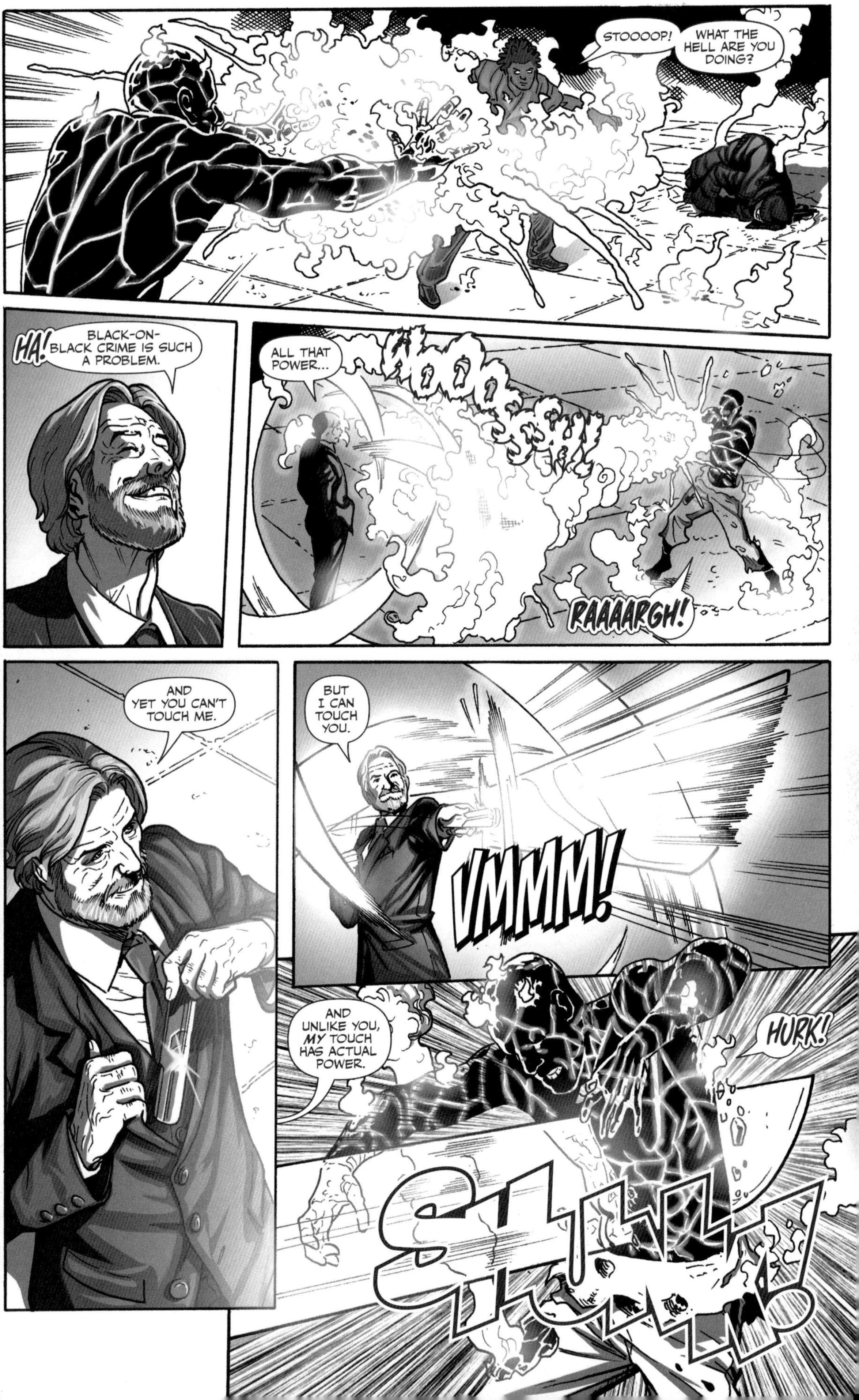
STOOOOP!
WHAT THE HELL ARE YOU DOING?
HA!
BLACK-ON-BLACK CRIME IS SUCH A PROBLEM.
ALL THAT POWER...
RAAAARGH!
AND YET YOU CAN'T TOUCH ME.
BUT I CAN TOUCH YOU.
VMMM!
AND UNLIKE YOU, *MY* TOUCH HAS ACTUAL POWER.
HURK!

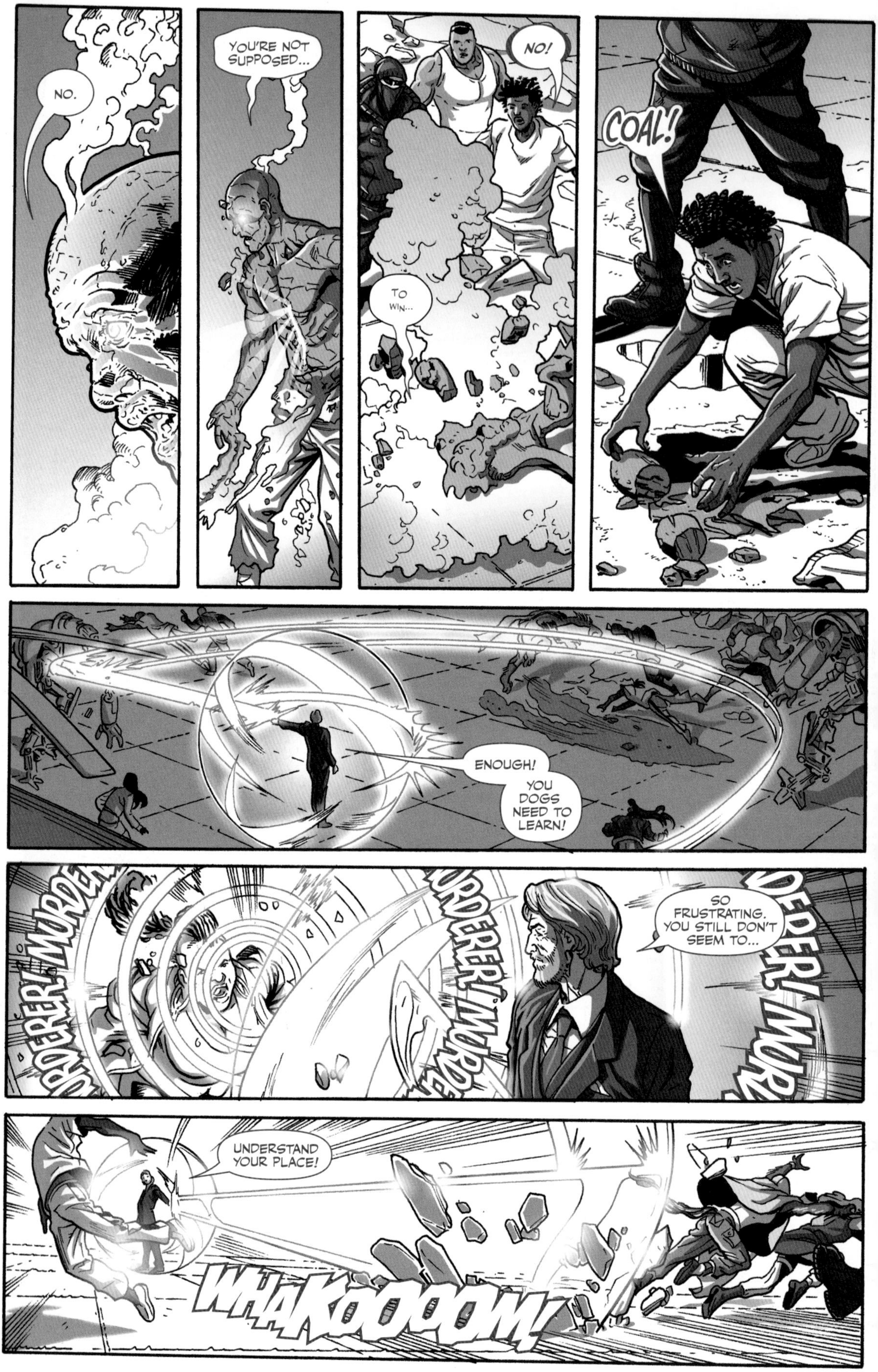
NO.
YOU'RE NOT SUPPOSED...
NO!
TO WIN...
COAL!
ENOUGH!
YOU DOGS NEED TO LEARN!
SO FRUSTRATING. YOU STILL DON'T SEEM TO...
UNDERSTAND YOUR PLACE!
WHAKOOOOM!

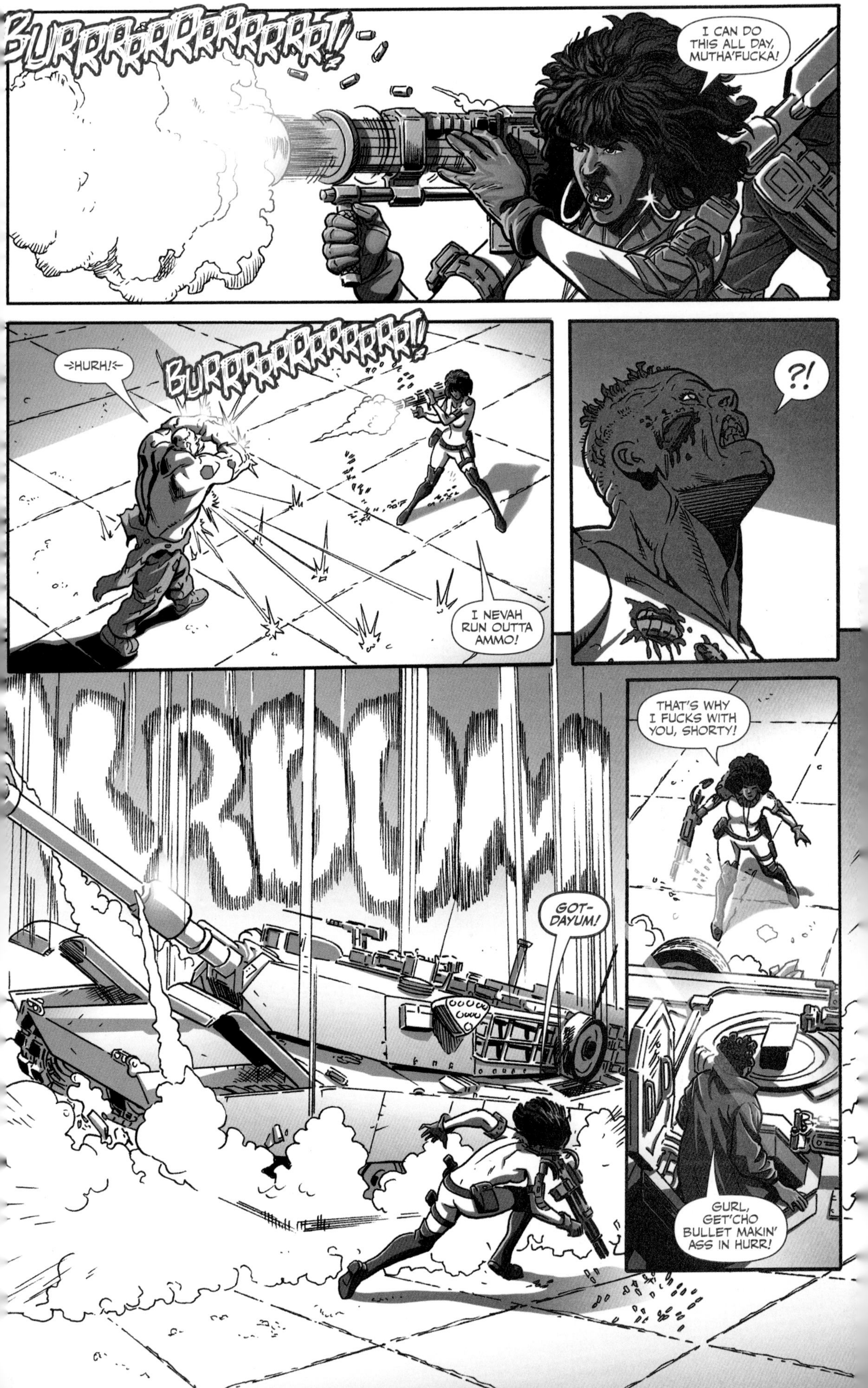
BURRRRRRRRRRRRT!
I CAN DO THIS ALL DAY, MUTHA'FUCKA!
BURRRRRRRRRRRRT!
HURH!
I NEVAH RUN OUTTA AMMO!
?!
KRBOOM
THAT'S WHY I FUCKS WITH YOU, SHORTY!
GOT-DAYUM!
GURL, GET'CHO BULLET MAKIN' ASS IN HURR!

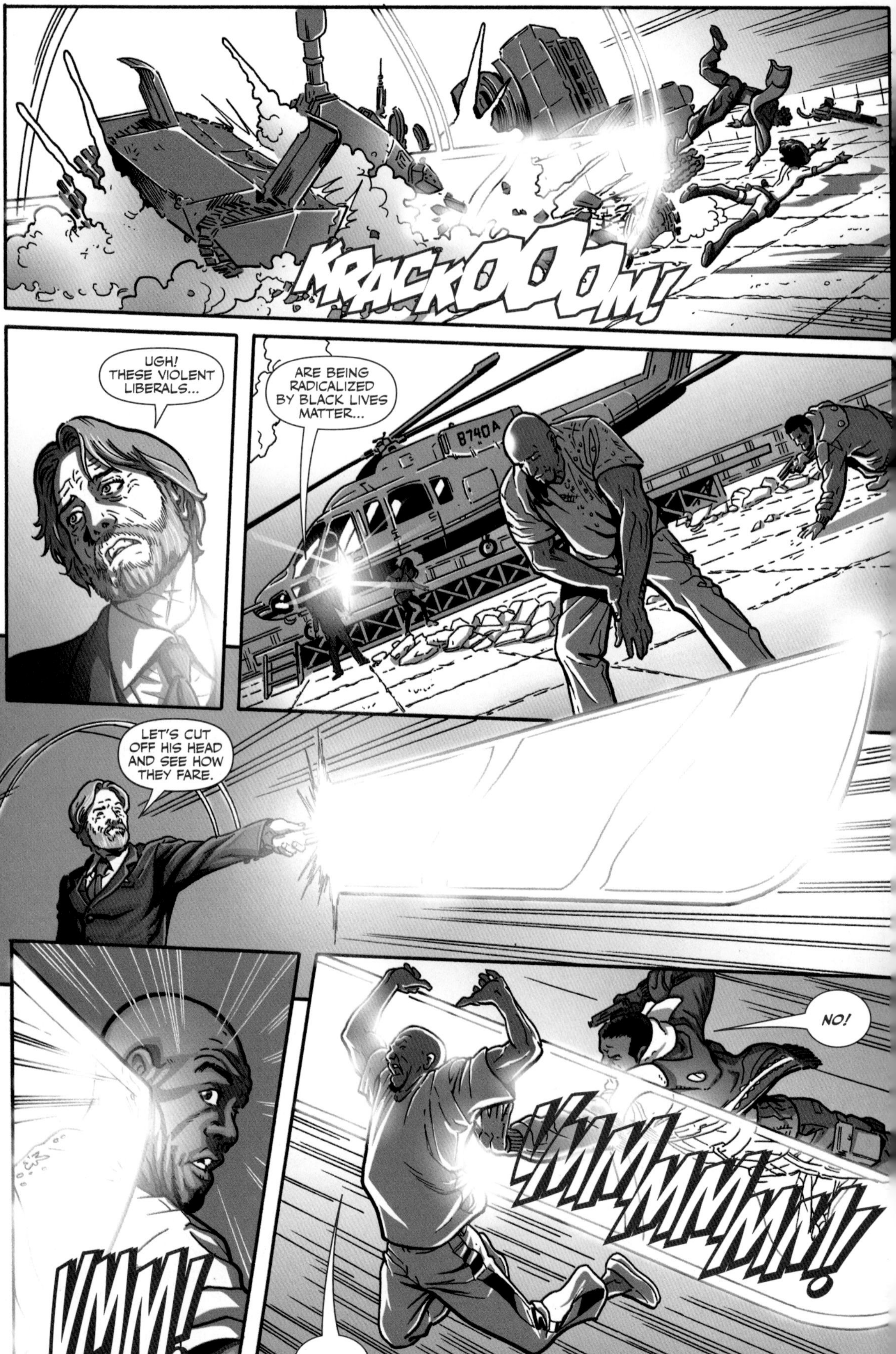
KRACKOOOOM!
UGH! THESE VIOLENT LIBERALS...
ARE BEING RADICALIZED BY BLACK LIVES MATTER...
8740A
LET'S CUT OFF HIS HEAD AND SEE HOW THEY FARE.
VMM!
NO!
VMMMMMM!
OOF!

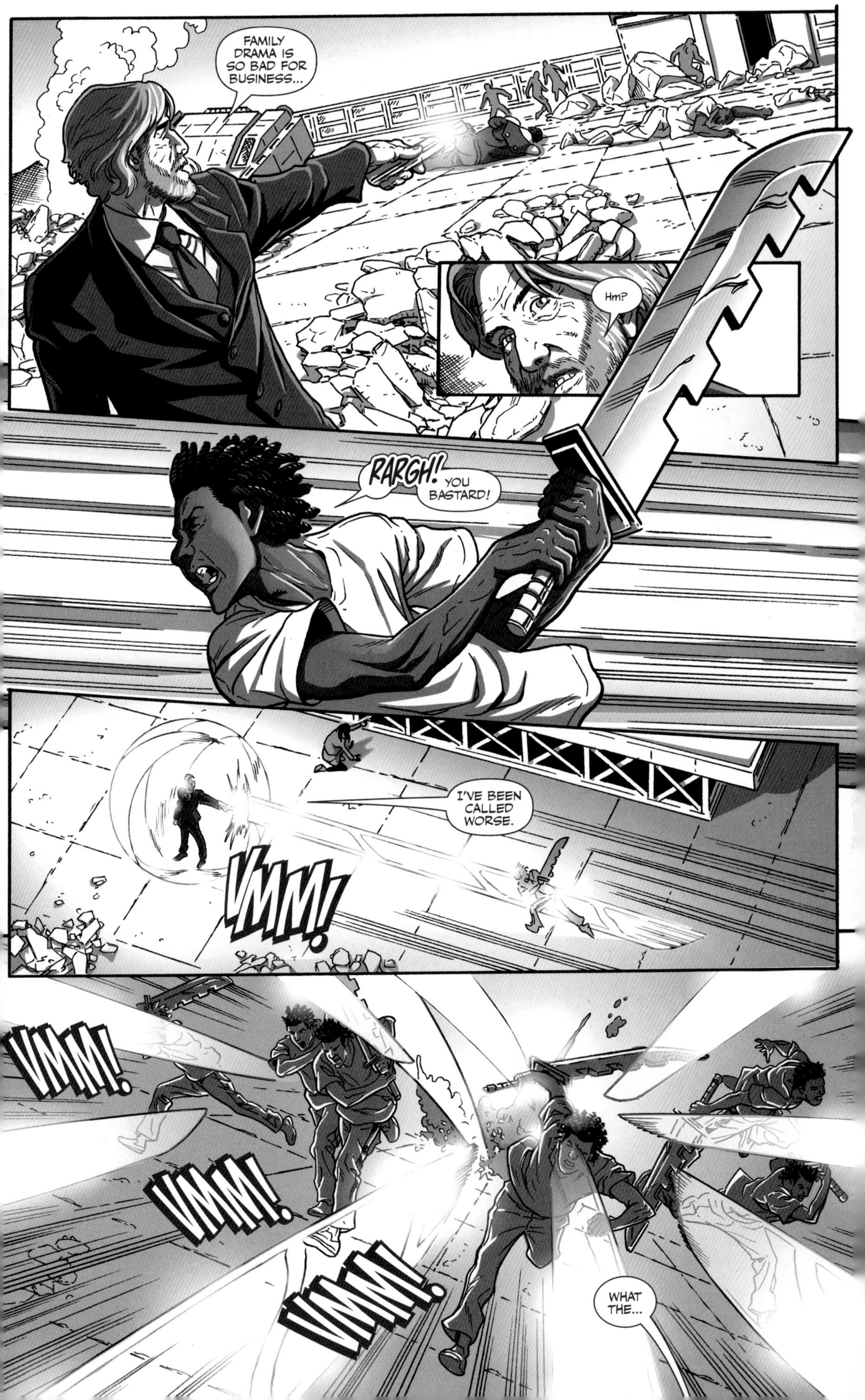
FAMILY DRAMA IS SO BAD FOR BUSINESS...
Hm?
RARGH!
YOU BASTARD!
I'VE BEEN CALLED WORSE.
VMM!
VMM!
VMM!
VMM!
WHAT THE...

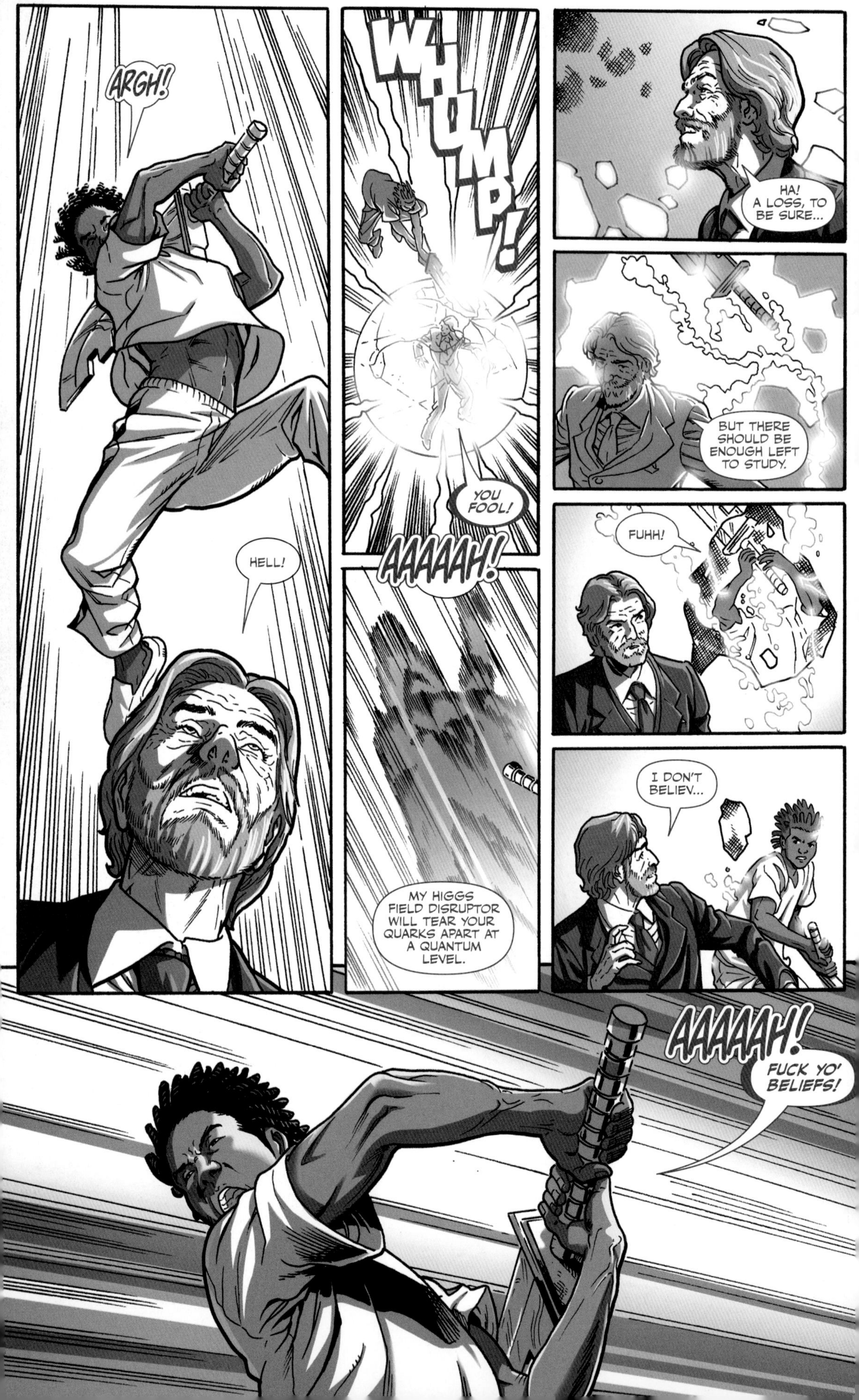
ARGH!
HELL!
WHUMP!
YOU FOOL!
AAAAAH!
MY HIGGS FIELD DISRUPTOR WILL TEAR YOUR QUARKS APART AT A QUANTUM LEVEL.
HA! A LOSS, TO BE SURE...
BUT THERE SHOULD BE ENOUGH LEFT TO STUDY.
FUHH!
I DON'T BELIEV...
AAAAAH!
FUCK YO' BELIEFS!

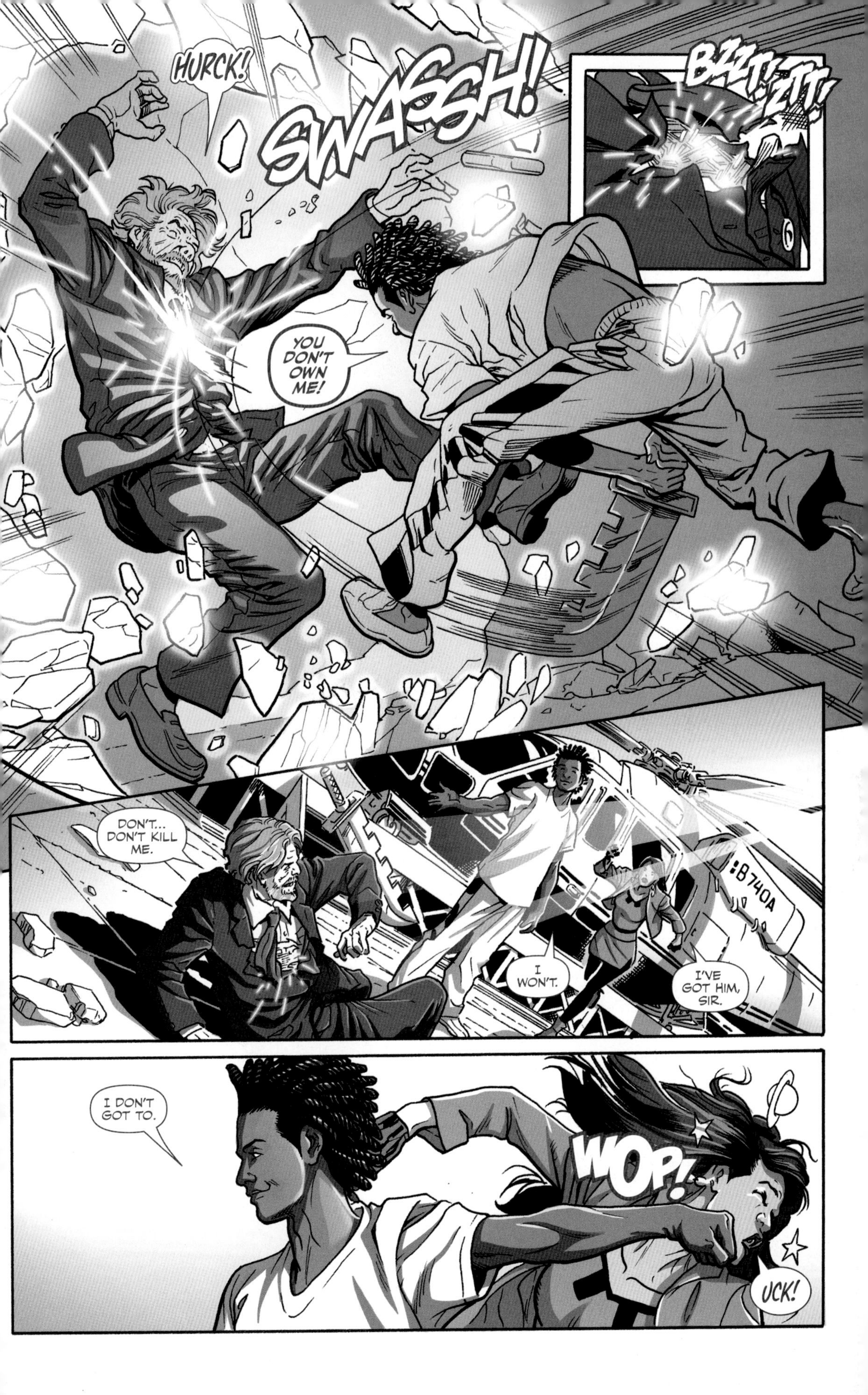
HURCK!
SWASSH!
BZZT! ZTT!
YOU DON'T OWN ME!
DON'T... DON'T KILL ME.
I WON'T.
I'VE GOT HIM, SIR.
I DON'T GOT TO.
WOP!
UCK!

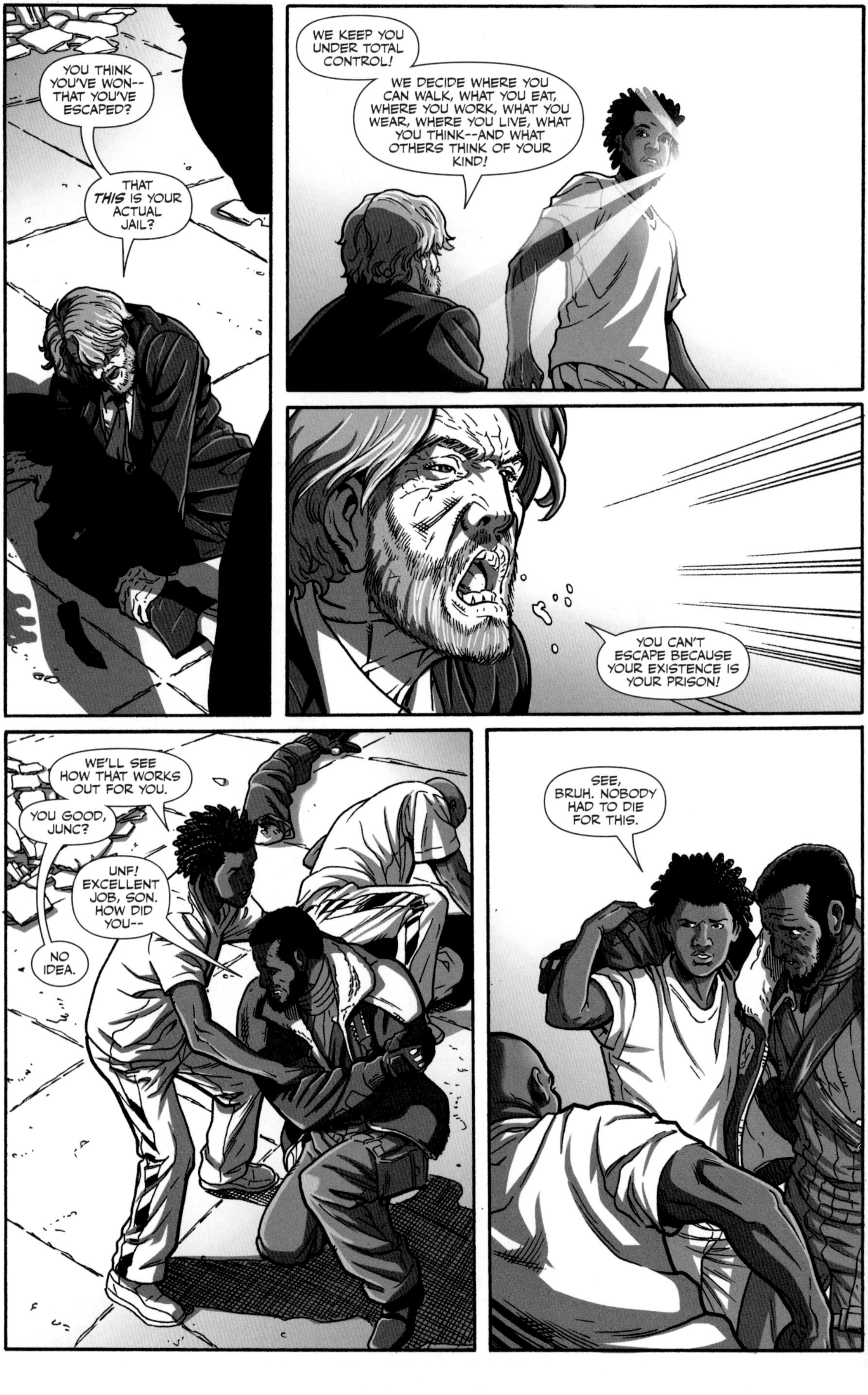
YOU THINK YOU'VE WON-- THAT YOU'VE ESCAPED?
THAT *THIS* IS YOUR ACTUAL JAIL?
WE KEEP YOU UNDER TOTAL CONTROL!
WE DECIDE WHERE YOU CAN WALK, WHAT YOU EAT, WHERE YOU WORK, WHAT YOU WEAR, WHERE YOU LIVE, WHAT YOU THINK--AND WHAT OTHERS THINK OF YOUR KIND!
YOU CAN'T ESCAPE BECAUSE YOUR EXISTENCE IS YOUR PRISON!
WE'LL SEE HOW THAT WORKS OUT FOR YOU.
YOU GOOD, JUNC?
UNF! EXCELLENT JOB, SON. HOW DID YOU--
NO IDEA.
SEE, BRUH. NOBODY HAD TO DIE FOR THIS.

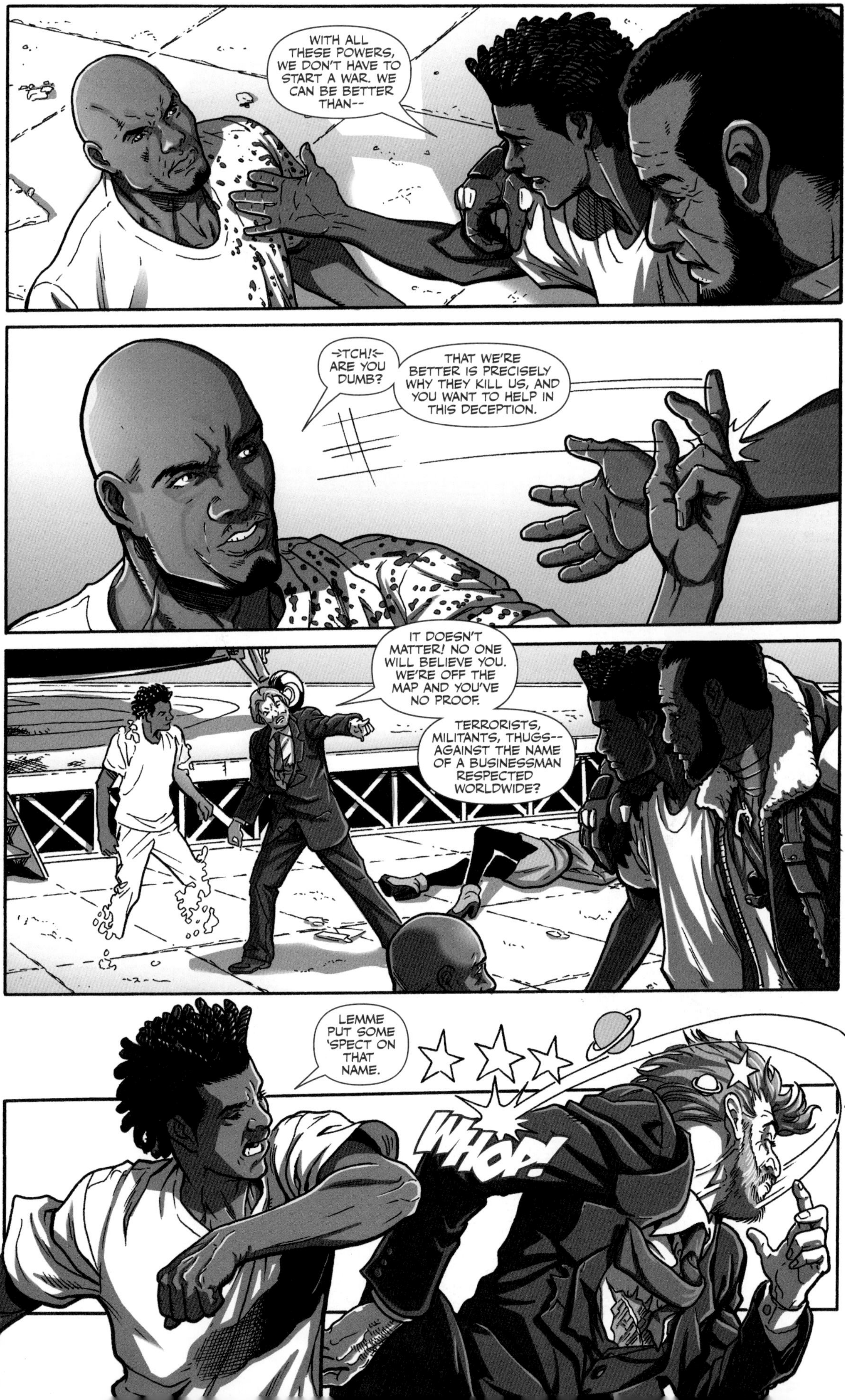
WITH ALL THESE POWERS, WE DON'T HAVE TO START A WAR. WE CAN BE BETTER THAN--
→TCH!← ARE YOU DUMB?
THAT WE'RE BETTER IS PRECISELY WHY THEY KILL US, AND YOU WANT TO HELP IN THIS DECEPTION.
IT DOESN'T MATTER! NO ONE WILL BELIEVE YOU. WE'RE OFF THE MAP AND YOU'VE NO PROOF.
TERRORISTS, MILITANTS, THUGS-- AGAINST THE NAME OF A BUSINESSMAN RESPECTED WORLDWIDE?
LEMME PUT SOME 'SPECT ON THAT NAME.
WHOP!

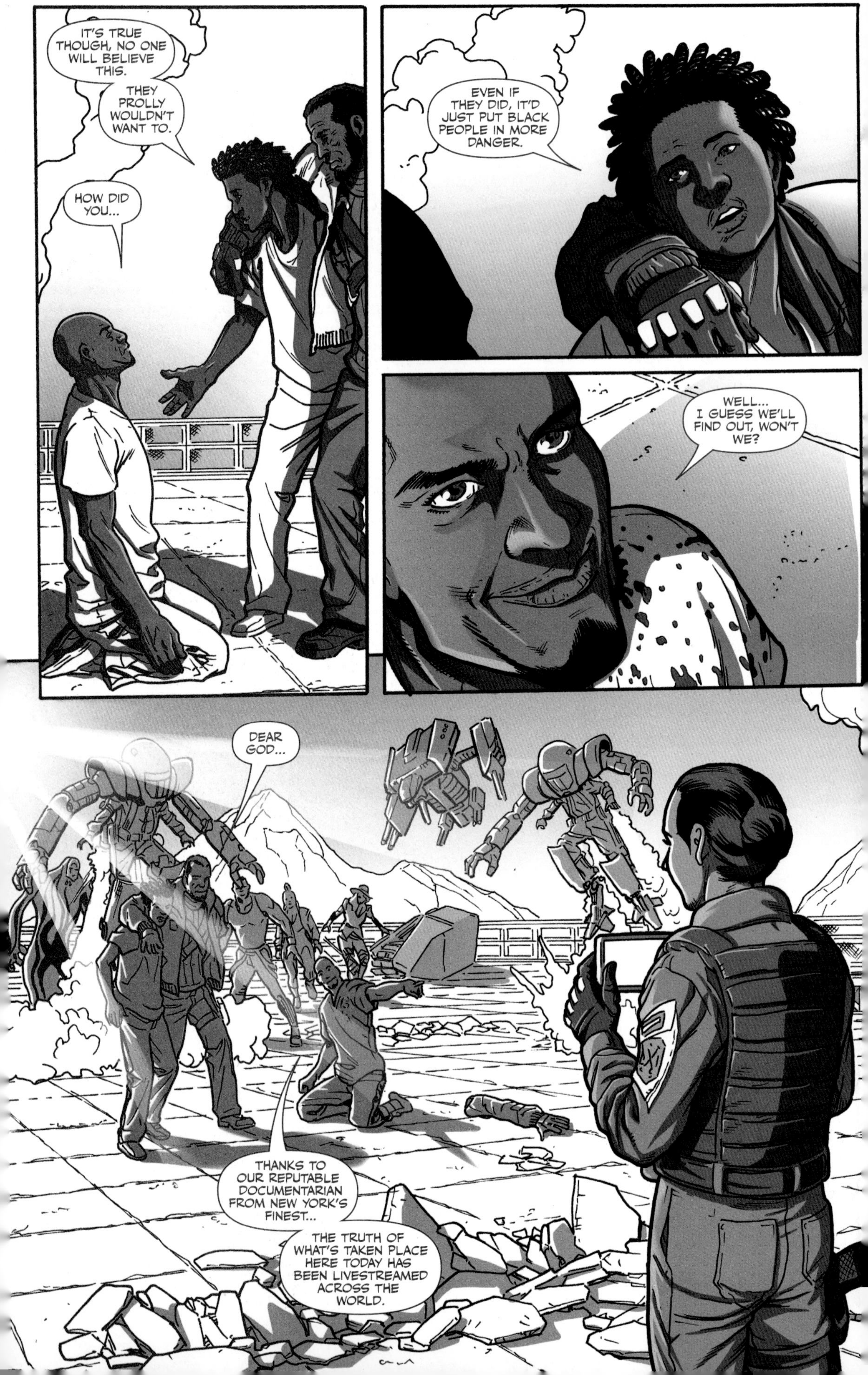
IT'S TRUE THOUGH, NO ONE WILL BELIEVE THIS.
THEY PROLLY WOULDN'T WANT TO.
HOW DID YOU...
EVEN IF THEY DID, IT'D JUST PUT BLACK PEOPLE IN MORE DANGER.
WELL... I GUESS WE'LL FIND OUT, WON'T WE?
DEAR GOD...
THANKS TO OUR REPUTABLE DOCUMENTARIAN FROM NEW YORK'S FINEST...
THE TRUTH OF WHAT'S TAKEN PLACE HERE TODAY HAS BEEN LIVESTREAMED ACROSS THE WORLD.

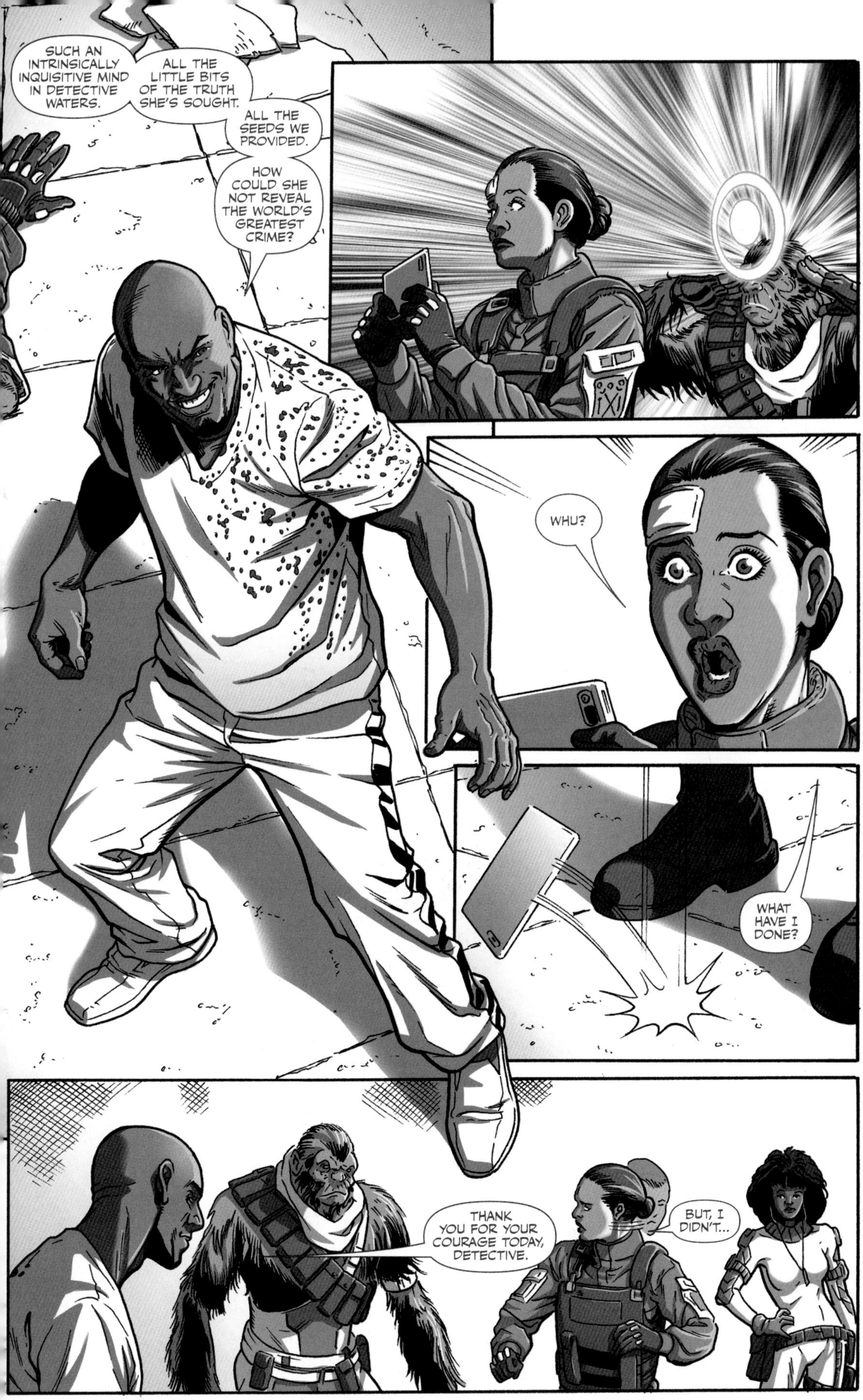
SUCH AN INTRINSICALLY INQUISITIVE MIND IN DETECTIVE WATERS.
ALL THE LITTLE BITS OF THE TRUTH SHE'S SOUGHT.
ALL THE SEEDS WE PROVIDED.
HOW COULD SHE NOT REVEAL THE WORLD'S GREATEST CRIME?
WHU?
WHAT HAVE I DONE?
THANK YOU FOR YOUR COURAGE TODAY, DETECTIVE.
BUT, I DIDN'T...

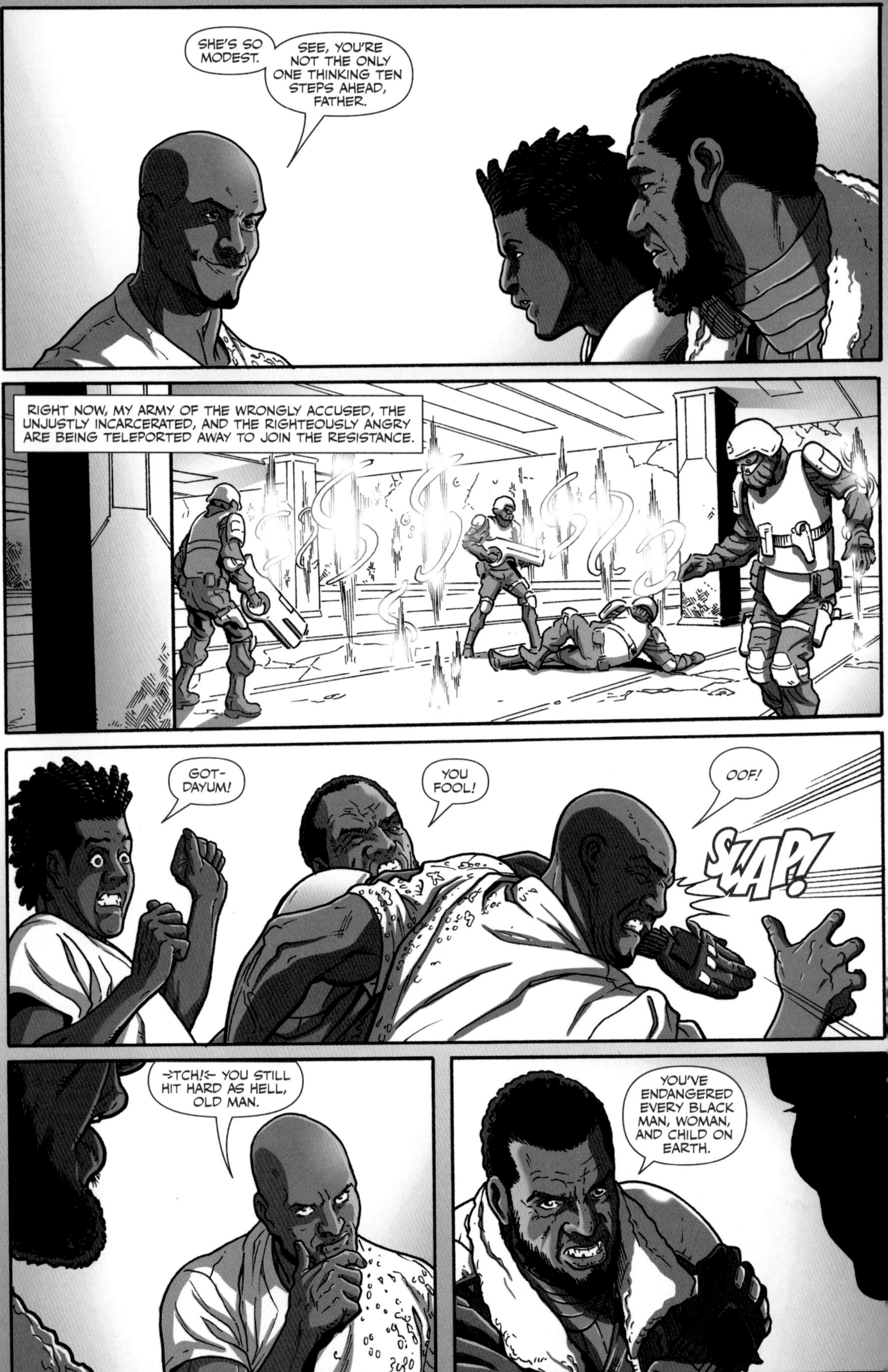
SHE'S SO MODEST.
SEE, YOU'RE NOT THE ONLY ONE THINKING TEN STEPS AHEAD, FATHER.
RIGHT NOW, MY ARMY OF THE WRONGLY ACCUSED, THE UNJUSTLY INCARCERATED, AND THE RIGHTEOUSLY ANGRY ARE BEING TELEPORTED AWAY TO JOIN THE RESISTANCE.
GOT-DAYUM!
YOU FOOL!
OOF!
SLAP!
>TCH!< YOU STILL HIT HARD AS HELL, OLD MAN.
YOU'VE ENDANGERED EVERY BLACK MAN, WOMAN, AND CHILD ON EARTH.

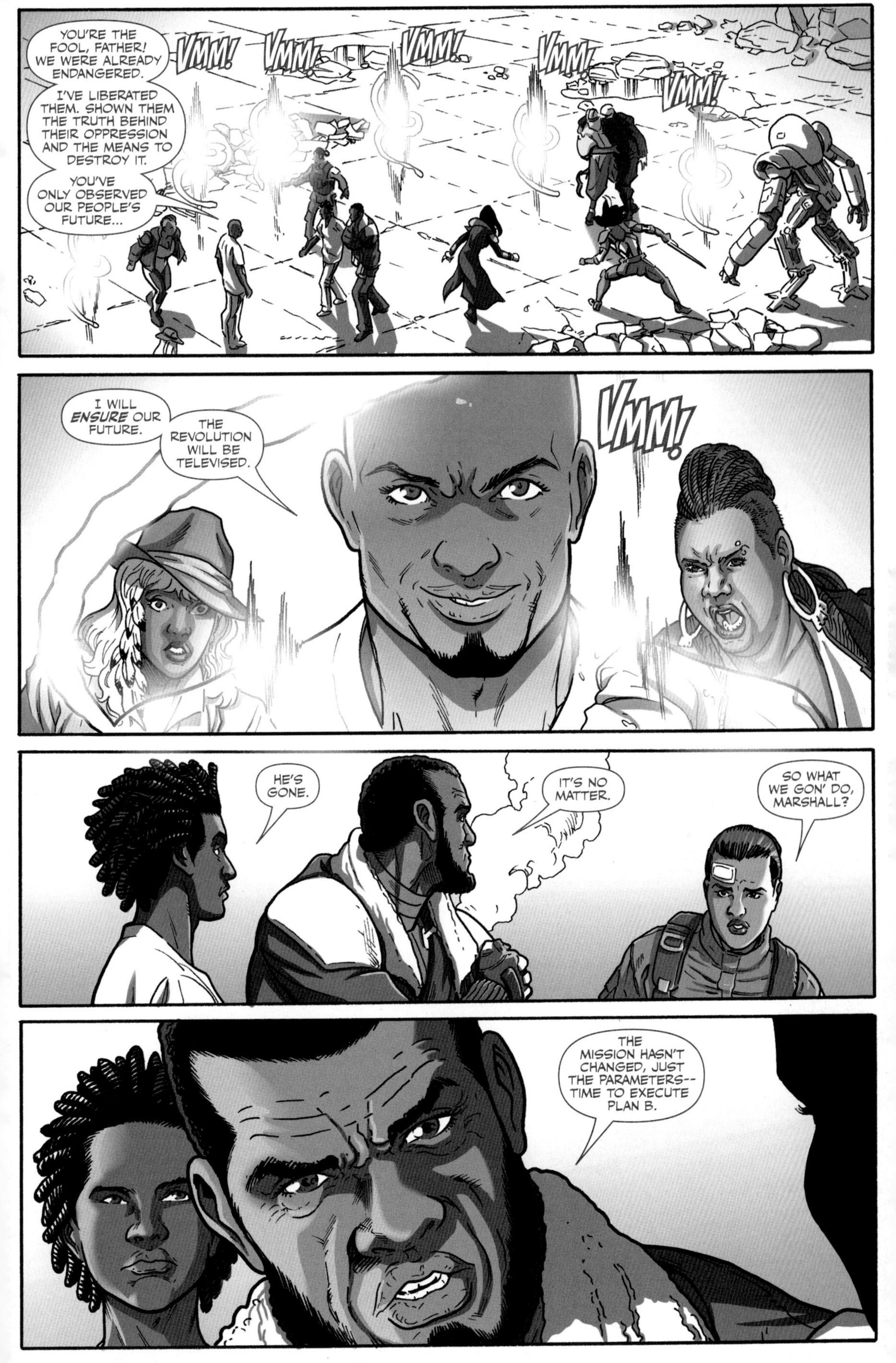
YOU'RE THE FOOL, FATHER! WE WERE ALREADY ENDANGERED.
I'VE LIBERATED THEM. SHOWN THEM THE TRUTH BEHIND THEIR OPPRESSION AND THE MEANS TO DESTROY IT.
YOU'VE ONLY OBSERVED OUR PEOPLE'S FUTURE...
VMM! VMM! VMM! VMM! VMM!
I WILL *ENSURE* OUR FUTURE.
THE REVOLUTION WILL BE TELEVISED.
VMM!
HE'S GONE.
IT'S NO MATTER.
SO WHAT WE GON' DO, MARSHALL?
THE MISSION HASN'T CHANGED, JUST THE PARAMETERS-- TIME TO EXECUTE PLAN B.

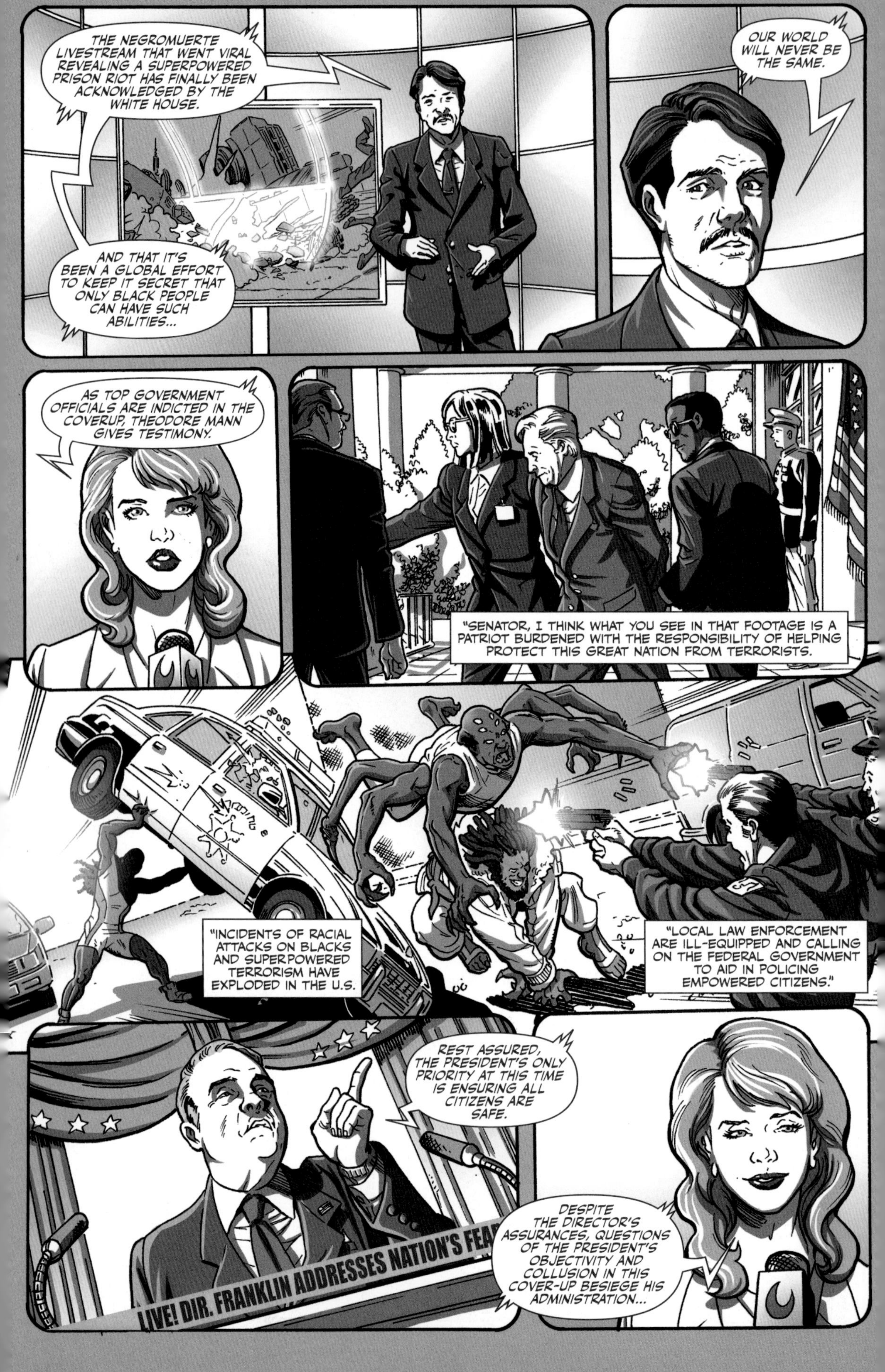
THE NEGROMUERTE LIVESTREAM THAT WENT VIRAL REVEALING A SUPERPOWERED PRISON RIOT HAS FINALLY BEEN ACKNOWLEDGED BY THE WHITE HOUSE.
AND THAT IT'S BEEN A GLOBAL EFFORT TO KEEP IT SECRET THAT ONLY BLACK PEOPLE CAN HAVE SUCH ABILITIES...
OUR WORLD WILL NEVER BE THE SAME.
AS TOP GOVERNMENT OFFICIALS ARE INDICTED IN THE COVERUP, THEODORE MANN GIVES TESTIMONY.
"SENATOR, I THINK WHAT YOU SEE IN THAT FOOTAGE IS A PATRIOT BURDENED WITH THE RESPONSIBILITY OF HELPING PROTECT THIS GREAT NATION FROM TERRORISTS.
"INCIDENTS OF RACIAL ATTACKS ON BLACKS AND SUPERPOWERED TERRORISM HAVE EXPLODED IN THE U.S.
"LOCAL LAW ENFORCEMENT ARE ILL-EQUIPPED AND CALLING ON THE FEDERAL GOVERNMENT TO AID IN POLICING EMPOWERED CITIZENS."
REST ASSURED, THE PRESIDENT'S ONLY PRIORITY AT THIS TIME IS ENSURING ALL CITIZENS ARE SAFE.
LIVE! DIR. FRANKLIN ADDRESSES NATION'S FEA
DESPITE THE DIRECTOR'S ASSURANCES, QUESTIONS OF THE PRESIDENT'S OBJECTIVITY AND COLLUSION IN THIS COVER-UP BESIEGE HIS ADMINISTRATION...

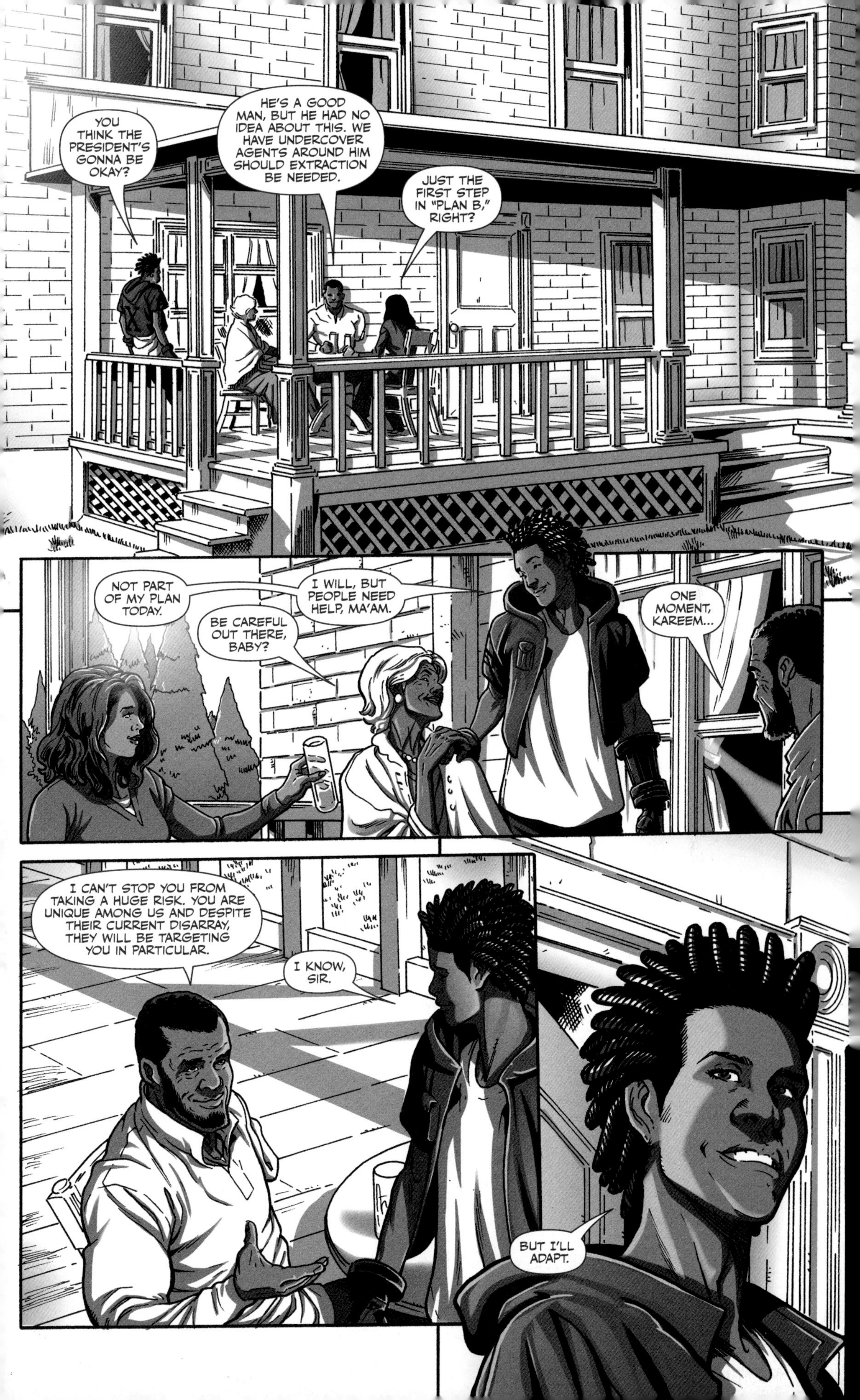

YOU THINK THE PRESIDENT'S GONNA BE OKAY?
HE'S A GOOD MAN, BUT HE HAD NO IDEA ABOUT THIS. WE HAVE UNDERCOVER AGENTS AROUND HIM SHOULD EXTRACTION BE NEEDED.
JUST THE FIRST STEP IN "PLAN B," RIGHT?
NOT PART OF MY PLAN TODAY.
BE CAREFUL OUT THERE, BABY?
I WILL, BUT PEOPLE NEED HELP, MA'AM.
ONE MOMENT, KAREEM...
I CAN'T STOP YOU FROM TAKING A HUGE RISK. YOU ARE UNIQUE AMONG US AND DESPITE THEIR CURRENT DISARRAY, THEY WILL BE TARGETING YOU IN PARTICULAR.
I KNOW, SIR.
BUT I'LL ADAPT.

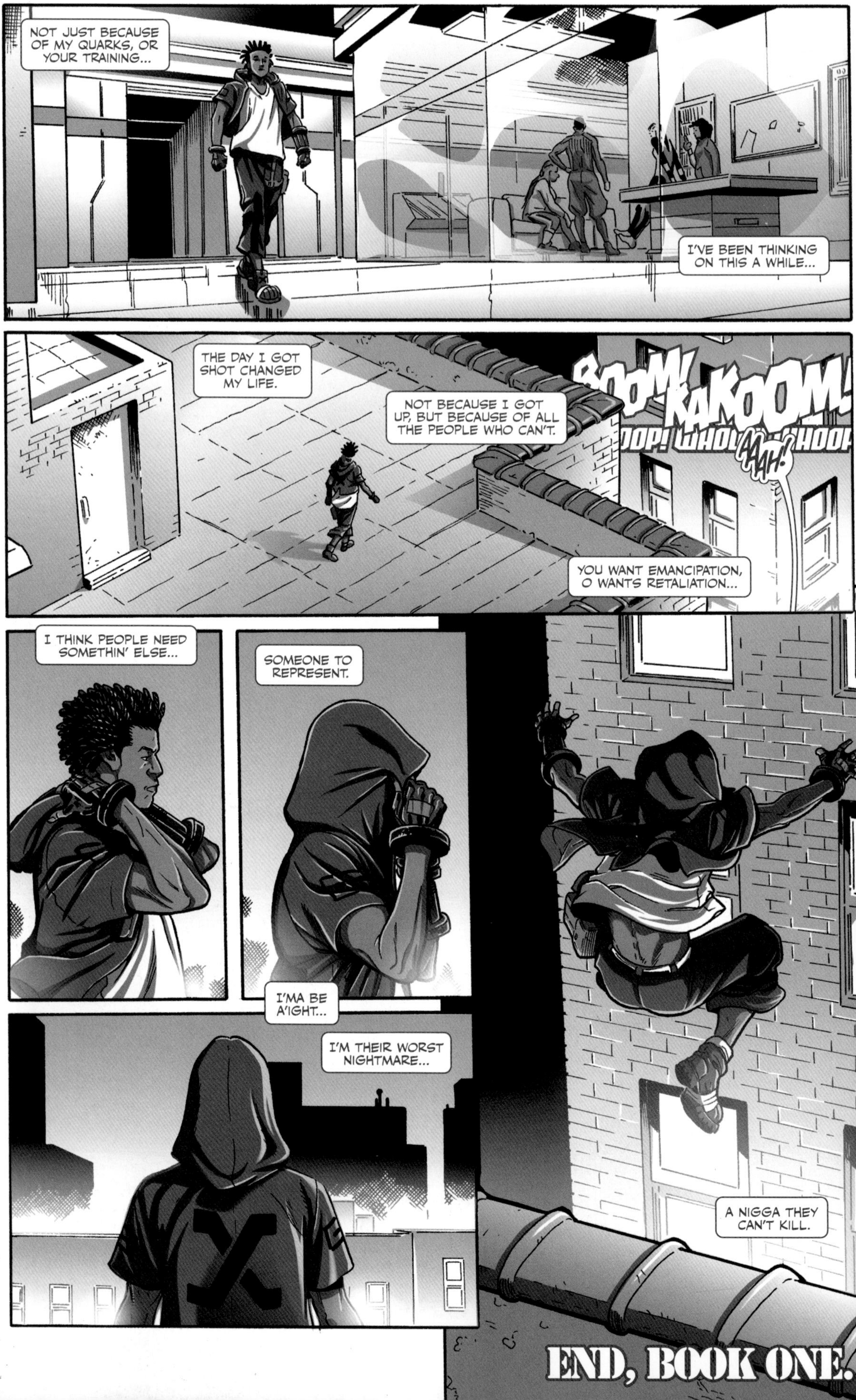

NOT JUST BECAUSE OF MY QUARKS, OR YOUR TRAINING...
I'VE BEEN THINKING ON THIS A WHILE...
THE DAY I GOT SHOT CHANGED MY LIFE.
NOT BECAUSE I GOT UP, BUT BECAUSE OF ALL THE PEOPLE WHO CAN'T.
BOOM! KAKOOM!
AAAH!
YOU WANT EMANCIPATION, O WANTS RETALIATION...
I THINK PEOPLE NEED SOMETHIN' ELSE...
SOMEONE TO REPRESENT.
I'MA BE A'IGHT...
I'M THEIR WORST NIGHTMARE...
A NIGGA THEY CAN'T KILL.
END, BOOK ONE.

DESIGNING BLACK X

AS THE MAIN CHARACTER, KAREEM, OR X, AS HE LATER CALLS HIMSELF, WAS THE DESIGN WE SPENT THE MOST TIME WITH. WE NEEDED TO CONVEY YOUTH WHILE ALSO GIVING HIM A UNIQUE SILHOUETTE TO STAND APART FROM THE REST OF THE CAST. THERE WERE A LOT OF REVISIONS, BUT WHERE WE FINALLY LANDED WITH X WAS A LOOK THAT FIT HIS PERSONALITY.

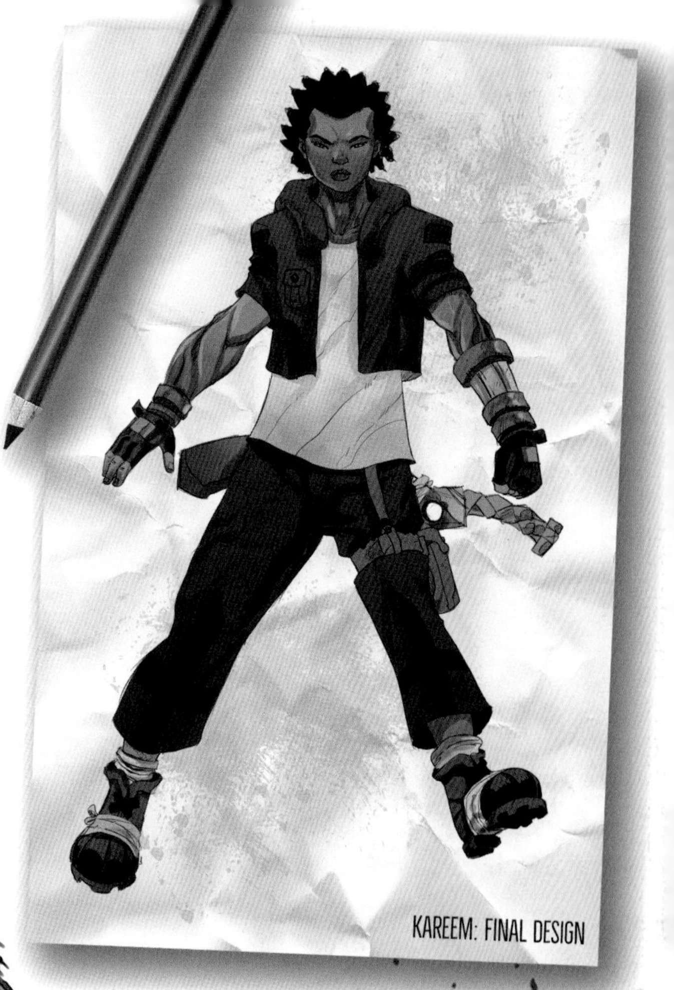

KAREEM: FINAL DESIGN

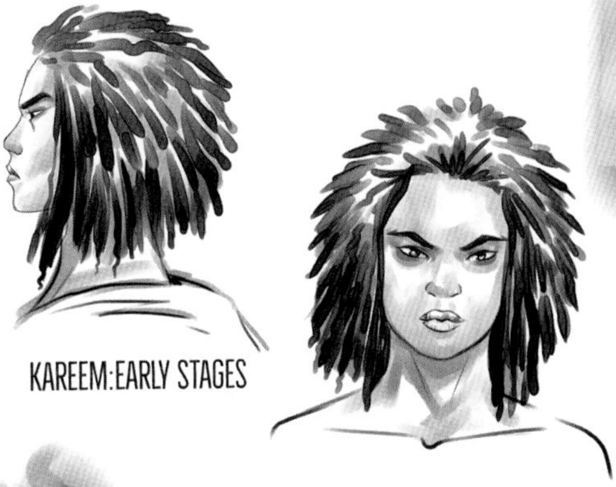

KAREEM:EARLY STAGES

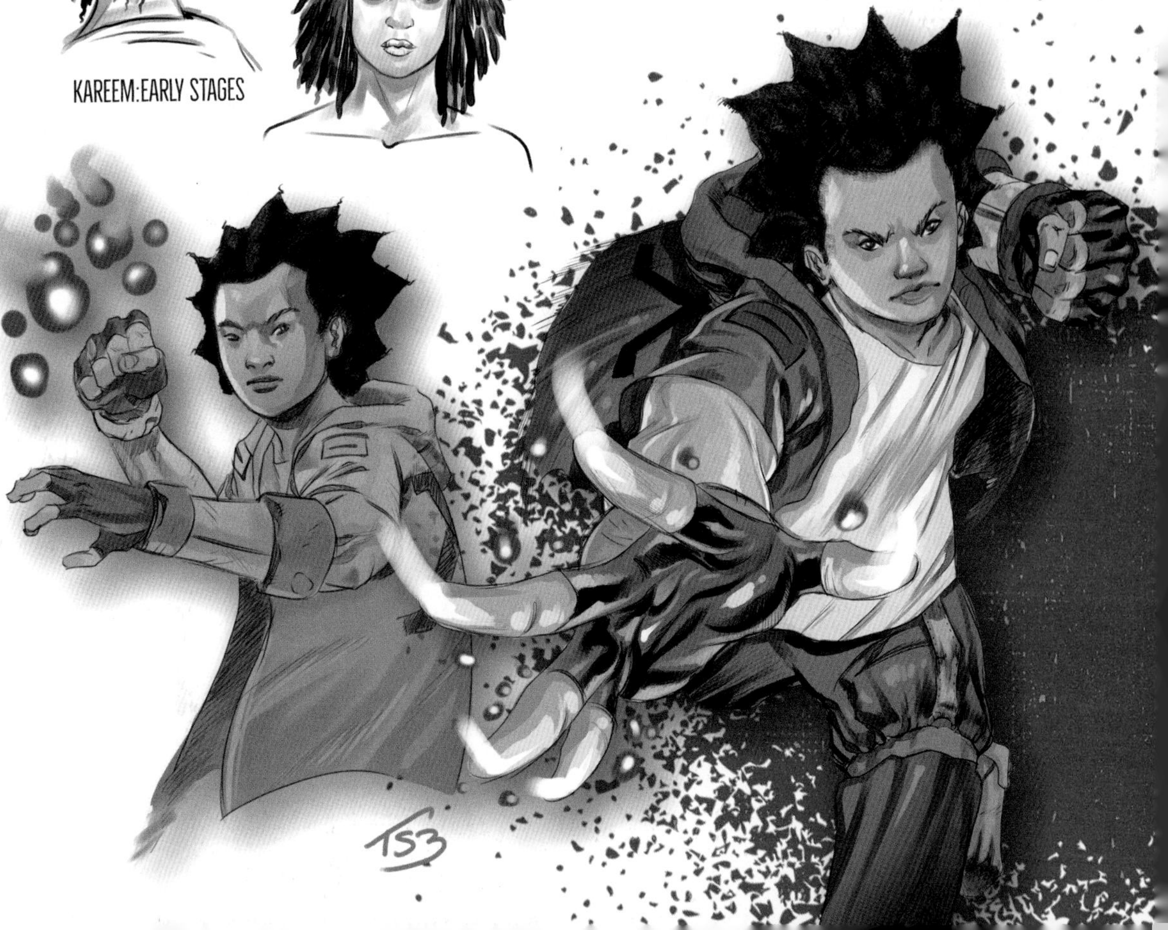
TS3

DESIGNING BLACK JUNCTURE

JUNCTURE'S DESIGN WAS ALMOST INSTANTANEOUS. A SEASONED WARRIOR, FIGHTING FOR PEACE SEEMED TO IMMEDIATELY INSPIRE A LOOK THAT GAVE JUNCTURE THE STATURE OF A PROTECTOR, BUT SOMEONE NOT TO BE TESTED.

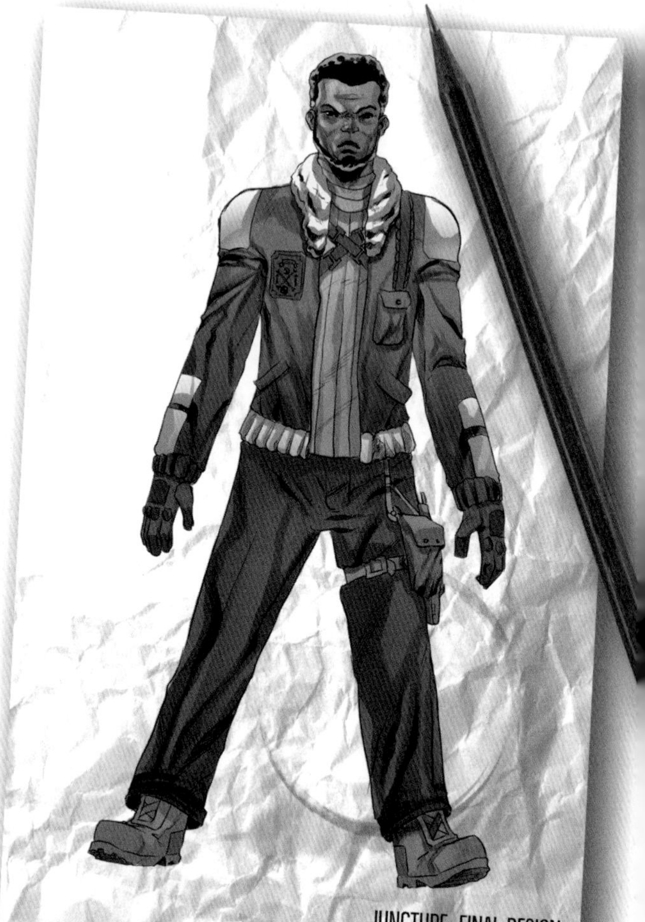

JUNCTURE: FINAL DESIGN

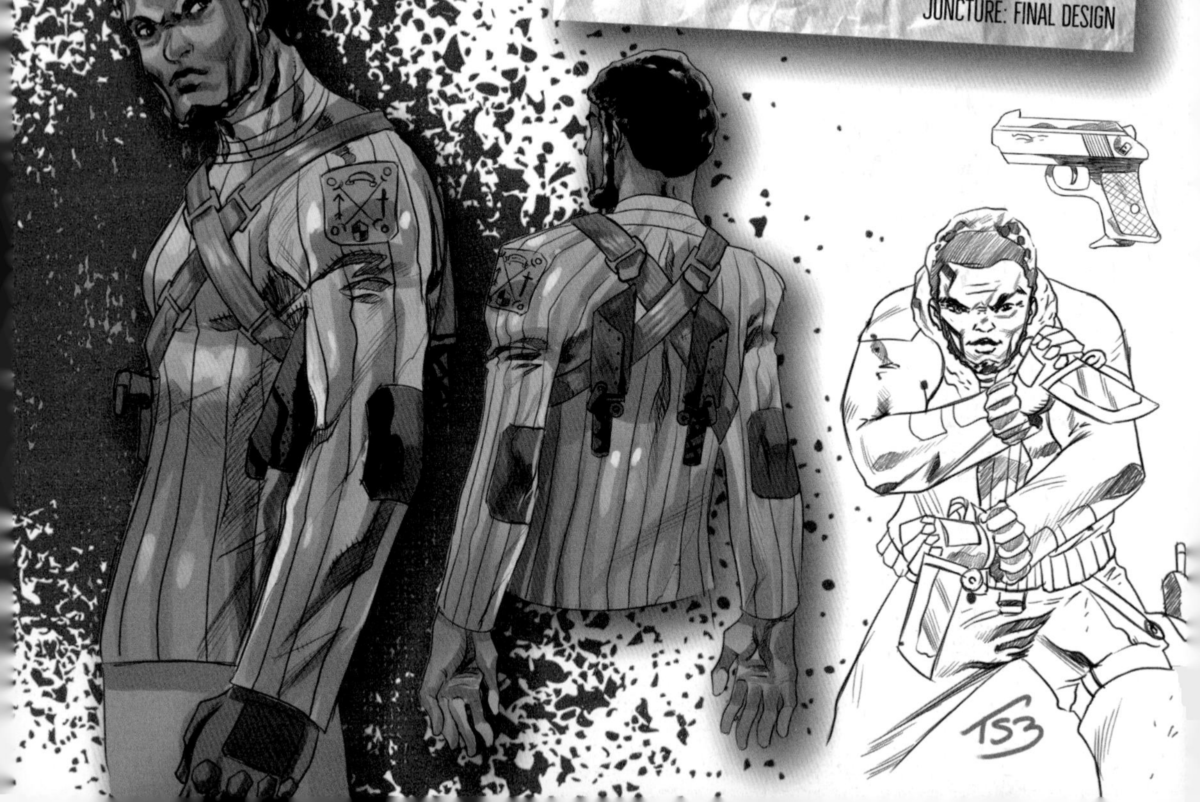

DESIGNING BLACK MANN

IT MIGHT SEEM EASY TO CREATE AN ANTAGONIST WHO IS SIMPLY A BUSINESSMAN, BUT WE DIDN'T WANT THEODORE MANN TO BE GENERIC. GIVING HIM A FULL BEARD AND HEAD OF HAIR FELT ATYPICAL AND VISUALLY EXPRESSED SOMEONE FROM OLD MONEY AND THE HIGHEST ECHELON OF PRIVILEGE.

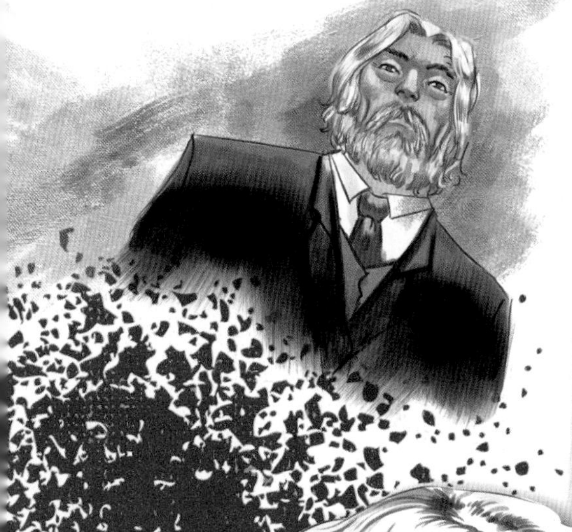

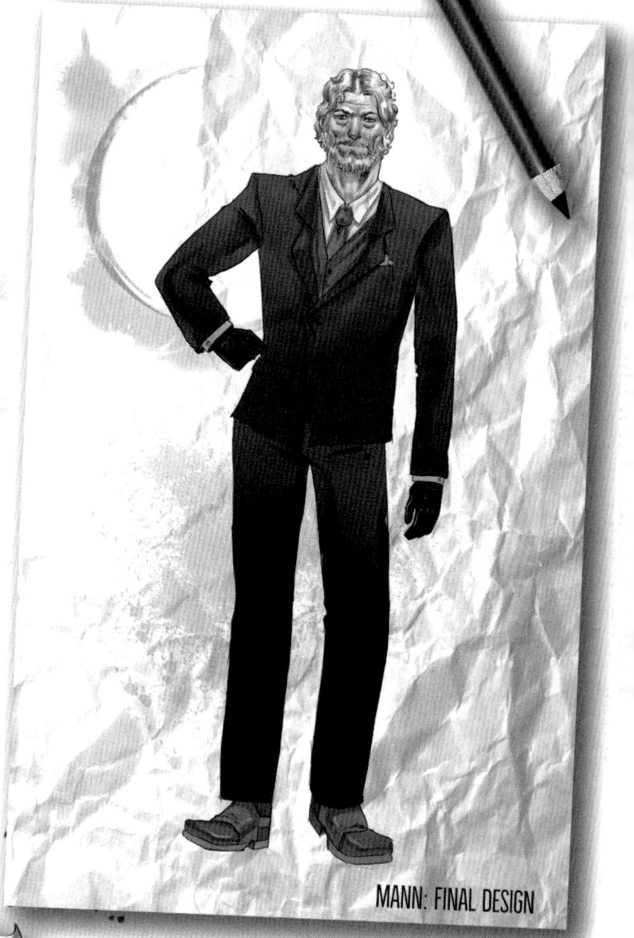
MANN: FINAL DESIGN

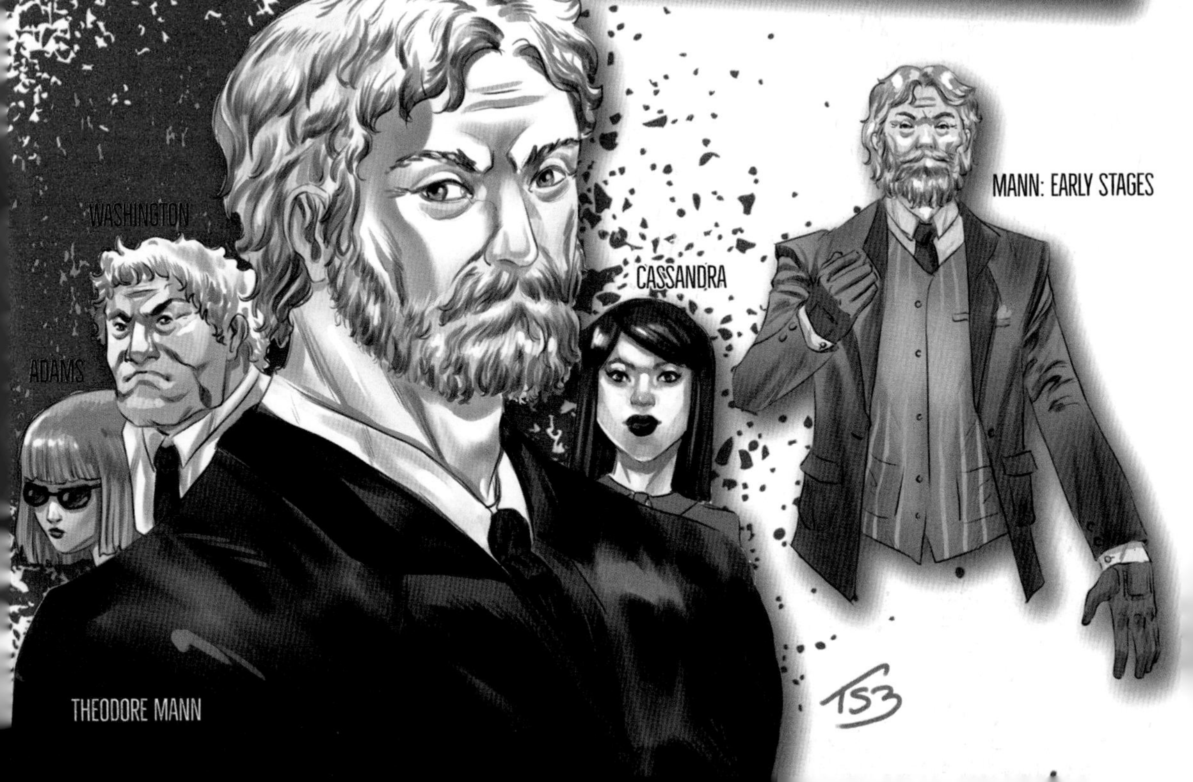
MANN: EARLY STAGES
WASHINGTON
CASSANDRA
ADAMS
THEODORE MANN

DESIGNING BLACK DET. WATERS

NAMED AFTER AND INSPIRED BY KWANZA OSAJYEFO'S MOTHER, ELLEN WATERS' DESIGN IS INTENDED TO COMMUNICATE CONFIDENCE AND DETERMINATION. AS A POLICE OFFICER, WE WANTED HER LOOK TO IMPART ALL THE BEST QUALITIES OF BOTH NEW YORK'S FINEST AND HER NAMESAKE.

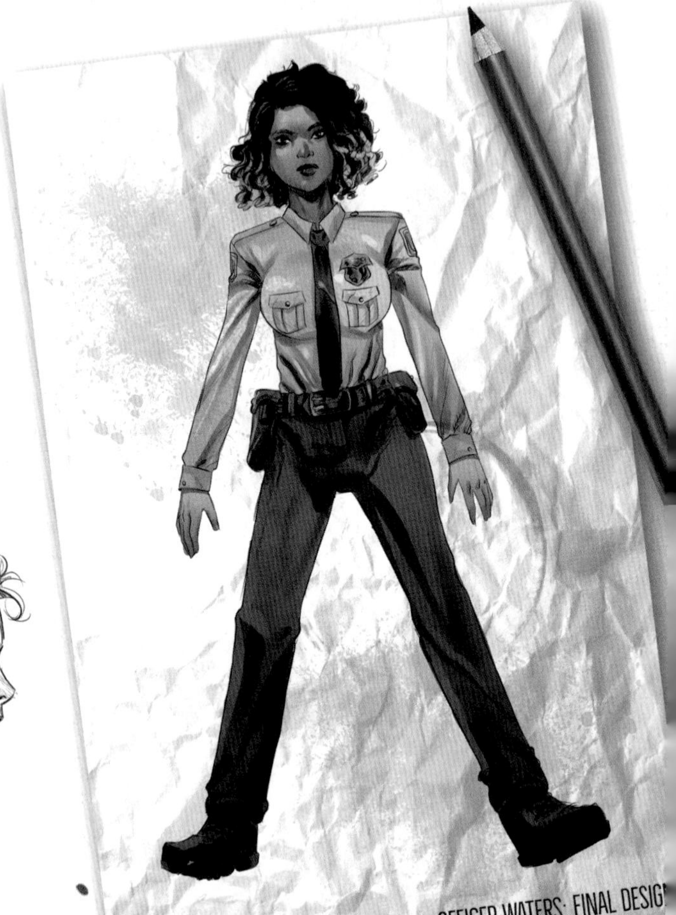

OFFICER WATERS: FINAL DESIG

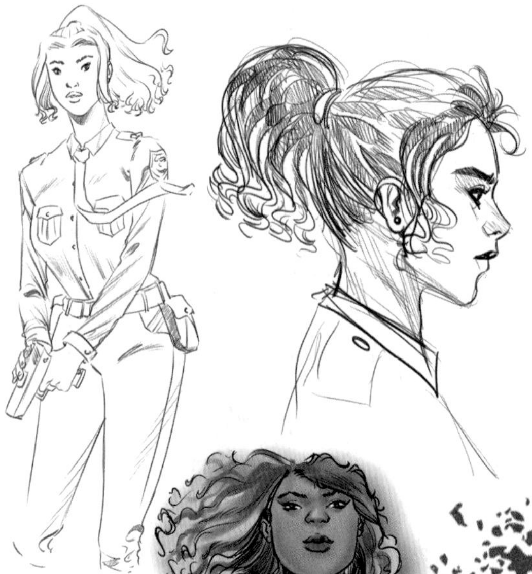

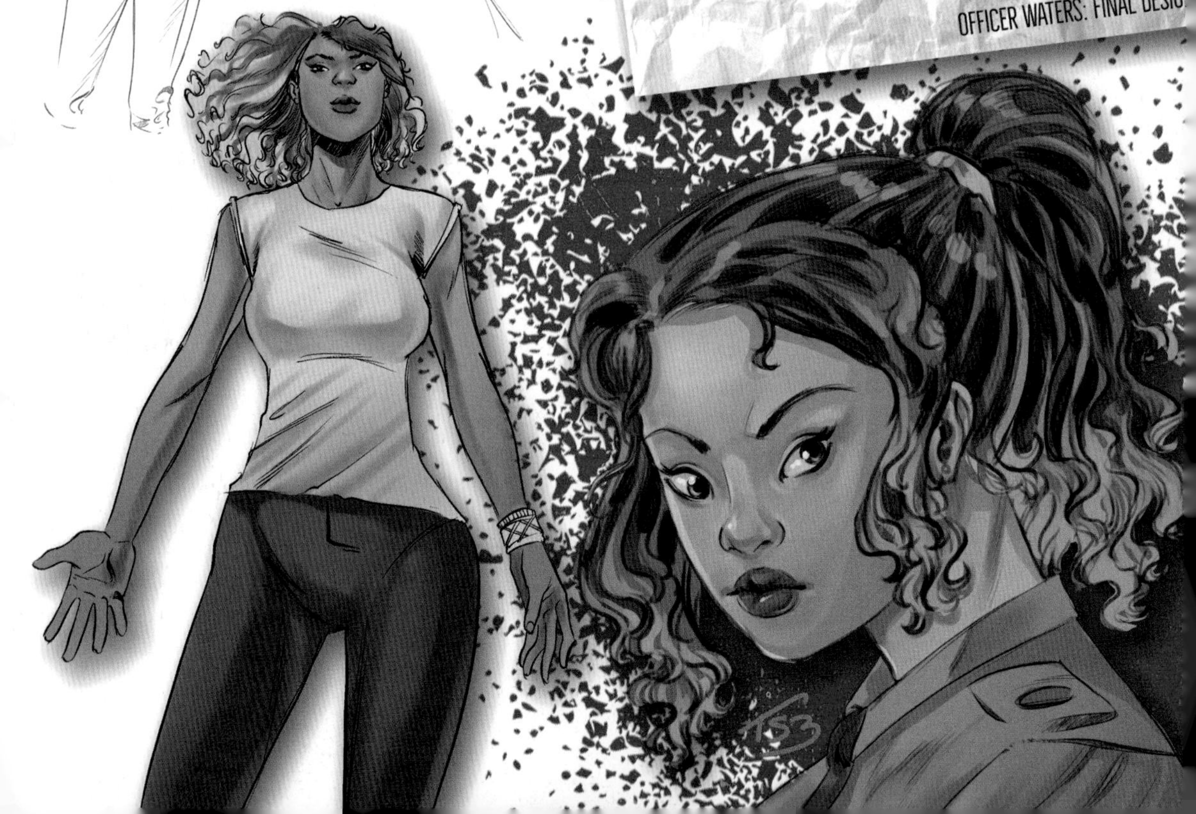

DESIGNING BLACK O

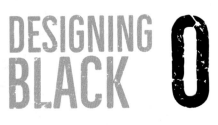

O'S APPEARANCE IMMEDIATELY NEEDED TO EXPRESS A MAN WITH A PLAN. SIMILAR IN PERSONALITY TO HIS FATHER, JUNCTURE, BUT WHERE O DEVIATES VISUALLY IS AS SOMEONE WITH UNFORGIVING INTENT. HE NEEDED TO LOOK LIKE SOMEONE WHO GIVES NO QUARTER IN THE PURSUIT OF HIS MISSION.

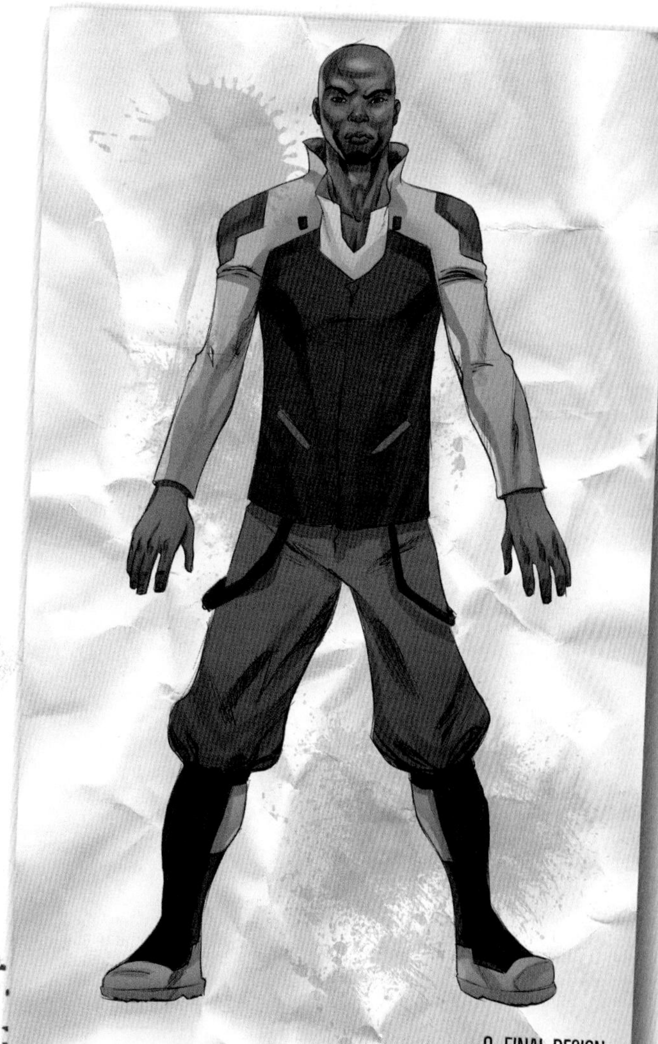

O: FINAL DESIGN

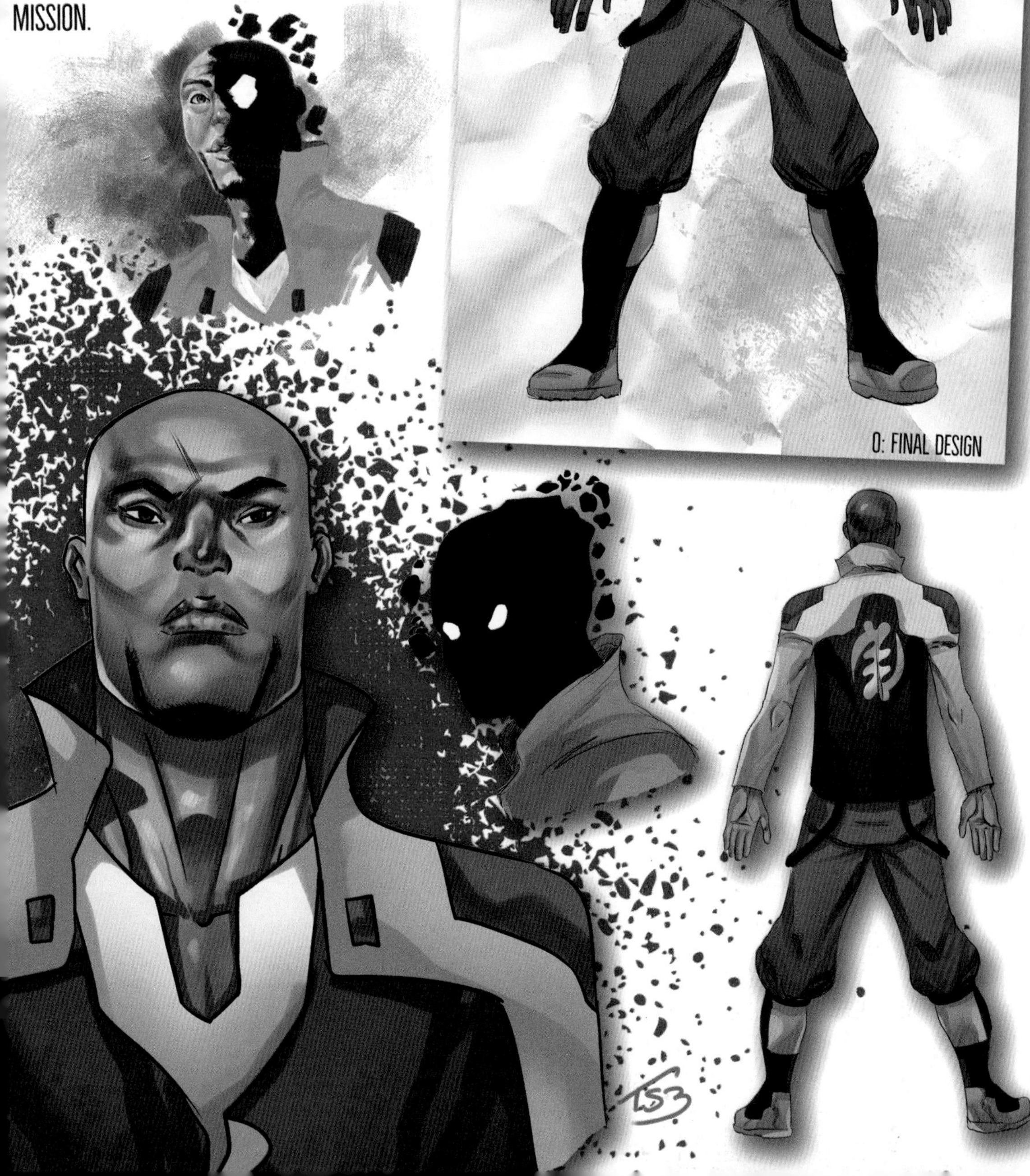

PANEL 1: CLOSE UP: ROLLED UP BLUE SLEEVES REVEAL A PAIR OF HANDS, LITTLE ROUGH; SHORT NAILS, - THEY'VE SEEN HARD WORK. A NYPD POLICE OFFICER PATROL HAT SITS TO THE RIGHT.

OFF PANEL VOICE
OFFICER WATERS...

PANEL 2: PROFILE OF OFFICER ELLEN WATERS, SHE'S TIRED, HEAD TILTED DOWN, BUT EYES STARE UP AT THE SPEAKER..

OFF PANEL VOICE
CAN I CALL YOU, 'ELLEN'?

PANEL 3: WATERS DOESN'T MOVE, HER FACE CHANGES VERY SLIGHTLY, SHE'S ANNOYED BY THIS VOICE.

ELLEN
NOPE.

PANEL 4: REVEAL FEDERAL AGENT ADAMS STANDS IN FRONT OF A TABLE WATERS IS SITTING AT, SUNGLASSES ON INDOORS, DOING THE INTIMIDATING FED THING. SHE'S WEARING A PANTSUIT BUT IT DOESN'T HIDE HER

ADAMS
WE'RE ALL FRIENDS HERE, OFFICER WATERS.

I JUST NEED TO KNOW WHAT TOOK PLACE TODAY.

PANEL 5: WATERS LOOKS AWAY, SILENT. SHE'S THINKING.

ELLEN
SURE...

PANEL 6: SHE TURNS HER GAZE BACK TO ADAMS, GIVING A SUSPICIOUS LOOK.

ELLEN
BUT I THINK YOU KNOW MORE THAN I DO.

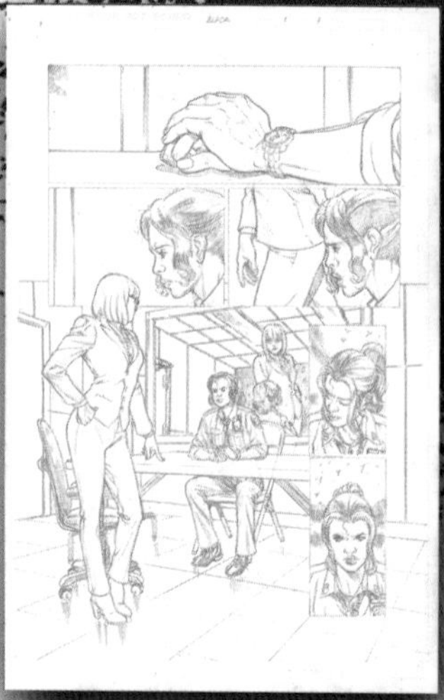

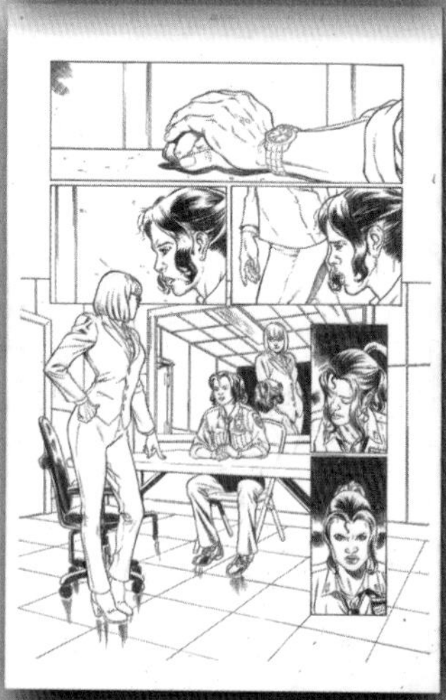

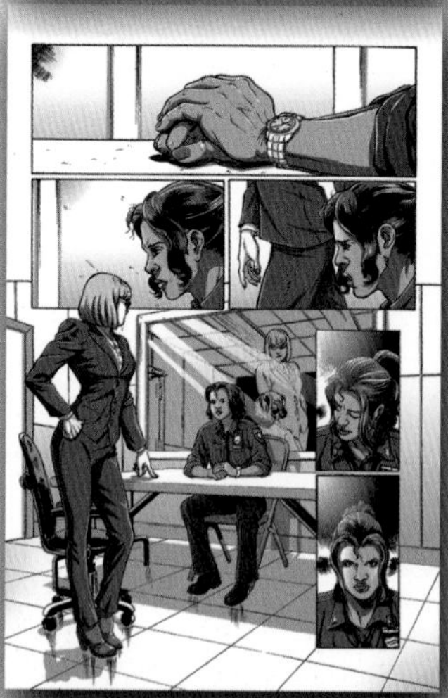

BLACK

SCRIPTS

CHAPTER 1, PAGE 1

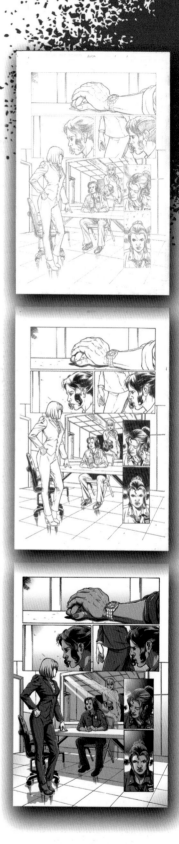

PANEL 1: WATERS SQUAD CAR, DRIVING AROUND, PATROLLING THE STREETS OF BED-STUY, BROOKLYN.

CAPTION
BED STUY IS MY BEAT.

PANEL 2: INSIDE THE SQUAD CAR, WATERS IN FULL NYPD UNIFORM LISTENS TO AN APB.

CAPTION
I GREW UP THERE...

SQUAD CAR RADIO
ALL CARS REPORT! THREE SUSPECTS JUST ROBBED A RESTAURANT AT GUNPOINT, HEADED SOUTH DOWN LEE AVE ON FOOT. BLACK MALES, 20S, IN BASKETBALL SHORTS AND T-SHIRTS.

PANEL 3: OFFICER WATERS IS ANSWERING HER RADIO.

CAPTION
A LOT OF OFFICERS DIDN'T...

WATERS
CAR 0122 REPORTING. HEADING NORTH UP NOSTRAND OFF MACON.

PANEL 4: KAREEM AND TWO FRIENDS, DRESSED IN BASKETBALL SHORTS AND T-SHIRTS ARE WALKING AWAY FROM THE BASKETBALL COURTS, SWEATY FROM A LONG GAME.

CAPTION
THEY PATROL THE PLACES, BUT DON'T KNOW THE FACES.

PANEL 5: KAREEM AND HIS FRIENDS SMILE AND JOKE AS THEY WALK. THEY JUST WON THEIR GAME AND ARE HAPPY.

CAPTION
THAT DESCRIPTION - COULD BE ANYBODY AROUND THERE...

BLACK

PANEL 1: A FEW SQUAD CARS CUT OFF KAREEM AND HIS FRIENDS PATH. THE BOYS STOP IN THEIR TRACKS, THEIR BASKETBALL BOUNCING AWAY.

SFX
WHOOP-WHOOP!

SQUAD CAR MEGAPHONE
DON'T MOVE!

CAPTION
TO SOME COPS, IT IS EVERYBODY...

PANEL 2: COPS CARS SURROUND THE BOYS, OFFICERS EXIT BARKING ORDERS.

OFFICER
GET YOUR HANDS UP, NOW!

CAPTION
I WAS SO CLOSE - IF I'D BEEN A LITTLE FASTER...

PANEL 3: THE BOYS ARE DUMBFOUNDED AND SCARED. THEY DON'T KNOW WHAT TO DO...

BOY NO. 1
YO, WE AIN'T DO NOTHING.

CAPTION
THEY WERE JUST KIDS - BABIES...

PANEL 4: THE COPS DRAW THEIR WEAPONS, TAKING AIM AS PEOPLE STOP AND STARE IN THE BACKGROUND.

COP NO. 1
I SAID, PUT YOUR GODDAMNED HANDS UP!

CAPTION
I COULD HAVE STOPPED IT...

PANEL 5: THE BOYS ARE SURROUNDED. POLICE LIGHTS FLASH AT THEM, OVERWHELMING,

BOY NO. 1
WHAT DO WE DO?

KAREEM
BE CHILL-

BOY NO. 2
NUH UH! THESE MUH'FUCKAZ GONNA KILL US.

BLACK

SCRIPTS
CHAPTER 1, PAGE 3

PANEL 1: THE MORE FEARFUL BOY BOLTS OFF. KAREEM SCREAMS AFTER HIM.

BOY NO. 2
FUCK THIS!

KAREEM
NO!

PANEL 2: CLOSE UP OF A COP'S MOUTH SCREAMING.

COP NO. 2
FREEZE!

PANEL 3: CLOSE UP ON KAREEM.

PANEL 4: CLOSE UP ON WATERS, SHE'S SCARED OF WHAT'S ABOUT TO HAPPEN.

WATERS
OH, NO...

PANEL 5: WATERS QUICKLY EXITING HER SQUAD CAR.

WATERS
NO!

PANEL 6: ALL THREE BOYS ARE TORN TO SHREDS IN A HAIL OF BULLETS, BLOOD ERUPTS FROM THEIR WOUNDS AS THEY FALL.

CAPTION
I WAS TOO LATE...

SFX
POP! POP!POP!POP!POP! POP! POP!POP!POP!POP!POP! POP!POP! POP! POP!POP! POP!POP!POP! POP! POP! POP!POP! POP!

BLACK

SCRIPTS
CHAPTER 1, PAGE 4

PANEL 1: EKG LINE DISPLAYS A WEAK ELEVATION.

SFX
BEEP!

PANEL 2: THE SAME EKG DISPLAY, SAME WEAK ELEVATION.

SFX
BEEP!

PANEL 3: THE EKG ELEVATION SPIKES.

CAPTION
AT LEAST I THOUGHT I WAS TOO LATE...

SFX
BEEP BEEP BEEP!

PANEL 4: KAREEM SPRINGS TO LIFE, GASPING FOR BREATH ON A GURNEY IN THE BACK OF AN AMBULANCE, SCARING THE SHIT OUT OF THE EMT. HIS SHIRT IS FULL OF HOLES, BUT HIS BODY IS NOT.

KAREEM
HUAAAAAAH!

EMT
AAAH! WHAT THE FU-!

PANEL 5: KAREEM AND THE EMT LOOK AT EACH OTHER AND SCREAM.

KAREEM AND EMT
AAAAAAAAAH!

PANEL 6: KAREEM RUSHES FOR THE AMBULANCE BACKDOOR.

BLACK

SCRIPTS
CHAPTER 1, PAGE 5

COVER VARIANT

ISSUE 1

1B PRINTING

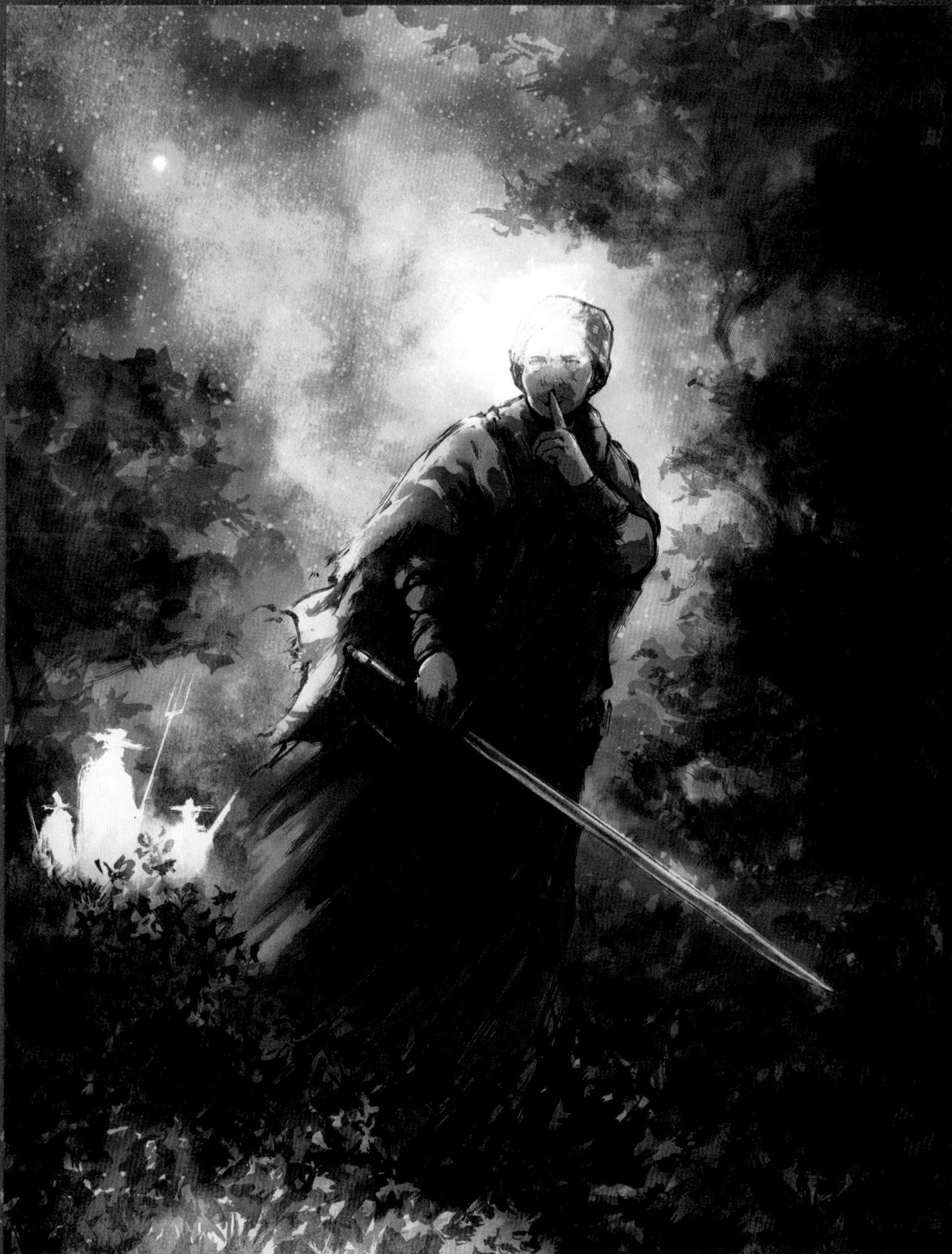

ASHLEY WOODS

COVER VARIANT

ISSUE 1

2ND PRINTING

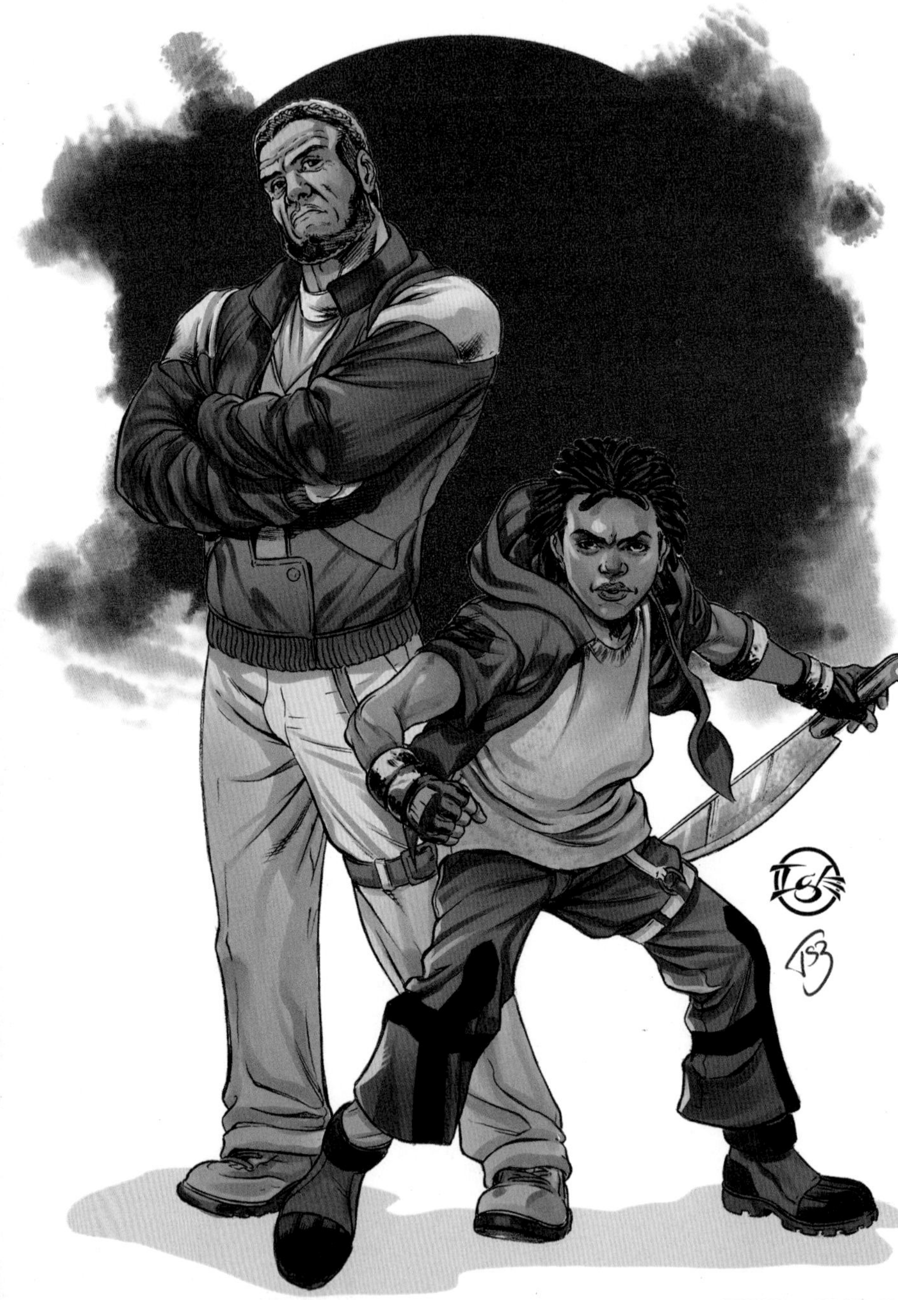

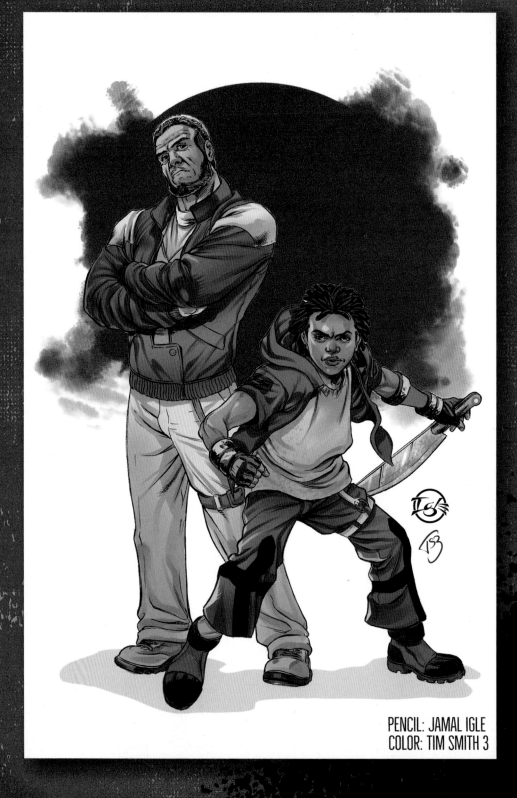

PENCIL: JAMAL IGLE
COLOR: TIM SMITH 3